JAPANESE IMPERIALISM 1894–1945

JAPANESE IMPERIALISM
1894–1945

W. G. BEASLEY

CLARENDON PRESS · OXFORD

Oxford University Press, Walton Street, Oxford OX2 6DP
Oxford New York Toronto
Delhi Bombay Calcutta Madras Karachi
Petaling Jaya Singapore Hong Kong Tokyo
Nairobi Dar es Salaam Cape Town
Melbourne Auckland
and associated companies in
Berlin Ibadan

Oxford is a trade mark of Oxford University Press

Published in the United States
by Oxford University Press, New York

© W. G. Beasley 1987

First published 1987
Reprinted 1989

British Library Cataloguing in Publication Data
Beasley, W. G.
Japanese imperialism, 1894–1945.
1. Japan—Foreign relations—1868–1912
2. Japan—Foreign relations—1912–1945
3. Japan—Colonies—History
I. Title
325'.32'0952   DS885.48
ISBN 0–19–821575–4

Library of Congress Cataloging-in-Publication Data
Beasley, W. G. (William G.), 1919–
Japanese imperialism 1894–1945.
Bibliography: p.
Includes index.
1. Japan—Foreign relations—20th century.
2. Japan—History—20th century.   3. Imperialism.
I. Title.
DS885.48.B43   1987   952.03   86–28544
ISBN 0–19–821575–4

Printed in Great Britain
at the Alden Press, Oxford

PREFACE

WHILE collecting material for this book I have received valuable advice from many scholars. I would like to thank in particular Professor Iwao Seiichi, Professor Oka Yoshitake, and Professor Hosoya Chihiro. The staff of the Japanese Foreign Ministry Archives (Gaikō Shiryōkan) have always been exceptionally helpful whenever I have had occasion to consult the records in their care. In London I owe many debts of gratitude to former colleagues and students at the School of Oriental and African Studies, especially to Mr Brian Hickman of the School's Library. The School has on several occasions contributed to the cost of my research visits to Japan. So did the British Academy (Leverhulme Visiting Professorship) and the Japan Foundation. To them all I express my thanks.

W. G. B.

London, 1985

CONTENTS

List of Maps		ix
List of Tables		ix
Note on Personal Names, Place-names, Transliteration, and Abbreviations		x
1.	Introduction: **Explanations of Imperialism**	1
2.	**The Treaty Port System and Japan**	14
	The nature of the treaty port system	14
	The treaty port system in Japan	20
3.	**Modernization and Imperialism**	27
	Japanese responses to the West	27
	Wealth and strength	34
4.	**Intervention in Korea, 1894–1895**	41
	Japan and Korea before the Sino-Japanese War	42
	Japanese policy in Korea, 1894–1895	48
5.	**The Peace Settlement with China, 1894–1896**	55
	Liaotung and Taiwan	56
	The commercial provisions	60
6.	**New Imperialism and the War with Russia, 1895–1905**	69
	Spheres of influence: Korea and Fukien	71
	The conflict with Russia	78
7.	**Formal and Informal Empire in North-east Asia, 1905–1910**	85
	The annexation of Korea	86
	Japan's sphere of influence in Manchuria	90
8.	**Chinese Revolution and World War**	101
	The Chinese Revolution and the powers	102

    The Twenty-one Demands   108
    The origins of co-prosperity   115

9. **Overseas Trade and Investment, 1895–1930**   122
    Foreign trade and colonial trade   123
    Foreign investment   132

10. **Japan's Territorial Dependencies, 1895–1930**   142
    Colonial government and society   143
    Colonial economies   149

11. **The Treaty Port System in Jeopardy, 1918–1931**   156
    Japan and the Russian Revolution   158
    Japan and the treaty powers   163
    Japan and Chinese nationalism   169

12. **The Making of Manchukuo, 1931–1932**   175
    Nationalism and militarism   176
    Japan and Manchuria before 1930   182
    The Manchurian Incident   188
    Manchukuo   194

13. **Japan's New Order in North-east Asia**   198
    The advance into China   199
    The New Order   203
    The industrial heartland   210

14. **Advance to the South**   220
    South-east Asia and economic self-sufficiency   222

15. **The Greater East Asia Co-prosperity Sphere**   233
    Political structures   233
    Ideology and economics   243

16. **Conclusion: The Nature of Japanese Imperialism**   251

    Bibliography   259
    Index   271

LIST OF MAPS

1. East and South-east Asia   xii
2. Korea and Manchuria   xiv

LIST OF TABLES

1. Japan's foreign trade 1890–1929: imports and exports   125
2. Japan's foreign trade 1890–1929: percentage shares by
   commodity groups   126
3. Japan's foreign trade 1890–1929: percentage shares by
   countries   127
4. Japan's colonial trade 1895–1929: percentage shares of
   total foreign trade by territories   131
5. Foreign investment in China 1902–1931: distribution by
   countries   133
6. Japanese and other foreign investment in China, 1914   138
7. Japanese and other foreign investment in China, 1930   140
8. Japan's colonial and mainland trade, 1929 and 1931   189
9. Japan's foreign trade 1925–1939: percentage shares by
   countries   211
10. Japanese investment in China and Manchuria, 1931–1944   215

NOTE ON PERSONAL NAMES, PLACE-NAMES, TRANSLITERATION, AND ABBREVIATIONS

Personal names. Chinese and Japanese personal names are given in the order traditionally used in China and Japan: family name, followed by given name, e.g. Li Hung-chang, where Li is the family name; Itō Hirobumi, where Itō is the family name.

Place-names. Many of the place-names to which reference is made in this book exist in more than one version. Some of these represent differences in linguistic readings (in Chinese, Japanese, and Korean, respectively). Some are differences of usage (e.g. Chinese and western versions of the names of treaty ports). Some reflect changes of name at different periods. The choice between them has been made on grounds of convenience, i.e. the name most likely to be familiar in the context of this book's subject-matter has been chosen and used throughout. Variants are given in the index.

Transliteration. Since the Chinese, Japanese, and Korean languages are written by means of ideographs or syllabaries, which do not correspond exactly with the Western alphabet, there have been considerable differences from time to time in the way in which words are transcribed in Western-language works. The problem applies to personal and place-names, as well as ordinary vocabulary. The systems of transliteration adopted in this book are those most commonly found in use before 1945: for Chinese, the Wade–Giles system; for Japanese, Hepburn; for Korean, McCune–Reischauer. Some diacritical marks are omitted, e.g. on familiar place-names. Variants (especially in the Chinese Pinyin system, now widely used) are given in the index.

Abbreviations. Where works cited in the notes have long titles, literal abbreviations have sometimes been used. In each case the abbreviation, in addition to the full description of the work, is inserted at the appropriate point alphabetically in the bibliography.

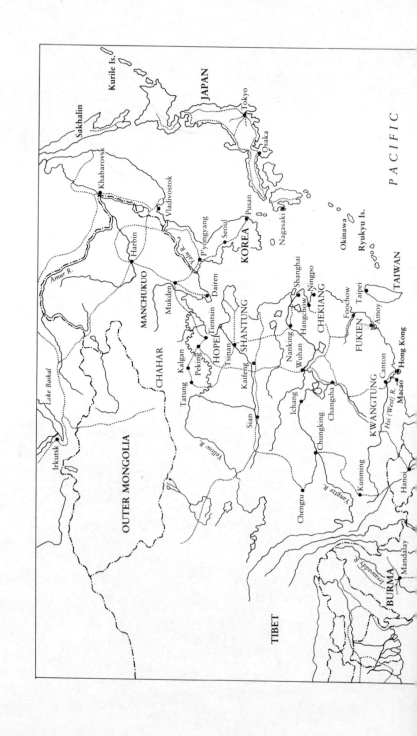

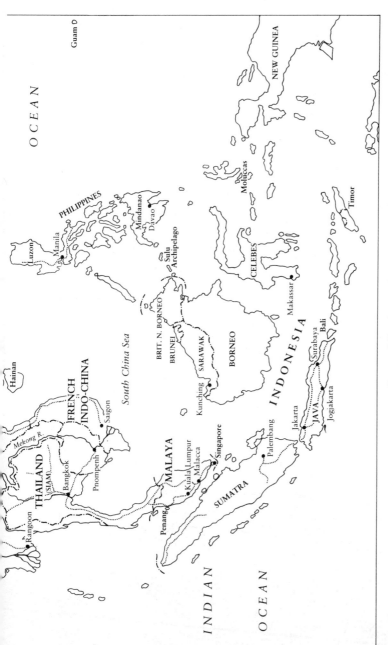

1. East and South-east Asia

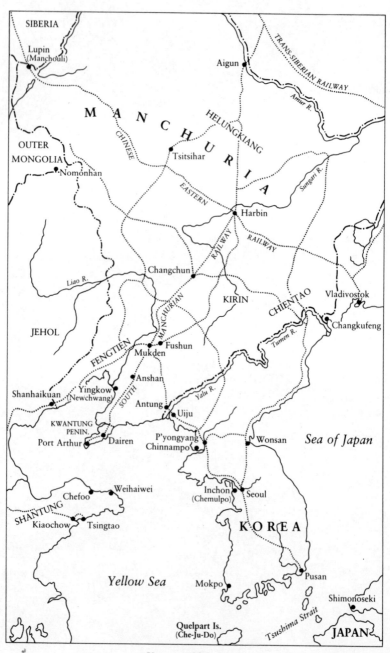

2. Korea and Manchuria

I

Introduction: Explanations of Imperialism

THE word 'imperialism' is now most often used to designate a phase
of Western expansion which began with the partition of Africa in the
1880s. The usage is not strictly accurate, because the phenomenon
had existed in various forms for much of history—Lichtheim starts his
account of it with the Roman Empire[1]—but it will serve well enough
for the purposes of this discussion. Japanese imperialism dates from
the Sino-Japanese War of 1894–5. It is therefore with modern Western imperialism that one tends to compare it.

Characteristically, this is 'economic imperialism', so called because
it is held to derive from a particular stage in the economic development
of Western society. The argument was first stated at length by Hobson
in 1902. He identified 'the tap-root of imperialism' as being overproduction, leading to a surplus of capital seeking investment:

Overproduction in the sense of an excessive manufacturing plant, and surplus
capital which could not find sound investments within the country, forced
Great Britain, Germany, Holland, France to place larger and larger portions of
their economic resources outside the area of their present political domain,
and then stimulate a policy of political expansion so as to take in the new
areas.[2]

It was investors, notably bankers and financiers, who in Hobson's view
most profited from this policy: 'To a larger extent every year Great
Britain is becoming a nation living upon tribute from abroad, and the
classes who enjoy this tribute have an ever-increasing incentive to
employ the public policy, the public purse, and the public force to
extend the field of their private investments.'[3] Such investors, 'essen-

---

[1] George Lichtheim, *Imperialism* (1971).
[2] See extract from Hobson's *Imperialism: a study* (1902), printed in Boulding and
Mukerjee (edd.), *Economic Imperialism* (1972), at p. 8. Another useful volume of extracts
and articles is H. M. Wright (ed.), *The 'New Imperialism'* (1961), in which there is some
duplication, but also a wider spread.
[3] Quoted in Wright, op. cit., p. 16.

tially parasites upon patriotism', were able to rally support from groups which could anticipate 'profitable business and lucrative employment' as a result of empire. They included those who looked forward to securing military or civil posts in the colonies, those who traded there, those who manufactured armaments for colonial wars, those who provided the capital for transport and colonial development.

This pejorative analysis of imperialism, which was by no means universally accepted in Hobson's time, has since become in large part orthodox, at least among intellectuals. Lenin put it into a Marxist framework in 1916. Imperialism, he maintained, was the inevitable product of capitalism in its monopoly stage. As industry raised the production of goods to a point at which domestic markets could no longer absorb them, capitalism ceased to be dynamic. Competition was replaced by monopolies and cartels, which served to maintain profit margins within protected markets. One result was surplus capital. To use it to raise the standard of living of the masses would have reduced profits. Hence it seemed more beneficial to Western capitalists to export it to areas where profits remained high because capital was scarce, labour was cheap, and the cost of raw materials was low. These conditions could best be ensured when the territories concerned were subject to political direction, that is to say, in colonies, protectorates, and spheres of influence. Political domination also made it possible to secure the basic requirements for investment: the development of railways and ports; financial stability; law and order.[4]

The Hobson–Lenin concept has been criticized on a number of grounds. One is that is does not accord with the financial facts, as subsequently determined. Before 1914 Britain had the largest empire and the greatest total of overseas investment. Yet the bulk of that investment was not in the colonies acquired after 1870, so much as in the independent countries of Europe and the Americas, or the older white settlement colonies, like Canada and Australia.[5]

Recognizing this disparity between the expectation and the event, several writers have tried to shift the emphasis from the 'push' that Lenin's 'crisis of capitalism' provided to the 'pull' of external circum-

[4] See extract from Lenin's *Imperialism: the highest stage of capitalism* (1916) in Wright, op. cit., pp. 33–8. On Marxist ideas on capitalism and imperialism more generally, see Mark Blaug, 'Economic imperialism revisited' (1972), and Michael Barratt Brown, 'A critique of Marxist theories of imperialism' (1972).
[5] Brown, 'A critique', 54–5; Blaug, 'Economic imperialism', 144–9; D. K. Fieldhouse, 'Imperialism: an historiographical revision' (1972), 195–9.

stance. Langer, writing in 1935, identified the economic motives of the
powers as being chiefly the protection rather than the extension of
markets and investment opportunities. He therefore attached priority
to international rivalries as an explanation of imperialism, especially
the rivalries that arose from the challenge to Britain's former commercial supremacy by the emerging industrial states of Western Europe.[6]
Landes, examining the subject in 1961, argued that the economic
motivation for imperialism was 'important but nevertheless insufficient'. He preferred to define Western expansion as 'a multifarious
response to a common opportunity that consists simply in disparity of
power'. This led to the conclusion that the West's overwhelming military and economic superiority encouraged a recourse to political or
financial controls whenever its economic aims were obstructed overseas, whether directly by opposition or indirectly by disorder.[7] Fieldhouse put the two strands together in a book published in 1973. He
agreed that after 1880 statesmen chose 'imperialist' solutions to problems with increasing frequency. The reason, however, was not in his
view a change in the nature of capitalism. It was a change in the situation with which the powers had to deal: the occurrence of multiple
crises, geographically dispersed, which reflected partly 'a fundamental
disequilibrium between Europe and the rest of the world', partly a failure to find any system of control, short of annexation or protectorate,
in areas where 'indigenous states were too weak to provide a satisfactory framework for European enterprise and where rivalry between
European states was excessive'.[8]

Interpretation of economic imperialism has been modified in a different way by writers who broaden the chronological basis of discussion. In a seminal article, published in 1953,[9] Gallagher and
Robinson identified three stages of development. The first was early
modern mercantilist imperialism. In this the homeland secured economic advantage through the exploitation of its political authority in colonies directly to the benefit of its own revenue and commerce. The
third stage was that of Hobson's analysis: the search for monopoly
markets and investment opportunity. Between them came the imperialism of free trade, exemplified above all by Britain. Since it was charac-

[6] Extract in Wright, op. cit., 68–76.
[7] David Landes, 'The nature of economic imperialism' (1972).
[8] See D. K. Fieldhouse, *Economics and Empire 1830–1914* (1973), at pp. 459–77.
[9] J. Gallagher and R. Robinson, 'The Imperialism of Free Trade' (1953).

terized by a willingness 'to limit the use of paramount power to establishing security for trade', in many parts of the world—China and
Latin America are the outstanding examples—where these ends could
be attained without colonial rule, the result was 'informal empire': protectorates, spheres of influence, or privileges embodied in treaties. Nor
was there any reason why formal and informal empire should not
coexist. Both were 'variable political functions of the extending pattern
of overseas trade, investment, migration and culture'. Britain profited
from the one in India, from the other in Latin America, during much
of the nineteenth century.

This view of imperialism was compatible with that of Langer and
Landes, in so far as it identified the progression from the second stage
to the third with an intensification of international rivalries, not a
transformation of the metropolitan economies. Once Britain's wishes
ceased to be paramount outside Europe, because its trade was successfully challenged, then, it was argued, informal empire no longer
worked. Even men like Salisbury and Chamberlain were forced to
accept territorial acquisitions as 'a painful but unavoidable necessity'.

The Gallagher–Robinson thesis, too, has been subject to criticism,
but as many of the objections to it focus on points concerning the
interpretation of British history, rather than the nature of imperialism,
we can disregard them here. There is, however, an elaboration worked
out by Cain and Hopkins[10] which opens up a new approach to it.
Examining British expansion over the whole span from 1750 to 1914,
they introduce two variables into the analysis. The first is the changing
influence over time of different sectors of the British economy—
agriculture, industry, finance—on the shaping of external policy. The
second is the relevance of British economic relations with Europe and
the United States to the character of British imperialism in different
periods. The result is to suggest a pattern in which relative failure to
penetrate the more advanced economies of Europe and America
becomes an explanation of expansion elsewhere: between 1815 and
1859, for example; then after 1875.

So far this discussion has focused on the economic elements in
imperialism. Most of the scholars who have been quoted above agreed
that these were decisive, no matter how much they disagreed about
interpreting them. Nevertheless, there were others who preferred

---

[10] P. J. Cain and A. G. Hopkins, 'The political economy of British expansion overseas, 1750–1914' (1980).

explanations that were much less obviously economic, or not economic at all. Staley, considering pre-revolutionary Russia, attributed its expansion to 'political ambition, dynastic megalomania, military lust for conquest'.[11] Carlton Hayes saw imperialism as 'a nationalistic phenomenon', a search for prestige abroad which developed once the powers found it hard to come by in a Europe newly stabilized after the wars of 1854 to 1870. Colonies were acquired for political reasons, he believed; economic justification was asserted *ex post facto*.[12]

The most influential of such arguments was Schumpeter's.[13] Writing after the First World War, he defined imperialism as 'the objectless disposition on the part of a state to unlimited forcible expansion'. It was not a manifestation of capitalism, which Schumpeter, like Herbert Spencer, thought to be rational, hence unwarlike. Rather, it was atavistic, reflecting the continued influence in society of a military, landowning aristocracy, whose traditional ideology, which included elements of protectionism and territorial expansion, had not been wholly replaced by that of the bourgeoisie. In other words, where Lenin took imperialism to be the consequence of a capitalism past its apogee, Schumpeter ascribed it to a period of capitalist immaturity.

He was no doubt moved towards this by his own Central European origins. Germany loomed much larger in his consciousness than Britain. Indeed, Germany also makes the better starting-point for a discussion of Japan, since both countries were 'late developers' in industry and empire. Japanese imperialism, as we shall see, possessed some of the features to which Schumpeter referred.

It can also be related to the kind of social tensions that Wehler takes to be the key to Bismarck's policies.[14] As Wehler describes it, the social tensions deriving from industrialization, especially working-class unrest, were widely thought to threaten the stability of the Bismarckian structure inside Germany. Expansion had two attractions as a means of reducing them. First, it could divert discontents from domestic grievances to the pursuit of prestige overseas. Second, it could provide the resources with which to improve the lot of the economically disadvantaged, so helping to reconcile them to the regime's blemishes.

[11] Eugene Staley, extract (1935) in Wright, op. cit., 77–80.
[12] Carlton Hayes, extract (1941) in Wright, op. cit., 81–8.
[13] Joseph Schumpeter, extract (1919–27) in Wright op. cit., 47–61, and in Boulding and Mukerjee, op. cit., 34–59.
[14] Hans-Ulrich Wehler, 'Industrial growth and early German imperialism' (1972).

Despite Bismarck's own preference for a free trade version of imperialism—because it minimized both costs and risks—these considerations led him to use the authority of the state ostentatiously to promote foreign trade and acquire colonies. His purpose was political, that is, to win support and foster unity at home. Thus he made imperialism into a weapon for holding back revolution: 'an integrative force in a recently founded state which . . . was unable to conceal its class divisions'. There were Japanese conservatives in the early years of the twentieth century who would gladly have made Bismarck in these respects a model for themselves.

It is apparent that the student of Japanese imperialism has no lack of Western examples from which to choose for purposes of comparison. They differ from one another partly because of the choice of countries from which supporting data are drawn. By the same token, when considering Japan one must take account of differences between its historical experience and the West's. Whether one sees imperialism as a phenomenon determined by the nature of the metropolitan society, or as a response to international circumstance, it matters that Japanese imperialism came into existence in a way quite unlike that of Britain or France or Germany or the United States.

In the middle of the nineteenth century Japan was incorporated into the treaty port system, which the powers, led by Britain, had devised to regulate their access to the trade of China on advantageous terms. It imposed on the countries of East Asia a number of commercial and political disabilities, such as have led Chinese and Japanese scholars to describe the position of their countries within it as 'semi-colonial'. The Japanese reacted vigorously to this situation. A political revolution in 1868 brought to power a group of leaders determined to make Japan strong. Within a generation they had dismantled feudalism, substituting an emperor-centred bureaucratic state; created a modern army and navy; instituted legal codes and education of the Western type; and taken the first major steps towards industrial development. Using the bargaining-power this gave them, they successfully demanded revision of Japan's 'unequal treaties'. Thereafter they built an empire: Taiwan, taken over from China in 1895; the southern half of Sakhalin (Karafuto) and a sphere of influence in south Manchuria, acquired from Russia in 1905; Korea, made a protectorate in 1905, a colony in 1910.

The nature of its origins gave a special character to Japanese imperialism. This is evident in writings about it by both Japanese and foreigners. For instance, in so far as the processes of social and economic change which made Japanese expansion possible can be described as the development of capitalism in Japan, the way is open to an interpretation of it based on Marxist thought; but the application of that thought to the Japanese case has produced analyses that are not quite orthodox in European terms. As stated by Tanin and Yohan in 1934, [15] the initial stage of Japanese expansion after 1894 derived from *samurai* desires to extend Japanese influence on the Asian mainland as a means of resisting 'white' imperialism. Japan's weakness within the treaty port system made this practicable only in unequal partnership with Britain. Until the Russo-Japanese War, therefore, Japanese actions were not a product of finance capitalism, but an opportunistic attempt to increase 'primitive capitalist accumulation' in order to enhance the country's strength. Even after 1905, when Japanese imperialism became more obviously capitalistic in its motivations, its social base was still an alliance between the military and the emerging bourgeoisie under the aegis of the monarchy. This balance of political forces reflected the fact that the preceding bourgeois revolution had been incomplete. In fact, late nineteenth-century modernization had been made politically acceptable in Japan only by a compromise between the modernizing bureaucrats and the former feudal ruling class. Because of this, it had been impossible, Tanin and Yohan argue, for the bourgeoisie wholly to do away with the medieval structure of agriculture, with the result that the growth of Japan's domestic economy was impaired by lack of purchasing power, so forcing industry to look outward for markets. Japanese imperialism was therefore 'immature', concerned more with trade and sources of raw material than with exports of capital.

This analysis has been modified and elaborated by Japanese Marxist writers since 1945, but not basically rejected. In an article published in 1956, [16] Fujii Shōichi described Japanese imperialism before 1904 as 'feudal, militarist and dependent', a product of 'the traditional ambition of the emperor system for territorial acquisition . . . reinforced by the emergence of industrial capitalism'. Its early successes, manifested in wartime profits, reparations, and the opening of new markets, made possible a rapid advance in Japanese capitalism, especially for those large-scale companies, the *zaibatsu*, which had

[15] O. Tanin and E. Yohan, extract (1934) in Marlene Mayo (ed.), *The Emergence of Imperial Japan* (1970), 69–73.
[16] Fujii Shōichi, extract (1956) in Mayo, op. cit., 76–82.

strong government links. They quickly evolved into examples of monopoly enterprise. It was such companies that took the lead in promoting
Japanese economic expansion overseas after 1905. Japanese finance
capitalism, however, remained weak. Accordingly, in the years before
the First World War Japanese imperialism was still characterized by
'the concentration of power in the hands of the military', and showed
itself 'dependent upon and subordinate to the imperialism of other
powers'.

In effect, Fujii identified two distinct sources of imperialism in
modern Japan. One was domestic: the 'absolutist' alliance of bureaucrat, landlord, and bourgeois, which was to keep the masses in subjec-
tion. The other was international: the need for Japan to conform with
'a world structure dominated by capitalism and imperialism' in order
to survive as an independent state. Inoue Kiyoshi, the most influential
Marxist writer on the subject,[17] associated these two concepts with the
'internal' and 'external' types of imperialism which in Lenin's view
existed side by side in Tsarist Russia: the first designed to maintain
Tsarist autocracy over the subject peoples of the Russian empire; the
second aimed at the extension of Russian power in Persia, Mongolia,
and Manchuria.

Inoue, like his predecessors, acknowledged the importance of the
Russo-Japanese war as a turning-point, marking the transition from a
pre-modern feudal to a modern capitalist stage of Japanese imperialism, but he chose to treat Japan's partnership with Western imperialism as belonging to the capitalist stage—that is, based on community
of interests—rather than as simply a response to *force majeure*. In one
sense, he argued, Japan fought the war against Russia as a proxy for
Anglo-American imperialism, opening up Asia more completely to
exploitation. Its reward was economic privilege, the gains from which
increased the influence of capitalists at home. Yet this was not accompanied by a decline in the power of the military. On the contrary, their
power grew, because of Japan's involvement in international rivalries.
Defence was vital to national policy; colonies contributed to defence;
the military had a key role in the government of colonies. Moreover,
although territorial expansion, which the military urged, was not always
the policy the *zaibatsu* would have chosen, such companies derived
profits from military expenditure and secured access to markets over-

---

[17] Inoue Kiyoshi, *Nihon teikokushugi no keisei* (1968). Much of the argument is incorporated into Jon Haliday, *A Political History of Japanese Capitalism* (1975), especially
100–2, 111–13.

seas from the use of military force. Consequently, the alliance between
the bourgeoisie and the military bureaucracy held firm. It follows that
the Japanese social order was not typically that of the 'final' stage of
capitalism even after 1905.

Marxist writers about Japanese imperialism have thus had to come
to terms with the fact that it did not quite relate to capitalism in the way
required by Leninist theory. They have done so by a process of implicit
intellectual borrowing. Modifying Schumpeter, they hold that the
weakness of the bourgeois element in nineteenth-century political
change left Japan with a military bureaucracy—ideologically, if not
genetically, the heirs to a feudal class—which exercised an exceptional
influence on policy. Equally, they maintain that the existence of an
international imperialist structure, by which Japan was threatened,
provided an external impulse working in the same direction. So Japanese imperialism becomes the illegitimate child of *Western* capitalism,
with international rivalry as midwife.

Inevitably, eclecticism of this kind increases the overlap between
Marxist and non-Marxist interpretations. The latter, too, recognize
the importance of the military and of the international environment.
They accept that Japanese capitalism was weak and that this has implications for the nature of Japanese expansion. Indeed, were it not for
the different theoretical propositions underlying them, Marxist and
non-Marxist arguments could in the case of Japan be treated as part of
a single spectrum of ideas.

The most recent statement of a non-Marxist viewpoint has been
made by Jansen.[18] His emphasis is not on 'the defensive and reactive'
characteristics of Japanese expansion—countering European domination of East Asia—but on the fact that imperialist ambition was a logical response to awareness of living in an imperialist world. At the end
of the nineteenth century, he believes, 'most articulate Japanese were
prepared to accept the argument that Darwinian selection and competition in the international order made imperialist expansion the
expected path for a vigorous and healthy polity that expected to compete'. The relevance of Japanese domestic society to this is that it contained no significant inhibitions against the growth of such an attitude.
Religion tolerated or supported it, as did the monarchy. The emerging
parliamentary system developed in an atmosphere that equated empire

---

[18] Marius B. Jansen, 'Japanese imperialism: late Meiji perspectives' (1984).

with patriotism. Hence outright opposition came only from those who were on the periphery of contemporary society, mostly socialists and romantic idealists. This makes imperialism the social norm, not an aberration to be excused or defended: there is no need to seek 'some special center of political, military or economic conniving on which to fasten the blame'.

Not everyone is willing to be so positive. Iriye, whose books and articles constitute the most convincing body of English-language writing on the subject in the last ten to fifteen years,[19] agrees on the importance of the West's example, but identifies a variety of Japanese responses to it, the relative importance of which changes over time. One was broadly economic: an attempt to secure Japan's position in the world through trade and emigration. Another was military and territorial: the pursuit of strength through the direct control of overseas bases and resources. In the early phase of Japanese imperialism, he argues, the two strands existed side by side. As Japanese industry grew stronger, notably during the First World War, so it became common to give priority to economic aims, pursued in rivalry with other powers, but within an international framework to which both they and Japan were willing to conform. Only after the trading crisis of 1929–30 did Japan decisively reject this form of co-operation. From that time on, a renewed sense of national danger, seen primarily in economic terms—that is, of a Japan shut out by its rivals from markets for its manufactures, from outlets for its surplus population, from access to the raw materials it required—brought back a commitment to military solutions. The consequence was the plan to build a Co-prosperity Sphere, necessitating war.

Both Jansen and Iriye have been influenced by a corpus of historical writing on the origins of the Pacific War, stimulated by the war crimes trials. After 1945 the search for scapegoats, both by victors and vanquished, focused attention on the power of the Japanese military and the inability of political institutions to restrain it in the years before Pearl Harbor. This is the aspect of Japanese expansion most familiar to Western readers. All the same, the many books concerning it deal more with foreign affairs—Japan's relations with the powers—than they do with the nature of Japanese empire, or the relationship between the Japanese and other peoples within the Co-prosperity

[19] See especially, Akira Iriye, *Pacific Estrangement. Japanese and American expansion 1897–1911* (1972); 'The failure of economic expansionism, 1918–1931' (1974); and 'The failure of military expansionism' (1972).

Sphere. Even the recent history of Japan's colonial empire by Myers and Peattie[20] defines its subject-matter in such a way as to leave out Manchuria and the other territories into which Japan expanded after 1931.

The first wide-ranging study of the Co-prosperity Sphere, based on evidence assembled for the war crimes trials, was that by F. C. Jones.[21] As he described it, there were two competing themes in Japanese external policy: Western-style imperialism, and Asian solidarity. There would have been no important conflict between them had the Western powers consented to Japanese hegemony in East Asia, but since they did not, foreign relations became the subject of a struggle within Japan between adherents of the two. A central element in it was 'the effort of the Army to regain for itself that pre-eminence in the shaping of national policy . . . which it had appeared to be losing in the nineteen-twenties'. The actions to which this gave rise rested on a number of attitudes and motivations: a heritage of feudal attitudes towards civil authority; a literal belief in the constitutional provisions concerning the emperor's command prerogative and the functions of the General Staff; and the prevalence among groups of younger officers of ideas deploring the changes brought about by industrialization and urbanization, whether in Japan or in the world at large.

This assessment of the military roots of Japanese imperialism after 1931 was refined and given more detailed application by Japanese scholars in the 1960s and 1970s, working from newly available official archives. One important series of volumes was published in 1962–3 under the title *Taiheiyō Sensō e no Michi* (*The Road to the Pacific War*), an English version of which has been prepared under the editorship of James Morley.[22] Morley has also edited a compendium on modern Japanese foreign policy, including a long article by Crowley on the military element in it.[23] Two Japanese historians, Tsunoda Jun and Kitaoka Shinichi, have examined military involvement in the formulation of mainland policy for the years before 1918.[24]

---

[20] Ramon Myers and Mark Peattie (ed.), *The Japanese Colonial Empire, 1895–1945* (1984).

[21] F. C. Jones, *Japan's New Order in East Asia: its rise and fall 1937–45* (1954), especially 2–13.

[22] James Morley (ed.), *Deterrent Diplomacy* (1976); *The Fateful Choice* (1980); *The China Quagmire* (1983); *Japan Erupts* (1984).

[23] James Crowley, 'Japan's military foreign policies' (1974).

[24] Tsunoda Jun, *Manshū mondai to kokubō hōshin* (1967); Kitaoka Shinichi, *Nihon rikugun to tairiku seisaku 1906–1918* (1978).

Taken together, these books have greatly increased our knowledge of the part played by military considerations in the extension of Japanese authority overseas. They have also made some of Jones's conclusions about policy-making out of date. Despite this, there are still important gaps. One concerns the political structure of the Greater East Asia Co-prosperity Sphere and Japanese aims concerning it. There are useful studies of parts of the subject,[25] but not enough for confident generalization. Another is the role of banks, companies, and business organizations, both before and after 1930. Almost everyone makes some reference to economic factors: trade, government loans, railway rights, mining operations. Yet it is only quite recently that there have begun to appear the specific studies that can elucidate (or in some cases, provide) the bare statistics on these matters.[26] Until such weaknesses in the literature are made good the interpretation of Japanese imperialism in its later stages will remain in some respects unbalanced and unsatisfactory.

One purpose of this introduction has been to indicate briefly the problems and issues that arise in a discussion of Japanese imperialism. I hope that the rest of the book will provide enough facts and narrative to enable the reader to make a judgement on them. Before entering upon it, however, it is proper that I should make clear the personal prejudices and preconceptions with which I start (so far as I am aware of them).

First, I do not believe in mono-causal explanations of complex historical phenomena, especially those which endure over long periods of time. Even a concept as broad as economic determinism, central though it is to this subject, does not seem to me a *sufficient* basis on which to analyse imperialism, either in the case of Japan, or more generally. Hence I do not find it necessary to make a choice between the theories of internal 'push' and external 'pull'. Both are relevant. Second, I do not believe that the human impetus towards imperialism needs explaining. Men, acting individually or in communities, have

---

[25] For example, on China, J. H. Boyle, *China and Japan at War 1937–1945* (1972); on economic policies, Kobayashi Hideo, *Dai-Toā-Kyoeī-Ken no keisei to hōkai* (1975), and Asada Kyōji (ed.), *Nihon teikokushugi-ka no Chūgoku* (1981); on aspects of Japanese central government organization, Baba Akira, *Nitchū kankei to gaisei kikō no kenkyū* (1983).

[26] On the South Manchuria Railway Co., Andō Hikotarō, *Mantetsu: Nihon teikokushugi to Chūgoku* (1965); on the Ōkura company, *Ōkura zaibatsu no kenkyū: Ōkura to tairiku* (1982).

always sought to establish dominion over others, where they could. What the character of a society, or the international circumstances with which it has to deal, does indeed determine is the timing and direction of the impetus, the degree of its success and failure, the kind of advantages that are sought, the institutions that are shaped to give them durability. That is what I understand by the nature of imperialism. That is what I propose to examine with respect to Japan.

2

The Treaty Port System and Japan

THE most distinctive feature of Japanese imperialism is that it originated within the structure of informal empire which the West established in East Asia during the nineteenth century. In 1850 Japan was politically feudal and economically backward. This made it an easy prey for powerful intruders like Britain, Russia, and the United States, which imposed upon it the same kind of legal and commercial disabilities as had been devised to serve their needs in China. That is to say, Japan was incorporated into the treaty port system. By 1860 it had thereby taken its first steps towards integration into the world economy.

This circumstance was to be important to the development of Japanese imperialism in two ways. First, it conditioned Japanese responses and the international ambitions to which they gave rise. Treaty privilege in China became a Japanese definition of success. Second, it provided an ineluctable context for action. For most of modern history, Japanese leaders had to choose between seeking satisfaction within an imperialist framework of the West's making, or devising an alternative to it. Whichever they chose, the treaty port system could not be disregarded. For these reasons it is appropiate to begin this study by considering that system's nature and its particular implications for Japan.

The nature of the treaty port system

The main thrust of Western imperialism in East Asia during the early and middle years of the nineteenth century was maritime and commercial. Its instrument was Britain, the world's first industrial nation and leading naval power. Its institutional structure was therefore British-made.

Europeans and Americans have always been ready to believe that trade with China holds a potential for profit greater than the reality at any given time has justified, with the result that there has been a gap between expectations and performance. It has been variously explained. Before 1833, when the British share of China's trade still fell within the East India Company's monopoly, the explanation had two facets, one directed towards British faults, the other to Chinese. The first was a criticism of monopoly, deriving from the economic ideas associated with *laissez-faire*. The second was a complaint about the restrictions which the Chinese government imposed, both in confining trade to south China—initially to Canton—and in limiting the rights, personal as well as commercial, that could be exercised by foreign merchants there. To many in contemporary Britain, freedom of trade and freedom for traders were so axiomatic as to justify the use of force to secure a more liberal entry to the Chinese market. Such men were rapidly becoming powerful in British politics. It is no accident that a ten-year period, starting with the Reform Act of 1832, witnessed both the abolition of the East India Company's monopoly and the first Anglo-Chinese War.

Britain in fact fought two wars for the sake of commercial privilege in China: the Opium War of 1840-2 and the Arrow War of 1856-8. The treaty settlements which ended those wars in 1842-3 and 1858-60, respectively, created a pattern of relationships that was to endure into the twentieth century. They had to meet three conditions. First, they were required by mercantile opinion, acting through chambers of commerce and the House of Commons, to guarantee access to the trade of China as widely as possible and with the minimum of constraint. This was the prime objective of British policy. Second, they had to afford foreign merchants a measure of protection against what were held to be the unjust and arbitrary acts of Chinese officials. Third, they had to be readily enforceable. Britain's power in East Asia rested on the strength, especially naval strength, which industrial technology gave it. Even so, the exercise of force at a distance of several thousand miles was neither easy nor cheap. Hence it became an article of faith among British policy-makers that the possession of influence in China must not be dependent upon interference in the domestic administration of that country, such as characterized Britain's role in India. Interference was costly. The point of having an 'informal' empire was that it should be economical to run.

The specific clauses in the treaties which were designed to give effect to these principles reflected the historical experience of the British in China. It is not necessary here to trace their origins. Nor is an account of the China wars particularly relevant. The treaties themselves, however, need to be summarized.

The Opium War ended with the Treaty of Nanking, imposed on a defeated China by Sir Henry Pottinger and signed on 29 August 1842. Its terms, leaving aside such matters as claims for compensation, followed closely the advice pressed upon the Foreign Secretary, Lord Palmerston, by the China coast merchants, which he had embodied in his instructions to British representatives in China at the outbreak of hostilities. The five ports of Canton, Amoy, Foochow, Ningpo, and Shanghai were to be opened to British trade, which was to be carried on 'without molestation or restraint'. British consuls were to be appointed to those ports and were to have a relationship on terms of equality with local Chinese officials. In addition, the island of Hong Kong was to be ceded to Britain 'to be possessed in perpetuity'. In Pottinger's words, this was because it would provide 'an emporium for our trade and a place from which Her Majesty's subjects in China may be alike protected and controlled'.[1] A separate commercial agreement, signed on 18 October 1843, added to these gains. It fixed customs duties for both imports and exports, averaging 5 per cent *ad valorem*; it provided for the establishment of consular courts, at which all civil or criminal cases involving British subjects as defendants were to be tried in accordance with British law; and it introduced a most-favoured-nation clause, whereby any further privileges that might subsequently be granted to other countries would accrue similarly to Britain.

The effect, when taken in conjunction with the terms of parallel French and American agreements, signed in 1844, was to establish the salient features of the treaty port system as it was to apply thereafter, not only in China, but also in several neighbouring countries. Foreigners were to be allowed to trade at specified ports. They would pay low custom duties, which the Chinese government could not change at will, because they were embodied in formal diplomatic documents. The legal provisions, known as extraterritoriality, ensured that foreign residents would be subject only to their own country's law, administered through consular courts. That was so, at least, if their home government set up such courts. If it did not, they were in most respects outside the law entirely. They could rent or buy houses and places of business in designated areas of the open ports, known as foreign settlements. There they could practise their own religions and follow their own ways of life, enjoying—in the words of the American

---

[1] Quoted in W. C. Costin, *Great Britain and China* (1937), 101–2. Costin provides a detailed narrative of British policy in China 1833–1860, based on Foreign Office records.

treaty—'the special protection of the local authorities of government, who shall defend them from all insult or injury on the part of the Chinese'.

These privileges involved a diminution of Chinese sovereignty. They were not reciprocal, that is, did not grant equivalent rights to Chinese in Britain or elsewhere. They have for this reason come to be called 'unequal'. More important for our present purpose is the fact that they brought into existence a kind of 'co-operative' imperialism. Because a gain made by one foreign power was, by virtue of the most-favoured-nation clause, shared by all the rest, treaty rights were not exclusive to any particular signatory. This made it relatively easy for the powers to co-operate in extending them. It also made them willing to let others join their ranks. In the middle years of the century, treaty powers multiplied: to those who signed agreements at the end of the Arrow War in 1858, namely, Britain, France, Russia, and the United States, were added Prussia (1861), Portugal (1862), Denmark and Holland (1863), Spain (1864), Belgium (1865), and Italy (1866). It is not surprising that Japan came to see its own accession to the list as a much-desired symbol of equality.

In the shorter term, what had been achieved at Nanking did not prove wholly satisfactory to the foreign community. Chinese officials continued to be obstructive. The trade of the newly opened ports was disappointing, except at Shanghai. This was usually explained by their remoteness, not only from the areas producing tea and silk, but also from the main population centres of the Yangtze valley. In January 1854 the Manchester Chamber of Commerce concluded that 'without permission to go to the interior of the country our trade with China must remain stunted and crippled'.[2]

During 1854 these considerations led the Foreign Secretary, Lord Clarendon, to formulate proposals for revision of the treaties. He sought diplomatic representation at the capital, in order to afford a means of appealing to the Manchu government over the heads of its officials at the ports, together with access to the interior, especially the Yangtze region, for the sake of expanding the trade. Both proposals were rejected by China. The outbreak of the Crimean War prevented any immediate British response to this rebuff, but once that war ended

---

[2] Memorial to Foreign Office, quoted in Nathan A. Pelcovits, *Old China Hands and the Foreign Office* (1948), 14–15. Pelcovits examines in some detail British business attitudes to China in the nineteenth century.

the approach was made again, this time in the context of a fresh dispute at Canton (the *Arrow* afffair). As the repercussions of the dispute carried Britain and China once more into hostilities in the winter of 1856–7, Clarendon took matters out of the hands of Sir John Bowring, the Superintendent of Trade at Hong Kong, and entrusted the conduct of affairs in China, both military and diplomatic, to Lord Elgin, former Governor-General of Canada. He was to work closely with the French envoy, Baron Gros. He was also to secure Chinese consent to the treaty revision proposals made in 1854.

This he did, despite an interruption occasioned by the Indian Mutiny. Canton was captured at the end of December 1857. In the following spring, Elgin and Gros moved north, first to Shanghai, then to Tientsin. At the latter city, negotiating under the guns of French and British gunboats, Chinese plenipotentiaries were forced to concede Elgin's demands. The treaty they concluded on 26 June 1858— Gros signed a similar one next day—became the authoritative statement of foreign rights in China for thirty years or more. Essentially, it added the principle of indefinite geographical extension to the original concept of the treaty port. Access to the interior and the north was achieved, not by opening those areas to foreigners indiscriminately, but by creating new treaty ports along the Yangtze river and on the coasts of the Yellow Sea. Thereafter, whenever the powers demanded entry to new areas, the same practice was followed. By the 1920s there were over seventy places designated as 'treaty ports' (some of which were in fact railheads in the interior).[3]

Nor was the process limited to China. In 1855 Bowring concluded a treaty with Siam (Thailand), establishing a similar system there, but on a more modest scale. Japan, as we shall see, followed in July 1858, this time at America's initiative. The United States was also the first Western power to secure treaty port privileges in Korea (May 1882), though Japan had led the way with a more restricted agreement in 1876. In all these cases, the first treaty to be signed became a model for others, ensuring that most of the countries which had come to terms with China were able to trade comparably with China's coastal neighbours.

Elgin's negotiations also made clear the political relationships on which this kind of informal empire was to rest. His treaty was manifestly a product of military victory. From one point of view Britain and

---

[3] A list of treaty ports and foreign concessions is given in G. C. Allen and Audrey Donnithorne, *Western enterprise in Far Eastern economic development* (1954), Appendix D.

France welcomed the fact, because it ensured, if only for a time, that there would be a compliant regime in the Chinese capital. On the other hand, such a situation had its dangers, as Elgin recognized. Speaking to the Shanghai Chamber of Commerce in January 1859, he referred to the treaties recently concluded with China and Japan as follows: 'Uninvited, and by methods not always of the gentlest, we have broken down the barriers behind which these ancient nations sought to conceal from the world without the mysteries, perhaps also, in the case of China, at least, the rags and rottenness of their waning civilisations.'[4] The risk was that, by so doing, the powers might destroy political stability in the region to their disadvantage. As Elgin put it in a letter to a member of the British cabinet, humiliating the Chinese emperor and impairing his authority might 'kill the goose that lays the golden eggs, throw the country into confusion and imperil the most lucrative trade you have in the world'.[5]

Accordingly, during the next few years the British Foreign Office and its principle advisers in China tried to identify a middle path, namely, a policy that would not draw Britain into territorial control, as in India, but would avoid the opposite extreme of having to fight occasional wars to reassert its interests. Positively, their conclusion was that China must be helped to undertake reforms: of the tax system, in order to provide a stable revenue; of administration, to eliminate endemic corruption and irresponsibility; and of the military establishment, to provide the means for suppressing unrest.[6] Such measures would benefit foreign trade, as well as China. Negatively the powers should refrain meanwhile from actions that would undermine the Manchu dynasty's position. They must uphold the treaties by negotiation with the central government, not by browbeating local officials. They must give no countenance to rebels.

These principles were embodied in an announcement issued in December 1868, known as the Clarendon Declaration. It gave cautious support to the idea of reform, provided China was not pressed 'to advance more rapidly . . . than was consistent with safety and with due and reasonable regard for the feelings of her subjects'. It made a forthright statement of the rights and duties of Peking: 'It is with the

[4] Great Britain, *Parliamentary Papers*, 1859, XXXIII [2571]; IUP edn.,*China*, vol. 33, 877–8.

[5] Quoted in Douglas Hurd, *The Arrow War* (1967), 198.

[6] See proposals by Robert Hart and Thomas Wade, cited in Mary C. Wright, *The last stand of Chinese conservatism* (1957), 263–8.

Central Government . . . that Foreign Powers have entered into Treaties, and it is for the interest of the Central Government that Foreign Powers should recognize its supreme authority over its provincial Governors, and that the Central Government should assume, and . . . be prepared to exercise that authority.'[7] In other words, if the West were to derive maximum benefit from its treaties, Manchu rule would not only have to be pliable. It must also be effective.

It did not follow, of course, that military force would no longer be employed against China or other countries in which the treaty port system existed. London had no wish to be obliged to send a gunboat every time an aggrieved merchant or an angry consul wanted one, but it was not difficult to envisage occasions when to refrain from doing so might imperil the treaty structure as a whole. In 1864 Sir Rutherford Alcock, British minister in Japan, defending himself against the accusation that he had been too ready to call upon the navy as an instrument of diplomacy, set out an argument that was to underlie much of Western policy in East Asia during the next fifty years. The 1858 treaties with Japan, he said, had not been signed willingly. So it was vain to expect that they could be maintained 'by a religious abstinence from the use of force as a means'. Nor was it wise:

It is weakness, or the suspicion of it, which invariably provokes wrong and aggression in the East, and is a far more fertile cause of bad faith and danger among Asiatics than either force or the abuse of strength. Hence it is that all diplomacy in these regions which does not rest on a solid substratum of force, or an element of strength, to be laid bare when all gentler processes fail, rests on false premises, and must of necessity fail in its object.[8]

Clearly, the world into which Japan was being introduced in the 1850s and 1860s was one in which gunboat diplomacy, though brought under discipline, had by no means been abandoned.

The treaty port system in Japan

In the European and American literature of the mid-nineteenth century it was commonly asserted that 'Asiatics', whether Turks or Arabs, Indians or Chinese, shared certain ideas and institutions which made them behave similarly—that is, made them devious, dishonest,

---

[7] Pelcovits, *Old China Hands*, 53–4.
[8] Alcock to Russell, 19 Nov. 1864, in *Parliamentary Papers*, 1864, LVII [3428]; IUP edn., *Japan*, vol 2, 312.

irrational—when dealing with westerners.[9] Since Asian peoples were in this respect alike, it followed that the policies appropriate to one Asian country were in substance applicable to another. Gunboat diplomacy and the treaty port system, though devised for China, should have the same usefulness if employed elsewhere.

The application of this doctrine eventually provided Japan with treaties on the Chinese model. Nevertheless, the manner in which that end was attained differed a good deal from what happened in China, because it had a different starting-point. In the 1630s, following nearly a century of commercial relations with Europe, Japan's *de facto* rulers, the Shōgun of the Tokugawa house, had closed their ports to all foreigners except Dutch and Chinese, who were allowed to remain at Nagasaki. Originally the decision had been taken in order to exclude influences—chiefly Christianity—which were thought to undermine the social order; but by the end of the eighteenth century, when Pacific exploration and the growth of the China trade began to stimulate renewed Western interest in Japan, the policy of the 'closed country' (*sakoku*) had become axiomatic, a matter of 'ancestral law'. In consequence, 'opening' Japan, if it could be achieved at all, was soon seen by the West to involve bringing about a major shift in Tokugawa attitudes and policy. This, many believed, was likely to require initiatives by governments, backed by force.

British interest in undertaking an initiative was half-hearted. During the Napoleonic wars, when Java was temporarily taken over from the Dutch, the British Lieutenant-Governor, Thomas Stamford Raffles, tried without success to substitute a British trade with Nagasaki for that of Holland. His superiors in India gave him no encouragement. Those in England did little more, with the result that his abortive missions of 1813 and 1814 were never followed up. Indeed, for the next forty years, while London occasionally paid lip-service to the idea of promoting trade with Japan, it did nothing much to bring it about. Palmerston's instructions to the Superintendent of Trade in China in 1834 included an injunction cautiously to ascertain 'whether it may not be possible to establish commercial intercourse with Japan'. Aberdeen wrote in rather more positive language to Sir John Davis in 1845, but concluded, discouragingly, that failure in such an enterprise 'could scarcely draw along with it any serious national damage'. Clarendon, writing to Bowring in 1854, aware that an American expedition was

---

[9] Western attitudes are discussed in V. G. Kiernan, *The Lords of Human Kind* (1969).

already on its way to Japan, expressed the view that if America suc-
ceded, Britain could profit from its example. If it failed, 'it might be
better to wait awhile'.[10] Given the lukewarm tone of all these statements, it is not surprising that Britain's representatives found more
important things to do in China.

Russian interest in Japan was also peripheral, though in a different
sense.[11] It focused on the potential importance of Japan to Russian
expansion in the Amur and Siberian regions, rather than on prospects for Russo-Japanese trade. Any maritime supply route from
Europe to the Russian settlements on the Sea of Okhotsk would, it
was recognized, benefit from the opening of Japanese ports. Japanese
agriculture might well be able to provide foodstuffs for the settlements. There were also potential boundary problems concerning the
islands north of Japan, into which the hunters and fishermen of both
countries had begun to move. For these reasons Nikolai Rezanov was
sent to Nagasaki in 1804 formally to seek a relaxation of Japan's seclusion laws in Russia's favour. He met with refusal and scant cour-
tesy. The incident precipitated a number of local clashes in the
Kurile Islands, but it seems also to have had the effect of discouraging further Russian approaches to Japan, for in the middle years of
the nineteenth century Russia, like Britain, remained content to wait
on American action, showing a concern principally to protect its
interests in the north from any possible British or American incursions.

The United States had stronger motives than either Britain or
Russia for seeking relations with Japan.[12] Whaling vessels, many of
which were American, regularly fished off the Japanese coast. They
had need of ports of refuge and supply. Moreover, plans had been discussed in America for a Pacific steamer route, linking California and
China, which depended to some extent on being able to obtain stores
and fuel in Japan. The idea was given greater substance after 1840 by
the opening of Shanghai, as well as by the extension of American
sovereignty to Oregon and California. Pressures on Washington to
send a naval expedition to Japan increased.

[10] The quotations are given in W. G. Beasley, *Great Britain and the opening of Japan*
(1951), 15, 62, 97.
[11] See generally, George A. Lensen, *The Russian push toward Japan* (1959).
[12] On American relations with Japan, see Payson J. Treat, *The early diplomatic relations
between the United States and Japan* (1917); and T. Wada, *American foreign policy toward
Japan during the nineteenth century* (1928).

The fact that these pressures were not much related to the prospects for trade in that country was reflected in the expedition's results. When Commodore Matthew C. Perry took his squadron of four warships to Uraga at the entrance to Edo Bay (now Tokyo Bay) in July 1853, he had instructions to deliver a letter from the President of the United States, which asked for a treaty of friendship and commerce. In fact, however, the text dwelt more particularly on facilities for shipping. This accorded with Perry's own inclinations and experience as a naval officer. When he returned for the Japanese reply in March 1854, negotiating at Yokohama under cover of his squadron's guns, he concluded a treaty which opened two ports, Shimoda and Hakodate, to American ships; provided for the future appointment of an American consul at Shimoda; but included no specific permission for trade.

As was to be expected, the British and Russian naval commanders in Chinese waters soon found opportunities to follow Perry's example, signing conventions with Japan in October 1854 and February 1855, respectively. All the same, neither they nor Perry gained much credit within the Western mercantile community for what they had done. In the matter of trade their agreements fell so far short of what had been imposed on China that they aroused a chorus of disapproval on the China coast. They were for the same reason almost equally unpopular in London and New York. The effect was for the first time seriously to turn American and British policy towards obtaining proper commercial treaties with Japan, to replace the ones already made. It was clear from the outset that 'proper' in this context must mean 'in the Chinese manner'.

Townsend Harris arrived at Shimoda in August 1856 as America's first consul. He had travelled via Siam, where he had concluded a treaty based on Bowring's. He therefore had some notion of how to go about modifying the China treaties so as to fit conditions elsewhere. He had also had some experience on that occasion of using Britain as a stalking-horse. This was to be useful to him, for his own negotiations during the next two years—undertaken without naval support, as he constantly complained—would not have succeeded without it. Especially important to him were reports of the capture of Canton in the winter of 1857–8, reaching Japan through Nagasaki, since these enabled him to persuade Japanese negotiators to accept his own proposals as a form of insurance against the British wrath to come. 'There will be a great difference', he told them, 'between a treaty made with a single individual, unattended, and one made with a person who should bring fifty men-of-war to these shores.'[13]

This modification of gunboat diplomacy—using the threat of someone else's gunboats—enabled Harris to overcome Japanese reluctance and secure a treaty. Signed on 29 July 1858, it included most of the features which Elgin had been demanding at Tientsin. True, there was to be no trade in opium. Unaccountably, there was no most-favoured-nation clause. The rest was there, however: a fixed import and export tariff, mostly at 5 per cent *ad valorem*; extraterritoriality and foreign lawcourts; a resident minister in Edo (Tokyo); consuls at the treaty ports. Five ports were to opened to trade on dates between 1859 and 1863: Hakodate, Nagasaki, Hyōgo (Kobe), Kanagawa (Yokohama), and Niigata. In addition, foreigners were to be admitted to the cities of Osaka and Edo in 1862 and 1863, respectively.

In effect, Harris had transplanted the treaty port system from China to Japan. Representatives of other countries quickly moved to share in his achievement. In August, treaties were signed by Holland and Russia. Elgin, arriving a few days later, but without the threatened fleet, had to negotiate in a hurry because he wanted to get back to China. He borrowed both Harris's secretary and his treaty's stipulations, except that he inserted a most-favoured-nation clause. Gros came in October, adding France.

There were still to be some adjustments to the pattern of the agreements. Japanese opposition to them led to several attacks on foreigners, individually and collectively, in the next few years. Reacting, the powers, led by Britain, at first proved willing to make allowances for the difficulties in which the Tokugawa government found itself, agreeing in the summer of 1862 to defer for five years the opening of Hyōgo, Niigata, Edo, and Osaka, provided all restrictions on trade at the ports already open be abolished. This proved insufficient to stabilize the situation in Japan, however. Fresh attacks on foreigners soon brought the first large-scale use of force against Japanese coastal cities, a British bombardment of Kagoshima in 1863. A joint foreign expedition against Shimonoseki followed in 1864.

One result was to convince many Japanese activists that Western military strength was irresistible. Another was to open the way to a reaffirmation of foreign rights. A tariff convention, signed on 25 June

---

[13] Quoted in W. G. Beasley, *Select documents on Japanese foreign policy* (1955), 163–4. The text of the treaty Harris concluded is ibid., 183–9,

1866, adjusted some customs dues and tidied up minor points of difficulty in the original treaties. Yet perhaps its most significant article was
the one in which the Japanese government was made to declare that
'Japanese merchants and traders of all classes are at liberty to trade
directly, and without the interference of Government officers, with
foreign merchants, not only at the open ports of Japan, but also in all
foreign countries.' (Article IX.)[14] Japanese, it was agreed, were to be
allowed to travel abroad for purposes of trade and study, subject to the
provisions of a passport system.

The Chineseness of the arrangements made in Japan did not consist
only in the terms of these treaties and the attitudes underlying them.
Giving naval support, when required, was usually the task of squad-
rons based in China. Appeals from the British consular courts in Japan
were to a Supreme Court at Shanghai. Many of the Western merchants in Yokohama, Kobe, and Nagasaki came in the first place from
the Chinese treaty ports, often as agents of firms already trading there.
They brought with them their Chinese personal servants and commercial staff (in such numbers that Chinese made up half the foreigners
resident in Japan in 1894). They occupied settlements much like those
at Canton or Shanghai, though on a smaller scale; communities with a
social life which focused on the club—and intermittently the race-
course—having their own foreign-language newspapers and even a
semblance of municipal government.[15]

For many years after the opening of the ports Western merchants,
living in these settlements, controlled almost the whole of Japan's
foreign trade. As late as 1890 four-fifths of silk exports were said to be
in foreign hands, though Japanese were by that time beginning to overcome the disadvantages of inexperience and inadequate credit by
which they had at first been handicapped. The value of the trade, of
course, was small by Chinese standards, totalling less than a quarter of
China's in the 1880s. In fact, Rutherford Alcock's biographer, Alexander Michie, himself an Old China Hand, described it in its early
days as being on 'such a lilliputian scale . . . that to merchants accustomed to the large transactions of China the whole affair wore something of the air of a comic opera'.[16]

Notwithstanding this patronizing view of it, Japan's trade had much

---

[14] Text in *Parliamentary Papers*, 1867, LXXIV [3758]; IUP edn., *Japan*, vol. 2, 493–6.
[15] On the treaty port communities, see Allen and Donnithorne, *Western enterprise*,
chap. xii; and J. E. Hoare, 'The Japanese treaty ports' (1971).
[16] A. Michie, *The Englishman in China* (1900), II, 27.

the same character and functions as China's. It opened a market in
Japan for Western manufactured goods: mostly texiles, but also
weapons and a growing quantity of machinery. A large proportion of
these things came from Britain. Exports, like China's, with which they
competed, were mainly silk and tea, though they also included coal.
Raw silk had quickly found buyers in France and Italy in the 1860s,
but went increasingly to America after about 1885. Tea also found its
best outlet in America. As a result, the United States became Japan's
best customer, taking 30 per cent of Japanese exports by value, sometimes more.[17]

Thus Japan, following China, took on a trading role as primary producer, relying on Europe and America for manufactures. These were
the familiar concomitants of the West's informal empire in East Asia.
They did not last. Whereas China's place in the world economy was to
remain essentially unchanged into the middle of the twentieth century,
Japan's was being revolutionized by a programme of modernization
even before 1900. The origins of the change lie in Japanese reponses
to the events we have been describing.

[17] For Japan's export trade before 1900, see S. Sugiyama, *Japan's industrialization in
the world economy* (forthcoming). Trade is discussed further in Chapter 9 below.

3

Modernization and Imperialism

JAPANESE modernization was not exclusively the product of western imperialism by any means. For three hundred years before the opening of the ports Japan had been developing a form of commercial capitalism which bequeathed to the modern economy an essential groundwork of attitudes and expertise. During the same period the feudal polity had become more centralized, turning its *samurai* into bureaucrats. In its early years the Meiji state did little more than take that process one stage further, albeit in alien guise. What is more, Japan's literacy rate in 1850 seems to have been as high as that in many parts of Europe, perhaps higher than some. None of these things depended for their existence on Western pressure or example.

Yet if one takes modernization to be a policy, rather than a process, Western imperialism had much to do with bringing it about, for it constituted a danger against which radical reform appeared to be the only promising defence. Equally, it afforded an example of the use of power that encouraged emulation. In this sense, modernization was a link between the treaty port system and the emergence of Japan's own imperialism. More specifically, the manner of it had the effect of shaping certain ideas, institutions, and interest groups, which were not only necessary to expansion, but also influences on the way it was carried out. These need to be examined before we turn to an analysis of Japan's relations with its neighbours.

Japanese responses to the West

It was to be expected that there would be Japanese hostility towards the treaty port system. Nor is it surprising that those Japanese who were in a position to form an opinion and express it almost all shared certain assumptions on the subject. One was that their country was too weak to be able to match the Western powers. From this there derived a sense of threat which was to remain not far from the surface in Japanese life for a hundred years, even in periods of success and apparent self-confidence. A second was that it would not suffice merely to lament the situation. Something had to be done about it. Trying to decide what this should be was the point at which political debate began.[1]

One strand in the debate had its beginning in curiosity about the outside world. Towards the end of the eighteenth century a number of Japanese scholars had begun to take an interest in the mysterious occident, from which they were shut off by the seclusion laws. The availability of a limited number of books, brought in by the Dutch through Nagasaki, enabled them to make some progress in acquiring a knowledge of it, particularly of those aspects of Western civilization which did not require a subtle understanding of European languages for their study: anatomy, mathematics, astronomy, cartography, art. As a result, by the time the Opium War gave notice of the dangers which Western expansion held for Japan, there were already a few Japanese who had a grounding in modern science and technology.

Fear and resentment gave this curiosity a new direction. From about 1840 onwards, Japanese study of the West increasingly acquired a military emphasis. It also gained a greater measure of official patronage. Sakuma Shōzan (1811–64) is an example of both tendencies. As a senior *samurai*, whose lord became a member of the Tokugawa council, Sakuma was made adviser on coast defence, a post for which he had earlier equipped himself by studying Western gunnery and cannon-founding. He exerted himself to propagate the idea that defending Japan involved learning what foreigners could teach: 'not theories of government and ethics, but highly ingenious techniques and machinery, borrowed so that we might be prepared to ward off indignities from the West'.[2]

Such statements seemed convincing to the small number of Tokugawa officials who recognized that commitment to a Western style of international behaviour was becoming unavoidable for Japan. Their most lucid and powerful spokesman was Hotta Masayoshi, head of the council at the time of Townsend Harris's negotiations. In a memorandum written at the end of 1857, Hotta stated two propositions: that 'military power always springs from national wealth'; and that wealth is 'principally to be found in trade and commerce'. This being so, he argued, Japan's aim must be 'to conclude friendly alliances, to send ships to foreign countries everywhere and conduct trade, to copy the foreigners where they are at their best and so repair our own short-

---

[1] The debates are considered in detail in W. G. Beasley, *The Meiji Restoration* (1972), especially chaps. 3, 5, 7, 8.
[2] Quoted in Richard T. Chang, *From Prejudice to Tolerance* (1970), 181.

comings, to foster our national strength and complete our armaments'.[3]

In so far as this argument concerned defence and the nature of weaponry it was broadly acceptable to *samurai* at large. They were, after all, members of a military ruling class. Nor was there a great deal of objection, except, perhaps, on grounds of practicality, to the gloss added by Yoshida Shōin (1830–59), one of Sakuma's pupils. Defence, Yoshida believed, required territorial expansion: 'to protect the country well is not merely to prevent it from losing the position it holds, but to add to it the positions which it does hold'. He identified them: 'Taking advantage of favourable opportunities, we will seize Manchuria, thus coming face to face with Russia; regaining Korea, we will keep watch on China; taking the islands to the South, we will advance on India.'[4] One can readily understand why Yoshida's memory was cherished by Japanese expansionists in the twentieth century.

Nevertheless, there was an alternative view, which was equally significant for our purposes. It was associated especially with scholars serving the Tokugawa lord of Mito, one of whom, Aizawa Seishisai (1782–1863), wrote a much-praised book expounding it in 1825. The book was called *New Proposals* (*Shinron*). To study the West, it claimed, was to risk contaminating Japanese culture: 'the weakness of some for novel gadgets and rare medicines . . . has led many to admire foreign ways'. Nor was disapproval of this just a matter of cultural conservatism. The 'treacherous foreigner' might well take advantage of this situation to 'lure ignorant people to his ways', with results that could be 'harmful and weakening'.[5] At worst, they might end in foreign invasion and the conquest of Japan.

One purpose of Aizawa's argument was to persuade men that defence did not depend solely on weapons and technology. It also involved leadership and morale. Morale, in turn, rested on the preservation of traditional attitudes and values. As his lord, Tokugawa Nariaki, put it in a memorandum on the subject of the Perry negotiations in 1853, a government's first task was to set an example of resolution. Without it, 'the gun-batteries and other preparations made will . . . be so much ornament, never put to effective use'.[6]

[3] Beasley, *Select documents*, 167.
[4] Quoted in David M. Earl, *Emperor and Nation in Japan* (1964), 173–4.
[5] R. Tsunoda (ed.), *Sources of Japanese Tradition* (1958), 601.
[6] Beasley, *Select documents*, 106.

Once the ports had been opened in 1859 this debate between those who espoused and those who resisted the use of Western methods and ideas was subordinated to more urgent disputes about the locus of authority. There followed a decade of turbulence, marked by assassinations, attempted *coups d'état*, local rebellions, civil war. Their nature and complexities need not concern us here. Their outcome does, however. In 1868 they brought to power—finally, as it proved—new leaders, acting in the emperor's name, who overthrew the Tokugawa and launched Japan upon a programme of modernization in the Western manner. Central to it was the concept of 'wealth and strength' (*fukoku-kyōhei*). This provided the background to a renewal of the debate about the West in more sophisticated terms.

The treaties had not only opened Japanese ports to trade. Agreements like that of 1866 had also made it possible for Japanese students to go to American and European universities, for Japanese scholars to acquire and translate a wider sample of foreign books, for Western experts to be brought to Japan as teachers and advisers. In consequence, there was available in Japan after 1868 a much greater range of knowledge about the West than earlier generations had been able to call upon. One thing this made clear was that Western strength was not a simple matter of technology and trade. Behind technology stood science; behind trade, industry; behind them both, particular kinds of law and institutions and philosophy.

Some men wanted Japan to go wholeheartedly down the path of adopting them. Fukuzawa Yukichi (1835–1901) was the most famous of these. He had begun life as a student of Dutch; transferred to English when the ports were opened; visited Europe and America with official missions in the 1860s; written a best seller on Western customs and society; then settled down after 1868 to a career as educator and writer. His overriding purpose, according to his autobiography, was 'to lead the whole country into the ways of civilization, and to make Japan a great nation, strong in military might, prosperous in trade'.[7] To this end, he believed, it was necessary for Japan to acquire the 'spirit' of the West, namely, that of self-reliance and rationality, in addition to its material trappings. To do so would have two consequences. First, it would contribute to the development of the national will and a proper understanding of science, thereby affording 'the best possible means of guaranteeing the safety and integrity of Japan from rapacious and

---

[7] Quoted in Carmen Blacker, *The Japanese Enlightenment* (1964), 121.

unscrupulous foreigners'.[8] Second, it would make it possible for Japan to move towards the stage of 'enlightenment,' defined in Social Darwinist terms, which some countries in the West had already reached.

This argument did not by any means make Fukuzawa an uncritical admirer of all things Western. In the newspaper, *Jiji Shimpō*, which he founded in 1881, he set out his ideas as follows: 'We want our learning independent, not licking up the lees and scum of the westerners. We want our commerce independent, not dominated by them. We want our law independent, not held in contempt by them. We want our religion independent, not trampled underfoot by them'.[9] Yet he did not equate this independence with traditionalism. To achieve it, Japan would have to stand aside from Asia, he wrote, not only culturally, in the search for Western-style sources of strength, but also politically, in order to provide the kind of leadership which Asia seemed unable to furnish for itself. In this sense, Japan must 'quit Asia' (*Datsu-A*): 'We cannot wait for our neighbour countries to become so civilized that all may combine together to make Asia progress. We must rather break out of formation and behave in the same way as the civilised countries of the West are doing'.[10]

It was another writer of the period, Tokutomi Sohō (1863–1957), who most clearly extended this argument into a justification for Japanese expansion. His first book, published in 1886, had accepted Herbert Spencer's thesis that an industrial society was one which by its nature renounced war and aggression. By 1893 he had moved away from that position. Notwithstanding all that Japan had achieved by way of reforms in politics, law, and education, plus substantial progress in commerce and industry, the West, he complained, still refused to revise the treaties which were 'our shame, our dishonour'. For all that they made up the 'most progressive, developed, civilized, and powerful nation in the Orient', Japanese could not escape 'the scorn of the white people'.[11] War, ironically, afforded an opportunity to change that state of affairs. As Tokutomi saw it, victory over China in 1894–5 gave his country the kind of international respect that more peaceful policies had never done. The powers had been shown that 'civilization is not a monopoly of the white man'. They had been made to realize that Japanese, too, had 'a character

---

[8] Ibid., 33.
[9] Ibid., 11–12.
[10] Ibid., 136.
[11] Quoted in John D. Pierson, *Tokutomi Sohō* (1980), 229.

suitable for great achievements in the world'.[12] Building on this,
Japanese must use their new-found strength to establish domination
over their neighbours, both for the sake of winning security, reputation
and economic advantage for themselves, and in order to bring civilization to other countries in East Asia under Japanese protection.

This strand of thought might be described as being in the line of
descent from that of Sakuma Shōzan and Yoshida Shōin, save that it
used Western values to justify Japanese expansion, as well as Western
technology to make it feasible. It was to be a leading element in the
ideology of Japanese imperialism in the twentieth century. That ideology, however, also had a secondary theme, which had its antecedents
in the writings of Aizawa Seishisai and the Mito school.

During the 1880s there was a general slackening of Japanese enthusiasm for Western ways. In part, this took the form of a more judicious
approach to cultural borrowing, such as Fukuzawa showed. On 11
February 1889, for example, the first issue of the newspaper *Nihon*
(Japan), announcing Japan's new Western-style constitution, commented: 'We recognize the excellence of Western civilization. We
value the Western theories of rights, liberty and equality; and we
respect Western philosophy and morals. . . . Above all, we esteem
Western science, economics, and industry. These, however, ought not
to be adopted simply because they are Western; they ought to be
adopted only if they contribute to Japan's welfare'.[13] Simultaneously
there was emerging a greater concern for the preservation of Japan's
own philosophical traditions, conceived as a *mélange* of Shintō and
Confucian ideas, such as Aizawa and his colleagues had put together.
Thus the constitution of 1889 incorporated a specifically Shintō exposition of the emperor's authority. The Education Rescript of 1890 gave
priority to Confucian precepts as the basis for moral teaching in
schools.

From this traditionalism there was fashioned an approach to Japan's
relations with the outside world which emphasized Japanese values,
not Western ones. What is more, Japanese values were increasingly
seen to be Asian values. It followed that one purpose of establishing
Japanese power in East Asia was to defend Asia's soul, not merely its
territory.

One can illustrate this from the writings of Okakura Kakuzō

---

[12] Ibid., 235–6.
[13] Quoted in Kenneth B. Pyle, *The New Generation in Meiji Japan* (1969), 94.

(1862–1913). Okakura's central argument was that there was a single Asian culture, composed of different regional ingredients—Arab chivalry, Persian poetry, Indian religion, Chinese ethics—of which Japan had over the centuries become the chief repository. The qualities that had made it possible to synthesize these various components into a harmonious whole—to Okakura, an 'instinctive eclecticism'[14]— had also saved Japanese society from being overwhelmed by Western influence. Yet in the process many Japanese had become so eager to identify themselves with European civilization 'that our continental neighbours regard us as renegades'.[15] Consequently, in order to save Asia, Japan must reaffirm a commitment to its own inherited ideals. Only in this way would it be possible to restore 'the old Asiatic unity' and give Asia the self-reliance to assert itself against the West.

Clearly, Okakura envisaged a different kind of Japanese influence in East Asia from that which Fukuzawa and Tokutomi were proposing. His insistence on being 'Asian', on creating an anti-Western partnership between Japan and its neighbours, reflected a determination to pursue national interests by means that had little to do with the treaty port system and the 'civilizing' mission associated with it. Many of his contemporaries shared that determination. After 1914 their views were to carry increasing weight, particularly in the shaping of policy towards China.

Meanwhile, there were some points, apart from the overriding need for national strength, on which the majority of Japanese were able to agree. One was revision of the treaties.[16] This had first been mooted in 1872, but the powers, led by Britain, had proved unwilling at that time to relinquish any substantial part of their privileges. Further talks took place on several occasions during the 1880s, always with the same result. Japanese resentment therefore grew, manifesting itself in inflammatory speeches, newspaper articles, even a bomb attack on the Foreign Minister. Despite all this it was not until 1893 that negotiations with Britain began to make progress, opening the way to the first genuinely reciprocal foreign treaty, signed in July 1894. It abolished extraterritoriality, subject to the implementation of new Japanese legal codes, and ended the special rights of foreign settlements. Both changes were to take effect from 1899. However, it also provided for treaty control over tariffs to continue for a further twelve years there-

---

[14] Okakura Kakuzō, *The Ideals of the East* (1904), 222–3.
[15] Okakura Kakuzō, *The Awakening of Japan* (1905), 101.
[16] On treaty revision, see F. C. Jones, *Extraterritoriality in Japan* (1931).

after, that is, until 1911. Thus, although Japan had at last won nominal freedom from its 'semi-colonial' status—the other powers quickly signed similar agreements—not all the symbols of inequality were immediately removed. Vestiges remained, to act as an irritant to Japanese opinion throughout a period in which, paradoxically, two major wars were won and the nucleus of a colonial empire was established.

Wealth and strength

If one consequence of semi-colonial status in Japan was to prompt attitudes of mixed hostility and emulation towards the West, another, as we have indicated, was to provide motivation for a programme of reform under the slogan 'wealth and strength'. This was of importance to the development of Japanese imperialism in various ways.

Most obviously, it brought about disparities between Japan and its neighbours, making imperialism easier to pursue. By 1894, the year in which the treaties were revised, Japan had already put into effect the basic policies which the powers had been urging unsuccessfully on China since the Treaty of Tientsin.[17] The country had stable political leadership: power was chiefly in the hands of former *samurai* who had played a major part in overthrowing the Tokugawa, several of whom were to remain key figures until the First World War. Their subordinates comprised a centralized bureaucracy, chosen and promoted by examination, which was staffed at first by other former *samurai*, then after about 1890 increasingly by graduates of the newly established universities. They operated a tax system which provided a dependable revenue; worked within a structure of laws and lawcourts which the powers were willing to accept as 'civilized'; and had the backing of well-trained police. In fact, Japan, unlike other countries of East Asia, had the government machinery to marshal its resources for any chosen end. It was also free of serious unrest. Police action and censorship, coupled with a modicum of representative institutions, nationally and locally, ensured that all but a recalcitrant minority supported the regime.

Popular support was given psychological intensity by the emperor system. The emperor had long been the theoretical source of authority in Japan, even for the Tokugawa and their feudal predecessors. In the

---

[17] Japanese modernization in this period is surveyed in W. G. Beasley, *The modern history of Japan* (1981), chaps. 6, 7, 8.

Meiji period (1867–1911), as often in the past, his role was to bestow legitimacy on those who had seized power by force: taking little personal part in government, he was invoked in its business at every turn. Public occasions were arranged to emphasize the dignity and awe that surrounded his office. The constitution recognized his divine descent. Imperial rescripts revealed him as a Confucian monarch, benevolent and deeply concerned about the moral behaviour of his people. In schools, the ethics course trained every child in reverence and loyalty to him. He was the focus of national unity, the personification of tradition. Everything possible was done to make the men, women, and children of Japan aware of it.

The imperial institution therefore deserved much of the credit for the orderliness with which the Japanese endured the upheavals of modernization. It also provided them with a vocabulary of expansion. Time-honoured phrases about an imperial line 'coeval with heaven and earth', bringing 'the four corners of the world under one roof', lent themselves readily to the idea of creating an empire overseas. That, too, was accomplished in the emperor's name.

Yet what was done, and how it was done, depended in reality much more on the policy of 'wealth and strength'. This was evident, first, in the building of a military establishment, able both to win victories and to influence Japanese policy.[18] From as early as 1873 it was decided that an efficient army had to be a conscript army, like those of France and Germany, not one composed of *samurai*. Steps towards training it were taken initially with the advice of a French military mission, which concentrated on producing a core of officers and NCOs to command units that would have a law-and-order function within Japan; but the difficulties encountered in suppressing a *samurai* rebellion in 1877 cast doubt on the wisdom and effectiveness of this. Accordingly, from 1878 the emphasis shifted towards the making of an army able to operate as a fully military force, both at home and overseas. The conscription rules were revised to provide for three years' active service, seven years (later nine years) with the reserves. Peacetime strength was raised to seven divisions, totalling 78,000 men, rising on a wartime footing to 120,000, including artillery and cavalry. Using reserves, the army was able to put 240,000 men into the field in 1894–5. Their weapons were

[18] On military reform, see Ernst L. Presseisen, *Before Aggression* (1965); the articles by Yamagata Aritomo and Yamamoto Gombei in S. Ōkuma (ed.), *Fifty Years of New Japan* (1910), vol. 1; and the standard Japanese work, Matsushita Yoshio, *Meiji gunsei shiron* (1956).

modern, though not quite up the best European standards; their training and degree of specialization thoroughly professional.

One reason for the rapid increase in efficiency that was evident in
the 1880s was the decision, taken in 1878, to create an Army General
Staff on the German model. Its principal German adviser, Major Klemens Meckel, initiated the study of strategic planning, intelligence,
mobilization, communications, and supply, thereby educating the
Japanese army's commanders to a new level of performance. His discussions of strategy also gave a generation of them an acute awareness
of the military importance of Korea to Japan.

The fact that the Army General Staff was independent of the War
Ministry was to be of great significance in twentieth-century politics.
The Chief of Staff, unlike the War Minister, had direct access to the
emperor, because the General Staff was the channel through which
the emperor's prerogative as Commander-in-chief was exercised.
Yamagata Aritomo, the Meiji period's senior military bureaucrat,
emphasized the high standing of the new office when he resigned as
War Minister in order to assume it in 1878. All the same, one should
not conclude from this that the object of the arrangement was to give
the army a voice in politics. As one of the central group of government
leaders—he was twice Prime Minister—Yamagata *controlled* the
General Staff. He was not its spokesman. It was only as government
authority became fragmented after the Russo-Japanese War that sections of the bureaucracy, including the army, began to believe that
administrative independence gave them a monopoly of decision-
making in certain areas.

The navy, despite the fact that no overseas expansion could take
place without it, had a less prominent part in the shaping of Japanese
imperialism. It had to wait unti 1891 to get its own General Staff,
which only achieved equality of status with the army's after the Sino-
Japanese War. It possessed, however, a modern and efficient fleet. By
1894 this included twenty-eight steam vessels, totalling 57,000 tonnes.
Most of these had been bought abroad, but it was no longer necessary
to place all new orders outside Japanese yards, which were well able by
then to build major warships. Advanced equipment like quick-firing
guns and torpedoes was also being manufactured in Japan.

Although the navy was an effective instrument of empire, its senior
officers seem not to have been preoccupied with using it in that way. In
matters of foreign policy they had the reputation of being moderates,
that is, less concerned than their army colleagues with opportunities

for territorial acquisition, more interested than them in trade and emigration. This made them natural allies as a rule of those groups in Japanese society whose influence and ambitions derived from the growth of national wealth.

The history of Meiji industry and commerce, which was central to that growth, falls into three parts.[19] The first, ending about 1880, was one in which policy was directed in particular to protection: measures for earning foreign currency and enabling Japanese producers to compete with foreign goods in the domestic market. Direct government investment, following the lead given by the Tokugawa and some feudal lords, continued to be substantial in strategic industries—shipyards, munitions plants, transport, and communications—but it also went to establish model factories in the textile industry and to finance initiatives in manufacturing import substitutes, like cement, bricks, and glass.

The next phase, lasting until the war of 1894–5, saw the benefits of this begin to show. In the silk industry, reeling was more and more transferred from the farm household to small factories, over half of which were using machine filatures. Standardization of quality contributed to better penetration of export markets. Production more than doubled. In the cotton industry growth came rather later, for yarn imports did not reach their peak until 1888, but by that date Japan already had one or two Western-style spinning-mills of moderate size. Their number increased rapidly in the next few years.

In the third phase, covering the period 1894 to 1914, a continuation of these trends gave Japan for the first time a non-agricultural sector in the economy capable of exerting considerable influence on both statistics and the country's way of life. Raw silk output trebled; filatures overtook hand-reeling, accounting for 70 per cent of production towards the end; and the average size of silk factories greatly increased. In cotton textiles, yarn output rose from an annual average of 177 million lb. in 1894–8 to 492 million lb. in 1909–13. The national total of spindles, standing at 382,000 in 1893, reached 2.4 million in 1913. Exports of textiles—silk to the United States, cotton goods to China and Korea—were over 50 per cent of total exports throughout the period. Imports included an increasing share of raw materials, especially cotton.

---

[19] The best surveys of economic history are G. C. Allen, *A short economic history of modern Japan* (1972), and W. W. Lockwood, *The economic development of Japan* (1968).

Moreover, government, which had sharply reduced its direct investments after 1881, now set out to establish the heavy industrial base
appropriate to Japan's international stature. The Industrial Bank,
founded in 1900, provided a means of directing capital for this purpose. A huge plant at Yawata, starting production in 1901, quickly
came to supply a significant proportion of the country's needs in pig-
iron and steel. Shipbuilding expanded, helped by government subsidies and naval contracts. Factory consumption of coal rose from just
over a million tonnes in 1894 to 8.3 million tonnes in 1914. A start was
made on the development of electric power.

It is easy to exaggerate these achievements. Japan's silk filatures
were still quite small by European standards, as were most of its cotton
mills. Pig-iron production was less than half a million tonnes in 1914
and the annual average of shipping launched from Japanese yards in
1909–13 was only 50,000 tonnes. Japan was not yet an industrial
power. All the same, it had moved far enough towards becoming one to
make it reasonable that we should discuss its imperialism in economic
terms.

It is important in this context to make it clear that not all those who
benefited from the changes in the economy had the same interests,
where overseas expansion was concerned. The new entrepreneurs
were of two kinds.[20] There were the pioneers: men of varied social origins, including many former *samurai*, who had committed themselves
to the Meiji government's policies and built up their businesses in
association with them. These were innovators in both organization and
type of enterprise. They participated in industries of 'national importance', making their patriotism evident and accepting that profits might
be a long time coming through. Because of this they worked closely
with officialdom, deriving advantage from subsidies and government
contracts and from access to scarce capital. They proved right: when
Japan's industrial society eventually took shape, they were on its commanding heights.

There was a second, larger segment, consisting of those who held
back from modern enterprises until they were shown to be profitable.
Often the possessors of pre-modern merchant capital, as likely as not
to be resident outside Tokyo—in the silk-producing areas, or round
Osaka and Nagoya—they made up the ranks of the smaller industrial-

[20] See Johannes Hirschmeier, *The Origins of Entrepreneurship in Meiji Japan* (1964),
especially 213–91.

ists, especially in textiles. Individually they lacked official contacts, though as voters and as members of chambers of commerce they gradually acquired a collective voice in public policy. They looked to government for patronage, to be sure. Their source of strength, however, was that they had learnt to compete with the West in terms of the price and quality of their products. What they had done in Japan, many were reasonably confident they could also do abroad.

This rather schematic description of the business world has a bearing on foreign affairs. Once Japan had gained equality with the West in China by virtue of victory in 1894–5, those who had built up the country's textile industry were able to develop substantial markets there. The privileges available within the treaty port system were as useful to them as to Americans and Europeans. They even found it possible to transplant some of their operations overseas, establishing a cotton industry in China's ports, which was Japanese-owned and Japanese-managed, but used Chinese labour. By contrast, the pioneers of large-scale industry in Japan found that they still needed specific government support—at least for a number of years—if they were to repeat their domestic successes on the Asian mainland. When it came to international comparisons at the highest level, their companies seemed undercapitalized, inexperienced, technologically backward. It was natural for them to think of 'spheres of influence'—areas in which government backing could serve to overcome these disabilities—as the sensible solution. There were, after all, French, German, and Russian business men who thought the same. The attitude was not wholly unknown among British and Americans.

This distinction between two economic interest groups is, I believe, a valid one to make in a discussion of Japanese imperialism, despite being much oversimplified as a piece of social analysis. Not all Japanese entrepreneurs wanted the same kind of imperialism, any more than all army leaders did. This will become apparent. Yet there is one important qualification that needs to be made on the subject here. Among those I have called pioneers there were a few concerns, known as *zaibatsu*—Mitsui, Mitsubishi, Sumitomo, Yasuda, and a handful of others—whose interests were in the twentieth century to become so enormous, and so widely spread in finance, industry, and commerce, that they cannot be fitted into the same scheme of categories as the rest. Since they were bankers and leaders in heavy industry, manufacturers of munitions, exporters of silk and cotton goods, they stood to gain from *any* extension of Japanese power overseas. It is no longer fashionable, as it once was, to treat them as the 'fine Italian hand' behind every Japanese advance. Nevertheless, their role was pervasive; and because it does not quite match Western stereotypes, it needs special attention in any attempt to assess the character of Japanese imperialism.

4

Intervention in Korea, 1894–1895

THE treaty port system was not the only means by which Western imperialism acted on China. During the nineteenth century the European empires closed in from the landward side as well. In 1858–9 France had acquired a foothold at Saigon, from which it had extended its power into Cochin China and Cambodia. Thereafter spasmodic expansion brought French influence into Tongking, precipitating a war with China along the borders between the two in 1883–5. In the south-east, a British advance into Burma, ostensibly for the protection of India, culminated in the annexation of Upper Burma in 1886. This gave Britain a common frontier with China, though one which was difficult to cross. In central Asia, the gradual eastward movement of Russian political authority produced Sino-Russian conflict over control of the Ili valley in 1871. It took ten years to resolve the dispute. More important was what happened in the north. A series of negotiations in 1858–60, when China was engaged in war with Britain and France, enabled Russia to establish a claim to former Chinese territories north of the Amur river and east of the Ussuri, plus navigation rights on the rivers themselves. As a result, Russia and China became uneasily contiguous over several hundred miles, bordering Manchuria.

One consequence of these events was a contraction and delimitation of Chinese frontiers. China's relations with its neighbours had traditionally been much less concerned with questions of line or space than those to which Europeans were accustomed, being based, not on the concept of national sovereignty, but on that of cultural unity. In theory the Chinese emperor ruled 'all under heaven'—the Chinese expression describing the known world—as an intermediary between the gods and man. It followed that his subjects need not be ethnically Chinese: they included all those who would subscribe to the Confucian values to which the emperor was himself committed. In reality, of course, his power was much less universal; but even outside the lands in which he was the acknowledged monarch, he was thought to have a certain ill-defined authority that constituted an organizing principle for China's foreign affairs.

It was manifested in what was called the tribute system. Rulers of nearby territories, entering into relations with China, were accorded titles, seals of office, rank. This established them within the Chinese political order. They were expected to use the Chinese language and the Chinese calendar in their official correspondence. They were to send periodic tribute to China, consisting of appropriate products from their countries. In return they received gifts. Better still, they were granted rights to trade, which were exceptionally valuable. Thus they ostensibly became 'vassals', favoured, in some respects privileged, and rarely subject to interference from their overlord.

Some of the early disputes between China and the maritime powers, from which the treaty system had emerged, arose from Chinese attempts to impose elements of this tribute system on Western diplomats and merchants. They were rejected with indignation. Instead, China itself was brought within a diplomatic structure based on Western law. The change did not apply *ipso facto* to China's relations with other countries in East Asia; but as the latter were increasingly subsumed within the West's formal or informal empires, their role in China's traditional world order crumbled away. Tongking, Annam, Cambodia, Cochin China, and Burma, together with the Moslem and Mongol tribes of the west and north-west, all began to find their old relationships with China incompatible with the new ones forced upon them by France, Britain, and Russia.

There was one exception: Korea. The 'hermit kingdom' maintained its aloofness longer than any other part of the region. It remained loyal to its Confucian values and its tribute missions even after Western countries concluded treaties with it. Indeed, it was Japan, not the West, that changed this situation. In doing so, Japan entered upon the road to imperialism in a manner quite different from that which its recent experience might have led one to expect.

Japan and Korea before the Sino-Japanese War

Japan had for many centuries been included in the list of China's vassals, along with Korea, though it had not in fact sent tribute missions since 1549. One consequence had been to make possible a Japanese–Korean relationship on terms of supposed equality. It had continued throughout the Tokugawa period, marked by the occasional visit of Korean envoys to Japan and a desultory exchange of goods at the south Korean port of Pusan, mostly under the patronage of the feudal lords of Tsushima. The overthrow of the Tokugawa, however, introduced a note of acrimony. In announcing to the Koreans the political change which had taken place in 1868, the Japanese used terminology which by implication likened their own ruler to China's and relegated Korea's to a lower place. The Koreans took offence at this and rejected the document. From that time on, paths diverged: Japan became increasingly Western in its diplomatic habits as it modernized its society; Korea clung persistently to the old ways, including its tribute relationship with China.

These circumstances provided ample excuse for conflict, if one were needed. Some Japanese actively sought it. During the early years of the new regime, the idea of an armed confrontation with Korea had attractions both as a means of diverting unrest at home and as a convenient outlet for the ambitions of dispossessed *samurai*. A 'war party' emerged in Japan, insisting that the continuing rebuffs from the Korean court must be dealt with by a punitive expedition. More cautious leaders saw two objections in particular to such a plan.[1] It would, they argued, be dangerously wasteful of resources, diverting energies from reform at home. It would also provide the powers, especially Britain and Russia, with an opportunity to fish in troubled waters to Japan's inevitable disadvantage. The record of these two powers elsewhere in Asia suggested they would seize it with alacrity.

In 1873, caution won. The advocates of an expedition departed from the government council, their opponents set about the task of securing some concession from Korea by methods short of war. They eventually succeeded in this by a form of gunboat diplomacy, not unlike that to which Japan itself had been subjected by Commodore Perry. Following a clash between Japanese surveying vessels and Korean coastal batteries in September 1875—deliberately stage-managed, it has been said—a squadron, backed by several thousand troops, was sent to demand an apology and the opening of Korean ports. Care was taken to prevent the incident from escalating: British and American representatives were briefed on the advantages their countries could expect to gain, while a senior diplomat was sent to Peking in order to remove any Chinese fears about what Japan intended. The result was

---

[1] The disputes concerning Korea are summarized in Beasley, *Meiji Restoration*, 372–8. The fullest English-language account of Japanese–Korean relations in the period to 1894 is Hilary Conroy, *The Japanese seizure of Korea* (1960), chaps. 1–4.

the treaty of Kanghwa, signed on 26 February 1876. It opened three Korean ports to trade; gave permission for the continuation of coastal surveys; and described Korea as an independent state, enjoying 'the same sovereign rights as does Japan'. The last of these provisions was to be a subject of contention between Japan and China.

The treaty made it possible for Japan to begin establishing its influence in Korea, partly by encouraging the growth of a pro-Japanese faction in Seoul, partly by such measures as sending promising young Koreans to Japan to receive a modern education. Korean conservatives reacted to this with considerable hostility. So did the Chinese. Li Hung-chang, who had responsibility for China's relations with Korea from 1881 to 1894, set out to dilute Japanese influence by the conclusion of treaties between Korea and the Western powers. Through his mediation, commercial agreements were negotiated with the United States, Britain, and Germany in 1882, then with Italy, Russia, and France in the next few years. Simultaneously, Li strengthened China's political links with members of the Korean royal family, building a pro-Chinese faction more powerful than that which favoured Japan.

Neither Tokyo nor Peking wanted this rivalry to go too far, because of possible repercussions on their relations with the West. Consequently, when a group of Japanese radicals and Korean reformers, acting with the help of the Japanese legation, carried out a *coup d'état* in Seoul in December 1884, both governments acted quickly to bring the situation under control. Chinese troops ejected the insurgents from the palace. Japanese cabinet ministers denied official involvement. Li Hung-chang and Itō Hirobumi, meeting at Tientsin in April 1885, agreed that both sides would withdraw their troops and refrain from sending them back to Korea without advance notice to the other. Nor would they engage in the training and reorganization of the Korean Army.

None of these actions quite has the air of an emerging Japanese imperialism. Korea had always been involved in the rivalries of its more considerable neighbours. It had been a base from which the Mongols launched attempted invasions of Japan in 1274 and 1281, then the route by which Hideyoshi sought to conquer China three centuries later. In Japanese history books these were memorable events, often recalled during the late Tokugawa and Meiji periods in nationalist writings. The Japanese saw nothing wrong with meddling in Korea. The Chinese, for their part, although they had recently added to their traditional prejudices an awareness of weakness in the face of French and Russian frontier incursions, were not induced thereby to moderate their stubbornness when dealing with Korea. After 1885 it was reflected increasingly in economic policy. Under the newly appointed Chinese Resident in Seoul, Yüan Shih-k'ai, successful efforts were made to use political pressure as a weapon in developing China's trade. Korean imports from China—substantially, they were Western manufactured goods, re-exported by Chinese merchants from the treaty ports—rose from 19 per cent of the country's total in 1885 to 45 per cent in 1892.[2]

It was during these years that the character of Sino-Japanese rivalry changed, largely because Japanese modernization was beginning to show commercial results. Japan's imports from Korea, in which rice and gold were the principal items, were not much at issue, though fears that they might be cut off because of Korean hostility occasionally caused alarm in Tokyo. More critical was the question of exports to Korea. Before 1882 some 76 per cent of these had, like China's, consisted of Western textiles, bought in Shanghai and transhipped in Japan for Korean destinations. As Japan's own textile industry grew, however, re-exported Western goods were replaced by Japanese products, which amounted to 87 per cent of the total by 1892. This fact made Japanese cotton textile manufacturers into a pressure group, seeking government action to tip the balance against their Chinese competitors, and it has led some historians to claim a primarily capitalist motivation for Japanese policy in Korea on the eve of war. On the other hand, it has to be recognized that the large-scale export of Japanese cotton goods was still at that time more a prospect than a reality: the whole of Japan's exports to Korea in 1893 were valued at only 1.7 million yen. Most scholars have concluded that economic interests on this limited scale did not constitute a sufficient reason for hostilities.[3]

Certainly the economic argument for expansion deriving from potential profits seems to have been less persuasive in Japanese government circles than the military one concerning the Russian threat. It was in 1885 that Major Meckel arrived from Germany to teach in the army's new staff college and advise on the reorganization

[2] Conroy, *Japanese seizure*, 193–6, 460–2.

[3] Ibid., 442–62, surveys the economic evidence and interpretations of it. The most detailed account of Japanese–Korean economic relations before 1894 is in Hō Takushū, *Meiji shoki Nichi–KanShin kankei no kenkyū* (1969), 279–330. Recent works by Japanese historians, discounting the economic motive, include Nakatsuka Akira, *Nisshin sensō no kenkyū* (1968), 30–6, 89–96; and Yamabe Kentarō, *Nikkan heigō shōshi* (1966), 109–16.

of defence. One consequence of his teaching was to reinforce the concern of Japanese strategists with Korea and the mainland, focusing on the Russian presence in the north. In March 1890 Yamagata Aritomo, formerly Chief of the General Staff, now Prime Minister, gave expression to this concern in a memorandum on foreign policy. It was a fundamental principle, he said, to maintain Japan's 'line of sovereignty', that is, to defend the Japanese islands. Beyond this, however, Japan must also hold a 'line of advantage', an essential element in which was Korea. Once Russia completed the planned Trans-Siberian railway, Korea would be at risk; and with Korea at risk the whole of the east would be threatened with disorder. It followed that 'measures to guarantee the independence of Korea' were 'crucial to our line of advantage'.[4]

It appears that what Yamagata had in mind was an international agreement on the subject of Korea. Some military planners went well beyond that. There is in existence a General Staff discussion document of 1887, drafted by the head of the bureau responsible for China and Korea, which examined the implications of a possible attack on China by one of the Western powers. It argued that such an attack would threaten the peace of East Asia and hence Japan's independence. This justified Japanese countermoves, which could appropriately take the form of a two-pronged Japanese strike into China, using one force to advance on Peking from the north, another to land at Shanghai. The desired outcome would be a peace settlement which would create an independent Manchuria, ruled by the Manchu dynasty; transfer Taiwan and much of north China to Japan; and establish a Japanese protectorate over China farther south. Preparations for such an operation, it was envisaged, would take five years, that is, until 1892.[5]

This document is cited, not as evidence of a 'plot' which might account for Japanese actions in 1894, but to indicate the kind of ambitions which were already to be found in army thinking at this time. It is significant that the author of the 1887 memorandum, Colonel Ogawa Mataji, became Chief of Staff to Yamagata's First Army in 1894–5, which suggests that his ideas had some respectability.

The specific origins of the crisis in the summer of 1894 lay in the Korean government's failure to suppress the anti-foreign activities of

---

[4] Text in Ōyama Azusa, *Yamagata Aritomo ikensho* (1966), at 197. See also Roger Hackett, *Yamagata Aritomo in the rise of modern Japan* (1971), 138–9.

[5] Nakatsuka, *Nisshin sensō*, 77–80.

armed insurgents called Tonghaks during the early part of the year. At the beginning of June, Seoul asked for Chinese military assistance in this task. It was promptly given. Japan just as promptly invoked the 1885 agreement as grounds for sending troops of its own. Both countries then refused to withdraw. Indeed, Mutsu Munemitsu, Japan's Foreign Minister, was under heavy pressure not to compromise on the question. Army officers, newspapers, the elected representatives of the people in the Diet, all clamoured for 'strong' action. Mutsu himself—if one is to judge by the memoirs he wrote immediately after the war— was not averse to this. China, as he saw it, 'had always maintained that matters relating to Korea must be handled in terms of her tributary relationship with China'. Its representatives insisted that 'no other country should enjoy a position of equality with them in Korea'.[6] This he found intolerable.

However, he recognized that it did not constitute a pretext for war which the West was likely to find acceptable. Accordingly, he drafted a set of proposals for joint Chinese and Japanese action to secure reform in Korea, which he was confident that the powers would welcome and China would reject. As finally approved by the cabinet and communicated to the Japanese minister in Seoul,[7] these called for the removal of 'old, deep-rooted abuses', which 'endangered peace and order' in Korea, so posing a threat to the country's independence and the stability of the region as a whole. Japan, Mutsu argued, could not allow such a situation to continue, whether from motives of neighbourliness, or 'out of consideration for our own security'. He therefore required Korea to ensure 'effective control' of its administration; to improve its judicial system; to revise its tax structure so as to prevent 'misappropriation of funds by corrupt officials'; to create an efficient army and police force; to reform the currency, the disorder of which caused 'extreme inconvenience to foreign trade'; and to take steps to 'facilitate transport and communications'. These were all policies which the Western powers had tried to get adopted in China at various times.

In a separate telegram of the same date Mutsu added some provisions concerning what Japan wanted more particularly for itself.[8] 'All the privileges that Chinese subjects have been enjoying hitherto to the exclusion of the nationals of other countries' were to be enjoyed also by

---

[6] Mutsu Munemitsu, *Kenkenroku*, trans. Berger (1982), 25.
[7] Mutsu to Ōtori, 28 June 1894; trans. in M. Kajima, *The Diplomacy of Japan 1894–1922* (1976–80), I, 43–6.
[8] Ibid., I, 46–7.

Japanese. In addition, 'talented young people of good families' were to be sent by Korea to study abroad—mostly, no doubt, to Japan—'for the purpose of bringing civilization to Korea'.

As a diplomatic device these demands had the desired effect. When they were presented in Seoul—'to give provocation to China', as Mutsu said in another telegram[9]—they were duly rejected. Hostilities followed at the end of July. Yet one should not on this account dismiss the issue of reform as something that was brought up merely to provide a *casus belli*. It *was* that, to be sure; but it also expressed the genuine aspirations of many Japanese, who wanted to have the satisfaction of seeing Korea follow Japan's example, rather than China's, in responding to western imperialism, as well as to enjoy the benefits that might flow from such a change. The Japanese consul in Seoul, Uchida Sadatsuchi, sent Tokyo a long dispatch on the subject of Korean reform on 26 June 1984. It ended with an exposition of Japanese aims as he saw them. They were, he said,

to conclude a treaty under which Korea accepts Japanese protection, then intervene in Korea's domestic and foreign affairs so as to achieve progress and reform, leading to wealth and strength; for thereby we will on the one hand make Korea into a strong bulwark for Japan, while on the other we extend our influence there and increase the rights enjoyed by our merchants.[10]

Much of what Japan actually did in Korea during the course of the war was in line with Uchida's thinking.

Japanese policy in Korea, 1894–1895

By the time Japan declared war on China on 1 August 1894 Japanese forces were already established in and around Seoul. On 16 September they captured Pyongyang. A naval victory next day gave them command of the Yellow Sea. Thereafter Yamagata's First Army crossed the Yalu river into south Manchuria (25 October), while Ōyama's Second Army landed in the Liaotung peninsula (24 October), capturing Port Arthur (Lushun) four weeks later. In effect, therefore, Japan had secured control of most of Korea within two months of the opening of hostilities. The royal palace had been seized even earlier

---

[9] Mutsu to Ōtori, 11 July 1894; English text in the Japanese Foreign Ministry collection of published documents, *Nihon Gaikō Bunsho* (1936– , in progress), 27:1: 595. The series is hereafter cited as *NGB*.

[10] *NGB* 27:1: 562–7, at 567.

(23 July), opening the way for talks with a government that could no longer afford to be anti-Japanese.

The Japanese minister in Seoul, Ōtori Keisuke, at once set about the task of negotiating a treaty with Korea. Some of its provisions, according to a draft dated 1 August,[11] were designed to give Japan what his superiors had called 'every possible material advantage': the option to build railways linking Pusan, Seoul and Inchon (Chemulpo), if Korea did not do so; the right to maintain telegraphs between those places; and the opening of another port in the south. In addition, Korea was to promise to undertake such reforms as were recommended by Japan and employ Japanese advisers in carrying them out.

Ōtori met with persistent opposition to these proposals. In fact, it soon became apparent that the cabinet in Tokyo would have to make up its mind how far it was prepared to go in imposing its will on Seoul. On 17 August, therefore, Mutsu set out a range of possibilities in a memorandum for the Prime Minister, Itō Hirobumi.[12] One was to observe strictly Japan's public aim of securing Korea's independence. This would have the disadvantage, Mutsu observed, that it would solve none of the underlying problems, so making another Sino-Japanese clash likely at some time, probably quite soon. A second was to make sure that reform would be effective by putting Korea under Japanese protection 'for many future years or even forever'. The problem with this was that Japan might not have the resources to maintain such a policy against opposition from both Russia and China. A third possibility was to seek an international guarantee of Korea's integrity, either from just China and Japan, or from all the interested powers. Mutsu doubted whether this would work. He also thought that it would be unacceptable to Japanese opinion, given the expectations that the war had already aroused. The cabinet, it appears, agreed with him (though we only have Mutsu's word for it). It believed a Japanese protectorate to be the most attractive plan, but recognized that Japan's ability to enforce it would depend on the outcome of the fighting. Meanwhile, care would have to be taken not to alarm the powers. As Mutsu told Ōtori in a secret dispatch on 23 August, 'we must be extremely cautious not to take any action which may substantially overstep the rules of international law either diplomatically or militarily.'[13]

---

[11] Text in Kajima, *Diplomacy*, I, 103–5. For a general account of Japanese policy in Korea in 1894–5, see Conroy, *Japanese seizure*, 261–324.
[12] Text in Kajima, *Diplomacy*, I, 108–11.
[13] Ibid., I, 112–14.

Against this background, Ōtori was constrained to accept some modification of the agreement he proposed. The reference to Japanese 'protection' was taken out. So was the statement about Japanese advisers, which was to become the subject of a separate (and less-binding) communication from the Korean government. In this form the document was signed on 20 August. It was supplemented by a treaty of alliance six days later. Mutsu considered this enough. By concluding an offensive and defensive alliance, he commented, Korea had demonstrated its independence of China. What is more, the existence of such a treaty would 'prevent Korea from turning elsewhere for advice and thus keep the Koreans firmly under our control'.[14]

Nevertheless, it remained difficult to make headway in matters of substance. Japanese business men, who had been making representations about railway development in Korea, proved reluctant, when put to the test, to provide the money for it without direct or indirect financial assistance from their government. When this was not forthcoming, Mutsu noted, 'their earlier enthusiasm suddenly waned'.[15] Nothing useful was done. In Seoul, projects for administrative reform foundered on Korean obstruction and factional strife, aggravated—to quote Mutsu again—'by the deeply suspicious animosity and unscrupulous recourse to treachery which are characteristic of the Korean people'.[16]

The unfortunate Ōtori was blamed for much of this, so it was decided to replace him by a man of more stature. The choice was Itō's close associate, Inoue Kaoru, who had twice served as Foreign Minister and had been sent as envoy extraordinary to Korea in the crisis of 1884–5. Inoue arrived in Seoul to replace Ōtori on 25 October 1894. He at once set about removing hostile officials from the Korean court and substituting nominees of his own. A few weeks later he sent Mutsu a detailed list of the measures he wanted these men to implement. In central government, the authority of the court was to be separated from that of the cabinet, and the functions of the various departments were to be clarified. New legal codes were to be introduced, administered by an independent judiciary and an efficient police force. Steps were to be taken to eliminate nepotism, sale of office, peculation, and bribery. The army was to be reorganized, being made into an instrument chiefly for the maintenance of order within the country. Taxation

---

[14] Mutsu, *Kenkenroku*, 93.
[15] Ibid., 100.
[16] Ibid., 95.

should be reformed, so as to provide a stable revenue. There was to be a new budgetary system and a ban on debasement of the currency.[17]

Inoue, as one of the architects of Japanese modernization, was obviously drawing on that experience in framing his actions in Korea. But one must beware of making too much of the comparison. For one thing, a condition of the plan was that it be carried out under Japanese tutelage: Inoue envisaged the use of Japanese advisers at every level, supported by what was to all intents and purposes a Japanese army of occupation. In Japan, that was precisely what Meiji modernization had been designed to prevent. Nor was Meiji Japan in every respect the model Inoue had in mind. In a letter to Itō at the end of the year he described what he was doing as 'the policy which England follows in Egypt'.[18] The point was a valid one. Korea's finances, like Egypt's a decade earlier, were in chaos, partly because of years of inefficiency and neglect, partly because of recent political disorders. There was no evidence that tax revenue was sufficient to sustain the kind of reforms that were held to be necessary. What was required, Inoue concluded, was a susbtantial foreign loan. Japan in its own interest should provide it. And it should do so soon, for once the war was over its influence in Seoul was likely to diminish.

During December, therefore, Inoue proposed a Japanese loan to Korea of 5 million yen, made available in bullion and repayable in eight years. It was to be secured on the revenues of Korea's three southern provinces, and Japanese advisers were to be employed to supervise tax collection there until the loan had been repaid. Without some such arrangement, he wrote early in January 1895, 'I cannot move a step', not even to pay the army or get the Koreans started on building railways.[19]

On the face of it, Inoue's policy is a classic example of economic imperialism. If that is so, one must also accept—and there is evidence for it, not only in Japan—that bankers showed less commitment to this kind of imperialism than politicians. Despite his influence in Tokyo, Inoue found it impossible to get an allocation of the funds he wanted. First he was told there would be a delay while the bankers were

[17] Dispatch of 24 Nov. 1894, in *NGB* 27: 2: 108–15; partly translated in Kajima, *Diplomacy*, I, 120–4.
[18] Inoue to Itō, 25 Dec. 1894, in the biography of Inoue, *Segai Inoue Kō Den* (1933–4), IV, at 441.
[19] Telegram to Mutsu, 8 Jan. 1895, in *NGB* 28:1:315–16.

consulted. Then he heard privately from Mitsui that while some were willing to put up the money, they required an effective rate of interest of 10 per cent. Such terms, Inoue exploded, 'I cannot morally allow'. They would drive the Koreans into the arms of the British, who would thus be able to seize 'the whole financial power' in Korea, which was presumably what Tokyo wanted for itself.[20]

Mutsu was not altogether helpful, with the result that 'a satisfactory settlement', as he called it, was still some time in coming. Early in February Inoue was told that he could have only 3 million yen, payable in Japanese paper money, and that the loan was to be secured on Korea's customs revenue. He protested again: the sum was too small for the needs he had identified; to pay it in paper money would simply compound the fiscal difficulties; to secure it on the customs instead of on tax revenue would deprive him of one lever by which to bring about administrative reform. Only part of this argument was accepted. And it all took time. It was not until 30 March 1895 that a loan agreement was at last concluded: 3 million yen, half in silver, half in notes, to be made available initially by the Bank of Japan; repayment over five years at 6 per cent; the whole to be secured on the tax revenue of the central government.

It is clear that during his months in Korea, Inoue, like proconsuls in other times and places, had developed ideas that were at odds with those prevailing at home. He was well aware of it. On 17 February 1895 he wrote a dispatch to Mutsu[21] complaining of the kind of proposals concerning Korea that had emerged in Japanese public discussion. They were selfish and self-defeating, he said. Their sole object seemed to be 'to pursue our own advantage in trade and industry, by the opening up of mines at our hands, or by planting colonies of our people in the interior, or by establishing fishing stations, or whatever'. There was nothing wrong in itself with advancing Japanese interests in this way; but how could one 'achieve the reality of independence for Korea', he asked, by pursing *only* 'the interests of the Japanese people', that is to say, 'by entrusting Korean interests entirely to Japanese'? Japan's aim should be higher than this: 'to co-operate in the pursuit of common interests, neither robbing Korea of benefits, nor sacrificing our own.'

In the long term, such sentiments were to contribute to the concept

---

[20] Telegram to Mutsu, 16 Jan. 1895, in *NGB* 28:1:318–19.
[21] Text in *NGB* 28:1:341.

of 'co-prosperity'. More immediately, they led Inoue to struggle—
unsuccessfully—to maintain a form of enlightened imperialism in
Korea while all the circumstances were turning against it. Peace with
China followed shortly after the signing of the Korean loan agreement.
Almost at once Russia organized an international protest against some
of its terms (see Chapter 5). Coupled with this were Russian warnings
against Japanese political interference in Korea, making it clear that
Japan was expected to observe that country's independence in fact as
well as in name. Accordingly, on 25 May 1895 the cabinet resolved—
in English, apparently for publication—that it would base its actions in
Korea solely on the maintenance of treaty rights. On 4 June another
resolution, adopted on Mutsu's initiative, renounced the decisions in
favour of Japanese protectorate and Korean reform, taken in August
1894. The new approach was to be 'passive', that is, 'refraining from
any intervention in Korean affairs as far as possible and letting Korea
achieve autonomy'.[22] A specific corollary was that Japan would no
longer press Korea on the matter of railways and telegraphs.

These decisions brought Inoue back to Tokyo for consultations.
While there he put his views about Korea into writing once more.[23]
The existing loan, he argued, should if possible be increased, both to
win Korean goodwill and to leave some money for railway development. Only two Japanese battalions should remain in Korea, preferably
with the Korean government's consent. Other troops should be withdrawn. Something should also be done to impose stricter controls on
Japanese merchants and other residents, whose arrogance and profi-
teering were causing hostility. Moreover, Japan should act cautiously
with respect to creating foreign settlements at the newly opened ports
of Mokpo and Chinnanpo. As to railways, the Seoul–Pusan line was
not really vital, and insistence on it tended to arouse suspicions about
Japan's future plans. It would therefore be wiser to concentrate on the
Seoul–Inchon (Chemulpo) line, arranging a Japanese loan to enable
the Korean government itself to build it (with the help of Japanese
machinery and technicians). And although Japanese military telegraphs in Korea should be retained, others, which had been controlled
by Japan while the war lasted, should be handed back.

What this amounted to was a proposal for a backward step in Japanese political ambitions in Korea: for the next few years Japan would

[22] Trans. in Kajima, *Diplomacy*, I, 387–8.
[23] Memorandum of 2 July 1895, in *Segai Inoue*, IV, 482–91.

have to set its eyes on something much more like a sphere of influence than a protectorate. Nor was the reason far to seek. The international repercussions of the peace settlement with China left little scope for any further advance immediately. Mutsu was well aware of it. 'The plain truth of the matter', he commented in his memoirs, 'is that our policy toward Korea was always under external constraints.'[24] It was to remain so until victory over Russia in 1904–5.

In the short term even Inoue's revised objectives seemed overoptimistic. While he was in Japan his Korean allies in Seoul had been dismissed from office and the court had resumed many of its former powers. Tokyo decided to replace him, perhaps because he was so closely identified with policies that were now to be abandoned. In August Miura Gorō was named as his successor. All the same, Inoue did not willingly let go. It took explicit orders from the new Foreign Minister, Saionji Kimmochi, confirmed personally by the Premier, to get him out of Korea when Miura arrived, while at his farewell audience with the king on 12 September he delivered yet another lecture on financial and administrative reform. Like many other Japanese in positions of influence, Inoue clearly did not mean peace with China to put an end to Japanese expansion on the mainland.

[24] Mutsu, *Kenkenroku*, 99.

5

The Peace Settlement with China, 1894–1896

THERE is no evidence that in declaring war on China in 1894 the Itō government had had any expectations of territorial gain, but the ease and rapidity of Japanese victories soon prompted them. Public feeling during the war ran high. Newspapers and politicians, 'intoxicated with pride', as Mutsu put it, insisted on such varied and excessive items for inclusion in the terms of peace that a plan capable of pleasing everyone would have produced 'a list of the most exorbitant conditions conceivable'. It would have provided for annexation of most of the coastal provinces of China as far south as Fukien, together with much of Manchuria. It would also have required China to sign a commercial agreement on terms 'even more favourable than those contained in China's treaties with the European powers'.[1] The British minister in Tokyo, reporting the clamour, commented that nothing less than 'the conquest and absorption by Japan of the entire Chinese Empire is now freely spoken of'. Indeed, he added, it seemed to some sections of the public that Japan might well hope during the course of the next century 'to become the greatest Power in the world, just as she now undoubtedly is the greatest in Asia'.[2]

Against this background, what had begun as a war over Korea developed into the first stage of Japanese imperial expansion. Its components, as Japanese leaders envisaged them, were worked out in the course of framing the peace terms to be demanded from China in the winter of 1894–5. Some were territorial, focusing on south Manchuria and Taiwan. Others were economic, anticipating commercial privileges for Japan in Chinese ports. China was in no position to refuse them, as the negotiations of 1895 made clear; but in the conditions obtaining in East Asia it was not so much China as the powers that had to be persuaded. For the most part, they were. As a result, Japan

---

[1] Mutsu, *Kenkenroku*, 145–6.
[2] Trench to Kimberley, 16 Nov. 1894, in Foreign Office, General Correspondence, *China* (hereafter cited as FO 17), vol. 438.

acquired its first colony, Taiwan; and it entered into the co-operative imperialism of the treaty ports by the consent of those who already enjoyed its advantages.

Liaotung and Taiwan

Spokesmen for Japanese government departments, who had some voice in the drafting of peace terms, were less ambitious than the public and the press, but not by very much. Officials of the Finance Ministry wanted an indemnity large enough to pay Japan's war expenses. The army discovered reasons for annexing Port Arthur and Liaotung: that Japanese blood was being shed to win control of them; that having a foothold there would enable Japan to protect Korea's land frontiers and command 'the gateway to Peking'. The navy, by contrast, developed an interest in Taiwan. It was true that the island had not been involved in the military operations so far undertaken, but Japan had had cause to intervene in the territory twenty years earlier, which provided a pretext of sorts for taking it. More immediately, there was a risk that in the confusion caused by the war France or Britain might seize Taiwan as a means of ensuring the safety of their China coast trade. Such action would pose a threat to Ryukyu and southern Japan. It would also block any future Japanese move towards south China or the Philippines.[3]

Itō and Mutsu, conducting private discussions about peace terms in the latter part of 1894, took account of these ideas, but kept it in mind, nevertheless, that Japan's freedom of action was not as great in reality as the heady atmosphere in Tokyo suggested. Mutsu's first memorandum on the subject, sent to Itō on 8 October, included references to a possible commercial treaty (which will be discussed in the next section of this chapter) and an indemnity, but was cautious on territorial issues. It identified as one possibility a Chinese recognition of Korean independence, which could be given substance by the cession of Port Arthur and Liaotung. Another would be to get a much wider guarantee of Korea's territorial integrity. If that could be arranged, Japanese possession of Liaotung would become unnecessary, so it would be possible, Mutsu thought, to demand the cession of Taiwan instead. Itō preferred the first plan, that of an undertaking by China. However, he

---

[3] On official opinion, see Mutsu, *Kenkenroku*, 143–5. Japanese interest in Taiwan is discussed in Edward I-te Chen, 'Japan's decision to annex Taiwan' (1977), and Leonard Gordon, 'Japan's interest in Taiwan' (1964).

advised that nothing be said to link it with the occupation of Liaotung until Port Arthur had actually been captured.[4]

After this preliminary exchange the two men got down to the business of preparing drafts. There are four in existence, all undated, three of which appear to have been made before members of the cabinet were asked to consider the proposals in January 1895. The first, presumably, was that which left blanks for some place-names and other details. It followed Itō's preference in calling for Chinese recognition of Korean independence, backed by a cession of territory (not specified at this stage). In addition, there was to be an indemnity for Japan's war costs, the amount also unspecified, which was to be payable over five years. Associated with the indemnity—apparently as a supplement to it, though conceivably as an alternative[5]—was the cession of Taiwan. In the later drafts, which were presumably drawn up after the capture of Port Arthur on 21 November, Liaotung was inserted as the place to be handed over in order to ensure the protection of Korea from China. Taiwan remained attached in some way to the indemnity. It was only after the papers had been seen by the cabinet that cession of the island was transferred to the same clause as that of Liaotung, thus becoming established as a territorial demand in its own right.

By the time Itō and Mutsu met Li Hung-chang in peace talks at Shimonoseki on 20 March 1895[6]—leaving aside earlier overtures as irrelevant to this discussion—there was every indication that the territorial items had become non-negotiable in the Japanese view. The draft treaty presented on 1 April required China not only to recognize Korean independence, pay an indemnity, and promise a commercial treaty, but also cede the Liaotung peninsula (generously defined), plus Taiwan and the islands of the Pescadores (which lie between Taiwan and the Fukien coast). Li Hung-chang protested. To relinquish Chinese sovereignty over these areas, he said, would 'awaken in the Chinese people a spirit of hostility and revenge'. It would prevent any co-operation between China and Japan, making them both ' a prey to

---

[4] On this exchange, see Tabohashi Kiyoshi, *Nisshin seneki gaikōshi no kenkyū* (1951), 391–2. The texts of the letters are in the standard biography of Itō, *Itō Hirobumi den* (1940), III, 140–6.

[5] The text of the draft, given in Nakatsuka, *Nisshin sensō*, 258–63, is so worded as to imply at one point that cession of Taiwan might have been acceptable as an alternative to the indemnity; but no such statement was made directly, so one cannot be sure. The rest of the drafts are discussed by Nakatsuka, ibid., 265–74.

[6] Kajima, *Diplomacy*, I, 198–260, gives long extracts from an English-language record of the discussions kept by Mutsu's son, Hirokichi, who was present as interpreter.

outside enemies'. The argument brought little response from Itō and Mutsu. They eventually accepted a narrower definition of what was meant by Liaotung. They reduced the size of the indemnity by a third. But to the plea that Taiwan should not be included, because Japan had never occupied it, they were quite impervious. Nor, despite the uncertainties suggested by Mutsu's earlier drafts, did they rise to the bait when the Chinese plenipotentiary hinted that the potential for economic development in Taiwan, which had both coal and petroleum resources, justified at least a further reduction in the indemnity. In fact, the Treaty of Shimonoseki, as signed on 17 April 1895, was no more than a minor revision of the original Japanese draft.[7]

The whole tone of the discussions with Li Hung-chang made it clear that the true restraint on Japanese ambitions was not the ability of China to defend itself, but the possibility of objections by the powers. During November 1894 reports from Japanese diplomats in Europe and America had warned that there might be hostility towards any action likely to bring about 'dismemberment of China' or 'destruction of the present dynasty'. Japan, it was plain, would undermine the political foundations of the treaty port system at its peril. Nishi Tokujirō in St Petersburg spelt out the implictions for the peace negotiations in a secret dispatch on 1 December.[8] If Japan were to demand territory in Korea, he stated, Russia would do so, too. Territorial gains in south Manchuria would be opposed by both Russia and Britain. A claim to Taiwan would provoke Britain and France. This being so, it would be best 'to consider territorial acquisition as unattainable' and concentrate on securing the largest possible indemnity. Were this to be politically unacceptable within Japan, however, then the lesser evil would be to seek the cession of Taiwan. Russia would not object, as far as he could tell. Britain would react unfavourably, but probably not to the point of intervening.

During the early weeks of 1895 Nishi's analysis received confirmation from several quarters, including the Russian minister in Tokyo, who put particular stress on Japanese promises not to 'injure' Korea's independence. He also observed that it would be 'impolitic' for

---

[7] The English text (which both sides agreed would be the basis for settling any disagreements, though as a matter of national dignity it was the Chinese and Japanese texts that were signed) is given in Kajima, *Diplomacy*, I, 262–71. For Chinese and Japanese texts, see *NGB* 28:2:363–72.

[8] Kajima, *Diplomacy*, I, 147–50.

Japan to acquire territory on the Asian mainland. The German minister was more forthright: any such demand, he said, would provoke European intervention. Mutsu seems not to have taken these warnings at face value, or to have been more willing to incur such risks than to arouse the wrath of Japanese opinion. At all events, he made no attempt to modify the terms that were to put to Li Hung-chang.

There is no doubt that Russian policy-makers were seriously disturbed at the prospect of Japan being established in Korea and Liaotung. At a meeting on 11 April 1895 the Finance Minister, Sergei Witte, went so far as to say that if nothing were done to prevent it he foresaw the day when 'the Mikado might become the Chinese Emperor and Russia would need hundreds of thousands of troops . . . for defence of her possessions'.[9] The meeting concluded that force must be used, if necessary, to turn Japan back. France and Germany for reasons of their own proved willing to join Russia in a protest at the Shimonoseki terms, made in similar notes to the Japanese government on 23 April. All three countries insisted that Japanese occupation of Liaotung would be 'a constant threat to the capital of China', rendering the independence of Korea 'illusory'. They 'advised' that this clause of the treaty be renounced.

The Triple Intervention, as it is called, left Japan with few options, especially as there was no indication that British or American help would be forthcoming. Mutsu made an attempt to persuade Russia to accept continued Japanese occupation of the extreme southern tip of Liaotung, but when this failed he carried out the cabinet's orders to renounce possession entirely. The curt note in which he did so was sent on 5 May. It remained only to negotiate compensation from China in the form of an increased indemnity.

Territorially, Japan kept Taiwan as prize of war, though this was because nearly all concerned, including Japanese, thought it not worth a quarrel. For the time being, Liaotung was abandoned. In Korea, as we have seen (Chapter 4), the intervention by the powers had so weakened Japan's position that Tokyo decided to lower its expectations there. That left commerce as Japan's most feasible avenue of development in the immediate post-war period.

---

[9] Krasny Archiv, quoted in Conroy, *Japanese seizure*, 294–5. Generally, on the Triple intervention, see W. L. Langer, *The Diplomacy of Imperialism* (1951), 176–87; and on Russo-Japanese relations more widely in this period, Ian Nish, *The Origins of the Russo-Japanese War* (1985), chap. 2.

The commercial provisions

When Li Hung-chang pointed out the value of Taiwan's natural resources during the Shimonoseki talks, Itō Hirobumi's response was not encouraging. 'Perhaps,' he said, 'we may have to spend on the lands more than we can reap from them.'[10] No doubt Itō intended by this to set up a bargaining position, but it is also possible that he had in mind Mutsu's failure to persuade Japanese business men to finance Korean railway-building, or Inoue's experience with the banks over his proposed Korean loan. Certainly there is not much evidence at this time of Japanese interest in the *investment* opportunities that might be made available by victory. For example, Yamamoto Jōtarō of the Mitsui company assessed the economic advantages of holding Liaotung in terms of the access it would give to Manchuria's soya beans, not its minerals.[11] Apparently trade, rather than mining or railways, was what attracted the Japanese business world. And trade meant China.

Extending Japan's commercial privileges in China was an enterprise which had respectable antecedents. In September 1870 Japan had sent an envoy to Tientsin to propose that the traditional trade between the two countries be given a treaty framework similar to that governing their relations with the West. Li Hung-chang, acting for China, had welcomed the idea in principle—possibly because he anticipated a degree of Sino-Japanese co-operation against the powers—but had in practice insisted on a greater measure of reciprocity than appeared in any of the 'unequal' treaties. This was so especially with respect to consular jurisdiction. Moreover, the agreement signed in Tientsin in September 1871 contained no most-favoured-nation clause. It thereby deprived Japan of the opportunity to share automatically in any further gains, such as the opening of additional ports, which might be made by Western negotiators from time to time.[12]

Improving on this arrangement remained a desideratum of Japanese policy for the following twenty years, though nothing worth while was achieved. It was particularly in the minds of Itō and Mutsu during the second half of 1894 because Japan was still much involved in negotiations for revision of its own unequal treaties, that is, in persuading other powers to accept the sort of terms agreed by Britain in July.

[10] Kajima, *Diplomacy*, I, 245.
[11] Nakatsuka, *Nisshin sensō*, 271–2.
[12] There is an accout of the negotiations in Grace Fox, *Britain and Japan* (1969), 274–80. The treaty opened fifteen ports in China, seven in Japan.

Moreover, both men were aware of the steady flow of papers from Japanese representatives at Peking and Shanghai in the months before the war. These had not just kept commercial relations with China at the forefront of Foreign Ministry thinking, but had been specifically concerned with the disadvantages which arose from Japan's lack of a most-favoured-nation clause.

One issue which had occasioned a good deal of correspondence was China's refusal to permit the import of steam-powered machinery for use in cotton-ginning at the treaty ports. This had been taken up by the diplomatic and consular body in China as a whole; but as Ōkoshi Narinori, the Japanese consul-general in London, pointed out in November 1893, if the moves to end the ban succeeded, Japan would not necessarily benefit. For lack of a most-favoured-nation clause, it would be necessary for Japan to negotiate separately with China, or revise the Sino-Japanese treaty, before a change could benefit Japanese business men. Later, writing this time as consul-general at Shanghai, just before the beginning of hostilities with China, he extended this into an argument for early treaty revision. Apart from the question of permission to bring in machinery and carry on textile manufature at the treaty ports, he identified Japanese grievances as chiefly the absence of any formal right to trade in the interior and exclusion from those places which had been opened since 1871. 'Removing our disadavantages in these matters', he wrote, 'is what all our merchants in Shanghai most desire.'[13]

Given this background, it is not surprising that ideas for a commercial treaty with China appeared in Mutsu's first draft of peace proposals late in 1894. The general proposition was that such a treaty should embody the same terms as China had already granted to European countries, which is what Japan's representatives had tried to obtain in 1871. More specifically, Japanese were to be allowed to import machinery for the purpose of establishing factories in China's treaty ports. They were also to be relieved of internal transit tax (*likin*), that is, any impost additional to customs dues, on goods brought into China.[14] Both were privileges which had been demanded by Britain and the United States at one time or another.

[13] Ōkoshi to Mutsu, secret, 12 July 1894, in *NGB* 28:1:196–7. See also his report from London, 23 Nov. 1893, in *NGB* 26:492–5.
[14] The draft is in Nakatsuka, *Nisshin sensō*, 260–3. The Chinese practice of taxing imports after they left the treaty ports on their way to China's domestic markets had been a recurrent issue in Sino-Western relations, and was long to remain so.

Itō expressed some reservations about these proposals on the grounds that they might arouse distrust among the powers, but he did not press the point when Mutsu disagreed. Subsequent drafts added greater detail without much change in substance. Then at some stage after the cabinet saw the documents in January 1895 this section was expanded to include two important new items: the opening of seven extra ports to trade; and the extension of river navigation rights in the interior.[15] Under the most-favoured-nation clause, of course, these gains would have been shared by all existing treaty signatories, just as Japan itself would have acquired the rights previously accorded only to the West.

It is widely held that this fact constituted the reason for much of what Japan sought. Itō and Mutsu were well aware by the beginning of 1895 that the territorial demands they were making on China were likely to arouse the hostility at least of Russia and Germany. They hoped that by securing commercial rights for all the powers, additional to those in existing treaties, they would encourage Britain and America to look on the settlement as a whole with favour, so improving their chances of getting it accepted internationally. In particular, the item about machinery and manufacturing seems to have been included more on tactical than economic grounds. Ōkoshi, the consul-general in Shanghai, had pointed out in March 1894 that 'Japan's interests differ somewhat from those of other countries in this matter.' If China's opposition could be overcome and 'foreign merchants given permission to import machinery and establish factories', it was likely that they would do so, he believed; but combining European and American capital with Chinese labour would produce goods at low prices, 'competing not only with Europe's products, but also with those of Japan'.[16] Leading Japanese entrepreneurs, as we shall see, found the objection cogent. Japan's policy-makers certainly knew about this.

By contrast, an improvement in Japan's trading position on the mainland was almost universally desired in Tokyo. This was made clear by Komura Jutarō, former minister in Peking, now head of the Foreign Ministry's Political Department, when he set out a detailed list

[15] Nakatsuka, *Nisshin sensō*, 267–9.
[16] Ōkoshi to Mutsu, 30 Mar. 1894, in *NGB* 26:495–9. Policy concerning this question, as well as business attitudes, is considered in Nakatsuka, *Nisshin sensō*, 275–87.

of Japan's requirements in March 1895.[17] Because the yen was silver-based, he observed, the decline in the value of silver in relation to gold had greatly improved Japan's competitive position *vis-à-vis* the West, thereby stimulating Japanese exports to China, especially textiles. To seize the present opportunity for putting Japanese treaty rights on a footing of equality with those of their competitors would reinforce this trend, making China a major market for Japanese manufactures. In addition, Japan would benefit commercially, as well as diplomatically, from taking the lead in improving foreign access to the China market. For this reason he proposed the opening of river ports in Hupeh, Hunan, Szechwan, and Kwangsi, plus Peking itself; steamer navigation on the upper Yangtze and inland from Canton as far as Wuchow; and railway-building to link Peking and Newchwang with the Tientsin–Shanhaikuan line, which would complete a route from the Chinese capital to the borders of Liaotung.

There are interesting differences between this memorandum and the draft treaty handed to Li Hung-chang shortly after.[18] The latter retained the references to manufacturing rights and exemption from payment of inland taxes (*likin*), neither of which had been mentioned by Komura. On steamer navigation the two were the same. The treaty draft had two additions to Komura's list of ports to be opened: Soochow and Hangchow, both fairly near Shanghai. However, it omitted all reference to railways. This may have been from fear of British and Russian protests—both powers had an interest in the lines to South Manchuria—or else because of a Japanese lack of enthusiasm for investment as such. In any event, one must assume that these final changes were made by Itō and Mutsu while in Shimonoseki, for Mutsu found it necessary to send a telegram to Tokyo on 4 April, telling the Foreign Ministry what they were. He also sent a summary to the Japanese minister in London with instructions to release it to the press 'without giving any appearance that the information has been furnished by you'.[19] There can be no doubt that this was in order to deny

---

[17] His memorandum is printed in *NGB* 28:1:193–6, where it is dated March 1894. However, Komura was not in the Foreign Minstry at the time. Moreover, the text in the Foreign Ministry archives in Tokyo is undated (as well as unsigned). On balance, it seems likely that the paper was drawn up for the Shimonoseki negotiations, i.e. in March 1895, especially as it contains a reference to 'hostilities' in China, which did not begin until July/August 1894.

[18] The text of the draft treaty is in Kajima, *Diplomacy*, I, 220–2.

[19] Mutsu to Katō, 4 Apr. 1895, telegram in Japanese Foreign Ministry file 2. 2. 1. 1, vol. 4.

Li Hung-chang the chance to suppress information which might influence Britain's view of the proposed Sino-Japanese treaty.

During the course of the subsequent negotiations Li Hung-chang argued vigorously to limit the Japanese gains. He accepted the idea of a commercial treaty on the western model, though he tried to avoid the word 'European', because the American treaties were a little more favourable to China. He attempted without success to make the most-favoured-nation clause reciprocal, that is, applying equally to China's rights in Japan. He rejected the claim for exemption from *likin*. He also objected to Japanese establishing factories in the treaty ports, because this would 'destroy the livelihood of the Chinese', but on this point, as on the most-favoured-nation clause, he found Itō adamant. Indeed, his most notable achievement was in reducing the number of new open ports to four by the omission of Peking and two others from the original list. River navigation from Canton to Wuchow was deleted as well. The rest stood, except for a few points of detail. Li Hung-chang was far from pleased: the commercial provisions of the treaty, he said, were 'unreasonable . . . and derogatory to the sovereignty of an independent nation'.[20]

In sum, the terms signed on 17 April 1895 included an undertaking by China to negotiate a commercial agreement on the basis of those existing between 'China and European Powers'. Pending its conclusion, Japan was to enjoy most-favoured-nation treatment. In addition, China made forthwith a number of specific concessions: Chungking, Shashih, Soochow, and Hangchow were to be opened to foreign trade; steam navigation was to be extended to the upper Yangtze (from Ichang to Chungking) and permitted between Shanghai, Soochow, and Hangchow; and Japanese were to be allowed to engage in manufacturing industry 'in all the open cities, towns and ports of China'. As was also true of the territorial clauses, which we discussed earlier, it was a treaty in the making of which Chinese wishes had played little part.

Despite that, a specific commercial agreement confirming it proved difficult to secure. This was partly because the Triple Intervention brought about a reduction in Japanese prestige, which encouraged China to put obstacles in the way. It was partly because the European powers, seeing Japan for the first time as a serious trade rival, were

[20] Kajima, *Diplomacy*, I, 241–2.

willing to give China a degree of support in offering resistance to it. Mutsu's memoirs record the German Foreign Minister as having said to Aoki Shūzō that 'Japan enjoyed advantages of cheap labour and propinquity, which would allow us under the new treaty arrangements to establish *de facto* an impregnable position in China over the trade and commerce of the European nations'.[21] Mutsu himself dismissed this as 'infantile'. Nevertheless, it was an attitude increasingly to be found among the Western representatives in Peking.

Even Britain was not wholly persuaded of the desirability of what Japan had achieved or proposed. In London the Board of Trade, while welcoming 'freer access to China', expressed doubts about whether the Treaty of Shimonoseki would bring 'any great and rapid development either of Chinese foreign trade generally or of Chinese trade with the United Kingdom and the British Empire specially'. The indemnity, in particular, was 'a great danger', because 'enforced poverty' might lead China to seek to raise its customs dues with crippling effect on trade. There was also a danger that in the new situation Japanese goods 'may compete seriously with our textile imports into China'.[22]

Once the detailed Japanese proposals and Chinese counter-proposals for a commercial treaty became known, the British minister in Peking sent home a report commenting on Chinese attempts to circumvent the promise made at Shimonoseki about establishing foreign factories in the treaty ports. To tax the products of such factories, as China wanted to do, would clearly put them at a disadvantage compared with goods bought from Manchester and India. On the other hand, British manufacturers at home 'should have no reason to be dissatisfied with this proposal to throttle manufactures on Chinese soil'.[23] The Board of Trade admitted the force of the argument. In March 1896, in response to a Foreign Office enquiry as to whether Britain should support Japan on the subject of manufacturing rights, it replied firmly that it should not. The reasons given are worth quoting, because of their relevance to the concept of economic imperialism generally:

There is . . . a considerable conflict between the British interests involved, for while on the one side there might be a profitable opening for the investment of capital as a result of any additional encouragement being given by China to the

[21] Mutsu, *Kenkenroku*, 240.
[22] Board of Trade to Foreign Office, 12 July and 16 Dec. 1895, in FO 17, vols. 1254 and 1256, respectively.
[23] Encl. in Beauclerk to Foreign Office, 5 Dec. 1895, in FO 17, vol. 1240.

establishment of manufactories, the interests of home manufacturers and exporters (especially of textile goods) are in the main directly opposed to any such encouragement being given. The larger and more prominent interest at the present time is in every way that of the home manufacturer.[24]

In Japan, too, it was recognized that a combination of foreign capital with cheap Chinese labour, though profitable to Shanghai business men, might well threaten the export trade in textiles which had been built up over the previous decade. Shibusawa Ei'ichi, the country's outstanding modern entrepreneur, wrote as President of the Tokyo Chamber of Commerce in 1896 to set out that body's views on the subject for the information of the new Foreign Minister, Ōkuma Shigenobu. Li Hung-chang, he said, had tried to justify the plan to tax manufactured goods from foreign-owned factories in China by the argument that it was necessary to increase revenue for the purpose of servicing loans, raised to pay Japan its indemnity. Such a tax would obviously be to the detriment of industrial development in the treaty ports. But would it therefore be to Japan's disadvantage? Shibusawa thought not. Development of China's textile industry could threaten Japan in two ways: by reducing exports of cotton goods to China; and by challenging Japan's silk market in the United States. On both counts it seemed wiser 'to prevent as far as possible the growth of manufacturing industry in China, while greatly developing our own'.[25]

The existence of such doubts in Britain and Japan implied that converting the fairly simple statements of the peace treaty into a full-scale commercial agreement might not prove to be as straightforward as it had appeared in the spring of 1895. Nor was it. In August 1895 the Japanese cabinet approved a draft in forty articles—mostly derived piecemeal from existing Western treaties with China—to serve as a basis for negotiation. The substance of the document was what had been outlined at Shimonoseki; but this did not prevent China from producing a set of counter-proposals, which omitted some clauses, set out more restrictive wording for others, and introduced into several the principle of reciprocity, which Japan had earlier rejected.[26]

The detail of the disagreements, or of the talks that followed from

[24] Board of Trade to Foreign Office, 27 March 1896, in FO 17, vol. 1287.
[25] Shibusawa memorandum of 8 Oct. 1896, in *NGB* 29: 518–20. See also Inoue, *Nihon teikokushugi*, 58–9.
[26] The Japanese proposals, dated 13 Aug. 1895, are in *NGB* 28: 1: 200–9. The Chinese counterproposals are ibid., 28: 1: 230–42.

them, need not greatly concern us here. The general tenor of the Chinese draft, unlike the Japanese one, was to seek to limit Japan to the enjoyment of existing privileges and conformity with existing rules, as previously agreed by the West. That is, China sought to prevent any extension of the treaty port system, except in so far as the opening of additional ports expanded it geographically. For example, Chinese negotiators refused to reduce tariffs on some goods, as demanded by Japan. They also made difficulties about easing the regulations concerning river traffic.

In this context, Chinese insistence on imposing a ten per cent tax on goods produced by foreign factories in China was logical. It was, as we have seen, not unacceptable to business circles in Tokyo. However, since it was contrary to the wording of the Shimonoseki treaty, which put such manufactures on the same footing as imports, the Japanese Foreign Ministry felt bound to oppose it. Only after prolonged argument did it drop its opposition, in return for concessions on other points. Lack of British support played a part in this.

The issue of reciprocity was a more central one. Indeed, in the Japanese view it was fundamental. China claimed, as Li Hung-chang had done in the peace talks, that the most-favoured-nation clause should apply equally to Chinese subjects in Japan, giving them the same rights with respect to trade, travel, and extraterritoriality as Japanese enjoyed in China. This, according to Foreign Minister Saionji Kimmochi, struck at the very heart of the treaty port relationship. The essence of it, he said, was 'intercourse with China in China'. There was no reciprocity with the West. Nor could there be between China and Japan. In no circumstances would the Japanese government consent 'to be placed in their relations with China in a more disadvantageous position than European powers'.[27] He held steadfastly to this determination throughout; and successfully so, for it was not a matter on which China could expect help from elsewhere. There was no reciprocity in the document that was finally signed on 21 July 1896.

Saionji's choice of words echoes those which Mutsu had used when the crisis began in the summer of 1894, save that Mutsu had been talking of equality with China in Korea, not with the West in China. The difference is a measure of how much Japan's standing had been changed by victory. True, in Korea and Liaotung its territorial

---

[27] Telegram of 14 Dec. 1895, in *NGB* 28: 1: 260–1.

advance had since been halted by Russia. Against that, in China Japan had become in the full sense a treaty power. Making good the territorial set-back on the mainland and exploiting the rights that had been gained in the commercial settlement were to be the main strands in Japanese imperialism during the next few years.

6

New Imperialism and the War with Russia, 1895–1905

JAPAN's victory over China in 1894–5 at once undermined the stability of the treaty port system. By demonstrating that China's weakness was much greater than had been thought it encouraged the powers, led by France, Germany, and Russia—ostensibly seeking compensation for 'defending' China against Japanese claims to Liaotung—to insist on demands which China had previously been able to refuse. Following patterns worked out elsewhere in the world during the previous decade, they concentrated on railway and mining rights, by which some areas of China outside the treaty ports could be opened to Western enterprise: the provinces contiguous with French and Russian territory to north and south; and, in the case of Germany, the province of Shantung, in which there had been German interest for several years.

Awareness of China's weakness was also relevant to the way in which the other powers reacted to these moves. It was clearly unreasonable any longer to believe that China was capable on its own of resisting such demands. There was, indeed, a real possibility that the country would be partitioned as a result of them. Consequently Britain and the United States, whose economic strength and economic attitudes were such as to make them prefer access to the whole of China, not just part of it, had to choose between opposing the trend, or coming to terms with it.

The contrasts were not quite as stark in reality as this summary makes them seem. Within France and Germany and Russia there were those—often the financiers—who thought in terms of continued Chinese unity: investment in national railways, for example, not provincial ones. It was commonly the military and the less self-confident merchants who wanted to control limited areas. By the same token, there were some officials and business men in Britain and America who believed China's collapse to be inevitable, so that they opted—against the majority view—for as large a segment of a dismembered market as was feasible. Thus the debate was within countries, as well as between them.

The outcome in the years 1895 to 1900 was a compromise. One ingredient in it was the creation of spheres of influence. These had three characteristics: the acquisition of special railway and mining concessions in the Chinese province or provinces concerned; the addition of a small leased territory, including a naval base, from which those interests could be protected; and an undertaking by China not to alienate the region or grant comparable privileges in it to any other power. Such arrangements were entered into by France with respect to Yunnan, Kwangsi, and Kwangtung in 1895–6; by Germany with respect to Shantung in 1897–8; and by Russia with respect to Manchuria at various dates between 1896 and 1898. The Russian rights, which were of direct concern to Japan, comprised permission to build an east–west railway across central Manchuria (the Chinese Eastern Railway), linking Vladivostock with the Trans-Siberian line, plus a spur running south to terminate at the Liaotung peninsula (Port Arthur). The peninsula itself became Russian under a twenty-five-year lease.

British policy in face of these developments was indecisive. Proposals for making the middle and lower Yangtze valley into a British sphere eventually came to nothing officially, though some important railway concessions were acquired there. Weihaiwei on the north coast of Shantung, held by Japan between 1895 and 1898 as security against payment of the Shimonoseki indemnity, was taken over as a British naval base to balance Russia's possession of Port Arthur. Some territorial gains were made at Hong Kong. Apart from this, Britain contented itself with advising China not to grant spheres of influence to other powers.

The ambiguities of British policy meant that it was left to the United States to work out the second ingredient in the compromise, which was the concept of the Open Door. As framed by Secretary of State John Hay in 1899, this rested on two assumptions. The first was that nothing could effectively be done to prevent the exploitation of monopoly investment rights within established spheres of influence. The second was that a formal reaffirmation of existing treaties was required, in order to prevent the exclusive privileges being extended to trade, which had hitherto been open to all on a footing of equality. Hay asked, and in part obtained, a promise from the powers that they would not try to use their spheres of influence in China to implement differential freight rates, or put up other barriers against the trade of their competitors. Britain actively supported him, as did Germany in later years, though the actions of Russia and Japan in Manchuria, as we shall see, left a measure of uncertainty about how much such international promises were worth.

It was into this environment that Japan was thrust by the Treaty of Shimonoseki. The situation was significantly different from the 'co-operative imperialism' the Japanese had thought to join, within which treaty signatories shared their privileges through the most-favoured-nation clause. Instead, there were fierce imperialist rivalries, as much about territory as about trade. One of the most powerful predators, Russia, was established at Japan's doorstep. And this fact posed a crucial dilemma. By all economic logic, Japan as an industrial late-developer should have belonged with Germany and Russia, seeking the protected markets and investment opportunities that a sphere of influence might afford. Yet the only region in which Japan could hope to create a sphere was precisely that in which to do so would be to challenge Russia. Challenging Russia, as the Triple Intervention had made plain, could only be attempted with some indication of support from Britain and America. The price of this was accepting the Open Door.

Spheres of influence: Korea and Fukien

The Triple Intervention, as we saw in the previous chapter, was a check to Japanese ambitions on the Asian mainland. It led to the formulation of plans for a programme of rearmament, designed to strengthen Japan in any future confrontation of the kind. It also brought back the caution which had characterized Japanese foreign policy before 1894. For several more years, Japanese imperialism involved nothing more than seeking modestly to exploit the gains already made in Korea and Taiwan, drawing back at any sign of serious opposition.

In Korea, it was not just that the climate had become unfavourable to establishing a Japanese protectorate—as even Inoue Kaoru had been forced to recognize in the summer of 1895—but also that Russia had begun to intervene on its own behalf. Inoue's successor was Miura Gorō, a former soldier, lacking diplomatic experience. Faced by an emerging pro-Russian faction in Seoul, he allowed himself to become involved with Japanese adventurers and Korean collaborators in an attempted *coup d'état* in October 1895. It was badly mishandled. When the palace was seized, the queen, whose family had consistently taken an anti-Japanese stance, was murdered. Japanese involvement in the incident was allowed publicly to appear.

One result was a winter of confusion and disorder, culminating in the king's escape from the palace to take refuge in Russia's legation in February 1896. Another was that Miura was disavowed, then replaced by a senior diplomat, Komura Jutarō. Komura's task was to mend fences. This did not prove easy, since Tokyo would not countenance further interference in Korean politics. In fact, it became clear that nothing much could be done in Korea until there was agreement at government level between Japan and Russia. The first step towards it was taken in March 1896, when Itō Hirobumi had talks with the Russian minister in Tokyo, agreeing the outline of a settlement: Japan would renounce any desire for 'exclusive interest'; Russia would be satisfied with an arrangement ensuring that Korea did not become 'a weapon against Russia in the hands of other Powers'.[1] More formal discussions were to take place in St Petersburg, when Yamagata Aritomo went to attend the coronation of Tsar Nicholas II.

The instructions Yamagata was given for this mission envisaged a solution to the Korean problem not unlike that which had been offered to China in the summer of 1894, that is, an informal joint protectorate.[2] Japanese and Russian representatives in Seoul, it was proposed, should work together to ensure the appointment of suitable Koreans to office, as well as advising on financial reform and foreign loans. Both countries would keep armed forces in Korea, sufficient to preserve public order, though that task should eventually be taken over by a reorganized Korean Army and police. If it were necessary for Russia and Japan to intervene, either to maintain order, or to defend Korea against external attack, their troops should co-operate, though possibly occupying separate zones.

In meetings with the Russian Foreign Minister during May and June, Yamagata tried to specify these zones, proposing a division into north and south, but Lobanov refused. He also refused to insert a clause which would 'guarantee' Korean independence. For his part, Yamagata objected to the king having a Russian-trained guard, but agreed that arrangements for the king's 'safety' would not be changed (he was still in the Russian legation). He accepted that Russia should

[1] Kajima, *Diplomacy*, I, 432–4. For events in Korea, see Conroy, *Japanese seizure*, 299–324.
[2] For these instructions, together with the agreement signed by Yamagata, see Kajima, *Diplomacy*, I, 436–46.

have the right to install a telegraph between Seoul and the Russo-Korean border. A document embodying these terms, part of it secret, was signed on 9 June 1896.

Russia's more positive approach to Korean questions was exemplified in December of that year, when the Russo-Chinese Bank made a loan, secured on Korean customs revenue, for the purpose of repaying the 3 million yen borrowed from the Bank of Japan during 1895. A small Russian military mission was sent to Seoul as well. Thereafter, however, the balance began to tilt back towards Japan again. One reason was that Koreans resented Russian interference, just as they had resented Japan's. In February 1897 the king was persuaded to return to his palace, weakening Russia's influence. Moreover, as the scramble for concessions developed in China during the next twelve months, Russia became more concerned about rivalry with Britain than about its position in Korea. Thus, once Liaotung had been taken over in the winter of 1897–8, the Foreign Minister, Muraviev, showed himself ready to reach an accommodation with Japan about Korea on rather more generous terms than in the past. The Nishi–Rosen agreement of 25 April 1898, while it required Japan and Russia equally to refrain from interference in Korean affairs and to consult each other before nominating military or financial advisers, included a Russian promise not to hinder the development of Japan's 'predominant' economic interests in that country.

This meant that Inoue's ideas of July 1895 for creating a Japanese sphere of influence in Korea could at last make progress.[3] In banking, for example, Japan was now able to assert superiority. Shibusawa Ei'ichi's Dai Ichi Bank had had a key part in financing Japanese trade with Korea ever since it had established a branch at Pusan in 1878. After 1894 it took on a new function, similar to that which foreign banks fulfilled in China, which was to furnish an alternative to the chaotic local currency. It did so at first by circulating yen coins and notes, but when Japan adopted the gold standard in 1897 this ceased to be practicable. For a time the bank minted silver yen coins specially for use in Korea. Late in 1901 it also began to print special yen notes for circulation there. Their popularity eventually made Dai Ichi in effect the country's

---

[3] On Japanese economic activities in Korea between 1895 and 1910, see Conroy, *Japanese seizure*, 448–52, 473–9; also Peter Duus, 'Economic dimensions of Meiji imperialism: the case of Korea', in Myers and Peattie, *Japanese colonial empire*, 148–61, plus the tables given at 164–71. Japanese economic expansion is discussed in more general terms in Chapter 9, below.

central banker, though it operated in these matters without specific authorization from the Korean government.

Railway rights were also directly related to the making of a sphere of influence. As an article in the Tokyo magazine *Taiyō* observed in July 1899, 'the means of extending one's territory without the use of troops . . . is railway policy'.[4] In 1894 Japan had secured an undertaking from the Korean government with respect to railway concessions for the Seoul–Pusan and Seoul–Inchon (Chemulpo) lines, but Japanese business had been reluctant to put up the necessary capital. No contracts were immediately signed. In March 1896, when Japanese influence was at its lowest because of Miura's abortive coup, the Korean government transferred the Seoul–Inchon concession to an American. He, too, experienced difficulty in raising capital, so sold his rights in 1897 to a private Japanese syndicate, headed by Shibusawa, in which four of the *zaibatsu* firms (Mitsui, Mitsubishi, Yasuda, and Ōkura) all had shares. Work on this railway was completed in 1901. It did not make real headway, however, until the Japanese government had departed from its original policy to the extent of contributing an interest-free loan of 1.8 million yen.

The Seoul–Pusan line took even longer to materialize, being much more expensive. Korean opposition prevented a start being made in 1896, though Japanese pressure was sufficient to ensure that the concession was not in this case transferred elsewhere. In fact, it was September 1898, following the Nishi–Rosen talks, before terms for building the railway were agreed. They included a stipulation that work must start within three years, which proved difficult to meet. Once again Shibusawa became head of the syndicate seeking capital. Once again it had to look to government financial backing, made available this time partly because of support from the army, which argued the strategic importance of the line. A company was formed in June 1901; work started in August, only a month before the concession would have lapsed; and it was still in progress when the enterprise was amalgamated in September 1903 with that of the company which owned the Seoul–Inchon line. Against a background of deteriorating relations with Russia, the government tried to speed up progress by injecting 10 million yen of additional capital in December. Even so, it took further reorganization and more government money to get the line finished by the end of the following year.

[4] Quoted in Inoue, *Nihon teikokushugi*, 65.

Thus the attempt to turn Korea into a Japanese sphere of influence had not been wholly successful by the time the Russo-Japanese War broke out in 1904. Between 1898 and 1903 Japan had provided on average a little over 60 per cent of Korean imports and taken about 80 per cent of exports.[5] This dominance in trade was reinforced by the ownership of railway lines connecting Seoul with Inchon and Pusan, the latter still incomplete. By a local agreement of 1896 it had the right to keep small detachments of troops at Seoul, Pusan, and Wonsan, as well as to operate some military telegraphs. On the other hand, the Japanese position was by no means a monopoly one. Russia had similar rights with respect to troops and telegraphs. Japan had no leased territory or naval base. And only at Wonsan was there a Japanese foothold in the northern half of the country. No foreign bids had been accepted by the Korean government for a railway between Seoul and Wonsan, though several had been made. For the line from Seoul to Uiju, the route to Mukden, a concession had been granted to a French concern in 1896; then, because no progress was made, it was offered to Russia, which declined it; and finally, after a Japanese bid had been rejected, work was begun—very slowly—by a Korean company.

Yet if what had been gained in Korea in these years fell short of Japanese hopes, it was a great deal more than had proved possible on the China coast, where the events of 1894–5 had also bred ambitions. There were a number of influential Japanese who saw the acquisition of Taiwan as opening the way for a Japanese 'advance to the south' (*nanshin*), especially through the Chinese province of Fukien. Katsura Tarō, Governor-General of Taiwan in 1896, was one of them. So was Kodama Gentarō, who held that office from 1898 to 1906. Not everyone shared their views—in 1898 there was considerable support for a proposal to sell the island to France, because it had proved expensive to pacify[6]—but the government was sufficiently persuaded of the prospects to make an attempt to secure special rights in Fukien during the scramble for concessions. Under some pressure, China agreed in April 1898 not to alienate the province to any other power. On the question of railways, however, it would do no more than give an undertaking to offer Japan first refusal, if it were ever contemplated that they should be built.

[5] See table in Inoue *Nihon teikokushugi*, 46. Almost all the rest of Korea's trade was with China.
[6] E. Patricia Tsurumi, 'Taiwan under Kodama Gentarō and Gotō Shimpei' (1967), 100–1.

So matters rested until 1900. In that year, as the Boxer outbreaks spread through north China, threatening once more the country's unity, Tokyo acted again. In the early part of the year the Japanese Foreign Ministry drew up proposals for securing railway concessions in Fukien and in the neighbouring provinces of Chekiang and Kiangsi, modelled on those Germany had secured in Shantung. These were presented to China in June, but rejected. Thereupon Katsura, who had become War Minister in Yamagata's cabinet, sent orders to Kodama in Taiwan to prepare an expedition to seize Fukien's chief port, Amoy, using as pretext various attacks that had been made on Japanese subjects in south China. In August steps were taken to carry these orders out. However, before the main body of Japanese troops could land, Tokyo called the operation off. According to Kodama's civilian deputy, Gotō Shimpei—who had actually been in Amoy, making arrangements for its occupation—there were two reasons for this. One was fear of the possible repercussions on Japan's relations with Britain. Another was the risk of a simultaneous dispute with Russia, arising from the ramifications of the Boxer crisis. In the cabinet's view, Gotō concluded, this was not a time to get embroiled in the affairs of Fukien.[7]

These events, coupled with what had happened in Korea, makes it clear that to Japanese policy-makers expansion, even in the diluted form of spheres of influence, still depended on the co-operation, or at least the acquiescence, of the major Euopean powers. In practice, this was likely to mean choosing between Russia and Britain, since the one dominated the area north of the Great Wall, while the other was the main participant in the trade and investment of the rest of China.

The question of which could least safely be offended was debated during 1901. The context was a proposal for alliance with Britain, but for the purpose of studying Japanese imperialism it is the nature of the arguments employed by Japanese leaders, not the alliance itself, that most concerns us. They began from the fact that in the summer of 1900, when the Boxers attacked Russian railway installations in Manchuria, Russia had sent in large numbers of troops to protect its interests. This indicated, Yamagata argued in April 1901,

---

[7] On Japanese policy concerning Fukien in 1896–1900, see Marius B. Jansen, *The Japanese and Sun Yat-sen* (1954), 99–101, and Ian Nish, 'Japan's indecision during the Boxer disturbances' (1961), 451–6.

that Russia was 'intent on permanent occupation'. As for China, he said, 'its partition is inevitable'. In these circumstances, Japan would have to leave aside its ambitions concerning Fukien (which could be pursued at a later opportunity) in order to defend the north. For this it needed British support.[8]

Katsura, who became Prime Minister in June 1901, took the reasoning a step further. He was convinced that Russia's advance would not stop with the occupation of Manchuria. Russia, he wrote, 'will inevitably extend into Korea and will not end until there is no room left for us'. It followed that any agreement with Russia would be only 'a short-term remedy'. His Foreign Minister, Komura Jutarō, saw the problem in much the same way: 'if Manchuria becomes the property of Russia, Korea itself cannot remain independent'. That made the issue for Japan 'a matter of life and death'. Compromise with Russia, Komura believed, would achieve nothing more than delay, while by destroying the 'affection and confidence' which Japan had built up among Chinese it would seriously hamper Japanese trade. By contrast, an alliance with Britain would not only serve as a warning to Russia. It would also improve Japan's commercial credit; afford access to Britain's financial resources; and open British colonies to Japanese trade. Such advantages 'would far exceed those to be derived from Manchuria and Siberia'.

The Anglo-Japanese alliance, which was signed in January 1902, was therefore in one sense a stage in the working out of Japanese imperialism. The treaty committed both signatories to 'maintaining the independence and territorial integrity' of China and Korea, as well as to 'securing equal opportunities in those countries for the commerce and industry of all nations'. However, it also recognized that Japan was 'interested in a peculiar degree politically as well as commercially and industrially' in Korea.[9] Hence endorsing the Open Door policy in China had obtained for Japan a measure of British support in defending its emerging sphere of influence on the mainland against the possibility of Russian attack. The corollary was that Japanese ambitions in Fukien were for some years to be set aside.

[8] Several documents relevant to these discussions, including those by Yamagata, Katsura, and Komura, quoted here, are translated in Ian Nish, *The Anglo-Japanese Alliance* (1966), 378–88.
[9] Texts of the document are given in Nish, *Anglo-Japanese Alliance*, 216–17, and Kajima, *Diplomacy*, II, 65–6.

The conflict with Russia

Since the Anglo-Japanese alliance provided for military help from Britain if Japan became involved in hostilities with more than one other power, it enabled the Japanese government to deal with the issues raised by Russian occupation of Manchuria without fear of another Triple Intervention. During 1902 and 1903 it used this advantage in an attempt to bring about the withdrawal of Russian troops from Manchuria and a settlement of Russo-Japanese disputes with regard to Manchuria and Korea. In the first it was partly successful, in the second not at all. At the end of 1903, therefore, the decision was taken to have recourse to war.

Early in February 1904 Japanese land and sea forces launched attacks on Russian positions in southern Manchuria, using Korea as a staging-area. The land fighting was heavy. There was a long siege of Port Arthur, which ended with its surrender on 1 January 1905. There were major battles in the vicinity of Liaoyang (August–September 1904) and Mukden (March 1905). In all these engagements Japan was successful, but suffered heavy casualties. At sea, local naval superiority was quickly established in the approaches to Port Arthur and Vladivostock. In an attempt to break the Japanese blockades the Russian Baltic fleet was sent from Europe in November 1904, arriving in the Straits of Tsushima in May 1905, where it was defeated by Tōgō Heihachirō. The event was decisive in persuading Russia to negotiate for peace.

For fifty years or more there has been controversy over the relevance of this war to Japanese imperialism.[10] There were certainly powerful pressure groups in Japan which saw a contest with Russia as the prelude to territorial expansion on the mainland. Outstanding among them was a patriotic association called the Kokuryūkai (Amur Society, better known as the Black Dragon Society), which was founded by Uchida Ryōhei in February 1901 to promote 'the mission of imperial Japan' and to 'check the expansion of the western powers'. Its manifesto declared that it was 'the urgent duty of Japan to fight Russia . . . and then to lay the foundation for a grand continental enterprise taking Manchuria, Mongolia and Siberia as one region'.[11] Many middle-ranking army officers gave enthusiastic backing to this view. So did

---

[10] The literature is surveyed in Shinobu Seizaburō and Nakayama Ji'ichi (ed.), *Nichi-Ro sensō-shi no kenkyū* (1972), 11–29. In English, the most detailed studies of the origins of the war are Nish, *Origins*, and Shumpei Okamoto, *The Japanese Oligarchy and the Russo-Japanese War* (1970).

[11] Okamoto, *Japanese Oligarchy*, 61.

newspapers and party politicians, who had much to say about 'revenge' for the Triple Intervention and for Russia's subsequent action in taking Port Arthur. Business sentiment was less clear-cut. One can find references to the long-term commercial gains which success against Russia would bring, but the weight of opinion seems to have been the other way.[12] War would penalize commerce and industry by raising taxes, it was pointed out; the most profitable markets were in China south of the Great Wall, not north of it; and Russia's occupation of Manchuria, by improving communications and political stability, might actually help Japan's trade with the area, rather than hinder it.

Official documents of 1902–3 reflect an interest chiefly in the task of defending what Japan already held. Komura Jutarō maintained that the danger in Manchuria was of Russia creating a sphere of influence which would exclude 'all foreign enterprises and ventures other than her own'.[13] Given Japan's need for British support, the only practicable counter to this was to insist on Russian observance of the Open Door. That was a policy which China favoured, too, in the hope that it might fend off Russian annexation of the territory by creating a kind of international vested interest in it.

Korea was a problem of a different order. After victory over China in 1895 Japanese military thinking had extended what Yamagata Aritomo had called the 'line of advantage' so as to bring the whole of Korea within it.[14] In other words, Korea became Japan's first line of defence, as well as a potential source of profit. It was for this reason that the army had given its approval to the building of Korean railways. It was also for this reason that the presence of Russian troops in Manchuria was seen, not merely as blocking future Japanese advances on the mainland, but also as a threat to the Japanese home islands. In consequence, the basis first put forward by Japan for a settlement of disagreements with Russia was *Man-Kan kōkan*, 'exchanging Manchuria for Korea', that is, offering a Japanese recognition of Russia's 'preponderant' rights in Manchuria in return for Russian recognition of Japan's in Korea. This was to put defence before expansion.

It is not necessary to consider in detail the diplomatic exchanges which followed, but for the sake of understanding Japanese aims on the mainland it is worth examining the documents in which the policy

[12] Shinobu and Nakayama, *Nichi-Ro sensō*, 180–6; Inoue, *Nihon teikokushugi*, 221.

[13] Komura to Uchida (Peking), 1 May 1903; *NGB* 36:1:110–14.

[14] The first step was a memorandum by Yamagata in April 1895: see Hackett, *Yamagata*, 168–9.

took its final form. The most useful of these is a memorandum prepared by Komura as Foreign Minister for discussion by the cabinet
and imperial conference in June 1903.[15] He began by pointing out that
Japan approached the continent most closely at two points: Korea in
the north, Fukien in the south. Fukien was important in the context of
a possible partition of China, but this problem was 'not at present of
great urgency'. Korea, by contrast, if occupied by another power,
would imperil 'the safety of Japan'. Russia, acting from an established
position in Manchuria, was bound to try to 'spread her influence to the
Korean peninsula and bring the court and government there under her
wing'. This Japan must at all costs prevent.

As the means of doing so, Komura proposed seeking an agreement
with Russia on the following lines. Both countries would promise to
observe the principles of territorial integrity and equal opportunity in
their dealings with China and Korea. They would recognize each
other's rights in Manchuria and Korea, respectively. Both would be
entitled to use troops to defend their interests or suppress 'regional
uprisings', if necessary, though the troops should be withdrawn 'as
soon as they achieve their object'. Finally, Japan would retain the right
of advising Korea on domestic reform and helping in its implementation. Thus both countries were to have rather more than a sphere of
interest in the accepted sense. Itō Hirobumi, in a conversation with the
British ambassador a few days later, seems frankly to have described
the plan as a division of spoils.[16]

Komura's proposals were approved and put to Russia, which
rejected them. By the end of 1903 war was therefore seen in Tokyo to
be unavoidable. Accordingly, on 30 December the cabinet again considered the policy to be adopted towards China and Korea, paying
attention in particular to whether those two countries should be
brought into the hostilities in any way.[17] With respect to China, the
decision was that it should not. For one thing, the cost of war, added to
the existing burden of indemnities, might put at risk China's financial
stability. This would be to the disadvantage of all the treaty powers,
including Japan. For another, a Sino-Japanese alliance against Russia

[15] Most of the text is translated in Ian Nish, *Japanese Foreign Policy* (1977), 277–8.
The Japanese text is in *NGB* 36:1:1–4. The imperial conference (*gozen-kaigi*) was a
meeting of elder statesmen (*Genrō*), service chiefs and cabinet ministers, held in the
emperor's presence.
[16] Nish, *Anglo-Japanese Alliance*, 264.
[17] Cabinet resolutions of 30 Dec. 1903, in Kajima, *Diplomacy*, II, 109–13.

might give substance to European fears of the 'Yellow Peril'. If, for example, it were to prompt popular attacks on white men, as had happened in the Boxer outbreaks, the powers might well intervene in China. In that event, Japan, preoccupied with fighting Russia, would not be able to defend its prospective interests in Fukien.

The other main element in Japanese policy was defined in this document as 'ensuring her security in the north by safeguarding the independence of Korea'. To this end, the cabinet resolved, it was necessary to keep Korea 'by force under our influence under whatever circumstances'. This made it desirable first to arrange an offensive and defensive alliance, or a treaty of protectorate, in order to provide public justification for Japanese intervention, if it were required.

There is nothing surprising about these decisions concerning Korea. They had been heralded, as we have seen, in the terms of the Anglo-Japanese alliance. More interesting is the absence from the documents of any reference to obtaining a special position for Japan in Manchuria, such as Russia was generally assumed to have been establishing. Indeed, what was said about China implied a commitment to the co-operative imperialism of the treaty port system, which would have been contradicted by possession of an exclusive Manchurian sphere. Victories changed that state of affairs, just as they had done with respect to Korea during the hostilities with China in 1894–5.

Komura was under considerable pressure to pursue extravagant war aims in 1904–5, as Mutsu had been a decade earlier. There were articles in the financial press, urging the government to exercise authority in Korea and Manchuria to compensate for the competitive weaknesses of Japanese business there.[18] There were petitions to the Foreign Ministry from Japanese residents in Seoul and Pusan, calling for the assimilation of Japanese and Korean currencies with Japan's, the acquisition of mining and property rights, plus improvements in the banking and telegraph systems under Japanese control, all with a view to the 'complete seizure of economic power'.[19]

Within the diplomatic service itself there were men with an even wider vision of Japanese economic empire. In the Foreign Ministry files in Tokyo there is a 'private' memorandum, dated 24 June 1904, written by Iwanaga Kakujū, one of the Russian-language specialists who had been serving in Vladivostock until the outbreak of hostilities.

[18] Shinobu and Nakayama, *Nichi-Ro sensō*, 284–8.
[19] Memorials of 23 March 1904 (Seoul) and 16 May 1904 (Pusan), in Japanese Foreign Ministry file 1. 1. 2. 33.

Its general argument was that in order to maintain stability in East Asia it would be necessary 'to bring Manchuria wholly within our sphere of influence'. This would entail something more than economic privileges, since it might be necessary to defend Japan's interests, not only against revenge from Russia, but also in the event of a conflict between the powers in China. Japan should therefore demand from Russia the handing over to Japan of the Chinese Eastern Railway, or at least its southern portion; the transfer of the lease of the Liaotung peninsula; an indemnity; a commercial treaty, giving Japan special tariff advantages in Russia's Far Eastern provinces, together with fishing and mining rights; and the cession of islands in the north. China should be required to confirm those parts of the agreement which related to Chinese territory; to grant mining and residential rights to Japanese in Manchuria; to carry out administrative reforms there, employing Japanese officers for military training and other Japanese in the customs service; and to promise not to extend similar privileges in Manchuria to any other power without Japanese consent. This apart, the region was to be opened to the trade and investment of all countries. An annex on railway development noted that Japan was not likely to be able to find the very considerable amounts of capital required for completing the Manchurian network, so investment by Britain and America would have to be encouraged. Railway competition with Russia should be avoided as far as possible, because of its expense.[20]

There is no evidence that Iwanaga spoke for anyone but himself, but it seems unlikely that a document which so clearly set out the main features of the eventual peace settlement—and, indeed, of Japanese policy in north-east Asia for the next twenty-five years—could have been the independent work of a thirty-one-year-old secretary. It may well have been drafted at Komura's request. Certainly it was the kind of proposal which one would expect to appeal to him. Komura, after all, had been partly responsible for the commercial sections of the Treaty of Shimonoseki. He had held senior posts in Seoul and Peking, which made him knowledgeable about the workings of the treaty port system. He was also doubtful about the competitiveness of the Japanese economy. In 1901, when China had proposed the 'opening' of Manchuria as a device for weakening the influence of Russia there, Komura had objected on the grounds that 'our commercial capitalists

---

[20] The memorandum is in Japanese Foreign Ministry file 1. 1. 2. 33. There are no minutes or any other indication of provenance.

have not yet reached the stage of development at which they could compete equally with those of other countries under such new privileges'.[21] This kind of thinking would have been reinforced by his knowledge of Russian actions in Manchuria. Much of what Japan eventually demanded paralleled what Russia had done, or was believed to have done, to ensure its own advantage against economically stronger competitors.

The first formal draft of peace terms was submitted by Komura to the Prime Minister, Katsura Tarō, in July 1904.[22] It identified four main aims. One was to maintain the independence of Korea and the territorial integrity of Manchuria for the sake of Japan's defence and security. The second was to 'extend our interests' in Manchuria, Korea, and Russia's Maritime Provinces, in order to maintain Japan's position in the contest between the powers for privileges in East Asia. Third, since China was destined for collapse and partition, it would be necessary to lay foundations for intervening effectively to protect Japan's interests when that time came. Finally, Japan's rights in Korea and Manchuria must be advanced a stage. Before the war, Komura argued, 'we would have been satisfied with making Korea our sphere of influence and simply maintaining our existing [treaty] rights in Manchuria'. Since the start of hostilities, that was no longer enough. Korea 'must be brought effectively within the sphere of our sovereignty', initially as a protectorate. Manchuria 'must be made in some degree a sphere of interest'.

In pursuit of these aims, Komura stated, undertakings would have to be secured from both Russia and China. In identifying the specific items to include in them, he followed very closely the memorandum drawn up by Iwanaga, which has been summarized above. The principal differences, in fact, were that Komura opted for the transfer only of Russian railways in south Manchuria, not the whole Chinese Eastern line; that he identified Sakhalin as an island to be ceded to Japan; and that he expanded the proposed agreement with China to include several commercial provisions, involving the opening of additional ports and cities in Manchuria to foreign trade, the grant of timber, mining, and fishery rights to Japan, and railway concessions designed to extend the existing Manchurian network.

These documents indicate clearly the Japanese government's

[21] *Komura gaikō-shi*, ed. Japanese Foreign Ministry (1968), 230–1
[22] There is an extensive summary in Okamoto, *Japanese Oligarchy*, 112–14. The Japanese text is in *NGB—Nichi-Ro Sensō*, V, 59–63.

aspirations on the Asian mainland. Yet Komura and his colleagues were always aware that only decisive victory would make it possible to attain them. In the event, they needed a modicum of diplomatic flexibility as well. By early 1905 the Japanese Army was warning the government that it could not long sustain the present rate of casualties. The cabinet was also becoming concerned about mounting international debt. As a result, when it was decided to accept American mediation in mid-April, the terms that it was agreed to put forward were a good deal more modest than Komura's earlier draft.[23] Those that were 'absolutely indispensable' consisted chiefly of a Russian acknowledgement of 'Japan's complete right of freedom of action in Korea', plus the transfer to Japan of the Liaotung lease and the spur of the Chinese Eastern Railway south from Harbin. This was justified on the grounds that Port Arthur and the railway had been 'a tool of Russian aggression, enabling it to exercise great influence over southern Manchuria and threaten the Korean border'. An indemnity had become 'not absolutely indispensable', as had the claim to Sakhalin. Komura's references to the fate of China were eliminated altogether. So were most of the demands for commercial advantages on the Amur and in the Maritime Provinces. In sum, Japan limited itself to the issues which had been the original *casus belli*, namely, Korea and Manchuria.

It was with instructions based on these decisions that Komura went as Japanese representative to the Portsmouth peace conference in August 1905. He negotiated rather more vigorously than his colleagues seem to have expected, securing the cession of the southern half of Sakhalin in return for waiving an indemnity, whereas Tokyo had been willing to dispense with both. For the rest, the treaty signed on 5 September followed very much the lines the Japanese cabinet had set out in April. It remained to persuade China to endorse its terms. It also remained to be seen whether Japan would be strictly bound by them, when giving the agreement practical effect.

[23] See Okamoto, 'op. cit.', 117–18; *NGB—Nichi-Ro Sensō*, V, 104–5.

7

Formal and Informal Empire in North-east Asia, 1905–1910

THERE was never any doubt that the Russo-Japanese War had left Japan in a strong position on the adjacent mainland. Less clear, even to Japanese, was what were now the limits to its ambitions. Korea having been occupied during the hostilities, there was no reason to expect a withdrawal there. As to Manchuria, Komura's peace proposals had hinted at claims that might put in question Japan's adherence to the principle of equal opportunity and the Open Door.

Important sections of Japanese opinion, influenced by strategic considerations as much as by economic ones, did indeed see Japanese interests on the mainland as being different in kind from those which informed the treaty port system in China. They did not conceive of Japanese authority in Korea and Manchuria as existing merely for the purpose of ensuring stable conditions for trade. Nor was it designed just to further the development of mining and railways under Japanese control. It had as one of its objects to 'preserve the peace of East Asia', which was part of the process of guaranteeing Japan's security.

For this reason, spheres of influence, such as the powers had acquired elsewhere, were not always thought by Japanese governments to be enough. Yet it was impossible for them to ignore the fact that establishing political power, going beyond the limits of the treaty port system, was likely to provoke opposition from Britain and America, who were in a position to deny, or at least hamper, Japanese access to international credit and the Chinese market. An attempt was therefore made to resolve this dilemma by making a distinction between two arms of Japanese imperialism. In China south of the Great Wall, Japanese policy rested on an acquiescence in Anglo-American ground rules for the sake of trade and investment opportunities. In Korea and Manchuria, however, it aimed at establishing a military and political foothold that would meet Japan's defence requirements, while giving Japanese economic interests an advantage over all competitors. The economic consequences of this policy will be considered in Chapter 9. Here we will be concerned with the processes of its formulation and the tensions to which it gave rise among decision-makers.

The annexation of Korea

The decision taken by the Japanese cabinet in December 1903, that in the event of hostilities with Russia it would be 'most convenient' to conclude an offensive and defensive alliance with Korea, was soon followed up. Against a background of substantial Japanese troop movements northward from the Korean capital, Hayashi Gonsuke, minister in Seoul, secured an agreement on 23 February 1904 by which the Korean government promised to place 'full confidence' in that of Japan; to accept advice concerning administrative reform; to afford facilities for any action Japan found it necessary to take to protect Korea from external attack or 'internal disturbances'; and to authorize Japanese occupation of 'such places as may be necessary from strategical points of view'.[1] In return, Japan guaranteed Korea's independence and territorial integrity (presumably against everyone else).

For Japan this was only a first step. At the end of May the cabinet took more detailed decisions, looking to the long-term future of the Japanese–Korean relationship.[2] They envisaged that Japan would take over responsibility for Korean security, both internally and externally, stationing a force in Korea for this purpose that would also be 'extremely useful as a means of maintaining our influence in time of peace'. There was to be supervision of the country's foreign relations through an adviser chosen by Japan, who would have access to all Korean Foreign Ministry documents. There was to be a Japanese financial adviser, concerned among other things with reform of the currency and tax structure. He could make a start on reducing expenditure by cutting the size of the Korean Army. In addition, Japan was to have effective control of transport and communications. It would seek to complete the Seoul–Pusan railway as soon as possible; to regularize the position with respect to the Seoul–Uiju line, running to the Manchurian frontier, which the army was constructing for its wartime needs; and to secure a concession for a line from Seoul to Wonsan,

---

[1] English text in *NGB* 37:1:343–4. On Japanese policy in Korea in the years 1904–10, see generally Conroy, *Japanese seizure*, 325–82; also Eugene and Han-kyo Kim, *Korea and the Politics of Imperialism* (1967), 121–218.

[2] Texts of 30 and 31 May 1904, in *NGB* 37:1:351–6.

though this would not be required immediately. Telegraph, telephone, and postal facilities were to be taken over and integrated with those of Japan.

Other objectives were outlined much more sketchily. In principle it was assumed that Korea would supply Japan with foodstuffs and raw materials in return for industrial products. One development designed to facilitate this would be the emigration of Japanese farmers to Korea, a step which would simultaneously increase Korean production (by using surplus land) and ease Japan's population problem. For this to be possible it would have to be made legal for Japanese to acquire land outside the treaty ports. Timber concessions would also have to be obtained. So must mining rights, though identifying the ones that were potentially profitable would require some preliminary study. Finally, Japan would seek to extend its fisheries into Korean coastal waters.

These documents set out so clearly the nature of Japanese aims in Korea that one can in large part treat policy during the next few years as being addressed to questions of ways and means. At a number of points the initial decisions were refined in the light of experience. They sometimes had to be modified to take account of Korean opposition. The general drift, however, remained the same until annexation in 1910.

The most debated issue after May 1904 was the way in which Japanese control should be exercised. In August the Korean government agreed to appoint advisers on finance and foreign affairs, the former a Japanese, the latter an American, long employed by the Foreign Ministry in Tokyo. The American was instructed by his former employers to use his powers in Seoul only in consultation with the Japanese minister there. In December, Japanese were given supervisory authority over the Korean police at both national and provincial levels. These measures were sufficient for Japan's purposes while the war lasted, but a different legal framework seemed necessary once peace had been concluded with Russia in September 1905. In the following month, having taken the precaution of sounding out Britain and the United States, in order to make sure that there was no risk of intervention by them, Tokyo decided to create a formal protectorate in Korea. This was preferably to be done with Korean consent, but would if necessary be enforced without it. In November, Itō Hirobumi went as special envoy to Seoul, exacting a treaty from a reluctant Korean court to provide for the appointment of a Japanese Resident-General. The holder of this office, who was to be responsible in diplomatic matters to the Japanese Foreign Minister, but otherwise to the premier, was given extensive powers. As defined in an imperial ordinance of 20 December, they included authority to use Japanese troops to maintain law and order; to supervise Japanese officials and advisers in Korea; to intervene directly in the decision-making of the Korean government, whenever he saw fit; and to issue regulations, enforceable by imprisonment or fines.

Itō himself was appointed to this post early in 1906. His staff at that time totalled a little over seventy Japanese in Seoul, plus a smaller number in each of the provinces. They were supported by a residency police force of 250 men and an army garrison of up to two divisions. In addition, there were Japanese representatives working with the Korean police. Through this machinery the Resident-General was able to supervise directly foreign relations, defence, and communications, while exercising an incontestable influence over the Korean cabinet on all other items of national policy. The Korean ruler himself—now using the title of emperor, not king—was effectively isolated from politics once Japanese police supplemented his palace guards in July.

Naturally enough, there was a good deal of Korean resentment at this state of affairs, not least within the court. This was made manifest in June 1907, when envoys were sent secretly to the Hague peace conference to ask for an international declaration of Korean independence. They were unsuccessful. The action did, however, provide Itō with grounds for tightening Japan's grip still more. On 19 July of that year he engineered the Korean emperor's abdication in favour of his son. This done, the Korean government was brought to accept an arrangement by which Japanese were introduced into the administration as chief secretary to the cabinet, chief of the Home Ministry police bureau, vice-ministers of departments, and judges. The Korean Army was to be disbanded, except for a battalion of royal guards. A Press Law, enacted in the same month, gave the Home Minister power to suppress any newspaper held to be 'injurious to public order or good morals'.

One result was to increase the number of Japanese in Korean official employment, especially in the Ministries of Finance and Justice. Another was that Itō's staff expanded, reaching over 4,500 by 1909, if one includes the two thousand or so Koreans in minor posts. One might have thought this sufficient to ensure docility. In the event, it was not. Starting with disaffected ex-soldiers, 'rebellion', as the Japanese called it, spread rapidly after the summer of 1907. Attacks on

Japanese civilians became frequent. So did large-scale punitive actions against Korean dissidents, hundreds of whom were killed.

To many Japanese in positions of responsibility, disorder on this scale implied that the mechanisms of control were still inadequate. The only measure that promised to make them stronger was outright annexation. In the spring of 1909 a decision was made in principle to take this final step. At the end of March, Foreign Minister Komura Jutarō recommended it to the cabinet in a memorandum arguing that Japanese power in Korea was still not firmly based: 'Korean officials and people have not yet been brought into a completely satisfactory relationship with us', he wrote. Japan must therefore act to strengthen its hold to the point at which 'it cannot be resisted from within or from without'. This meant annexation (*heigō*), once a suitable opportunity could be found for it.[3]

There was no dissent from this view in Japanese ruling circles. Itō and Yamagata, consulted privately, both agreed. The government approved the proposal in July. Komura was then authorized to proceed with detailed arrangements concerning the manner of an announcement, the future of the Korean royal family, and the appropriate diplomatic preliminaries. At no stage was the desirability of full Japanese control of Korea ever discussed or questioned. Nor had it been since May 1904.

It did not seem likely that annexation would bring objections from the powers. The Anglo-Japanese alliance, as renewed in August 1905, had recognized Japan's 'paramount political, military and economic interests' in Korea, together with its right 'to take such measures of guidance, control and protection' as might be thought 'proper and necessary to safeguard and advance those interests'.[4] The United States had made no difficulties about the Korean protectorate in 1905 and had shown no signs of doing so since. Nor was there much likelihood of public pressure on Korea's behalf in Washington. When the Korean emperor appealed to the Hague in 1907 the *New York Tribune* had commented that Japan's right to act as it did in Korea was 'at least as good as that of Russia, France, England or any other Power to deal as they have with subject nations'.[5] Russia, the other power with a stake in the region, had already signed a secret convention with Japan

[3] The text is in Yamabe, *Nikkan heigō*, 223–4. See also Conroy, *Japanese seizure*, 374–81.
[4] Nish, *Anglo-Japanese Alliance*, 332.
[5] Quoted in Conroy, *Japanese seizure*, 350.

(30 July 1907) concerning their respective ambitions in Korea, Man-churia, and Mongolia. In it there was specific recognition of Japan's desire to achieve 'political solidarity' with Korea.[6]

Given international 'understanding', Japan was confident enough of its ability to handle the only other likely obstacle, namely, Korean resistance. The assassination of Itō provided the excuse for putting matters in train. In October 1909, having relinquished office as Minis-ter-Resident in June, he visited Harbin, possibly to ensure that there would no misunderstandings with Russia over what was being planned. While there he was killed by a Korean patriot. Almost at once there was an attempt to marshal pro-Japanese sentiment in Korea as a pre-liminary to annexation, undertaken by the Kokuryūkai's Uchida Ryōhei through his links with a Korean organization called the Ilchinhoe. At Uchida's prompting, the Ilchinhoe presented a petition to both Korean and Japanese authorities in December, calling for the merger (*gappō*) of the two countries as the only way to protect Korea from predatory Western powers. 'If we stand alone we cannot exist', it argued, citing the examples of India, Burma, and Indo-China to prove the point.[7]

This petition was not altogether welcome in Tokyo, because it raised the question of what might be meant by 'merger', but it was in any case less directly relevant to Japanese intentions than the prep-arations being made to suppress such Korean opposition as might occur. On 30 May 1910 Terauchi Masatake, War Minister in the Kat-sura cabinet, was appointed concurrently Minister-Resident in Seoul. A force was put at his disposal sufficient for maintaining order in what-ever circumstances, as well as of exercising pressure on the Korean court to follow his instructions. As a result, a treaty of annexation, negotiated secretly, was signed on 22 August. It was made public seven days later. Terauchi himself became Japan's first Governor-General, a post which he held until he became Prime Minister in October 1916.

Japan's sphere of influence in Manchuria

Korea, though it had its own unequal treaties, had not figured very largely in the economic interests of the powers. Annexing it did not therefore cause a great furore. Manchuria, however, was a part of China. This meant that Japanese actions there, because they might

[6] Kim, *Korea*, 141–3.
[7] Quoted in Conroy, *Japanese seizure*, 430–1.

affect the treaty port system generally, had a more important international dimension. For the same reason they were controversial in
Japan.

Komura's inclusion in his first peace proposals in 1904 of the idea of
establishing a Japanese sphere of influence in Manchuria reflected a
sentiment that was widely held. To some Japanese, at least, there was
nothing in such a step that conflicted with the doctrines of the Open
Door. For example, Soeda Juichi, President of the Industrial Bank,
talking to a member of the British embassy in May 1904, emphasized
that Japan had no wish 'to incur continental responsibilities and
expense, which would result from the annexation of any part of Manchuria'. What mattered in his view was economic opportunity: it would
be against Japan's interests 'if Manchuria were closed to commercial
enterprise, as would undoubtedly be the case, if that province of China
came under the domination of Russia'.[8] Major-General Iguchi Shōgo
of the General Staff had come to a similar conclusion for different
reasons. Writing in June 1903, he had expressed the belief that once
Russia had been expelled from Manchuria it would be best to make the
region 'an open market for the commerce of all nations, so as to
balance their interests against one another'.[9] Such a strategy appealed
in particular to those Japanese military leaders who expected victory
against Russia to prompt a Russian war of revenge.

As Foreign Minister, Komura had good grounds for supporting this
kind of argument. The cost of fighting Russia was heavy; and despite a
sharp rise in domestic taxation, most of it had to be met by borrowing
overseas. At the end of 1903 the Japanese government's foreign debt
amounted to only 98 million yen. A year later it had risen to 312 million, by the end of 1905 to 1,142 million.[10] Almost the whole of this
represented loans raised in the money-markets of London and New
York. To obtain them it had been necessary to have the approval, or at
least the tacit consent, of the British and American governments. This
in turn rested on undertakings about Japan's future mainland policies.
Komura, writing about loans to his ambassador in London on 31
December 1903, had promised that 'if Japan wins the war, the fruits of

[8] MacDonald to Lansdowne, Confidential, No. 158, 27 May 1904, in FO 46, vol.
578.
[9] Quoted in Iriye, *Pacific Estrangement*, 82. See also Tsunoda, *Manshū mondai*,
238–40.
[10] *Meiji ikō hompō shuyō keizai tōkei*, ed. Bank of Japan (1966): Table of foreign investment in Japan, 1897–1941, at 317.

her efforts will be enjoyed equally by all the Powers having commercial relationships with Manchuria'.[11] In January 1905, when Theodore Roosevelt mooted the idea that Manchuria 'be returned to China to be made into a neutral area under the guarantee of the Powers', Komura had hastened to head him off with an assurance similar to that which he had given London. Japan, he confirmed, would 'uphold the principle of equal opportunity in Manchuria' and ensure that administration there remained 'in substance' in Chinese hands.[12]

Komura's plans for a peace settlement, as we saw in the previous chapter, envisaged a more advantageous position for Japan than these statements seem to imply. Claims for the transfer to Japan of the Liaotung lease and of the Russian railways in south Manchuria carried the implication of a sphere of influence in the Russian manner, that is, one which involved preferential rights. Moreover, what had been said to Roosevelt in January 1905 had included a sentence qualifying the recognition of China's territorial integrity: it was to be conditional on 'reform and good administration adequate to fully secure peace and order as well as protect lives and property'.

An important test of Japanese intentions came in the negotiations with China at the end of 1905. Though these were ostensibly for the purpose of getting Chinese confirmation of the arrangements made in the Treaty of Portsmouth, Japan entered into them on the basis of cabinet resolutions that sought quite a lot more. An agreement on the subject of Liaotung and the Russian railways was 'absolutely required', of course. In addition, however, Japan's representatives were to seek, as desiderata, administrative reforms designed to safeguard foreign residents and property in Manchuria; the opening of a number of cities there to foreign trade; Japanese management of the Fushun and Yengtai coal-mines; permission for Japan to extend the rail network by building a line from Changchun to Kirin; and a guarantee that China would not alienate Manchurian territory to any other power.[13]

Komura, who had devised these terms, went himself to Peking to negotiate them in November. China at once rejected the clauses relating to non-alienation and administrative reform. It agreed to open

[11] Kajima, *Diplomacy*, II, 124.
[12] Ibid., II, 205–6.
[13] Cabinet decisions of 27 Oct. 1905, in *NGB* 38:1:105–7. The English text of the slightly modified demands presented to China on 17 Nov. is ibid., 116–7. The negotiations are treated in *Komura gaikō-shi*, 680–709.

various places in Manchuria to trade and offered to build the Chang-chun–Kirin railway, using a Japanese loan. For the rest, it sought on many points of detail to adopt the narrowest possible interpretation of Japanese rights, including those relating to Liaotung and the railway zone. Bargaining on these issues was difficult and lasted several weeks. In the end, Komura withdrew the demand about non-alienation in return for a promise that China would take some initiative about reform in Manchuria; accepted the Chinese proposal for the Kirin railway; won some concessions concerning the improvement for com-mercial use of the wartime military railway, built between Mukden and Antung (linking the Korean lines with those in south Manchuria); and secured an agreement—recorded in the conference minutes, but not in the treaty text—that Japan would be consulted before China built any railways which might compete with those of Japan in southern Manchuria. A treaty, plus a supplementary convention, embodying most of these provisions, was signed on 22 December 1905.

Identifying the policies actually to be pursued in Manchuria remained nevertheless a matter of debate in Japanese government cir-cles. One strand of opinion, expressed most forcefully by Inoue Kaoru, started from the proposition that Japan, exhausted by war, lacked the capital to make the most of its newly won privileges. This was especially so, Inoue believed, with respect to Manchurian railways, on which a great deal of expenditure would be required. Accordingly, when an American railway magnate, E. H. Harriman, put forward plans for joint American and Japanese operation of them as part of a round-the-world transport system, involving also the Trans-Siberian Railway and a Pacific steamship service, he found Inoue receptive.[14] Finance Minister Sone Arasuke and representatives of the Mitsui and Mitsubishi companies also had talks with Harriman while he was in Tokyo during September and October 1905. They helped persuade the Prime Minister, Katsura, to come to a provisional agreement with him, subject to confirmation by Komura when he returned from the Portsmouth conference.

Komura, arriving in Tokyo a few days after Harriman left, objected strongly to these plans. In his view, Japan had no need to offer partner-ship as the price of obtaining Western capital, which was readily avail-able without such strings in London and New York. Moreover, he

[14] See *Segai Inoue*, V, 109–13. The Harriman incident is examined more generally in *Komura gaikō–shi*, 664–70.

pointed out, there was the question of Chinese sensitivity about the processes of consultation. This might easily wreck the negotiations he was about to undertake in Peking. His own preference, therefore, was to try to develop a sphere of influence in Manchuria in which only Japan and China were concerned.

In October 1905 Komura was able to muster enough support for this argument to get the Harriman proposal set aside. However, there soon emerged a different kind of threat to consensus over policy, because of the single-minded manner in which the army went about its duties in the districts of Manchuria which it still occupied, pending final Russian withdrawal. One of those duties, recommended to its attention by the Ministries of Finance and Foreign Affairs, was the promotion of Japanese economic interests. Another, identified by senior staff officers, notably in Liaotung (henceforward to be called Kwantung), was preparation to defend the region against any Russian attempt to regain control of it. This was a task, it was generally recognized, well beyond the capacity of the Chinese. It was also one which in the view of the newly established Kwantung headquarters required military and administrative rights in Manchuria much wider than those commonly given to railway guards.[15]

One consequence was a growth of Japanese carpet-bagging in Manchuria during the winter of 1905–6, facilitated by military actions apparently aimed at obstructing Western merchants. Japanese, for example, were admitted to some areas from which their Western competitors were excluded. There were suspicions that the customs service was not being administered even-handedly. All this brought British and American protests early in 1906, made to the new Japanese government, in which Saionji Kimmochi, Itō's protégé, was Premier. Nor were the complaints only about access to the region's trade. The whole question of China's territorial integrity and the treaty structure was said to be at issue. The American Minister in Tokyo reported the State Department's view as being that, if things went on as they were, 'China will find herself, at the end of Japanese occupation, the merely nominal sovereign of a territory the material advantages of which have been appropriated by the temporary occupants'.[16] The British ambassador wrote privately to Itō in even stronger terms. It appeared,

---

[15] Tsunoda, *Manshū mondai*, 280–2, 296–305. Strictly speaking, Kwantung meant 'east of the barrier', i.e. east of Shanhaikuan. Politically, this implied a wider frame of reference than the term Liaotung.

[16] Note of 2 Apr. 1906, in *NGB* 39:1:215–16.

he said, that 'the military party in Manchuria are using military reasons
to exclude foreign trade'. For Japan to allow this to continue, alienating
the sympathies of Britain and America, would be 'suicidal', bearing in
mind that those two countries had financed Japan's war against Russia
'on the distinct understanding that the door was to be kept open.' The
military had claimed that their actions were necessary, in order to
guard against a Russian war of revenge; 'but the war of revenge, if it
ever comes, should find Japan with friends at her back, which she certainly won't have if she tries to close the door now after all her prot-
estations to the contrary'.[17]

These complaints raised in an acute form the problem of Japan's
position in Manchuria in relation to the doctrine of the Open Door.
The Finance Ministry was already aware of unease about Japan's
financial credit in international banking circles, associated with doubts
about expensive proposals for nationalizing domestic railways. Inoue
Kaoru, who had close links with business, was much concerned about
this. So was Katō Takaaki—son-in-law to the founder of the Mitsubishi company—who had resigned as Foreign Minister in February
1906, partly over the railway issue, partly because of disagreements
over army policy in Manchuria. There was therefore significant pressure on Saionji to give Britain and America satisfaction.

Saionji duly gave the appropriate assurances to the diplomats in
Tokyo. Unhappily, the army showed itself stubborn, or at least dila-
tory, about giving them effect. Nor could its objections easily be over-
ridden. Action to counter a possible attack from Russia fell properly
within the army's prerogative. Arguably, it fell outside the powers of
the Foreign Ministry, perhaps even those of the cabinet. This being so,
Saionji tried to meet the difficulty by having recourse to an extra-con-
stitutional device. On 22 May 1906 he summoned a meeting of elder
statesmen (mostly former Prime Ministers), senior members of the
cabinet, and service Chiefs of Staff.

Itō, brought back for the occasion from his duties in Seoul,
addressed the meeting first.[18] He began with a reference to British and
American resentment at Japanese actions, quoting the British
ambassador's letter. He then turned to the possibility of China's even-

---

[17] MacDonald to Itō, private, 31 March 1906, encl. in MacDonald to Grey, No. 113,
7 June 1906, in FO 371, vol. 180.
[18] A text of Itō's statement and the decisions taken is in *NGB* 39:1:237–45. Tsunoda,
Manshū mondai, 319–31, gives a much fuller account of the rest of the discussion.

tual collapse, which, he said, would force Japan to choose between giving help and leadership to China, or participating in a division of spoils. He preferred the former. It would, however, depend on winning China's goodwill, which the army's policy in Manchuria was doing nothing to ensure. Indeed, maintaining order there without the co-operation of Chinese officials was impossible, as well as disadvantageous. It would be better by far to restore the administration to a peacetime footing, putting it back into Chinese hands.

It seemed at first that Itō's argument was going to be accepted without demur. Yamagata Aritomo, the doyen of the military contingent, endorsed Katsura's comment that it was for the government to lay down policy, the services to carry it out. Terauchi Masatake, the War Minister, defended what the army had done so far, but agreed that the time had come for a change. Even the army's Chief of Staff, Kodama Gentarō, though he was adamant that there were too many practical problems for the transfer from military to civilian control to be made forthwith, accepted that it must come before long. Saionji began to draft a resolution along these lines, Then, just as it appeared that consensus had been reached, there came a clash between Itō and Kodama which showed them still to be at odds over fundamentals. Pressed on the subject of some particular army decisions in Manchuria, the Chief of Staff replied that it was not such details that most concerned him. He was thinking rather of the future, when maintaining Japanese interests in Manchuria, which were different in nature from those of other treaty powers in places like Shanghai, would require 'management' (*kei'ei*) of a kind best entrusted to a single, coherent governmental organization, instead of being diffused through several Ministries. To Itō, this was to reopen the whole question. 'Management', he said, had nothing to do with Japan: 'Manchuria is in no respect Japanese territory. It is simply part of Chinese territory. Since there are no grounds for exercising our authority in a place which is not our territory, there is no need to create something like a colonial ministry to handle such duties. The responsibility for administering Manchuria rests with the Chinese government.'

On this occasion the argument was taken no further. Saionji said some soothing words; a resolution was drafted by which the army would be required to relinquish its special wartime powers; Itō returned to Korea. Yet the meeting had brought into the open a disagreement that was to recur in Japanese policy-making at times of crisis for a quarter of a century. There was one school of thought,

represented on this occasion by Itō, but more often expressed thereafter by the Foreign Ministry, which for the sake of Japan's economic
interests gave priority to co-operation with the powers, especially
Britain and America. To do so, it was argued, ensured continuing
opportunities in north and central China, the greatest treasure-house
of all. A necessary condition of it was that Japan should not press its
claims in Manchuria further than the advocates of the Open Door
would tolerate.

Business opinion for the most part agreed with this. The army, plus
its political allies, did not. As Kodama made clear in May 1906, it held
that Japan had interests in Manchuria that were properly strategic.
Maintaining them could not be done exclusively through economic
rights. It involved also controlling transport and communications, for
example, keeping civil order, and protecting the Korean frontier. To
do these things efficiently required actions that conflicted with the
policy of the Open Door.

Such arguments were not limited to the immediate situation in
1906, created by the threat of Russian revenge. In later years it was just
as possible to apply them to the dangers arising from Chinese turbulence or communist insurgency. That being so, the army continued to
insist throughout the period of the Chinese and Russian revolutions
and their aftermath that Manchuria was not just a problem for diplomats and their political masters. Soldiers, they claimed, rightly had a
share in decisions concerning it, preferably a dominant one.

Even in the shadow of Itō's victory, Kodama kept this idea alive. As
chairman of the committee formed to establish a company to run the
railways taken over from Russia—the South Manchuria Railway Company (see Chapter 9)—he worked actively for the appointment of Gotō
Shimpei as its president. Gotō, a strong advocate of Japanese expansion, who had been Kodama's civil deputy when the latter was Governor-General in Taiwan, was offered the post in July 1906. Saionji
explained to him that as president of the railway company he would be
responsible in some matters to the governor of Kwantung, an army
officer, and in others to the Foreign Minister. He did not apparently
comment on any possible conflicts of interest between them. Kodama
was more forthright. In an interview lasting over three hours, he set out
his own views on the future of Manchuria and the part the railway
company should play in it. What was needed, he said, was to put
Japan's position on such a solid footing that there would no longer be a
risk of Russian attack. The management of the railways, the opening

up of mines, the improvement of agriculture, the encouragement of Japanese settlers, all these would contribute to that end.[19]

The fact that Gotō accepted the post following this interview suggests that he was likely to be sympathetic to the army's version of Manchuria policy. So it proved. Nevertheless, in the short term it was the Foreign Ministry, backed by Itō, that had the greater influence. In September 1906 the governorship of Kwantung was given its peacetime form. Though the governor was to be a general and was to retain command of Manchurian railway guards, it was made clear that in diplomatic matters he must follow the orders of the Foreign Minister. This implied that he would not be allowed to act in a way that imperilled Japan's relations with China, in which commerce was paramount. Various army attempts to weaken this control during the next few years—in 1907, for example, there was a proposal, apparently originating with Gotō Shimpei, to put consuls in Manchuria under the governor's jurisdiction—were successfully resisted.[20]

Yet this is not to imply that Manchuria was unimportant in the eyes of Foreign Ministry officials, or that they were willing to sacrifice Japanese interests there. Certainly this would have been contrary to everything that Komura had done and written. In September 1908, when he returned as Foreign Minister in the second Katsura cabinet, he again set out his ideas on China policy and the place of Manchuria in it.[21] The powers, he observed, were no longer putting pressure on China to secure leases or exclusive railway and mining rights, but were seeking to placate Chinese opinion. Japan must do the same. Sino-Japanese co-operation, after all, was the key to Asia's stability. It followed that efforts must be made to persuade the Chinese that Japanese privileges in Manchuria were in no way contradictory to it.

What Komura intended in practice became clear during 1909 and 1910. An arrangement with China in September 1909 at last obtained for Japan mining rights in the Fushun and Yengtai coalfields in Manchuria, together with a number of concessions concerning railways. In July 1910 a secret agreement with Russia, prompted by American pro-

[19] Tsurumi Yūsuke, *Gotō Shimpei* (1937–8), II, 663–77, gives a detailed account of these discussions.

[20] On the disputes over administration in Manchuria in these years, see Tsunoda, *Manshū mondai*, 332–41, and Kitaoka, *Nihon rikugun*, 54–7.

[21] Memorandum, approved by the cabinet on 25 Sept. 1908, printed in the Japanese Foreign Ministry's collection of major diplomatic documents: *Nihon Gaikō Nempyō narabi Shuyō Bunsho* (1965), I, documents, 305–9. The collection is hereafter cited as *NGNB*.

posals for the internationalization of the South Manchuria and Chinese Eastern lines, laid down a division of spheres: Russia in the north of the region, Japan in the south. It recognized that each had the right to intervene in defence of its interests within its own sphere. It also provided for co-operation between them if they were challenged by any third power.

This was not at all what Britain and America meant by the Open Door, though there was not a great deal they could do about it. In 1911, when renewal of the Anglo-Japanese alliance came under discussion, Komura began by trying to win fuller British recognition of Japan's rights on the mainland—he described them as 'closely resembling the position which Britain had in India'—but found British commercial hostility to Japanese actions in Manchuria an obstacle to any such move.[22] Neither India nor Manchuria was mentioned in the treaty that was signed. All the same, the comments made by Sir Edward Grey in the course of the negotiations made it clear that Britain had no expectation of being able to check Japan's advance in north-east Asia.

Washington eventually came to the same conclusion, though it tried harder to avoid it.[23] There was evidence that sections of American opinion, especially among missionaries and consular staff in China, were beginning to see Japanese policy as inimical to Chinese 'progress', by which they set great store. More directly, Japan had been identified as a commercial rival in Manchuria. The growing sale of Japanese textiles, for example, was substantially at the expense of American exporters. Japanese and Russian railway monopolies, coupled with attempts to prevent the Chinese from building lines that might compete with them, blocked American investment in one of the few areas where there still seemed opportunities for it. Taft's efforts to pursue 'dollar diplomacy' in East Asia in these years was specifically related to Manchurian railway questions. Its failure partly reflected the scepticism of American bankers, faced by the entrenched interests of Russia and Japan.

Commercial rivalry produced irritation and occasional disputes. It

---

[22] Ian Nish, *Alliance in Decline* (1972), 57–8. On the subsequent negotiations, see ibid., 66–74.

[23] On the part played by Manchuria in American–Japanese relations, see especially Iriye, *Pacific Estrangement*, chaps. 7 and 8; also Michael H. Hunt, *Frontier Defense and the Open Door* (1973), chaps. 8, 11, and 12.

was reinforced from the Japanese side by resentment of American immigration laws. But these factors had to be set against others: that America had a larger economic stake in Japan than in China; that China's plans to help itself did not inspire great confidence; that East Asia was not yet an area of prime American concern. In these circumstances, Washington was not willing to have a confrontation with Japan. Former President Theodore Roosevelt aptly summarized the argument against doing so in a letter to Taft in December 1910:

Our vital interest is to keep the Japanese out of our country. . . . The vital interest of the Japanese, on the other hand, is in Manchuria and Korea. It is therefore peculiarly our interest not to take any steps as regards Manchuria which will give the Japanese cause to feel . . . that we are hostile to them. . . . Our interests in Manchuria are really unimportant, and not such that the American people would be content to run the slightest risk of collision about them.[24]

It is reasonable to conclude that in the period between 1905 and 1910 Japanese attempts to exclude Manchuria, in addition to Korea, from the scope of the Open Door policy had damaged its relations with Britain and the United States, but not yet to the point of requiring a fundamental reconsideration of how East Asia's international relations ought to work. That wider issue was to be raised by events in the next few years. The Chinese Revolution, starting in 1911, deprived the treaty port system of an essential element in its political base. The outbreak of the First World War in 1914 weakened the ability of some of the powers to intervene in China to protect their interests. In these conditions, Japanese imperialism began to take on a different character.

[24] Quoted in Hunt, *Frontier Defense*, 221.

8

Chinese Revolution and World War

THE overthrow of the Manchu dynasty in the winter of 1911–12 had the effect of destroying China's political unity for something like fifteen years. During most of that period there were rival regimes claiming to be the country's legitimate government: one in the north at Peking; another in the south, centred on Nanking or Canton. After 1916 both depended for support on coalitions of war-lords, each of whom exercised virtually independent authority in one or more Chinese provinces. Civil war was endemic. It continued in some areas until Japanese military intervention in the 1930s.

This was the kind of situation of which the powers had gone in fear since 1895. If China had no stable central government, on which pressure could be put, by whom were foreign privileges to be sustained? Recent history suggested two possibilities. One was co-operation among the powers to back some Chinese claimant to authority, who would recognize and implement the treaties. This implied a willingness to intervene collectively in Chinese politics. The other was to exploit the country's disunity, the inevitable corollary of which would be competition for exclusive rights by different powers in different parts of China.

Predictably, Britain and the United States opted for the first of these, though their actions often lacked conviction. Japan showed greater uncertainty. Its leaders, as we have seen, had for several years been divided over the relative attractions of an empire in north-east Asia and a less formal position of economic advantage in China generally. If Chinese revolution forced a choice between them, it was by no means easy to judge which way it would go. Moreover, there was a secondary strand in Japanese thinking about foreign affairs, which favoured an 'Asian' partnership between Japan and China, directed against Western imperialism as such, rather than any form of co-operation with the powers. Revolution in China strengthened it, by indicating that China was about to discard some of the traditional attitudes that had so far impeded a Sino-Japanese accord.

These divergences were made more pronounced by the outbreak of hostilities in Europe in the summer of 1914. The war diverted the attention of Europeans from East Asia and reduced their ability to take action there. It increased the relative strength of Japan and America, both of whom were able to expand their trade and investment in the region. One result was to encourage the exploration of new paths for the development of Japanese imperialism. Another was to stimulate Japanese–American rivalry.

The Chinese Revolution and the powers

The military rebellion in Wuchang, which marked the beginning of the Chinese Revolution on 10 October 1911, was a response to local police action, lacking an overall political plan. The best known of China's revolutionaries, Sun Yat-sen, was in America at the time. It is not surprising, therefore, that the foreign representatives were unprepared for the crisis. Despite the fact that they had for many years expressed concern about the possibility of a breakdown of authority in China, there is no evidence that they had concerted their ideas on the subject of what to do about it when it came. Nor was the situation they faced at all clear-cut. In particular, there was no smooth transfer of power to a successor regime, with which negotiation would have been possible. Until January 1912 it was by no means certain that the Manchu dynasty would fall.

When it did, a short-lived compromise emerged between the competing candidates for leadership. Sun Yat-sen, the chosen spokesman for the revolutionaries, agreed to serve under the former Manchu official, Yüan Shih-k'ai, who controlled China's most effective military force. Yüan, in turn, dropped his proposals for a constitutional monarchy and became president of the new republic, promulgated in March. The arrangement was not entirely welcome to either side. In the summer of 1913 Sun's supporters, now organized as the Nationalist Party (Kuomintang), took part in another rising, which Yüan quickly crushed. Yüan himself then set out to become the founder of a dynasty, only to be thwarted by domestic opposition, which was widespread by the end of 1915. His death in the following June left China fragmented: the south under a greatly weakened Kuomintang; the rest of the country under various war-lords, who had been Yüan's subordinate commanders.

The treaty powers threaded their way through these complexities with circumspection. Their first requirement was the maintenance of existing privileges. Recognition of the republic seemed to give them that. Their next was to get an undertaking that the republican regime would assume Manchu obligations, that is, the servicing and repayment of foreign loans. The means to this end was the so-called Reorganization Loan, first mooted in March 1912, concluded twelve months later. Under its terms a bank consortium, representing Britain, Germany, France, Russia, and Japan, made over to Yüan Shih-k'ai's government the sum of £25 million at 5 per cent for forty seven years, to be used for the following purposes: the payment of earlier indemnities and the redemption of outstanding provincial debt; the cost of disbanding troops; the current expenses of administration; and the financing of a number of reforms. The advance was to be secured partly on the surplus of customs revenue, to the extent that this was not already pledged, partly on salt revenue, which was for the first time to be brought under foreign supervision.

The implications were plain enough. Yüan was to be granted the funds by which to improve the efficiency of his administration and hence the effectiveness of his authority. In return, he would take over Manchu debts and permit a larger measure of foreign scrutiny of China's tax structure than before. The United States, which had participated in the discussions, found this unacceptable. President Woodrow Wilson, announcing American withdrawal from the scheme in March 1913, stated that he did so because the loan's conditions 'seem to us to touch very nearly the administrative independence of China itself'. They involved not only the pledging of particular taxes, but also 'the administration of those taxes by foreign agents'. They might at some time require 'forcible interference' in China's financial and political affairs.[1]

Japan had objections of another kind. One was the difficulty of finding capital on this scale: in practice, its share was mostly subdivided among other members of the consortium. More significant, the Japanese cabinet had never been sure that it wanted to see China ruled by Yüan Shih-k'ai. He had in the past opposed Japanese policy in Korea and Manchuria. If his current ambitions were realized, he might prove to be a stronger leader than Japan had any wish to see in China. And

---

[1] The American statement is in W. W. Willoughby, *Foreign Rights and Interests in China* (1920), 500–2. On the Reorganization Loan in general, see ibid., 502–6; also Charles Vevier, *The United States and China* (1955), chap. 9, and Peter Lowe, *Great Britain and Japan* (1969), 127–36.

there were influential groups both inside and outside the government in Japan whose ideas concerning China's political future were very different from those they attributed to Yüan.

Tokyo's first official response to news of the revolution came at a cabinet meeting on 24 October 1911. Previous policies were reiterated and confirmed: to maintain the gains already made in Manchuria, taking any opportunity that offered to extend the term of the Kwantung lease and settle outstanding railway questions; to co-operate with Russia in defending those interests; to take steps towards establishing a 'paramount' position in the rest of China, while working closely with Britain, France, and the United States.[2] What was to be done in the immediate crisis, however, was not so readily agreed. The elder statesmen expressed approval of Yüan's plan for a constitutional monarchy, which they saw as a way of bringing China and Japan closer together. Yamagata commented that 'the key to the peace of the Far East must be an alliance between our nation and a politically reconstructed China'.[3] The War Ministry, perhaps interpreting Yamagata's wishes, supported a Manchu request for military aid against the revolutionaries. The Ōkura company was induced to enter into a contract to supply munitions. By contrast, the Army General Staff proposed sending arms to Sun Yat-sen, an operation which won the approval of the Home Minister, Hara Kei, on the grounds that it would serve as an insurance in case the rebels won. And from Peking the Japanese minister, Ijūin Motohiko, urged Japanese military intervention to establish the independence of Manchuria and Inner Mongolia. He recommended that China be divided into three: the north, still to be ruled by the Manchus, plus separate regimes in the centre and the south.[4]

Under a Prime Minister, Saionji Kimmochi, who was not much given to making firm decisions, such disparities of advice had the effect of rendering Japanese policy incoherent. Those who felt confident enough to do so, or whose enthusiasms overrode caution, began to act on their own. For a short time, Japanese expansion displayed the characteristics that were to mark it after 1930: a diversity of sub-imperialisms, rarely checked and never co-ordinated by the central government.

---

[2] Masaru Ikei, 'Japan's response to the Chinese revolution of 1911' (1966), 214–15. The Japanese text is in *NGNB*, I, documents, 356–7.

[3] Hackett, *Yamagata*, 272.

[4] Ikei, 'Japan's reponse', 213–16.

Inevitably, Manchuria was the direction in which there was the most considerable pressure for advance. The military element in Japan's top leadership—the Genrō, Marshal Yamagata Aritomo; the former Premier, General Katsura Tarō; the Governor-General of Korea, General Terauchi Masatake—had all reached the conclusion by the beginning of 1912 that Japan should send reinforcements to Kwantung to defend Japanese interests from the consequences of the revolution. As Yamagata put it in a memorandum on 14 January, a suitable force—two divisions was what he had in mind—would make it possible to maintain order in southern Manchuria; to give protection to the Manchu court, if it should withdraw to the area from Peking; and to ensure equality with Russia, which was already taking steps to strengthen its position in Outer Mongolia.[5] This was not far from anticipating an independent Manchuria under Russian and Japanese sponsorship.

The cabinet recognized that any such movement of troops would arouse international suspicion. Consequently it decided on 16 January not to approve it, but to initiate talks with Russia with a view to arranging for co-operation in defending the interests of the two countries in those parts of Manchuria and Mongolia with which they were chiefly concerned. Continued military pressure for something more than this was ignored in the face of clear indications that Britain would object to intervention in Manchuria. However, there remained dissatisfaction among less senior army officers, who saw the revolution as an opportunity for additional Japanese gains. Their ideas, as formulated in 1911 by Utsunomiya Tarō, head of a section in the General Staff, and Kawashima Naniwa, attached to the Peking legation, envisaged separating Manchuria from the rest of China and retaining some kind of Manchu rule there in the form of a Japanese protectorate. They had similar plans to sponsor a Mongol regime in Inner Mongolia. The organization of an expedition to effect these aims, including the identification of suitable Manchu and Mongol princes to serve as figureheads, together with the conclusion of agreements with them for the extension of Japanese privileges once the operation had been carried out, was left to Kawashima.[6] It was thwarted, however, by fears in the

---

[5] Japanese discussions of Manchuria policy at this time are examined in Kitaoka, *Nihon rikugun*, 92–9; Tsunoda, *Manshū mondai*, 754–72; and Usui Katsumi, *Nihon to Chūgoku* (1972), 18–21. There is a summary in English in Ikei, 'Japan's response', 225–7.

[6] In addition to the material cited in note 5, see Jansen, *Japanese and Sun*, 137–40.

Japanese cabinet and Foreign Ministry about the diplomatic risks. Tokyo ordered the Kwantung Army to call the expedition off. Kawashima and his colleagues reluctantly obeyed.

The idea of an independent Manchuria was to recur regularly in Japanese army plans until it was finally achieved in 1931; but in 1912 and 1913 the emphasis shifted to a second strand in China policy, the pursuit of economic advantage by political means.[7] The obvious channel for this, at least to those who believed Sun Yat-sen was destined to play a major role in China's future, was the regime which he established at Nanking on his return to China in December 1911. The appropriate instruments were Japanese companies, acting, as the army did in Manchuria, independently, but under official patronage. In this case it came mostly from the Prime Minister, Saionji, and the Genrō, Inoue Kaoru.

Two *zaibatsu* concerns played a leading part in the arrangements: Mitsui, which had an important stake in foreign trade and coal-mining; and Ōkura, which had built up its earlier enterprises in the timber business and colonial public works. They were associated in the armaments industry through a joint affiliate, the Taiping company, in which another *zaibatsu* firm, Mitsubishi, also had a share. Financial backing, arranged with government approval, was available to them through a group of Japanese banks: the Yokohama Specie Bank, which was Japan's principal dealer in foreign exchange; the Dai Ichi Bank, which operated largely in Korea; and the Bank of Taiwan. At various times senior bureaucrats from the Foreign Ministry, the Finance Ministry, and the Bank of Japan took part in their discussions.

The nature of what they set out to do was simple: to provide Sun Yat-sen with arms and political funds in return for economic privileges, much as the other powers were doing with Yüan Shih-k'ai. The manner of doing it was sometimes very complicated. For example, both Mitsui and Ōkura had for some years been helping to finance the Hanyehping coal and iron company in the Yangtze valley, chiefly as a source of iron for Japan's Yawata plant (see Chapter 9). When Sun Yat-sen approached Mitsui's Shanghai office for a loan at the end of 1911, a plan was devised for increasing the capital of Hanyehping by an extra 10 million yen, of which half was to be provided through Mitsui. Hanyehping was to transfer the Japanese contribution to the revo-

[7] See especially Jansen, *Japanese and Sun*, 145–8, 161–7; same, 'Yawata, Hanyehping and the Twentyone Demands' (1954), 38–42; Usui, *Nihon to Chūgoku*, 12–14; and J. G. Roberts, *Mitsui* (1973), 178–84.

lutionaries, who would use some of it to buy arms, also through Mitsui. As a reward, Mitsui was wherever possible to be given preference in the future allocation of mining and railway concessions. Only part of this plan was actually carried out. The Yokohama Specie Bank, acting on the instructions of the Saionji government, put up three million yen in February 1912, of which most was promptly transferred to Sun's colleagues in Nanking. However, proposed arrangements for joint Sino-Japanese operation of Hanyehping were blocked in the end by Yüan Shih-k'ai. And the fact that Sun Yat-sen did not win control of China meant that his promises about future concessions carried no weight.

There was another similar exercise involving Ōkura. In January 1912, again at the request of the revolutionary leaders, the Ōkura company agreed to arrange a loan of 3 million yen, secured on the Shanghai–Soochow railway. Tokyo approved. Ōkura itself put up a third of the money; a consortium of five Japanese banks provided the other two-thirds in equal proportions; and at the end of the month most of the sum found its way to Nanking, where it was allocated for the purchase of arms through Ōkura.

Sun Yat-sen's decision to accept a subordinate position to Yüan Shih-k'ai in a Chinese republican government in March 1912 temporarily brought these machinations to a halt. Growing tension between the two men in 1913 revived them. Visiting Tokyo in the spring of that year, Sun had a round of meetings with politicians and business men, in which he made clear that he was willing to grant Japan considerable economic benefits. As an earnest of good intentions a new company, the China Industrial Company (later renamed the Sino-Japanese Industrial Company) was formed to promote the exploitation of China's raw materials, using Japanese capital. Sun was to be President. The Vice-president was Kurachi Tetsukichi, formerly a senior official in the Japanese Foreign Ministry. Capital was provided by four *zaibatsu* firms: Mitsui, Mitsubishi, Ōkura, and Yasuda.

Again, little came of the arrangement in the short term, because Sun Yat-sen was for the second time a political loser. Or perhaps one should say, because Japan refused to back him strongly enough. In July 1913, when the Kuomintang took up arms against Yüan Shih-k'ai, Mori Kaku of Mitsui offered Nanking a loan of 20 million yen and equipment for two divisions. Sun accepted. The Japanese government dithered. Yüan, given confidence by the Reorganization Loan, put the rising down before anything practical was done; and as he strengthened his grip on China in the months that followed, it began to look as if Japan had let slip its last chance of large-scale profit from the Chinese Revolution.

The Twenty-one Demands

During 1912 and 1913 the head of the Japanese Foreign Ministry Political Department, Abe Moritarō, prepared several versions of a memorandum on China policy.[8] Their theme was that Japan must proceed cautiously in China, pursuing its objectives—Abe categorized them at one point as 'economic peace'—without separating itself from Britain and Russia on the one hand, or giving offence to Chinese opinion on the other. To this end it would be necessary to maintain tight control over the actions of Japanese representatives, in particular those of the army with respect to Manchuria. What must be avoided at all costs was anything that might unite China behind Yüan Shih-k'ai in hostility to Japanese rights in the north.

In September 1913 his views made Abe a victim of assassination, for they were not in the least acceptable to 'patriots' within Japan. Yet if one examines his statement of what Japan's aims actually were, they turn out to be just as much a check-list of imperialist ambitions as the demands put forward by those who threatened him. He wanted to extend the duration of the Kwantung lease, which had originally, as negotiated by Russia, been for only twenty-five years. The leases for the South Manchuria Railway and its branch lines ought also to be extended, he believed. It was desirable that Japan's economic activities be pushed forward into northern Manchuria and eastern Inner Mongolia, though it should be made clear that no territorial gains were sought there. Elsewhere, joint Sino-Japanese commercial and industrial undertakings should be encouraged; financial organization should be strengthened, in order to make possible loans to China for economic development; and a special effort should be made to gain control of the Hanyehping coal and iron company, because of its importance to railway-building. Japan's own shortage of capital would make it necessary to work closely with British and French financiers in these matters.

This was in effect a blueprint for the treaty port version of Japanese

[8] The originals (undated) are in Japanese Foreign Minstry file 1. 1. 2. 78. The fullest—and presumably final—version is published in *NGNB*, I, documents, 369–76.

imperialism: a sphere of influence in Manchuria, gradually expanding; and economic privilege in the rest of China, broadly as defined by the Open Door policy and the operations of the international bank consortium. The difficulty, of course, was how such rights could be guaranteed. The Foreign Minister, Makino Nobuaki, identified it clearly enough in a memorandum written when he was about to leave office in April 1914.[9] The powers, he pointed out, had recently agreed to distinguish between 'political' investments, like the Reorganization Loan, and industrial ones; but there was a sense in which both were political, because they depended on the existence of a stable Chinese government. If that were to collapse, as seemed very possible, only direct intervention would serve to protect foreign investments. Japan needed as a matter of urgency to decide what to do in such an eventuality. It had not only to defend its railway and mining rights, but also to ensure access to raw materials like coal and iron, which were of increasing importance to Japanese industry.

In emphasizing means, rather than ends, Makino was right, for means were at the root of Japanese difficulties over policy. The weakness of the arguments regularly put forward by the Foreign Ministry was that 'co-operation' was not achieving the desired results. Britain, for example, despite the Anglo-Japanese alliance, had opposed Japan's attempts to secure railway concessions linking Fukien with the middle Yangtze. More broadly, Japan had not yet found a satisfactory basis for working with China's leadership. Sun Yat-sen, whom many Japanese favoured—on ideological grounds, as well as those of national advantage—lacked power. Yüan Shih-k'ai, who had it, had been offended by lack of Japanese support. Thus a year or more of political meddling had left Japan no better off. In these circumstances, men who had always preferred to uphold Japanese interests by direct intervention on the mainland, or by browbeating China, regardless of the diplomatic consequences, became more and more critical of the government.

The outbreak of the war in Europe gave greater momentum to their calls for change. It was immediately apparent, as much in London as in Tokyo, that the hostilities would upset the whole balance of power in East Asia, leaving Japan free to pursue its ambitions almost without check. In the course of discussions about whether Japan should declare war on Germany, the British Foreign Secretary urged—ominously—that care should be taken to avoid arousing 'unfounded mis-

---

[9] Cited in Usui, *Nihon to Chūgoku*, 41–2.

apprehension' about Japanese motives. Specifically, he proposed, 'it should be stated that the Japanese action will not extend beyond the China Seas to the Pacific Ocean, nor beyond Asiatic waters westward of the China Seas, nor to any foreign territory with the exception of territory on the continent of Eastern Asia which is in the occupation of Germany'.[10] This obviously did not preclude gains at Germany's expense in China, which on any realistic judgement seemed inevitable.

Taking over German rights in Shantung, which the government of Ōkuma Shigenobu certainly had in mind, was not the limit of Japanese expectations. The talk in official Tokyo during August and September 1914 was increasingly of an 'accord' between Japan and China, a term—in Japanese, *teikei*—which implied a broad understanding on a whole range of matters, not just a diplomatic settlement. Inoue Kaoru, who had helped to bring Ōkuma to power, saw this improved relationship chiefly in the familiar Foreign Ministry context of economic diplomacy. Much of what he wrote echoed the proposals made by Abe Moritarō a year or two earlier. Yamagata, however, who was closer to the critics of the Foreign Ministry, wanted something different. Declaring war on Germany, he argued,[11] made necessary a thorough reappraisal of China policy, involving a fresh approach to Yüan Shih-k'ai. One feature of it would be an appeal based on racial and cultural affinities: 'if the colored races of the Orient hope to compete with the so-called culturally advanced white races and maintain friendly relations with them, while retaining their own cultural identity and independence, China and Japan, which are culturally and racially alike, must become friendly and promote each other's interests'. As an earnest of this, Japan should promise to return Germany's Shantung lease (Kiaochow) to China. It should also offer China financial help, even though the capital would be difficult to find. For China, deprived of the chance of European loans, might otherwise fall into disorder, an outcome much to Japan's disadvantage, politically and economically. So would it be if China turned to America for help. In short, Yamagata concluded, the object of Japanese policy must be to attach China more closely to Japan, instilling in Chinese leaders a feeling of 'trust and reliance in our empire'.

Yamagata intended this to be done without breaking Japan's ties

---

[10] British *aide-mémoire*, 12 Aug. 1914, in Kajima, *Diplomacy*, III, 50–1.
[11] Memorandum of August 1914 in Ōyama, *Yamagata Aritomo ikensho* (1966), 340–5. It is partly translated in Tsunoda, *Sources*, 714–16, whence the quotations given here are taken. For Inoue's views, see *Segai Inoue*, V, 367–74, 377–92.

with Russia, Britain, or America, because he recognized that those powers must be expected to regain their influence in East Asia once the war in Europe was over. But there were other Japanese, including some who would have acknowledged Yamagata as their patron, who saw things quite differently in that respect. For example, at the end of October Uchida Ryōhei, representing the patriotic society, Kokuryūkai, sent a set of proposals to the Foreign Ministry for an alliance with China, such as would make Japan's position impregnable in face of the powers. It was to provide for the handing over of South Manchuria and Inner Mongolia to Japan; the transfer of German rights in Shantung; the acquisition by Japan of a naval base, plus railway and mining concessions, in Fukien; an agreement by China to use Japanese advisers in carrying out military and fiscal reforms; and an undertaking to seek Japanese consent before arranging leases or loans with any other power. As a corollary, Japan must try to bring into existence a friendly regime in China: in Uchida's view, Yüan Shih-k'ai was untrustworthy, a man who was likely to renounce any document he had signed if he saw a prospect of European support for something better once the war had ended.[12]

Army circles welcomed some of these ideas, but not all.[13] Akashi Motojirō, Vice-chief of the General Staff, recommended action to secure recognition of Japan's superior position in Manchuria and Mongolia; Japanese assistance in administrative reform in China; and acknowledgement by China of Japan's right to prior consultation about all foreign loans and leases. Leverage could be exerted on Yüan, he said, not only by refusing to withdraw from Shantung, but also by threatening to back the Manchurian war-lord, Chang Tso-lin, as an independent ruler. Recommendations from the military attaché in Peking were not dissimilar: an extension of Japanese railway and mining rights in Manchuria and Mongolia; the transfer to Japan of German privileges in Shantung, plus the acquisition of similar ones in Fukien; the appointment of Japanese military advisers in China. The War Minister, Oka Ichinosuke, put some of these pieces together in his report to the cabinet in November. He included the items about military advisers and consultation over foreign loans, but added some very precise claims with respect to Manchuria and Inner Mongolia, involving outright ownership of the South Manchuria Railway, new

[12] Usui, *Nihon to Chūgoku*, 58–60. See also Jansen, *Japanese and Sun*, 180–2.
[13] On army opinion, see Kitaoka, *Nihon rikugun*, 167–70, and Usui, *Nihon to Chūgoku*, 55–7.

residence and property rights for Japanese, further railway and mining concessions, and so on. Some of this probably emanated from the Kwantung Army.

Many of these matters were already on the table, in the sense that Hioki Eki, the Japanese minister, had discussed them with Yüan Shih-k'ai in Peking during August 1914. They included the Kwantung lease, various railway questions concerning Manchuria, rights of residence for Japanese, additional railway concessions in Chekiang and Kiangsi, and proposals for reform. Yüan, probably dishonestly, was encouraging. As Hioki reported him,[14] he believed that 'China, like Japan, is of the yellow race and should not at all make friends of Europeans and Americans who are of the white race'. Japan and China must expect to face 'more powerful white adversaries' after the war. In such a situation they would clearly need to stand together.

Given by this some expectation of making progress, the Foreign Minister, Katō Takaaki, recalled Hioki to Tokyo for consultations in November. While there, he was given the task, together with Koike Chōzō, Abe's successor as head of the Ministry's political department, of working the diverse proposals about China policy into a programme for negotiation. The result was the Twenty-one Demands, approved by the cabinet, the Genrō, and the emperor in the next few weeks.[15] On 3 December Katō transmitted them officially to Hioki with instructions to present the list personally to Yüan at some suitable future opportunity. As a sweetener, he was empowered to offer Yüan cash and Japanese decorations, as well as to promise stricter Japanese control over anti-Yüan Chinese revolutionaries in Japan.

In some respects the contents of the document were a statement of unfinished business. That is to say, it brought together those elements in imperialist policy which circumstances had prevented Japan from pursuing successfully so far. They fell into two segments. The first concerned Manchuria and Inner Mongolia (the two areas were by this time customarily elided in Japanese drafting). The lease of the Kwantung peninsula, originally for twenty-five years, was to be extended to ninety-nine years. So were arrangements for the South Manchuria

[14] Kajima, *Diplomacy*, III, 126–9.
[15] On the drafting and presentation of the Japanese demands, see Nish, *Japanese Foreign Policy*, 96–9, and Madeleine Chi, *China Diplomacy* (1970), 28–31. An English text of the demands, acquired by the British legation in Peking in May 1915, is printed in Lowe, *Great Britain and Japan*, 258–62. It is not quite complete. The Japanese text is in *NGNB*, I, documents, 381–4.

Railway, cancelling China's right to repurchase it after thirty-six years. Similar terms were to be attached to the Antung–Mukden and Kirin–Changchun lines. Japanese were to be given the right to hold land in Manchuria and to carry out mining operations; proposals for new foreign loans or railway-building in the region were to be subject to prior Japanese consent; and the Chinese administration was to give preference to Japanese subjects as political, military, and financial advisers. In sum, Manchuria was to be put under Japanese tutelage, much as Korea had been during 1904–5. Despite this, the instructions given to Hioki explicitly disclaimed any desire to separate Manchuria from the rest of China.

A second set of clauses were those which concerned Japan's position within the treaty port system in the rest of China. The Hanyehping coal and iron company was to become a joint Sino-Japanese enterprise, in which the Japanese investors were to retain certain veto rights. Japan was also to have railway concessions in Chekiang and Kiangsi, connecting with Nanchang. Foreign loans for railways, mines, and harbours in Fukien were to be subject to prior consultation with Japan.

There remained several other stipulations, some of which looked forward to establishing a wholly different relationship between China and Japan. The claim to German privileges in Shantung, together with a modest extension of them, was not really novel, in that it was in reality no more than the transfer from one treaty power to another of a type of advantage to which the system at large had already accommodated. The provision by which Peking was required 'not to cede or lease to any other Power any harbour or bay or any island along the coast of China' aroused more speculation, since it implied that Japan was willing to defend China from any further growth in Western imperialism, thereby carrying hints of an overall protectorate; but in 1914 the danger it claimed to guard against already seemed remote.

Japan's wider aspirations emerged more clearly from a number of items which formed part of the last section of the document, known as Group V. This was something of a rag-bag. It included the clauses about Fukien and the Nanchang railways, noted above, as well as one granting additional legal rights to Japanese hospitals and schools. It provided for Japanese to have the right to preach (the origin of which is obscure, though one is tempted to put it down to simple emulation). More important, it inserted an undertaking that the Chinese central government would employ 'influential Japanese as political, financial, and military advisers'; another that in certain areas of China, where difficulties had arisen, the police should be placed under joint Chinese and Japanese control; and a third that China would look to Japan for the supply of munitions (to perhaps half its needs). Many contemporary observers thought this to be uncommonly like the first step along a road which Korea and Manchuria had already travelled, notwithstanding the fact that Hioki was told to regard Group V as consisting of matters that were 'highly desirable', not 'absolutely essential' like the rest.

When Japan declared war on Germany, late in August 1914, it had rapidly moved forces to Shantung, acting in the name of the allies. It took a little more than two months for them to occupy the leased territory at Kiaochow, plus some two hundred miles of German-owned railway leading to the provincial capital, Tsinan. Once this operation was completed, Yüan Shih-k'ai had cautiously set out to arrange for the withdrawal of Japanese troops within the boundaries of the former German lease; and early in January 1915, on the grounds that all fighting was at an end, he abolished the war zone which China had previously declared in Shantung province. This 'unfriendly' announcement was the signal for Hioki to present the Twenty-one Demands.

Yüan made great efforts to involve the other powers in opposing the demands, but it was soon apparent that neither Britain nor the United States was likely to come to China's rescue. Indeed, a warning from London that Britain would not accept 'an occupation of Peking and the establishment of a virtual protection over all China'[16] was taken in Tokyo—rightly, one suspects—as a green light for virtually everything else. Within Japan Katō faced criticism on two counts. He had been politically unwise in failing to take the Genrō into his confidence before making his *démarche*. He had also been diplomatically clumsy: first, in the manner of his approach to Yüan; second, in keeping his ally, Britain, ignorant of those clauses which affected the Yangtze valley. In practice, such criticisms were easily overcome. By dropping Group V—which included the provisions about the Yangtze railways, as well as the items most offensive to Chinese opinion—Katō was able to secure acceptance of the rest, both in Tokyo and Peking. In May 1915 China signed treaties embodying with minor modifications almost all the demands except Group V.

In general, the texts of these treaties were more moderate in tone than the instructions first transmitted to Hioki, but they were not a

[16] Chi, *China Diplomacy*, 49.

great deal different in substance.[17] Concerning Manchuria, the various leases were extended and Japanese were given the right to rent land (not own it). Agreements about mining were stated in separate notes, as were those about foreign loans and foreign advisers (leaving it to China to decide whether it required them). Eastern Inner Mongolia was to be opened to trade, but nothing more. As to Shantung, China agreed to transfer German rights to Japan, to build a railway to Chefoo, using a Japanese loan, and to increase the number of places at which trade could be carried on. Japan promised that Kiaochow would eventually be returned to China, subject to being made an open port. There was no formal agreement respecting Fukien. Nor was there about Hanyehping, though in an exchange of notes China undertook to approve any arrangements made between the company and its Japanese creditors. It would not take steps without Japanese consent to 'convert the company into a state enterprise, nor confiscate it, nor cause it to borrow and use foreign capital other than Japanese'.

The outcome was a considerable expansion of Japanese interests in China, notably in Manchuria. Britain, whose commercial dominance was being challenged, found the settlement a tolerable price to pay for wartime naval assistance. It did not see anything in the 1915 agreements to cause irreparable harm to the treaty port system as such. When the war was over, London believed, a recovery could be made. Senior Japanese statesmen saw things in much the same way, though with a touch of trepidation. By the same token, those Japanese who had looked forward to startling advances, deriving from an 'accord' with China, were disappointed. Towards the end of the war they were to make an opportunity to try again.

The origins of co-prosperity

A good deal of what might be said to comprise Japanese imperialism between 1915 and 1918 was a consolidation of the gains made through the Twenty-one Demands. Economically, this meant exploiting new privileges in areas such as Manchuria and Shantung (see Chapter 9). Diplomatically, it involved putting pressure on the powers to recognize the Sino-Japanese treaties of May 1915, mostly by threats to cut back Japan's contribution to the war against Germany.[18] After mid-1917 even the United States was subject to this kind of blackmail.

---

[17] For the final terms and some comparisons with the original demands, see Willoughby, *Foreign Rights*, 331–8, 386–91, 411–17.
[18] See Chi, *China Diplomacy*, chaps. 4 and 5.

There was one novel theme, in that these years also saw the beginnings of an 'advance to the south' (*nanshin*).[19] In October 1914 Japan had occupied, in addition to Kiaochow, various German-held islands in the western Pacific, north of the equator: the Mariana, Palau, Caroline, and Marshall groups. The expectation was that these, too, would become Japanese at the end of the war. As economic assets they were not very valuable; but when linked in the public mind with a colony in Taiwan and commercial expansion into southern China, they served to stimulate a growth of interest in the whole 'south seas' (*nanyō*), including south-east Asia. Books and articles were written about the possibilities that were unfolding for Japanese expansion in that region. There were plans to increase the number of Japanese consulates, to establish branches of banks, to develop shipping routes. Companies were formed to trade in the islands and invest in Malayan rubber plantations. Trade exhibitions were organized. Courses were begun for the teaching of Malay and Dutch.

None of this amounted to a great deal by comparison with Japan's interests in Korea and China, for all that it had some importance as a preliminary to the creation of a south-east Asian co-prosperity sphere after 1936. Indeed, it was with respect to China, not to south-east Asia, that the Terauchi cabinet and its advisers first made co-prosperity into a feature of Japanese policy. One factor in their doing so was the death of Yüan Shih-k'ai in June 1916, which seemed to open up the prospect of a fresh departure in Sino-Japanese relations. Another was the impact of the war on the Japanese economy. As European competitors became preoccupied with military production, Japan was able to penetrate new markets and develop the industries to supply them. It thus became for the first time an international creditor, able to provide from its own resources the capital for economic expansion overseas.

During 1915 and 1916 Japan had been intervening more insistently in Chinese politics than before. Alarmed by proposals to make Yüan emperor, because such a step might give China unity at the cost of confirming its hostility to Japan, Japanese ministers took the lead in organizing diplomatic opposition to the move. They also made some attempt to arouse protests inside China, giving free rein to various Japanese adventurers willing to take action to that end. Once again, Kawashima Naniwa was one of them. By March 1916 he was in

[19] Yano Tōru, *Nanshin no keifu* (1975), 68–78.

Dairen, working closely with the Kwantung Army to prepare an expedition to put a Manchu, Prince Su, on the throne of an 'independent' Manchuria. The army made available weapons and released a number of junior officers for the enterprise. The Ōkura company put up money. Mitsui helped in providing ammunition. As a result a substantial force was soon launched into Manchuria, only to be halted and dispersed when Yüan Shih-k'ai's death brought a change in Tokyo's view of things.[20]

The government of Terauchi Masatake, who succeeded Ōkuma as Premier in October 1916, had to choose what line to follow in China's subsequent turmoil. It made two initial decisions. One was to avoid offending its Western allies, in order to improve Japan's chances of getting international recognition of the 1915 treaties. The other, taken in July 1917, was to mend fences in China by giving economic aid to the regime which Tuan Ch'i-jui was forming in Peking.[21] Tuan, after all, not only appeared to be co-operative, but was also in control of those parts of China which mattered most to Japan. This made him on balance the best Chinese partner available in any search for Sino-Japanese 'accord'.

The approach to him was through the so-called Nishihara loans: advances made to Tuan's government in 1917 and 1918 for a variety of purposes, including military support, administrative costs, and economic development, which totalled something over 140 million yen.[22] In Japan they were conceived by the 'Korea faction', consisting of Terauchi himself, former Governor-General of the colony; his Finance Minister, Shōda Kazue, who had been President of the Bank of Chōsen; and Nishihara Kamezō, one-time business man in Korea, who acted as Terauchi's personal representative in Peking. In making arrangements for the loans they bypassed the foreign ministries in both

[20] Jansen, *Japanese and Sun*, 196–7; Kurihara Ken, *Tai-Manmō seisaku-shi no ichimen* (1966), 148–59; and Kwanha Yim, 'Yüan Shih-k'ai and the Japanese' (1965).

[21] Cabinet decisions of 20 July 1917, in *NGNB*, I, documents, 437–8. See also Kitaoka, *Nihon rikugun*, 217–19, 226–8.

[22] In English, see William Morton, *Tanaka Giichi and Japan's China Policy* (1980), 29–33, and Hsi-ping Shao, 'From the Twenty-one Demands to the Sino-Japanese military agreements' (1978), 47–9. In Japanese, the most useful account is in Usui, *Nihon to Chūgoku*, 107–8, 118–27, 135–7. See also Kitaoka, *Nihon rikugun*, 220–6; Shōda Tatsuo, *Chūgoku shakkan to Shōda Kazue* (1972); and Suzuki Takeo, *Nishihara shakkan shiryō kenkyū* (1972). Estimates of the total value of the loans vary according to what is included, it being possible to exclude some items on the grounds that they were 'normal' loans, not special ones.

countries. Shōda's Finance Ministry took over responsibility for raising the necessary capital, preferring private sources (Mitsui, Mitsubishi, the Dai Ichi Bank), but also turning where necessary to a semi-
official consortium (the Yokohama Specie Bank, the Industrial Bank,
the Bank of Chōsen, the Bank of Taiwan). In Peking, Nishihara
worked closely with Tsao Ju-lin, a law graduate of Tokyo's Waseda
University, who had served under Yüan Shih-k'ai, then been Governor of the Bank of Communications. Tsao became both Minister of
Finance and Minister of Communications in Tuan's cabinet.[23]

Though modelled in some respects on what the powers had done
for Yüan Shih-k'ai, the loans were designed to give Japan more specific advantages. One was to make Japan a principal supplier of munitions and military advice. Another was to improve China's internal
transport and communications in co-ordination with Japan's. A third
was to give Japan privileges in the mining, timber, and textile industries, plus an extension of its railway rights, all within a financial framework which would open the way to a preponderant Japanese influence
over fiscal and currency decisions. In the event, not a great deal of this
was actually achieved, because most of the money was swallowed up by
Tuan's attempts to win a civil war. Since, like Sun Yat-sen earlier, he
failed, or at least did not succeed decisively, the investment turned out
to be neither politically nor economically sound. The Nishihara loans
were to this extent wasted money.

Yet they did mark a significant shift in Japanese ideas about what
imperialism should mean on the Asian mainland. What Terauchi
sought was sometimes called 'coexistence and co-prosperity' (*kyōson-
kyōei*), an expression which appears to have been first used in May
1915 by Yamagata Aritomo, when criticizing Katō's diplomatic inef-
fectiveness over the Twenty-one Demands. Though Katō's methods,
Yamagata said, had served dangerously to alienate Chinese sentiment,
in the long run it would be necessary for Japan and China to work
together if Asia were to be saved. True, Japan must expand into Manchuria for the sake of its own livelihood—Manchuria was 'Japan's lifeline'—but in pursuing its own interests in this way it must always bear
in mind the need to strive for 'the self-protection of Asians and for the
coexistence and co-prosperity of China and Japan'.[24]

[23] Madeleine Chi, 'Tsao Ju-lin' (1980), 141–9.
[24] Trans. in Tsunoda, *Sources*, 716–17. The translation is taken from a book published in 1925, which may well explain why phrases used by Yamagata in this passage
became widely current about 1930.

The same theme was taken up in a Kokuryūkai pamphlet, *Shina kaiketsu ron* (Views on a China settlement), published in November 1916. In it, Uchida Ryōhei argued that once the war was over there would inevitably be a clash between Japan and Britain over the domination of East Asia. To prepare for this, Japan must come to terms with China. Admittedly, Japan would have to take possession of Manchuria and Inner Mongolia; but such possession need not be an obstacle to Sino-Japanese friendship, since by demonstrating the benefits of Japanese rule—improved living standards and political stability, coupled with a degree of self-government greater than was accorded to Korea and Taiwan—it could actually serve to overcome the prejudices that had been manifest in China during recent years. Friendship could not in any case be on terms of independence and equality, because China had already been deprived of these attributes by Western imperialism. There would have to be Japanese 'guidance' (*shidō*). Within that framework, however, the relationship should be one of 'community and mutual benefit' (*kyōtsū-kyōsai*), both politically and economically. Another Japanese leader, Matsukata Masayoshi, writing at this time, added to the vocabulary the notion of Japanese 'tutelage' (*ikusei*) over China.[25]

During the war years such proposals for an unequal partnership between China and Japan were also being put into the context of the rapid growth of Japanese heavy industry. This was by no means confined to those who held that only economic forms of expansion were proper within the treaty port system. For example, Ugaki Kazushige, head of a section in the Army General Staff, described China in his diary as a key source of raw materials which were of strategic importance in terms of Japanese self-sufficiency: 'there is no way for the empire's industries to survive without access to China'.[26] Gotō Shimpei, who became Home Minister under Terauchi, put forward proposals for establishing a Sino-Japanese investment bank and creating an 'East Asian economic alliance'.[27]

Nor was it difficult to secure the goodwill of business men. In the records of the Sumitomo company there is a detailed study, dated 1915, of plans for carrying out an economic penetration of China

---

[25] On Matsukata, see Kitaoka, *Nihon rikugun*, 196–7. The summary of the Kokuryūkai pamphlet derives from a copy in the author's possession.

[26] Masaru Ikei, 'Ugaki Kazushige's view of China' (1980), 203.

[27] Shōda, *Chūgoku shakkan*, 79–84.

during the breathing-space afforded by the war in Europe.[28] It argued that it was not enough simply to acquire markets there. An injection of capital was also necessary, in order to develop China's natural resources. Since China lacked both the finances and the leadership for this task, it would have to be undertaken by the West or by Japan. If it were done by the West, the result would eventually be to produce a competitor capable of destroying Japan's export trade and the industries on which it was based; but if Japan took the lead, it could retain the key to all this wealth, co-ordinating the Chinese and Japanese economies for the sake of its own economic future. It followed that action must be taken by those Japanese companies that could raise capital on the requisite scale: the *zaibatsu* concerns, Mitsui, Mitsubishi, Sumitomo, Yasuda, and Ōkura.

The policies pursued by Shōda Kazue and Nishihara Kamezō fitted neatly into this pattern. Whereas the Terauchi government's objectives as a whole concentrated on the need for a *political* partnership with Tuan Ch'i-jui, reflecting the attitudes of Yamagata and Uchida, its financial advisers put their emphasis on economic forms of 'accord' (*teikei*) or 'community' (*kyōdō*). In other words, they set out to create a Sino-Japanese bloc, such as would give Japan privileged access to Chinese raw materials—especially coal, iron, and cotton—together with a measure of control over China's financial structure, but would not cause offence to Chinese susceptibilities to the same extent as open political interference or the seizure of Manchuria and Inner Mongolia would do. Nishihara described the objective as follows in a letter to Shōda in January 1918: 'to develop the limitless natural resources of China and the industry of Japan by co-ordinating the two, so as to make possible a plan for self-sufficiency under which Japan and China would become a single entity'.[29]

Although, as we have said, the plans of Shōda and Nishihara came to little at the time, they were nevertheless important in the development of Japanese imperialism. They were not simply a reiteration of old themes, that is, army insistence on the strategic importance of north-east Asia versus Foreign Ministry concern about the reactions of the powers, seen as a condition of Japan's economic progress overseas. They did not particularly address the question of how far a Manchurian sphere of influence within the treaty port system could accommo-

---

[28] Summarized in *Ōkura zaibatsu no kenkyū*, 1–3.
[29] Quoted in Usui, *Nihon to Chūgoku*, 125.

date Japan's military needs. Instead, they postulated a 'special relation-ship' between Japan and China, to which the treaty port system could be said to be irrelevant, or even an obstacle. What is more, they gave it an economic, as well as a political rationale. To some extent they were ahead of their time: Japan did not yet have the resources for what they proposed. Arguably, it never did. Yet a decade later, when world events made Japanese opinion still more disenchanted with the Foreign Ministry view of things, and when the treaty port structure itself was crumbling in the face of Chinese nationalism, the ideas put forward in 1917 and 1918 lay ready to hand to offer an alternative. One has to bear in mind that the time-span we are considering was short. Both Shōda and Nishihara were still alive—aged seventy-six and seventy-two, respectively—when the Greater East Asia Co-prosperity Sphere collapsed in 1945.

9

Overseas Trade and Investment, 1895–1930

By the end of the first decade of the twentieth century Japan had
established for itself a position of advantage *vis-à-vis* its neighbours in
much the same way as the Western powers had done. One aspect of
this, which will be considered in Chapter 10, was the acquisition of
colonies and other overseas dependencies. Another, to be examined
here, was the possession of economic privilege. This had rested
initially on the benefits to trade accorded by participation in the treaty
port system—benefits that were to continue throughout the period stu-
died in this book—but after the scramble for concessions in China
during 1897–8 it had also opened the way for Japan, like other powers,
to secure investment rights, mostly in railways and mining. Agreements were concluded with China, supplementing the old unequal
treaties, which defined these rights and gave them a measure of security. They provided a diplomatic framework for capital investment on a
considerable scale.

Investment was of two kinds, each having different political implications. Direct investments, by which foreigners put capital into industrial operations in China, either on their own or in partnership with
Chinese, involved foreign governments only in the sense that investors
expected some assurance of stability in the areas with which they were
concerned, plus a guarantee, as far as possible, against Chinese fiscal
exactions or the repudiation of loans. Indirect investments, by contrast,
were loans made to Chinese authorities, national or provincial, in some
cases for much the same industrial purposes, in others to finance
indemnities, administration, or currency reform. Loans of this kind
were commonly put together by a consortium of foreign banks, acting
under the auspices of their governments. They were secured on part of
China's revenue, from which interest and redemption payments were
made. China's tax structure thus became subject in these matters to
the supervision and sometimes intervention of foreign representatives.

Japan obviously stood to profit greatly from such arrangements: the
powers, acting together, could obtain far more than Japan could ever

hope to do alone. Indeed, in the broadest sense the way in which the Japanese economy developed during the first three decades of the twentieth century made a Sino-Japanese relationship within the treaty port system logical. China was a primary producer; Japan increasingly an exporter of industrial goods. However, in practice, as we shall see, Japan's economy had particular requirements which distinguished it from those of its Western colleagues. For example, it came to rely heavily on China as a supplier of raw materials for heavy industry. The Western powers did not. The consequence was tension and conflict of a kind which the treaty port system had not been designed to accommodate.

Such differences had a bearing on investment as well as trade. As a late developer, anxious for political reasons to avoid foreign borrowing wherever possible, Japan was notably short of capital, whether for domestic or for overseas investment, in the years before 1914. It had difficulty in finding its share of consortium loans to China, for example. Even when this disadvantage was overcome—first by arrangements for using Western capital, then by virtue of Japanese economic growth—the Japanese government preferred to guide investment into enterprises in which the country had an immediate stake, rather than to participate in international loans designed, as those of the consortium were, to regulate the gains that could be made by different contributors. In other words, Japan opted for a narrow interpretation of national economic advantage in this context, which did not accord easily with the co-operative emphasis implicit in the China treaties. Disagreements about the interpretation of phrases like the Open Door and equal opportunity became frequent and acrimonious. In the end, Japan turned away from the treaty port system almost entirely, seeking to co-ordinate economic policy within its formal and informal empires in such a way as to devise an international structure in East Asia that would better suit its needs. This development forms an important part of the story of Japanese imperialism after 1930.

Foreign trade and colonial trade

Several features of Japanese economic history between 1895 and 1930 have a bearing on overseas trade.[1] One was the growth of the cotton

---

[1] General statements about the Japanese economy made in this section are largely based on Allen, *Short economic history*; for statistics, see especially Tables X, XI, XIII, XVII.

industry, which continued throughout this period. Annual yarn output rose from 177 million lb. in 1894–8 to 1,026 million lb. in 1925–9. Reflecting this, cotton piece-goods, principally the cheaper and coarser grades, were being exported to a value of 412 million yen in 1929, compared with just under 6 million yen in 1900. This put Japan massively into competition with British and American manufacturers, especially in Asian markets.

A different situation obtained with respect to those items of Japanese exports which were also produced by China. In raw silk and tea, which still accounted for a little under 30 per cent of China's own exports in 1913, China was a competitor, not a market or a supplier. What Japan mostly bought from China in these early years, either on its own account or for shipment elsewhere, was raw cotton, soya beans, and bean products. This distinguished Japan from China's Western trading partners. However, a much more critical difference emerged as a result of the rapid growth of Japanese heavy industry in the second part of the period. The indices of Japanese manufacturing production by physical volume (1910–14 = 100) show an increase from 69 in 1905–9 to 313 in 1925–9. Textiles, metals, and machinery were a little below this average, chemicals and ceramics, electricity and gas, were far above it. The figures for iron and steel are particularly relevant. In 1906, Japanese production of pig-iron was 145,000 metric tonnes, that of finished steel 69,000 tonnes. By 1929 the totals had risen to approximately 1.1 million tonnes and 2 million tonnes, respectively. Since Japan had never been an important producer of iron ore—and after 1925 became a net importer of coal, despite continuing exports on a substantial scale—it was by this time looking to China (including Manchuria) to provide key materials for its heavy industry. By contrast, the Western powers, although they, too, had mining interests in China, saw them chiefly as a source of profit, serving East Asia's industrial needs, not theirs.

One unmistakable consequence of industrial growth was a very large increase in the total value of Japanese foreign trade (Table 1).[2] Annual averages of exports, valued in yen, almost quadrupled between 1895–9 and 1910–14, then quadrupled again by 1925–9. Imports increased a little more slowly before 1910–14, a little faster thereafter. Signifi-

---

[2] On foreign trade in this period, see Allen, *Short economic history*, chaps. 5 and 6, and Lockwood, *Economic development*, chaps. 6 and 7. Detailed trade statistics are given in the works cited as sources for Tables 1, 2, and 3 in this chapter.

Table 1. *Japan's foreign trade 1890–1929: imports and exports*

	Exports		Imports	
	Annual averages* (in yen millions at current prices)	Index (1910–14 = 100)	Annual averages* (in yen millions at current prices)	Index (1910–14 = 100)
1890–4	85.4	14.4	85.7	12.9
1895–9	161.5	27.2	212.0	32.0
1900–4	271.3	45.7	321.8	48.6
1905–9	407.5	68.7	475.4	71.8
1910–14	593.1	100.0	662.3	100.0
1915–19	1,599.9	269.8	1,413.7	213.4
1920–4	1,810.4	305.3	2,425.7	366.2
1925–9	2,391.2	403.2	2,841.3	429.0

* Includes Japan's trade with Japanese colonies

Sources: Ohkawa, Shinohara and Meissner, *Patterns of Japanese Economic Development* (1979), Tables A 26 and A 27.

cantly, in only one five-year period, 1915–19, did exports exceed imports. This reflected the exceptional opportunities created in overseas markets by the war in Europe, which led temporarily to a sharp decline in European competition in most parts of East and south-east Asia.

Industrialization changed the character of the trade, as well as its scale. Japan's role in the world's trading economy before the 1880s had been that of primary producer, like other colonial and semi-colonial areas. It was only because Japan was able to break away from this pattern that its exports increased at such exceptional speed: by 1914 Japan's foreign trade was approximately equal in value to China's, despite the enormous disparity in the agricultural resources of the two. Yet there continued to be important survivals from that first semi-colonial phase. Although tea was a declining item in Japanese exports after 1895, silk was an expanding one. It became the principal cash crop of farmers and kept pace with the remarkable increase in exports as a whole, accounting for 36 per cent by value of commodities exported as late as 1929. This underlines a dualism in the Japanese economy: it remained a supplier of agricultural products to advanced countries, while furnishing manufactured goods to backward ones.

Silk apart, the composition of Japanese foreign trade had become predominantly that of an industrial power by 1930 (Table 2). Cotton goods, sent mostly to Asian markets, plus silk for America, made textiles

Table 2. Japan's foreign trade 1890–1929: percentage shares by commodity groups (annual averages)

	Exports*			Imports*			
	Manufactures		Primary products	Manufactures		Primary products	
	Textiles	Other		Chemicals and metals	Other	Raw materials	Foodstuffs
1890–4	49.3	25.0	25.7	16.2	51.6	21.8	10.4
1895–9	53.1	25.7	21.2	18.6	43.8	25.9	11.7
1900–4	54.2	28.6	17.2	20.6	33.9	31.3	14.2
1905–9	52.4	34.1	13.5	27.3	30.7	30.4	11.6
1910–14	56.3	31.0	12.7	25.9	23.6	39.4	11.2
1915–19	54.3	36.8	8.9	31.2	13.4	41.6	12.8
1920–4	66.0	27.1	6.9	24.1	24.9	35.8	15.2
1925–9	66.9	26.5	6.6	19.0	21.9	39.6	19.5

* Includes Japan's trade with Japanese colonies

Sources: Ohkawa, Shinohara and Meissner, *Patterns of Japanese Economic Development* (1979), Tables A 26 and A 27.

much the largest component in exports: something over 50 per cent in the years to 1919, more than 65 per cent thereafter. The share of primary products like tea and seafood declined steadily throughout the period: over 20 per cent of exports in 1895–9, under 7 per cent in the 1920s. Among imports, machinery, which had been of major importance before 1900, when Western technology was being brought to Japan, was gradually reduced in value thereafter, as Japanese industry acquired the ability to produce its own. Simultaneously, foreign consumer goods were finding it more and more difficult to overcome the competition of those produced within Japan. Imports, therefore, came to comprise for the most part materials for industry—first, raw cotton, and iron ore; then coal, oil, pig-iron, and scrap-metal—together with foodstuffs for a population which was steadily outgrowing the productive capacity of Japanese agriculture.

The geographical distribution of the trade varied with its changing composition (Table 3). Britain, which had begun by being Japan's largest supplier of both machinery and consumer goods, was of relatively little consequence after the First World War. India was a major source of cotton, later of pig-iron, but there was difficulty in developing an export market there, at least until the 1920s. For the rest, only the United States was able to maintain and even expand its position in

Table 3. *Japan's foreign trade 1890–1929: percentage shares by countries (annual averages)*

	Exports		Imports			
	USA	China (including Manchuria)	USA	Britain	India	China (including Manchuria)
1890–4	37.3	8.0	8.6	32.1	9.7	15.1
1895–9	30.9	14.1	12.4	26.2	14.1	12.5
1900–4	28.7	18.8	16.1	18.4	15.8	12.3
1905–9	29.7	24.0	16.3	22.2	14.3	11.2
1910–14	28.2	24.7	14.6	16.2	20.4	12.8
1915–19	29.8	23.1	29.1	5.6	16.1	18.5
1920–4	34.7	22.8	26.6	9.9	12.8	14.9
1925–9	37.1	20.7	23.2	6.1	12.7	13.4

Sources: Oriental Economist, *Foreign Trade of Japan* (1935); *Nihon Kindaishi Jiten* (1958), Table 42. Percentages are of the totals in Table 1.

the Japanese import trade despite the effects of Japanese industrialization. This was because it was able to combine the supply of advanced industrial goods with that of raw materials—cotton, oil, metals—as Japanese requirements changed. What is more, it remained Japan's largest customer, taking something close to 30 per cent of Japanese exports in the period 1895–1919, about 35 per cent during the following decade. It is instructive to compare the composition of trade between Japan and America in 1913 and 1929.[3] In the first of those years, raw silk accounted for 68 per cent of Japanese exports to America; in the second, 82 per cent. Over the same period, Japanese imports of American cotton dropped from 52 per cent of goods bought from the United States to 42 per cent. By contrast, the proportion of imports attributable to oil, iron and steel, machinery and automobiles rose from 19.8 to 25 per cent.

Within this pattern of foreign trade China had an importance second only to the United States. In fact, promoting trade with China was something to which successive Japanese governments gave the highest priority. Partly this involved diplomatic negotiations designed to ensure that any commercial agreements made by the powers did not unduly disadvantage Japan by comparison with its Western

[3] Ohara Keishi, *Japanese trade and industry in the Meiji-Taisho era* (1957), 35–7.

competitors.[4] Partly it called for direct action by Japan's consular service on behalf of Japanese business men. Thus Komura, when he became Foreign Minister towards the end of 1901, wrote a memorandum urging that, since his fellow-countrymen were not yet altogether capable of competing successfully on their own, they must be given government protection and support in China. There would, for example, have to be a better commercial information service, provided by consuls, plus training facilities for those merchants who were unfamiliar with the Chinese and Korean markets. A representative of the Finance Ministry, sent to study the situation in the Peking and Tientsin area in 1902, made similar recommendations. Japanese exporters needed to study Chinese tastes more carefully, he observed. It would be useful to establish exhibitions and trade centres in the treaty ports; to encourage Japanese entrepreneurs to visit China in order to acquire a knowledge of conditions there; and to organize a China Association for businessmen in Japan.[5] Action along these lines became a regular part of the Foreign Ministry's work. The attention paid to it can be exemplified by a circular, sent to the legation and consulates in China in February 1912, calling for reports assessing how changes in Chinese interests and habits, due to the anti-Manchu revolution, might influence the market for Japanese goods.[6]

In view of all this, it is not surprising that Japanese exports to China grew more rapidly than imports from that country (Table 3). As a percentage of total exports they increased from only 8 per cent in the years immediately before the war of 1894–5 to 24 per cent in 1905–14. Given the simultaneous rise in Japan's exports as a whole from 85 million yen to over 593 million, the secular increase in exports to China was enormous: an annual average of 6.8 million yen in 1890–4 became 146.4 million in 1910–14. Thereafter the percentage figure dropped back a little as Japan's foreign trade became geographically more diversified, but the annual value still reached 494 million yen in 1925–9. Seen from the Chinese viewpoint the rate of growth was

---

[4] Japan, like the other powers, engaged in negotiations for new commercial treaties with China in 1902–3, following the Boxer disputes. Japan's treaty, which differed from the rest chiefly in making greater provision for open ports in Manchuria, was signed on 8 Oct. 1903; the English text is in *NGB* 36:2:145–50.

[5] Komura memorandum of late 1901, in *Komura gaikō-shi*, I, 206–15; report by Yamaoka Jirō of Finance Ministry, Dec. 1902, in Japanese Foreign Ministry file 3. 2. 1. 18.

[6] Japanese Foreign Ministry file 3. 2. 1. 32.

equally striking. Imports from Japan, accounting for just over 5 per cent of China's total in 1890–4, reached 28 per cent in 1925–9.[7]

By contrast, Japan's imports from China actually declined in percentage terms after the Sino-Japanese War. Only once thereafter did they exceed the proportion achieved in 1890–4, that is, during the war years of 1915–19, when conditions were exceptional. After 1905 they were usually by value between a half and two-thirds of Japan's exports to China, or between 11 and 15 per cent of total Japanese imports. These were still considerable figures: just under 13 million yen of imports from China in 1890–4; 84.6 million in 1910–14; 381.5 million in 1925–9. It remained true, however, that after 1900 Japan had a credit balance in its trade with China, as it did with the United States, which could be set off against unfavourable balances in other parts of the world. In 1929–30 there were credits of 175 million yen and 143 million yen in the American and China trades, respectively, against deficits of 233 million yen with Europe and 123 million yen with the rest of Asia.[8]

The composition of Sino-Japanese trade is very much what one would expect between a country which was becoming industrialized and another which was not. Cotton textiles, both yarn and cloth, played a major part in Japanese exports to China, though the value of yarn was declining by 1914 (mostly because of the growth of China's modern spinning-mills, financed by foreign capital). The bulk of the cotton cloth was of coarse grades, cheaper than those produced by Britain and America. In return, China shipped to Japan raw cotton (and eventually cotton yarn), though the market fluctuated with Indian and American competition. After 1895, still more so after 1905, there were substantial shipments of soya beans and bean products from Manchuria, consumed by Japanese as food and by world industry—largely supplied by Japan—as raw material. Manchuria and north China were also becoming exporters of coal and iron to Japan by the end of the period. In 1929 Japan had gross imports of 3.25 million tonnes of coal, 1.95 million tonnes of iron ore, and 0.65 million tonnes of pig-iron. China, excluding Manchuria, provided approximately 18 per cent of the coal, 45 per cent of the iron ore, and 10 per cent of the pig-iron. Manchuria furnished 60 per cent of the coal and 23 per cent of the pig-iron (more

[7] On China's foreign trade, including that with Japan, see C. F. Remer, *The foreign trade of China* (1926); also Hsiao Liang-lin, *China's foreign trade statistics 1864–1949* (1974).

[8] Lockwood, *Economic Development*, 531–2.

than that in 1928 and 1930). About 44 per cent of the iron ore came from Malaya and 60 per cent of the pig-iron from British India (rather less in 1928 and 1930).[9]

At this point it is convenient to turn from foreign trade to colonial trade. Manchuria might be said to fall into an intermediate category, having some of the characteristics of both. So does Korea, in the sense that its trade was 'foreign' before 1910 and 'colonial' thereafter. Official Japanese statistics complicate these difficulties of definition. They did not include Korea and Taiwan under foreign trade after those territories became formally Japanese, except in so far as they were trading with areas outside the empire. Their trade with Japan was not considered to be foreign once they were colonies. On the other hand, Manchuria—or more precisely, Kwantung, since this is how the trade was listed—was shown separately from China with effect from 1907.

Trade with these areas comprised a significant and increasing element in Japanese trade as a whole (Table 4).[10] Both exports to and imports from Taiwan increased as a percentage of total trade down to 1914. After that year exports did not quite maintain their relative strength, with the result that between 1920 and 1929 Japan had an annual balance of imports over exports in its dealings with the colony, amounting to more than 60 million yen. Over 80 per cent of Taiwan's exports went to Japan at the end of the period, while over 65 per cent of its imports came from there.

Exports to Korea seem to have expanded much more as a result of the establishment of the protectorate in 1905 than they did after annexation in 1910: a rise from 4.2 per cent of the Japanese total in 1900–4 to 6 per cent in 1905–9, then little change for the next ten years. It was after 1920 that Korea again developed rapidly as an export market for Japan. Imports from Korea also increased then, achieving an approximte balance. Like Taiwan, the colony sent over 80 per cent of its exports to Japan by 1929, but took a rather small proportion of its imports from that country.

[9] Figures derived from the Japanese government's annual statistical summary, *Nihon Teikoku Tōkei Nenkan*, vol. 50 (1931). The percentages are calculated on the basis of yen values, not quantities.

[10] In addition to the statistical sources identified in Table 4, see the following: George W. Barclay, *Colonial development and population in Taiwan* (1954), 21; E. B. Schumpeter (ed.), *The industrialization of Japan and Manchukuo 1930–1940* (1940), 287–99; Samuel Pao-san Ho, 'Colonialism and development: Korea, Taiwan, and Kwantung', in Myers and Peattie, *Japanese colonial empire*, 369–71, 396–7.

Table 4. *Japan's colonial trade 1895–1929: percentage shares of total foreign trade by territories (annual averages)*

	Exports			Imports		
	Taiwan	Korea	Kwantung* (Manchuria)	Taiwan	Korea	Kwantung* (Manchuria)
1895–9	–	3.1	–	–	2.5	–
1900–4	3.5	4.2	–	2.4	2.2	–
1905–9	4.6	6.0	–	4.6	2.1	–
1910–14	6.4	6.1	4.1	7.0	3.0	3.6
1915–19	4.0	5.9	4.9	7.0	6.9	5.3
1920–4	4.9	9.3	4.5	6.7	9.2	6.3
1925–9	5.4	11.4	4.4	7.6	11.5	5.5

* Trade figures given for Kwantung, starting in 1907, include trade from the territory's hinterland, which comprised chiefly Manchuria. They are included as part of Japan's trade with China in Table 3.

Sources: as for Table 3. Percentages are of the totals in Table 1.

About the significance of the figures for Kwantung there is some uncertainty, because of the problem of defining the trading area concerned. Strictly, the name Kwantung referred after 1905 to the Japanese-leased territory in the southern tip of Manchuria, formerly known as Liaotung. However, the territory's commercial port, Dairen, was the principal point of entry and exit for Japanese trade with a large hinterland, comprising much or most of Manchuria. Thus Japanese official statistics, listing trade with Kwantung, are usually treated as a statement of the country's trade with Manchuria as a whole, though the equivalence is not exact. They are so treated here.

Taken together, Taiwan, Korea, and Kwantung/Manchuria absorbed one-sixth of Japan's exports in 1910–14, more than one-fifth in 1925–9. In the same period their contribution to Japanese imports rose from one-seventh to nearly a quarter. Nor was this the only measure of their importance. As customers they were much like China: buyers chiefly of Japanese cotton textiles and other consumer goods. As producers, however, they provided Japan with almost all its imports of food: Manchurian soya beans and millet, Korean rice, Taiwanese rice and sugar. Some four-fifths of Taiwan's exports to Japan came under this heading. For Korea the figure was more than 70 per cent before 1914, dropping slowly to about 62 per cent by 1930. Thus they played a major part in sustaining Japan's modern economy by providing cheap food for a growing urban population. In 1925–9, when Japan's domestic rice production stood at approximately 60 million *koku* (1 *koku* equals 4.96 bushels), imports of rice were just over 10 million *koku*.

One can usefully conclude this section by summarizing some figures given by Lockwood for Japanese trade in 1930.[11] Of a total of 1,435 million yen of exports going to countries other than Taiwan and Korea in that year, fractionally more than half consisted of industrial products using mainly domestic materials. Raw silk and silk goods (496 million yen) comprised overwhelmingly the largest part of this. Another 45 per cent (648 million yen) was accounted for by industrial goods using mainly imported materials, more than two-thirds of which were textiles. Of exports to Taiwan and Korea, totalling 393 million yen, about one-quarter were made from domestic materials (despite the fact that silk and silk goods hardly appeared in the list at all). Imported materials were used in just over 60 per cent of the exports going to these two colonies, that is, items to the value of 246 million yen. About two-fifths were textiles.

Turning to imports, 1,545 million yen's worth of goods were brought in from outside the empire in 1930. Of these, food and fertilizer accounted for 22 per cent; metals and minerals for 19 per cent; cotton, wool, and rayon pulp for almost 30 per cent. Imports from Taiwan and Korea came to a further 461 million yen: foodstuffs 342 million (74 per cent); metals and minerals 22 million (4.7 per cent). No separate figures are given for Manchuria, which was very close to being a dependent territory. Adding its contributions of foodstuffs and minerals to the figures for Taiwan and Korea would clearly make a significant difference. Even so, it is evident that Japan's sources of primary products were diverse. The empire was not far from being self-sufficient in foodstuffs by this time, but it was by no means so in coal and iron, to say nothing of oil, tin, and other metals. This fact was to be of critical importance in the debates about expansion in the 1930s.

Foreign investment

Japan's overseas investment before 1930 contrasts sharply in one respect with its foreign trade: whereas trade was world-wide, investment was certainly not. All figures for international investment are approximations in some degree. Few of those cited in this chapter can be regarded as absolutely accurate. Nevertheless, they are reliable

---

[11] Lockwood, *Economic development*, Tables 28 and 32.

Table 5. *Foreign investment in China* 1902–31: distribution by countries (current prices)*

	1902		1914		1931	
	US $m	%	US $m	%	US $m	%
Britain	260	33.0	607	37.7	1,189	36.7
Russia	246	31.3	269	16.7	273	8.4
France	91	11.6	171	10.7	192	5.9
Germany	164	20.9	264	16.4	87	2.7
USA	20	2.5	49	3.1	197	6.1
Japan	1	0.1	220	13.6	1,136	35.1
(Others omitted)						
Total	788	100.0	1,610	100.0	3,242	100.0

* Includes Manchuria and Hong Kong

Source: Hou Chi-ming, *Foreign investment and economic development in China* (1965), Table 4.

enough to sustain a number of conclusions, one of which is that Japanese investment on the Asian mainland was inconsiderable by great power standards. In 1914 Britain was the largest investor in China, but its investments there, valued at some 600 million US dollars, were a mere 3 per cent of its foreign investments as a whole. British holdings of American railway securities alone amounted to 3,300 million dollars in that year. By contrast, Japan's investments in China, estimated at 220 million dollars, represented no less than 80 per cent of Japanese investment overseas. This proportion seems to have remained constant down to 1930.[12]

By Remer's calculations, foreign investment in China stood at just under 800 million US dollars in 1902. It slightly more than doubled between 1902 and 1914, then doubled again by 1931 (Table 5). These are estimates at current prices: allowing for inflation, one must discount the larger part of the apparent growth in the second half of the period. Britain retained first place in the table of investing countries, having a third of the total or a little more. The shares of France,

[12] See Higuchi Hiroshi, *Nihon no tai-Shi tōshi no kenkyū* (1939), 550–1, 566–7. Higuchi gives a wealth of detail on Japanese investment down to about 1936. In English, the most useful works are C. F. Remer, *Foreign investments in China* (1933); Hou Chi-ming; *Foreign investment and economic development in China 1840–1937* (1965); and Willoughby, *Foreign rights* (especially for information on specific rights and arrangements). On Manchuria, see Herbert P. Bix, 'Japanese imperialism and the Manchurian economy 1900–31' (1972).

Germany, and Russia declined considerably, reflecting the consequences of war and revolution. That of the United States increased, but was always very small. Japan's grew enormously: from negligible amounts in 1902 to 1,136 million dollars in 1931, that is, to 35 per cent, which was only slightly less than Britain's at that time.

One explanation for the Japanese advance is military. Victory over Russia in 1904–5 brought a substantial transfer of Russian investments in Manchuria to Japan. Similarly, the outbreak of war in Europe in 1914 opened the way for Japan to take over German interests in Shantung.[13] It is true that the political advantages secured in that province were surrendered as a result of international pressure in 1922, but many of the economic gains were left in the hands of Japanese business men and companies, often acting jointly with Chinese. Shantung was the third most important region of China for Japanese investors in the 1920s (after Manchuria and Shanghai). One result was that the geographical distribution of Japanese investment in China followed a different pattern from that of the Western powers. According to Remer, foreign direct investment as a whole was distributed as follows: in 1914, 22 per cent in Manchuria, 18 per cent in Shanghai, 32 per cent not allocated by region; in 1931, 27 per cent in Manchuria, 34 per cent in Shanghai, 20 per cent not allocated. Britain actually had over 75 per cent of its China investments in Shanghai at the latter date. For Japan, Hou Chi-ming gives these figures: in 1914, 69 per cent in Manchuria; in 1931, 63 per cent in Manchuria.[14] As for Japanese investment outside Manchuria, Higuchi, writing in 1939, divided it as follows: Shanghai and Hankow, 53 per cent; Shantung, 24 per cent; and Peking and Tientsin, 15 per cent.[15]

The growth of Japanese interests in China reflected in certain respects the development of the Japanese economy. Thus the war of 1914–18 was a turning-point for investment, as well as for trade. Since Europe's industry was heavily committed to war production, Japan profited: by the absence of European goods from Asian markets, by munitions orders from its allies, and by increased demand for its merchant shipping. Under these stimuli, Japanese industry grew rapidly in output and scale. The country's balance of payments moved for several years substantially into credit. What is more, although the end of hostilities brought a short-lived slump, some of the structural changes

---

[13] Tsing Yuan, 'The Japanese intervention in Shantung during World War I' (1978).
[14] Hou, *Foreign investment*, 17–18. See also Remer, *Foreign investments*, 71–4.
[15] Higuchi, *Nihon no tai-Shi tōshi*, 522–3.

proved irreversible. Japan after 1920 was more obviously an industrial society than it had been before the war.

For these reasons it is useful to look at Japan's overseas investment in two phases, divided at 1914. In the first, Japan always found it difficult to raise the capital which would enable it to play its full part in the arrangements by which the powers invested in China and made loans to the Chinese government. For example, during the negotiations about the Boxer indemnity in 1901, Britain had recognized, as did the Finance Ministry in Tokyo, that proposals for payment in the form of Chinese bonds, which the recipients could if they wished put on the market, would be likely to penalize Japan, because of the weakness of its international credit. Various devices were suggested in order to overcome this difficulty, but in the end the Katsura government accepted the scheme as it stood for the sake of gaining political goodwill.[16] Problems of this kind continued for several years. Thus despite its membership of the bank consortium which had a virtual monopoly of loans to the Chinese government, Japan had advanced less than 10 million US dollars under this head by 1914, a mere 1.8 per cent of the total. Most of its share was taken up by other members.

Both government and business circles in Japan recognized that the country lacked the capital to finance large-scale overseas projects, such as railway-building. The chosen solution was to borrow from abroad. One advantage of the Anglo-Japanese alliance was that it made this kind of borrowing much easier. Within a few months of the agreement being signed in January 1902 loans had been raised in London to develop railways in Korea and in Japan.[17]

The most notable instance of borrowing for investment overseas came after the victory over Russia. During 1906 the South Manchuria Railway Company (known in Japan as Mantetsu) was formed to run the railway and other interests acquired under the peace terms.[18] Of its initial capital of 200 million yen, one-half was provided by the Japanese government in the form of the facilities and rolling-stock received from Russia. A further 2 million yen was raised by the sale of shares to the public. For the rest, the company—relying on the fact that the government had guaranteed its dividends at a minimum of 6 per cent—looked to two banks: the Yokohama Specie Bank, which

[16] Nish, *Anglo-Japanese alliance*, 136–41.
[17] Ibid., 253–61.
[18] For the organization and early operations of the company, see Andō, *Mantetsu*, 37–46, 56–63, 92–5, 105–8; also Willoughby, *Foreign rights*, 364–7.

would conduct its financial business in Manchuria; and the Industrial Bank, which was to act as a channel for investment from the West. A good deal of capital was in fact needed. Much of the railway system had to be double-tracked during the next few years. A temporary military line, linking Mukden to the Japanese network in Korea, was made permanent. To meet the cost of these and other improvements, the Industrial Bank raised four loans in London on Mantetsu's behalf between 1906 and 1911, totalling £14 million (136 million yen).

The Japanese government's role did not stop at putting up capital and negotiating with China for additional privileges from time to time. The regulations establishing Mantetsu gave officials a veto on the company's operations and control over its freight rates. The president of the company was a government nominee. When Gotō Shimpei was appointed to the post in 1906 (see Chapter 8), he received confidential instructions directly from the Prime Minister, which made it clear that Mantetsu, plus the two banks with which it was required to work, would be Japan's 'most important economic instruments in Manchuria'.[19] The corollary was powerful official patronage. Indeed, there are indications that the men most closely concerned with bringing the company into existence—Kodama Gentarō and Gotō himself—had in mind for it a role like that which the English East India Company had performed in India.[20]

It is not surprising in these circumstances that Mantetsu quickly came to dominate Japanese investments in Manchuria. It was valued at four-fifths of the total for that region by 1914, or 55 per cent of Japanese investments in China as a whole. The length of its track, including several branch lines, was just over 700 miles. Freight, especially of soya beans and coal, accounted for most of its profits, which came to 7 million yen on a turnover of 81 million in 1914. The coal it carried came in large part from the company's own mines, of which the largest, Fushun, was producing over 2 million tonnes a year. Apart from Mantetsu, the Ōkura concern was also engaged in heavy industry in Manchuria, though on a much smaller scale. Mitsui had considerable interests in the soya bean trade. Other Japanese businesses tended to be small and connected with Japan's foreign trade or retailing.

The pattern of investment in the rest of China was quite different. In the first place, Japan had no economic agency south of the Great

[19] Saionji to Gotō, 13 Nov. 1906, in *NGB* 39:1:649–50.
[20] Tsurumi, *Gotō*, II, 649–53.

Wall at all comparable with Mantetsu. Instead, *zaibatsu* firms were
from time to time given special credits or low-interest loans to encourage them to invest in undertakings which were thought to be of
national importance. Often they worked together. For example, Tōa
Kōgyō (East Asian Industrial) was established in this way in August
1909, initially for railway development in the Yangtze valley. The syndicate included semi-official banks, as well as all the leading *zaibatsu*.
In 1908 Mitsui, Mitsubishi, and Ōkura, prompted by the War Ministry, formed an affiliate to promote overseas arms sales, called the Taiping (Taihei) company. It was active in supplying arms to China during
and after the revolution of 1911–12. Mitsui also made various loans to
Chinese revolutionaries, including Sun Yat-sen, presumably with the
knowledge of the Japanese government.[21]

In economic terms, the most important achievement arising from all
this was financial control over the Hanyehping coal and iron company.[22] The firm had been founded in 1894, comprising originally
three separate enterprises, concerned with the production of coal, iron
ore, and pig-iron, respectively, which had been brought together as a
single entity in 1908. The Japanese connection with it dated from
1899, when an arrangement was made for the supply of 50,000 tonnes
of iron ore from Tayeh to Japan's Yawata plant each year, in return for
coke, which the Chinese had difficulty in obtaining. In 1903, needing
capital for re-equipment, Hanyehping turned again to Japan, this time
for a loan (3 million yen), to be repaid by guaranteed sales of iron ore
to Yawata at a fixed price. This was followed by other loans in subsequent years, negotiated variously by Mitsui and Ōkura, financed
principally by the Yokohama Specie Bank. There were sixteen such
loans, totalling almost 39 million yen, by 1913. Several were associated
with contracts for the sale of iron ore and pig-iron to Japan. By the
beginning of the First World War Yawata, Japan's only major iron and
steel plant, was obtaining 60 per cent of its iron ore from this source, in
addition to large quantities of pig-iron.

Government commitment to the arrangement had been made specific as early as 1905. In August of that year, Katsura Tarō, as Prime
Minister, had given his approval to a memorandum on the subject, prepared by the departments of Finance, Foreign Affairs, and Agriculture

[21] Roberts, *Mitsui*, 178–84, 186–8, 196–8; *Ōkura zaibatsu no kenkyū*, 120–4, 134–9.
See also Chapter 8, above.
[22] See generally Albert Feuerwerker, 'China's nineteenth-century industrialization:
the case of the Hanyehping Coal and Iron Company Limited' (1964).

Table 6. *Japanese and other foreign investment in China, 1914**

Type of investment	All foreign investment		Japanese investment	
	Value (US $m)	% composition	Value (US $m)	% composition
Chinese government obligations	525.8	33.0	9.6	4.2
Direct investment of which:	1,067.0	67.0	220.0†	95.8
Transport	336.3	21.1	68.3	29.7
Import and export	142.6	9.0	42.5	18.5
Manufacturing	110.6	6.9	10.6	4.6
Mining	34.1	2.1	29.1	12.7

* Includes Manchuria and Hong Kong
† Includes Japanese investment in Chinese companies, amounting to US $17.5m

Sources: Hou Chi-ming, *Foreign Investment and Economic Development in China* (1965), Table 46; Remer, *Foreign Investments in China* (1933), 426–45.

and Commerce.[23] It set out a plan for providing Hanyehping with capital and technical assistance through the agency of Mitsui and Ōkura; it identified as the immediate objective securing control over the company's commercial management; and it stated the ultimate aim to be that Hanyehping's mining operations should 'at some future opportunity fall wholly into our country's hands'.

In north and central China, as in Manchuria, the great majority of Japanese enterprises were not of this kind, nor on this scale. Most of the manufacturing businesses were small, located in and around Shanghai or Tientsin. They produced cotton textiles and other consumer goods for the Chinese market, much as Western-owned factories in those areas did, though they constituted a less important investment sector for Japan than for the West. Indeed, if one compares the industrial distribution of Japanese investment in China in 1914 with that of foreigners as a whole (Table 6), other differences also become apparent. Most striking is the tiny part which loans to the Chinese government played in the Japanese case: just over 4 per cent of Japanese investment, but 33 per cent of foreign investment as a whole. Almost all Japanese capital in China before this date had gone into commerce and industry, rather than finance. Transport took the greatest share, chiefly because of Mantetsu. Next came import and

[23] The text is in *NGB* 38:2:207–8.

export businesses, in which Japan invested twice as much as the foreign average. Mining, proportionately, was enormously more important to Japan than to anyone else. Manufacturing was noticeably less so. These, it might be said, are the characterisitics of a late developer: not yet able to compete effectively in finance and heavy industry; investing on a larger scale where the interests of the state directed.

The period 1914 to 1930 was to change that situation, for the greater availability of capital for investment, generated by industrial growth at home, was to affect Japanese economic activity in China at every level. Lending to the Chinese government grew very quickly. Some of it was for railways, especially for lines in Manchuria that were not in Japanese ownership. Much more was political, in the sense that it was intended, whatever its ostensible purposes, to increase Japanese influence over Chinese leaders (see Chapter 8). The bulk of it was still concentrated in Manchuria. The South Manchuria Railway's total mileage did not increase very greatly, but its industrial ventures were extended much more widely than before. Heavy investment in new technology for the Fushun coal-mine pushed its annual production up from 2 million tonnes in 1914 to 7 million in 1929. Iron-mining was begun at Anshan after 1915, necessitating large injections of capital, especially in 1919 and 1920. By the mid-1920s it was well on the way to replacing Hanyehping as a supplier for Yawata. Yet Mantetsu no longer dominated Manchurian industry to the same extent as it had before 1914. Its share of Japanese direct investment there dropped from 80 per cent to 63 per cent, most of it in transport, mining, and utilities (gas and electricity). This relative decline was partly due to the fact that a few other large Japanese concerns had begun to establish themselves in the region: Mitsui's Ōji Paper subsidiary; Ōkura, engaged in iron-mining (at Penhsihu) and lumber. Partly it was because smaller firms had started businesses to service the requirements of these giants. A number of them were joint Sino-Japanese ventures.[24]

Elsewhere in China, Japanese railway and mining interests in Shantung continued to be important, but the most considerable change was in the expansion of cotton textile manufacture under Japanese control, especially in and near Shanghai. Of the foreign-owned mills in China, the Japanese share in 1919 was almost 60 per cent, measured by

---

[24] Andō, *Mantetsu*, 92–5, 105–8; *Ōkura zaibatsu no kenkyū*, 134–6, 326–41; Bix, 'Japanese imperialism', 436–40.

Table 7. *Japanese and other foreign investment in China, 1930**

Type of investment	All foreign investment		Japanese investment	
	Value (US $m)	% composition	Value (US $m)	% composition
Chinese government obligations	710.6	22.2	224.1	19.7
Direct investment of which:	2,493.2	77.8	912.0†	80.3
Transport	592.4	18.5	204.5	18.0
Import and export	483.7	15.1	182.7	16.1
Manufacturing	372.4	11.6	165.2	14.5
Mining	108.9	3.4	87.4	7.7

* Includes Manchuria and Hong Kong
† Includes Japanese investment in Chinese companies, amounting to US $38m
Sources: Hou Chi-ming, *Foreign Investment and Economic Development in China* (1965), Table 46; Remer, *Foreign Investments in China* (1933), 505–7, 548–50.

spindles in operation, and 40 per cent, measured by looms. Revised tariff arrangements in 1918 and 1922 stimulated a further increase. By 1930 Japanese factories had over 1.5 million spindles (90 per cent of those that were foreign-owned) and 13,000 looms (84 per cent). This meant that they had close to 40 per cent of China's modern textile plant.[25]

One consequence of these developments was that Japan's investments in China in 1930 no longer differed markedly in kind and industrial distribution from those of the West (Table 7). Its share of Chinese government borrowing was a little below that of the treaty powers generally, its share of direct investment a little above it. In transport and in the import–export business it was close to the average. Mining was still an above-average component, though far less so than in 1914. Manufacturing, thanks largely to textiles, had moved from being well below the norm to being significantly above it.

Simply put, this means that the growth of the Japanese economy had at last brought Japanese interests overseas into line with those of the countries which had in the nineteenth century taken the lead in devising the treaty port system and the policy of the Open Door. It followed that Japan's rivalries with them became more readily recognizable as a case of like against like. There are, however, important respects in which that statement needs to be qualified. First, Japan was

[25] Hou, *Foreign investment*, 86–8.

concerned to an exceptional degree with Manchuria: of the 270,000 Japanese resident in China in 1930, four-fifths lived north of Shanhaikuan. Second, Japanese economic interests were part of a larger complex of policy, in which colonies and strategic considerations also had a place. These facts, taken in conjunction with changes in international circumstance after the First World War, were to ensure that Japan did not simply fall into the role which conformity with Western notions of imperialism in East Asia would have assigned to it.

10

Japan's Territorial Dependencies, 1895–1930

WITHIN twenty years of negotiating an end to its unequal treaties with the West, Japan had become a substantial colonial power. It acquired the island of Taiwan, ceded by China at Shimonoseki in 1895 without ever having been occupied by Japanese troops; Karafuto—that is, the southern half of Sakhalin—taken over from Russia as spoils of war in 1905; and Korea, which had passed through successive stages as sphere of influence and protectorate before being annexed in 1910.

With these it is customary to include certain other territories, whose status was not strictly colonial. In 1905 Japan had secured by agreement with Russia and China the lease of Liaotung in southern Manchuria, containing the naval base of Port Arthur (Lushun) and the commercial port of Dalny (Dairen). Known subsequently as Kwantung, this area was to remain under Japanese jurisdiction, though nominally Chinese, until 1945. Then in 1914, having declared war on Germany, ostensibly in accordance with obligations under the Anglo-Japanese alliance, Japan seized the German installations and investments in the Chinese province of Shantung, which included the leased territory of Kiaochow and a naval base at Tsingtao. It also occupied German island possessions in the western Pacific north of the equator. The Shantung rights, except for some economic ones, were returned to China after the Washington Conference in 1922. Japanese occupation of the Pacific islands (the Mariana, Palau, Caroline, and Marshall groups) continued after the Versailles treaties in the guise of a League of Nations mandate.

These territories were not large—Korea, Taiwan, and Karafuto together had a total area which was only four-fifths of that of the Japanese home islands—but they were important to Japan in a number of ways. For an aspiring world power, colonies were a prestige symbol. Moreover, as a glance at the map will demonstrate, Japan's overseas empire, taken together with the Kurile, Ryūkyū, and Bonin (Ogasawara) islands, which were part of Japan proper, formed a defence zone in depth, as well as providing jumping-off points for further advances.

Both the army and the navy regarded the empire as strategically vital, though not for the same reasons. It was also a major economic resource. Its markets, its food supplies, and its industrial raw materials were to seem more and more valuable as the Japanese economy became 'advanced'.

Colonial government and society

Since Taiwan was Japan's first colony, establishing Japanese authority there became for a time the focus of debates about the principles of colonialism. There was from the start some doubt among Japanese policy-makers about which Western models it was best to follow, or even whether they were appropriate at all.[1] French ideas of assimilation, looking forward to a stage in which colonial peoples would be 'civilized' and made full members of the metropolitan state, had considerable appeal, not only because they fitted well enough with traditional Confucian concepts of a monarch's educative function, but also because they avoided the more unpleasant racial implications of colonial rule. The Taiwanese, it was pointed out—certainly the members of their dominant class—shared with Japanese a Confucian education and the use of the Chinese script. Thus they were already partly civilized. Against that, treating Taiwan as a separate and subordinate political entity in the British manner also had its attractions, since it would make it easier to deny the Taiwanese those rights under the Japanese constitution for which they were demonstrably unprepared. During the first months of Japanese rule, after all, many of them were in open rebellion against Japan. This made it difficult to treat them as being, like the Japanese, 'one people under one emperor'.

Such uncertainties were to persist throughout the history of the Japanese colonial empire. Different governments at different times were to prefer different emphases. However, there were some assumptions that were widely held, at least with respect to the 'sovereign' colonies of Taiwan, Korea, and Karafuto. One was the desirability of their being *ultimately* integrated with Japan, both culturally and politically. Another was that Japan had a civilizing—or perhaps one should say, modernizing—mission, which applied as much to promoting

[1] For Japanese views on colonialism, see Mark R. Peattie, 'Japanese attitudes toward colonialism' (1984), and Edward I-te Chen, 'The attempt to integrate the empire: legal perspectives' (1984). Much of the basic information on the Japanese colonial empire, summarized in this chapter, is to be found in the volume in which these articles appear, i.e. Myers and Peattie, *The Japanese Colonial Empire*.

education and public health and economic development as it did to political behaviour. With the passing of time there was a tendency to put such ideas into a traditionalist framework of Japanese political thought, that is, to relate colonies to the 'national polity' (*kokutai*), implying a special relationship with a divinely descended emperor.

The law which spelt out the nature of Japanese administration of Taiwan in 1896 evaded some of these issues by asserting the principle of Japanese political unity, while denying that the Japanese constitution applied within the colony. The Diet's legislative powers were delegated to the Governor-General in order to make this feasible. In due course similar provisions were made concerning Karafuto (1907) and Korea (1911). The effect was to give their governors immense authority, combining legislative and executive powers. They were also unusually free from ministerial supervision, exercised from the capital. A Colonial Ministry was formed in 1896 to administer Taiwan and Hokkaido, but was abolished after little more than a year. From 1897 to 1910 there was no central office responsible for overseas territories: Taiwan and Karafuto came under the Home Ministry, Kwantung in most respects under the Foreign Ministry. In June 1910 a colonial bureau was created, responsible to the Prime Minister, to deal with Taiwan, Karafuto, and non-diplomatic matters concerning Kwantung. It had a chequered history: abolished in 1913; revived in 1917; transferred to the cabinet secretariat in 1922; finally, absorbed into a full-fledged Colonial Ministry in 1929. At no time was Korea effectively subordinate to it.

Colonial governors accordingly enjoyed a large measure of independence. The Governors-General of Korea and Taiwan were responsible in theory to the emperor personally: through the Prime Minister in civil matters; through the War Ministry and Army Chief of Staff in military ones. In Kwantung, supervision was similarly shared, though in this case it was the Foreign Minister who exercised the civil function. All three governors were chosen after consultations between the premier, the elder statesmen, and senior army leaders. Partly this reflected the very high prestige attaching to these posts, which were often held by men of great political influence. Kodama Gentarō, for example, who was Governor-General of Taiwan from 1896 to 1906, served simultaneously as War Minister, later as Home Minister, during his term of office, then became Chief of Staff. Terauchi Masatake, the first Governor-General of Korea in 1910, had already been War Minister for several years, and left Korea to become Prime Minister in

1916. Such subordinates would have been difficult for any ministry to control.

They were especially so because they were required for most of the period we are here discussing to be serving officers with the rank of lieutenant-general or general. Taiwanese resistance to Japanese occupation in 1895 had meant that the first governor was in charge of a military campaign to suppress it. Kwantung and Karafuto had both become Japanese as a result of war. The governor of the former, like his more senior colleague in Korea, commanded forces that were important to national defence. Consequently, the army had successfully demanded that they be officers able to carry out such military duties. This gave the army a voice in choosing them. It also made them in some degree exponents of army policy, rather than government policy, where the two conflicted. Even though the Hara cabinet opened the posts to civilians in 1919, the change was not long-lived. Except for a few years in the 1920s, the characteristic pattern of Japanese colonial administration was that generals held office as governors and had civilians as deputies.

In the two largest colonies, Taiwan and Korea, these officials were served by a considerable secretariat, of which the senior members were recruited in Japan, the rest locally. The powers of the Governor-General were authoritarian. The functions of his subordinates covered all aspects of taxation, communications, public health, education, economic development, legislation, and law enforcement. Supervision was exercised directly from the colonial capital over the main units of regional government. At the local level use was made of institutions of control inherited from the pre-colonial period: landlords, village headmen, household groups. The whole structure was supported by a civil police force, in which the highest positions were held by Japanese. It was highly trained and tightly organized. Both regionally and locally its responsibilities extended beyond the maintenance of law and order to take in the regulation of the community and the monitoring of social policy, much as the police did in Japan itself. A particular task was the enforcement of censorship and the scrutiny of potentially subversive organizations.[2]

Much the same principles were observed in setting up administra-

---

[2] On colonial administration, see E. Patricia Tsurumi, 'Taiwan under Kodama Gentarō and Gotō Shimpei' (1967); Ching-chih Chen, 'Police and community control systems in the empire' (1984); Han-kyo Kim, 'The Japanese colonial administration in Korea' (1973); Jong Hae Yoo, 'The system of Korean local government' (1973).

tive machinery in Karafuto, Shantung (between 1914 and 1922), and the mandated Pacific islands, though in these areas, where Japanese interests were less substantial, the rank of the officials concerned, hence their independence, was reduced. Kwantung, however, was a special case.[3] As a territory it was very small, but those who governed it had duties stretching well beyond its borders. It was a key naval base; its garrison commander was also responsible for the guards on the South Manchuria railway line; and the fact that it was legally Chinese gave it a place in Sino-Japanese diplomacy. These circumstances had from the beginning caused tension between the army and the Foreign Ministry (see Chapter 7). It persisted throughout the period. At first on the grounds that it was necessary to take precautions against a possible Russian war of revenge, later by the more general argument that Manchuria was a vital Japanese interest, the country's military leaders sought to assert the priority of their own concerns, hence that of their representatives in Kwantung. When this was checked by the Foreign Ministry, pleading the importance of Manchuria to relations between China and Japan, the army gave its approval to the idea of creating a colonial bureau or ministry as a means of weakening the influence of the diplomats at source, that is, in Tokyo. This is a topic to which we shall have to return. Meanwhile, it is enough to note that the disputes had very little to do with colonial policy in the ordinary sense.

Framing colonial policy in Taiwan was in large part the work of Kodama Gentarō and Gotō Shimpei in the years 1898–1906.[4] One of its objects was to make the colony fiscally self-sufficient, or at least able to dispense with subsidies from Tokyo. To this end a reform of the land tax system was implemented, involving a comprehensive survey of agricultural land and a population census. Both had been completed by 1905. One consequence—as it had also been in Japan during the 1870s and 1880s—was to confirm the landlords in their domination of rural society, thereby smoothing the path of local government. Another was to double the area of land registered for tax and to treble the revenue taken from it. A similar increase in revenue was obtained by efficient management of monopolies in opium, salt, camphor, and tobacco. The financial stability which this ensured made it possible to

---

    [3] On Kwantung, see F. C. Jones, *Manchuria since 1931* (1949), 14–16; Tsunoda, *Manshū mondai*, 332–41.
    [4] On colonial policies in Taiwan, see especially Tsurumi, 'Taiwan under Kodama'; also the same author's *Japanese Colonial Education in Taiwan* (1977).

meet budget deficits by floating bonds, placed with the newly formed Bank of Taiwan.

Much of the revenue raised in this way was used for public works, including roads and railways. Some—though the amount was kept to a minimum—went to provide for an education system designed to make Taiwanese into useful citizens, reconciled to Japanese rule. Primary schools were established, in which the curriculum concentrated on teaching the Japanese language, useful skills such as arithmetic and letter-writing, and civic duty (a combination of Confucian ethics and loyalty). By 1918 something more than 15 per cent of the relevant age group was attending them. Alternatively, Taiwanese could go to local private schools, which were broadly Confucian in their approach to education, though they were required in all cases to teach Japanese in addition to Chinese. A separate primary-school system, better equipped and taught, existed for the children of Japanese residents.

During this period, further education for Taiwanese was limited to facilities for training primary-school teachers and doctors (the latter qualified to practise only in Taiwan). This accorded with Gotō's ideas of a gradualist approach to the process of assimilation. After 1918, in response to changes in Japanese society, as well as to unrest among colonial populations, especially in Korea, the emphasis changed. Regulations of January 1919 opened up opportunities for Taiwanese in secondary and higher education, including commercial and agricultural colleges. Applicants had to compete—on disadvantageous terms—with Japanese students, as they did also in the university which was established in 1928. The principal gain in practice was an increase in the number of primary schools.

The aim of this system, it has been said, was to create 'faithful Japanese followers, not able Japanese leaders', that is, to assimilate Japan's Taiwanese subjects only at the lower levels of the social order.[5] Certainly those Taiwanese who could afford it preferred to seek higher education in Japan, where they got a better training, but also in some cases an injection of ideas inappropriate to their status as colonials. Some of them founded a political association in 1920, designed to campaign for equality and partial home rule. Liberal rather than radical, its members accepted that the Japanese connection would be retained; but there were other groups in Taiwan itself, organizing peasant protests on the Korean model, which set their sights on

---

[5] Tsurumi, *Japanese Colonial Education*, 145.

independence. Effective and often ruthless action by the Japanese police denied both movements any real success.

Things were different in Korea, in that Japanese rule there met at all times with very much greater opposition. This to some extent reflected differences in pre-colonial political consciousness: Korea had for centuries been an independent kingdom; Taiwan was a remote and little-regarded Chinese province. It was also because Japanese officials failed to secure the acquiescence or co-operation of Korean élites in the way they were able to do in Taiwan. Yet the policies pursued in the two colonies were much the same.[6] In Korea, too, a land survey, carried out after annexation in 1910, increased government revenue and clarified ownership rights to the benefit of Korean landlords. In 1914 about half the arable land was owned by 2 per cent of rural households. It also made land available for Japanese purchase. Not a great deal of it was actually taken up by Japanese, despite strenuous efforts from Tokyo to encourage them: approximately 8 per cent of farm land was in Japanese possession in 1930. All the same, their privileges caused political resentment. So did the fact that the Korean gentry lost their hereditary access to government office, which became effectively a Japanese monopoly. In consequence, the discontents which had existed before 1910, manifested in bitter risings, continued in the colonial period. One nation-wide demonstration in favour of independence, which took place on 1 March 1919 (the March First Movement), was suppressed with over 2,000 casualties. Thereafter a Korean government in exile was established, first in China, then in the United States.

In these circumstances, Japanese attempts to create loyal subjects of the emperor in Korea through the education system were almost inevitably unsuccessful. Primary schools were set up, teaching much the same curriculum as in Taiwan, but only a tiny percentage of Koreans attended them. Private Korean schools in the Confucian tradition remained much more popular, despite close Japanese control of what was taught in them. They suffered a particular disadvantage, like their equivalents in Taiwan, from the fact that they afforded an inadequate

---

[6] On colonial policies in Korea, see the articles in Andrew C. Nahm, *Korea under Japanese colonial rule* (1973), especially Chul Won Kang, 'An analysis of Japanese policy and economic change in Korea', and Eugene C. Kim, 'Education in Korea under Japanese colonial rule'. See also Yunshik Chang, 'Colonization as planned change: the Korean case' (1971), and E. Patricia Tsurumi, 'Colonial education in Korea and Taiwan' (1984).

preparation for secondary and higher education, when this became available in the 1920s; but even Japanese pressure to bring them more into line with the state schools—including the use of approved textbooks and the teaching of a Japanese ethics course—did little to reduce their appeal. Nationalism proved a more powerful attraction than modernity in a society in which a Korean's opportunities were limited, whatever his skills.

Colonial economies

If Korea proved difficult for Japan to govern, its economic resources, like Taiwan's, made the effort worth while. In Chapter 9 we examined the nature of colonial trade, which was the most obvious index of the value of colonies to the homeland. It is now necessary to consider the economic development which made the trade possible. Many features of it were similar to those of Japan's own modernization after 1870. In particular, government played an important part in it: indirectly, by providing the legal and fiscal framework within which the economy operated; directly, by investing in infrastructure, especially transport and communications, and by facilitating the spread of new technology. Where industrial investment was needed on a large scale, it was commonly provided by major Japanese firms, many of which were *zaibatsu* subsidiaries or affiliates. Members of the colonial population, having restricted access to capital, were involved, if at all, in smaller operations, as were individual Japanese. The parameters of policy were set by Japan's own needs, above all those for markets and foodstuffs, rather than by any considerations of colonial welfare. By the end of the 1920s, over 90 per cent of Korea's exports went to Japan. Two-thirds were foodstuffs. For Taiwan, a smaller proportion of exports went to Japan (78 per cent), but even more was foodstuffs (85 per cent). The amount of food available daily to Koreans at this time (1925–9) has been estimated to have been on average 1,924 calories per person. This was about 10 per cent less than it had been in 1910–14. Taiwanese did a little better: 2,208 calories, which was about 10 per cent more than at the earlier date. These quantities were close to subsistence level—though the figure for Japanese in the home islands (at approximately 2,300 calories) was not much higher.[7]

Turning in more detail to Taiwan, the first point to note is that the

---

[7] Samuel Pao-san Ho, 'Colonialism and development: Korea, Taiwan, and Kwantung' (1984), 378–9, and Tables, 396–8.

Governor-General and his officials not only achieved fiscal self-sufficiency, but also ran an export balance in trade with the homeland.[8] This balance reached over 36 million yen from total exports of 130 million in 1915–19, then 65 million yen from exports of 256 million in 1925–9. One result was capital accumulation, which financed government investment. Between 1905 and 1930 it was usual for the Government-General to allocate one-quarter to one-third of its expenditure to capital projects. Of this, something like 50 per cent went to the development of railways and ports. By 1929 there were over a thousand miles of railway on the island, half of it government-owned. Expenditure on irrigation, the other main item, rose from three million yen in 1905–9 to 55 million in 1925–9. Until 1920 most of the funds came from government. Thereafter there was a sharp rise in the total, an increasing proportion of which (70 per cent at the end of the period) was provided by rural savings, mobilized through semi-official irrigation associations.

Better access to the ports, plus an increase in the area of land under irrigation, greatly raised the production of Taiwan's two main export crops, rice and sugar. In annual averages, the area planted to rice increased from 432,000 hectares in 1901–10 to 551,000 hectares in 1921–30. Production rose from 571,000 tonnes to 879,000 over the same period. This to some extent reflects improved export opportunities, due to the reduction of Japanese tariffs on colonial rice after urban rice riots in 1918. The growth in the amount of sugar produced was even more rapid: 82,000 tonnes a year from 30,000 hectares in 1901–10; 498,00 tonnes from 115,000 hectares in 1921–30. By value, Taiwan's total production of all goods doubled between 1915–19 and 1925–9. Throughout, just over 50 per cent was in agriculture, just under 40 per cent in manufacturing. Two-thirds of manufacturing, however, was accounted for by food products, including sugar. This emphasizes how much the colony remained dependent on its two main crops.

Sugar (like Japan's own silk exports) required processing. As the export of it grew, so the primitive methods of refining employed before

---

[8] On economic development in Taiwan, see the following articles in Myers and Peattie, *Japanese Colonial Empire*: Ho, 'Colonialism and development'; Ramon H. Myers and Yamada Saburō, 'Agricultural development in the empire'; Mizoguchi Toshiyuki and Yamamoto Yūzō, 'Capital formation in Taiwan and Korea'. More detailed studies are Barclay, *Colonial development*, chaps. 1–3; Samuel Pao-san Ho, *Economic development of Taiwan* (1978), chaps. 3–6; Hosokawa Karoku, *Gendai Nihon Bummei-shi: Shokumin-shi* (1941), part 2; and Mizoguchi Toshiyuki, *Taiwan Chōsen no keizai seichō* (1975).

1895 gave way to the use of modern factories, requiring inputs of capital and technology. The companies which established them were mostly Japanese, often linked with *zaibatsu* firms, such as Mitsui. By 1910 there were five large Japanese companies of this kind, representing private investment of the order of 20–30 million yen. Thereafter they continued to expand, largely, it seems, by the investment of retained profits. There were other comparable Japanese companies in construction and public works. Ōkura, for example, which started in the timber and construction business, then moved briefly into sugar-refining, had almost a quarter of its overseas investments in Taiwan in the years 1912–26, that is, approximately 10 million yen out of a total of 41 million.[9]

In 1929 the paid-up capital of joint-stock companies in Taiwan came to almost 288 million yen. The bulk of it (199 million yen) was in manufacturing companies, of which 90 per cent by value were Japanese-owned. Population figures tell a similar story. The 1930 census showed a population of just under 4.6 million, including 228,000 Japanese. Of Taiwanese males, 68 per cent were engaged in agriculture and forestry, 10 per cent in commerce, 2.7 per cent in government and the professions. Of Japanese males, 45 per cent were in government and the professions, 43 per cent in transport, manufacturing, and commerce. In other words, Japanese residents were predominantly officials, teachers, business men, technicians, and clerical staff. Taiwanese provided the agricultural and unskilled labour.

One difference between Taiwan and Korea was that the latter's economy had been much influenced by Japan for a decade or more before the country was annexed. By 1910 Japanese had begun to acquire farmland in Korea: the Oriental Development Company, formed in 1908 to facilitate Japanese settlement there, had already bought 8,500 hectares and rented 7,400 more. Through the Dai Ichi Bank Japanese financiers had for some years managed the Korean currency, a function later taken over by another Japanese bank, the Bank of Chōsen (Korea), which was established in 1909. Several Japanese agricultural and industrial banks also began operating in the peninsula during the protectorate. Japanese railways completed by 1910 included the main trunk route running from Pusan via Seoul to the Manchurian frontier at Uiju. Work had started on the line from Seoul to Wonsan, though it was not to be finished until 1914. These

---

[9] *Ōkura zaibatsu no kenkyū*, 85–96.

railways were run by private companies, but they came under Japanese government supervision after Japan's own main lines were nationalized in 1906. They were brought into public ownership after annexation.[10]

Accordingly, the new Government-General, replacing the Residency, inherited a situation in which some progress had been made towards reshaping the Korean economy. Much still needed to be done, however. Surveying the land and reorganizing taxation of it was to take until 1918. Moreover, although the country was better provided with railways than Taiwan—1,750 miles of government-owned lines in 1930—it had less irrigation. And there was no export surplus to use for funding an investment programme. Trade with Japan was consistently in deficit. Government expenditure proved much heavier than in Taiwan, partly because of the high cost of suppressing political unrest, partly because strategic considerations dictated more spending on transport and communications. Korea therefore continued to need an inflow of Japanese capital to provide for its investment needs.[11]

A relatively small part of the investment went into agriculture, which failed in consequence to match the growth of Taiwan's.[12] This was in spite of similarities in social background between the two. In Korea, tenancy and share-cropping seem to have done more to inhibit growth because of the absence of 'improving' landlords. In fact, it was not until the change in Japanese tariff policy concerning rice imports after 1918, coinciding with the completion of the land survey, that there was any significant degree of agrarian modernization in Korea (more irrigation; better seed strains; more widespread use of fertilizer). There was a 6 per cent increase in the area under rice cultivation between 1919 and 1929, a slightly larger increase in the crop. Already by 1929, however, a slump in farm prices in Japan was reducing Korean incentives. Though the total Korean rice crop in 1929 was 8 per cent up on that of 1919, its value had dropped by 38 per cent (from 516 million yen to 322 million).

Despite their technological backwardness, Korean farmers exported an average of 5.2 million *koku* of rice a year to Japan in 1925–9, com-

[10] On Korea in the period 1905–10, see Conroy, *Japanese seizure*, 448–52, 473–6, 480–4; and Duus, 'Economic dimensions', 148–61.

[11] Investment in Korea is discussed in Mizoguchi and Yamamoto, 'Capital formation', and in Young-Iob Chung, 'Japanese investment in Korea 1904–1945' (1973).

[12] On Korean agriculture, see chiefly Myers and Yamada, 'Agricultural development', and Chang, 'Colonization as planned change'. Schumpeter, *Industrialization*, 287–305, though concerned primarily with the years after 1930, also has useful material on the earlier period.

pared with 1.8 million in 1915–19. This was 50 per cent of Japanese imports, over 45 per cent of Korean production. It was made possible by a reduction in consumption among the Korean population. Yunshik Chang has calculated[13] that per capita consumption of rice in Korea, taking 1915–19 as 100, dropped to 63 in the worst slump years of 1930–4. Nor did the use of coarse grains as a substitute fully compensate for this, since consumption of these also fell towards the end of the period.

Little of Korea's agricultural production can be attributed to Japanese settlers, despite early hopes that they would provide an important stimulus to it. The Oriental Development Company, which continued to receive a modest government subsidy for several years after 1910, had been responsible by 1926 for the emigration of some 20,000 Japanese to Korea, about 85 per cent being farmer-cultivators, the rest small landlords. From 1917 it extended its activities into semi-colonial areas (Manchuria, China, the Pacific islands) and fields of investment other than land. Its capitalization was raised to 50 million yen in 1919 from the original figure of 10 million. In the event, however, it suffered heavily from the post-war slump and its fortunes did not revive until after 1930. True, it raised loans in America in 1923 and 1928 totalling almost 40 million dollars, but these chiefly paved the way for it to play a part in the next phase of Japanese expansion.

Most Japanese residents in Korea were not engaged in agriculture. In 1930 there were half a million of them, that is, two-and-a-half per cent of the population. They held three-quarters of the senior posts in government, three-fifths of the junior ones. They dominated the managerial and technical jobs in transport, communications, and manufacturing industry. They controlled the most important banking and export businesses. In other words, they did in Korea what their compatriots did in Taiwan.

There is nevertheless a distinction to be made between the two colonial economies. Korea's rice exports to Japan were much larger than Taiwan's—two-and-a-half times as much in 1929 and 1930—but Korea had no other crop as valuable as Taiwan sugar. Soya beans comprised the next largest item of Korean exports in 1929 (6.7 per cent), followed by raw silk (5.8 per cent). More significant for the future, though not yet fully exploited, was the country's mineral wealth. Korea had always been a producer of gold. Increasingly it was

[13] Chang, 'Colonization as planned change', 173–4.

becoming a source of coal and iron: iron ore, pig-iron, and coal together accounted for 3.3 per cent of exports in 1929. Coal sent to Japan topped 3 million tonnes that year. Such exports were to become of major significance when the emphasis within imperial policy shifted towards industrial self-sufficiency after 1930. .

Japan's other overseas territories can be examined more briefly. In economic matters, Kwantung cannot usefully be treated apart from Manchuria, which was discussed in connection with China in the previous chapter; but Shantung, which was also part of China, needs some additional comment. In 1914 Japan took over the German railway there and ran it profitably, using staff transferred from Manchuria. By 1917 its annual freight and passenger receipts came to over 8 million yen. Several large Japanese companies established branches in the province, including Mitsui and Mantetsu, as did the Yokohama Specie Bank and the Bank of Chōsen. However, the majority of Japanese enterprises in Shantung were small, engaged in salt production or the manufacture of consumer goods (flour, beer, soap, matches). There were no less than fifty-two Japanese companies in Kiaochow by 1918 and approximately 25,000 Japanese residents in the province as a whole. Shipping came to be dominated by Japan, largely at the expense of Germany. Thus the economic rights which Japan retained in the area, when agreement was reached with China about its political future in 1922, were valuable.[14]

The Pacific islands were much less so. They produced sugar, mostly through a Japanese company (Nankō), which used contract labour from depressed rural districts in Japan. They had a limited trade in tropical products, monopolized by another Japanese company (Nambō). They afforded a living to Japanese shopkeepers, restaurateurs, and brothel proprietors. None of this was as important as their potential strategic value, though it served to support almost 20,000 Japanese residents in the islands by 1930.[15]

Karafuto[16] was at first prized chiefly for its fisheries, which had been used by Japanese since the early nineteenth century. By 1915, ten years after the territory had been ceded by Russia, they accounted for

[14] Yuan, 'Japanese intervention in Shantung', 24–7. German economic penetration of Shantung before 1914 is examined in John E. Schrecker, *Imperialism and Chinese Nationalism: Germany in Shantung* (1971), chap. 6.

[15] See Mark R. Peattie, 'The Nan'yō: Japan in the South Pacific' (1984).

[16] John J. Stephan, *Sakhalin* (1971), 87–90, 98–107.

over 60 per cent of its income. Gradually, however, they were over-taken in value by forestry and pulp production, handled by a number of large Japanese companies, of which Mitsui, through its Ōji Paper sub-sidiary, had the greatest share. Mitsui also dominated the coal-mining in the island, though the development of this was handicapped by poor transport facilities before 1930. In addition, Karafuto became the means of access for Japan to the oilfields of northern Sakhalin, which was still in Russian possession. Negotiations, originally with the White Russian regime at Alexandrovsk, later with the Soviets, gave a Japan-ese consortium, which included the Mitsubishi and Kuhara com-panies, a concession to work some of the Sakhalin wells. Between 1920 and 1925 Japan took about 100,000 tonnes of oil a year from this source, that is, 12 per cent of its domestic consumption.

If one disregards the comparatively small amounts of coal and iron from Korea and oil from Sakhalin, Japan's dependent territories in 1930 remained primarily a market and a source of food. Tight political controls and superior economic organization enabled Japanese com-panies and individuals to take major profits from them. Something less than a million Japanese—excluding army units—had gone to various parts of the empire to make a living, one which was very much better than the colonial peoples had, or than they themselves would have enjoyed at home. The majority did not settle permanently. Like Euro-peans in Africa and India and south-east Asia, they went home when they retired. And despite talk of 'integration' and 'assimilation' in Tokyo, Japanese overseas tended to lead lives that were separate, as well as privileged. The regime they imposed on their subjects was harsh. In fact, there was little in Japan's colonial experience that led naturally to Asian partnership, or co-prosperity, or the co-ordination of industrial growth. For the origins of these we must look to the Japanese relationship with China.

11

The Treaty Port System in Jeopardy, 1918–1931

THE First World War gave Japan both the opportunity and the financial resources by which to build a new relationship with China: a bilateral one, falling outside the multilateral norms of co-operative imperialism. It proved abortive, as we have seen (Chapter 8). The presumption was, therefore, that earlier patterns would be reasserted, as soon as the end of hostilities left the powers free to resume their activities in East Asia.

This presumption proved to be in some respects misleading. True, Japanese policy-makers after 1918 faced a number of familiar dilemmas. What weight should they give to the Open Door in China and its implications of working with the West for the sake of Japan's commercial advantage? How far could Japanese strategic interests be given priority in Manchuria without putting economic interests at risk elsewhere? Could the powers, as well as China, be brought to accept the more prominent role which Japan had come to play on the mainland since 1915? Yet if the questions were familiar, the international context within which answers to them had to be found was not. There had been a major redistribution of strength and political influence in the previous four years. What is more, it was no longer possible to take for granted an unqualified acceptance of the treaty port system as the framework within which relationships must be set.

One prominent change related to Russia. The 1917 Revolution there had immediately posed a threat to Japan's position in Manchuria. Instead of a rival, who needed to be watched with care, but with whom it was possible to find common ground in defence of the notion of spheres of influence, there was now disorder. If, as seemed likely, the disorder ended in Bolshevik victory, the Amur frontier would pass into the hands of a regime hostile in principle to imperialism. China, still locked in civil war, was fertile soil for Bolshevik propaganda and political manoeuvring. In Korea there was continuing unrest. In Japan the post-war slump in manufacturing industry had prompted a wave of strikes and extensive unionization of labour. In such conditions the treaty port system seemed to many Japanese too loose an arrangement to guarantee security. More positive intervention in the affairs of north-east Asia, first to check the Bolsheviks, then to prevent the spread of Bolshevik ideology, was, they believed, a condition of their country's safety.

With respect to China Proper—the expression implied that Manchuria was not part of it—there had been other changes that increased the pressures on Japan. Germany and France, which had in the past been willing both to create spheres of influence and to tolerate those of others, had been weakened, the one by defeat, the other by the cost of victory. Their participation in China diplomacy was likely to be minimal for some time to come. Britain, a long-standing opponent of monopoly rights, must be expected to try to regain the ground it had lost in China; and since that ground had mostly been lost to Japan, the prospects for Anglo-Japanese relations were uncertain. There remained the United States, which had from the beginning been the chief spokesman for the doctrines of the Open Door. America was very much stronger, militarily and economically, than it had been before 1914. Nor did it show any signs of being willing to approve an adjustment of the treaty port system in ways that would suit Japan. Moreover, under Woodrow Wilson's leadership it was likely to demand much more insistently that Tokyo observe the principle of Chinese sovereignty. Thus Japan could no longer count on international concern for shared treaty rights as a support for its own ambitions. On the contrary, British and American statesmen were coming to see the treaty port system as a device for putting restraints upon Japan.

A third new factor was the enhanced importance and stridency of Chinese nationalism. Stimulated first by the Twenty-one Demands, then by Japan's attempt to incorporate provisions about Shantung into the peace settlement at Versailles, hostility to imperialism became a major element in Chinese politics. The fall of the Manchus had put the treaties at risk for lack of a Chinese government able to enforce them. Nationalism threatened them economically through anti-foreign strikes and boycotts. One part of the story of the 1920s is the failure of the powers to agree on what to do about this, so that the treaty structure gradually crumbled, leaving trade and investment without their customary props. Japan, in particular, was left with a stark choice: whether to acquiesce in a deterioration of its position in China, or to act unilaterally to prevent it. This chapter will examine the changes in international circumstance, in the light of which that choice was made.

Japan and the Russian Revolution

Despite the shifts in China policy under the Ōkuma and Terauchi cabinets, Japanese assumptions about the special importance of Manchuria had remained consistent. Apart from Shantung, it was the subject of the most explicit sections of the Twenty-one Demands. Three of the Nishihara loans had related to Manchurian mines and railways. In negotiations with Russia in 1916, Japan had successfully pressed for the right to purchase part of the railway line running northwards from Changchun, a move designed, as Foreign Minister Ishii Kikujirō described it, to ensure that 'all the natural resources in the Kirin plain will fall into our hands'.[1] A few months later Japan demanded that China approve the stationing of Japanese police in south Manchuria and the employment of Japanese army officers as advisers there. Peking refused. Tokyo let the matter drop. Nevertheless, the incident had shown that the aims set out in Group V of the Twenty-one Demands were not entirely forgotten.

Given these precedents, it is not surprising that Japanese leaders found some difficulty in deciding whether events in Russia at the end of 1917 were to be taken as an opportunity or a threat.[2] Yamagata Aritomo saw the revolution as confirmation that Japan would face greater problems over European rivalries when the war was over. Russia would no longer be a potential ally. It followed, he wrote in January 1918, that the Sino-Japanese connection should be made still stronger, even to the point of preparing plans for joint military action in the north. Terauchi went along with this, since it chimed with his desire for partnership with Tuan Ch'i-jui.

A different view was taken by Tanaka Giichi, who was Vice-chief of the General Staff under Terauchi, then War Minister under his successor, Hara Kei.[3] He had long held that Manchuria's economic resources were vital to Japan. In order to ensure access to them, he believed, it would be necessary to detach Manchuria from China and put it under Japanese control, preferably in association with Korea. Confusion and disorder along the Amur offered a means of bringing

---

[1] Quoted in Kajima, *Diplomacy*, III, 239.
[2] Views are summarised in Kitaoka, *Nihon rikugun*, 215–17.
[3] On Tanaka's role in Manchurian affairs before 1921, see Morton, *Tanaka*, 25–45.

this objective nearer. Hence he proposed that military assistance be offered to anti-Bolshevik Russians in the Siberian region, for the purpose of establishing an independent state which would be willing to co-operate with Japan. Behind such a buffer Japan could extend its hold on Manchuria and work with China to develop the region's wealth.

In practice, choosing between the cautious and the adventurous alternatives proposed by Yamagata and Tanaka involved an assessment of the likely diplomatic repercussions.[4] The army, prompted by Tanaka, refused to be held back by them. When news came of the Russian Revolution, it entered into direct negotiations with China's military leaders—it was only later that the Japanese Foreign Ministry gave its sanction to them—with the intention of arranging for defence of the northern frontiers. Some of the items it put forward proved unacceptable: for example, that Japan should exercise overall command; that operations should be zoned in such a way as to leave northern Manchuria to Japanese forces; and that any agreement should endure for as long as there existed an 'enemy' in Siberia. A Chinese counter-proposal that operations within China's borders be carried out only by Chinese troops was similarly objectionable to Japan. In May 1918, however, an agreement was at last reached, providing for close co-ordination of planning, military movements, and munitions, so long as both countries remained at war with Germany. Japan promised to withdraw as soon as the need for action ended.

These were not the only initiatives looking towards some kind of Japanese intervention in Asiatic Russia. During February and March 1918, Araki Sadao, then a lieutenant-colonel on the General Staff, arranged for arms to be supplied to an anti-Bolshevik Cossack force in a deal financed by the Kuhara *zaibatsu* company. Dmitrii Horvat, managing director of the Trans-Siberian Railway, also turned to Japan for help at this time, though when he found that Tanaka's promises of arms were not backed by the Foreign Ministry's spokesmen he did not pursue the matter. The Japanese Navy, not to be left out, sent two ships to Vladivostock under the command of Katō Kanji. His instructions—which, he was told, stated the navy's views, not necessarily those of the cabinet—included this sentence: 'To the Bolsheviks under Lenin we shall of course give no assistance, but shall destroy

[4] For discussion of Japanese policy debates concerning the subsequent Siberian expedition, see James W. Morley, *The Japanese thrust into Siberia 1918* (1957); Hosoya Chihiro, 'Origin of the Siberian intervention, 1917–1918' (1958); same, 'Japanese documents on the Siberian Intervention, 1917–1922, part I' (1960).

their power as quickly as possible and hope to establish a government under the moderates.'[5]

The army's intentions were very much the same. A secret committee under Tanaka's chairmanship produced plans in March 1918 for dispatching two separate forces to 'maintain peace in the Far East by occupying various strategic points in Russian territory east of Lake Baikal and along the Chinese Eastern Railway'.[6] One, consisting of two divisions, was to advance from Vladivostock to Khabarovsk, then move westward along the Amur and the Trans-Siberian. The other, mustering five divisions, was to pass through Manchuria and Mongolia to attack Chita. Both were to co-operate with Chinese units and give help to suitable groups of Russians.

All this was in the established tradition of army 'independence' in Manchuria. Equally familiar was the cabinet's preoccupation with the reactions of the powers. The first non-Japanese proposals for intervention in Russia had been made in December 1917 by France and Britain, who were concerned both to halt the Bolsheviks and to maintain the eastern front against Germany. They envisaged action by the United States and Japan to keep open a supply route for this purpose through Vladivostock. Neither Washington nor Tokyo responded favourably. Woodrow Wilson was opposed to intervention in principle and wanted 'the most explicit assurances' that Japan had no ulterior motives in Siberia. Hara Kei, who was to be Japan's next Prime Minister, made it clear that he was unwilling to act contrary to American wishes. So was Yamagata Aritomo, because he believed that Japan could not intervene effectively in Russia without outside help. 'Our armed forces are strong enough to combat the enemy single-handed', he wrote, but 'we should count greatly upon assistance from the United States and Great Britain so far as military *matériel* and financial backing are concerned.'[7]

Terauchi's Foreign Minister, Motono Ichirō, was an interventionist—like Tanaka, he looked forward to eventual Japanese control of the Amur basin through a White Russian puppet state—but he was reluctant to work with America from fear of opening the way to an extension of American influence. His successor, Gotō Shimpei, who came to office in April 1918, was committed to the same broad objec-

---

[5] Morley, *Japanese thrust*, 64.
[6] Text in Hosoya, 'Japanese documents', 34–5.
[7] Quoted in Hosoya, 'Origin', 102.

tives, though he thought more in terms of railway and mining rights, as befitted his experience in Manchuria.[8] He was also more flexible about how to get them. This made him willing to subscribe to a deviously worded undertaking to the United States, which denied any intention of interfering in Russia's internal affairs and limited the troops to be employed to approximately one division from each country. Since Wilson's objections were simultaneously weakened by allied proposals for rescuing Czech forces, which were known to be making their way eastward towards Vladivostock, plans for an expedition were finally put in hand in August 1918.

It proved to be a disaster in almost all respects. The operations of American and Japanese units were badly co-ordinated; their Russian collaborators gave the impression of being as hostile to each other as they were to the Bolsheviks; and none of them seemed to have popular support. As a result, the Soviets made steady headway against them. The only achievement on the credit side was that the Czechs fought their way to Vladivostock. Among the allies the enterprise fell apart in bickering and recrimination, not least because the Japanese were accused of bad faith on every side. They had 70,000 men in Russia by the end of the year, their earlier promises about limiting the number having been disregarded on grounds of 'operational necessity.' This force constantly interfered in the political and economic affairs of the region. Indeed, the instructions its commander had been given by the General Staff in August and September made it clear that this was what it was meant to do. He was 'to maintain peace and order'. He was to 'facilitate the activities of Japanese officials and civilians', including 'the conduct of business and the development of natural resources'. He was to work closely with the Chinese, 'so as to enhance Japan's position in its future competition with the Western powers in China'.[9] In other words, he was to carry out the substance of the plans which had originally been devised by Tanaka, Motono, Gotō, and their subordinates.

Such military adventures ominously foreshadowed later years. This time they failed, however. In June 1920, when the Americans decided to withdraw, the Japanese stayed on; but Yamagata's doubts about going it alone were to prove well founded. Faced by mounting costs and unacceptable casualties, Japan pulled back from the Amur in

[8] On Gotō, see Morley, *Japanese thrust*, 213–18.
[9] Hosoya, 'Japanese documents', 45–8, *passim*.

October 1922, then early in 1925 evacuated northern Sakhalin, which had been occupied in 1920. It left behind, not a puppet state, but a hostile Soviet, already firmly established. Even the Chinese Eastern Railway reverted to Russia, albeit shorn of its non-commercial rights and functions.

Since intervention in Siberia had been undertaken, not only by way of expansion, but also for the purpose of consolidating Japan's hold on Manchuria, withdrawal still left some issues unresolved. In the spring of 1921, when withdrawal had begun to seem likely, Hara Kei and his Foreign Minister, Uchida Yasuya, had turned their attention to them. Their options were limited. To rely on Tuan Ch'i-jui's goodwill as a defence against Chinese subversion or Soviet attack was demonstrably unwise, since his authority inside China was being widely threatened by the nationalists. Nor did the treaty powers seem likely to be of any more help in Manchuria than they had been in Siberia. The most practical course, therefore, appeared to be to look to Chang Tso-lin, who had emerged as a war-lord in south Manchuria after Yüan Shih-k'ai's death.[10] Chang had control of Mukden; he was an evident anti-Bolshevik; and he had shown himself willing to co-operate with Japan in return for supplies of arms. His principal disadvantage was political ambition, manifested in a readiness to compete with Tuan Ch'i-jui for possession of Peking. This was not only potentially embarrassing—it carried a risk of hostilities between two of Japan's friends—but might also drag Manchuria into China's civil war. Hence Japanese officials found it difficult to decide how to deal with him: whether to accept him as a substitute for Tuan in every sense, encouraging him to establish a government south of the Great Wall, as well as north of it; or to try to restrict him to Manchuria.

Hara and his colleagues settled for the latter, that is, a Manchurian puppet, dissociated as far as possible from the politics of the rest of China. Cabinet resolutions in May 1921 set out a number of basic pro-positions: that Japan had special rights in Manchuria, strategically and economically; that these rights had been established by treaties, con-cluded with China, and must be defended by upholding those treaties, not by separating the Manchurian provinces from the rest of the country; and that within these constraints Japan must seek to develop

---

[10] His career is examined in detail in Gavan McCormack, *Chang Tso-lin in Northeast China, 1911–1928* (1977); see especially chap. 2. On the Hara cabinet's policy towards him, see also John W. Young, 'The Hara cabinet and Chang Tso-lin, 1920–1' (1972).

the area's economy through 'coexistence and co-prosperity' (*kyōson-kyōei*).[11] Thereafter, a conference of officials concerned with north-east Asia quicky agreed that Chang Tso-lin's role should be that of maintaining Manchuria's stability. He would be provided with muni-tions and given help in manufacturing his own. He would receive financial and industrial support, preferably through joint Sino-Japan-ese companies. He would not, however, be encouraged to make a bid to become ruler of all China. In sum, the affairs of Manchuria were not at this time to be made the occasion for a challenge to the treaty port system as such, provided Japan's interests there could be sufficiently guaranteed within it.

Japan and the treaty powers

In renewing their commitment to the treaty port system in these terms, Japan's post-war leaders took it for granted that they were doing so on the basis of the improved position Japan had won since the Twenty-one Demands. The other treaty powers were not easily persuaded that this was appropriate. The United States, in particular, had come in the interval to regard Japan as a rival, rather than a colleague. Robert Lansing, Woodrow Wilson's Secretary of State, believed that the further development of the Chinese economy was a task for which America was uniquely equipped, technically and financially, but that it might well be deprived of the chance to carry it out by Japanese politi-cal hegemony there. He therefore directed his policy towards prevent-ing Japan from securing exclusive rights, except in Manchuria, where it seemed already too late to do so.

He also sought a Japanese undertaking, denying monopoly inten-tions. The occasion for this came in 1917, when Ishii Kikujirō was sent to Washington to win American recognition of the gains Japan had made in China in the previous two or three years. Ishii offered a pro-mise that American economic activities would not be hindered by Japan. He welcomed the co-operation of the United States in develop-ing 'China's vast natural resources'. He insisted, however, on Japan's 'special interests' in that country. These were not exclusively econ-omic, he said. They included also an element of Japanese tutelage:

Internal disturbances in, or a collapse of, China would have no direct

---

[11] Cabinet resolution of 13 May 1921, in *NGNB*, I, documents, 523–4. See also reso-lutions of 17 May, ibid., 524–5.

consequences for other countries, but were of vital concern to Japan . . . [because] if Japan cannot see sound administration for the defence and general safety of China, she cannot feel secure in her own defence. This is why Japan deems it a natural obligation, without prejudice to China's independence, to counsel that country in administrative reform and assist by supplying instructors.[12]

A corollary was that the powers should not seek to influence China against Japan, nor challenge Japanese leadership in East Asia.

Lansing was willing to go some way towards compromise on the issue of Manchuria, but even on this his freedom of action was limited by Wilson's insistence that the question of the Open Door was one of 'high moral principle'. As a result, the Lansing–Ishii talks produced little more than platitudes, expressed in a dangerously vague joint statement of 2 November 1917. It affirmed that 'territorial propinquity creates special interests between countries'. And it acknowledged that Japan had such interests in China, 'particularly in the part to which her possessions are contiguous'.

When the war ended, Lansing went with Wilson to Versailles, convinced that the only way of ensuring a welcome for American enterprise in China was by openly defending Chinese interests against Japan. On these grounds he was prepared to oppose the Japanese claim to German rights in Shantung. Wilson, on the other hand, because he was more anxious to secure a world settlement and set up the League of Nations, wanted Japanese co-operation. Accordingly he accepted a compromise formula whereby Japan agreed, though without specifyng a date, 'to hand back the Shantung peninsula in full sovereignty to China, retaining only the economic privileges granted to Germany'. Since China rejected this clause in the peace treaty, however, the issue remained an obstacle to both Sino-Japanese and American-Japanese accord.

The tension between Japan and America emerged also in attempts to reconstitute the international bank consortium.[13] The United States had withdrawn from it in 1913 because of the political implications of the Reorganization Loan (Chapter 9), but by the later years of the war

[12] Kajima, *Diplomacy*, III, 310–11. On Lansing, see Burton F. Beers, *Vain Endeavor* (1962).
[13] See Warren I. Cohen, 'America's New Order for East Asia: The Four Power Financial Consortium and China, 1919–1946' (1982); and Roberta A. Dayer, *Bankers and Diplomats in China 1917–1925* (1981). These two works differ sharply on the interpretation of American policy, but not in ways that greatly affect a discussion of Japanese imperialism.

it was being urged—by China, among others—to reverse that decision. Lansing favoured the idea of rejoining the consortium, because this would not only make sure that China had a source of funds other than Japan, but would also create openings for American business. Despite Wilson's continued misgivings—he insisted that steps be taken 'to protect the Chinese government against such unconscionable arrangements as were contemplated by the former consortium'—talks during 1917 and 1918 led to an agreement with the French and British banks. The Japanese were admitted early in the following year. One motive for this was a British belief that membership would make Japan susceptible to pressure: as the Foreign Secretary, Lord Curzon, put it, once in, Japan could be told 'that she must fall into line . . . or else the Powers concerned would fight her commercially'.[14]

In the event this turned out to be overoptimistic. The American government's plans included one for centralizing the Chinese railway system, preferably under the supervision of American engineers, using American equipment, and paid for by an American loan arranged through the consortium. One difficulty about it was that American bankers, faced by a variety of attractive investment opportunities elsewhere in the world—including Japan, which they knew was politically stable—were unwilling to put up the sort of capital needed in China without a guarantee from their government. Another was that American and European business men were much more ready to accept a partnership with Japan on the Asian mainland than the State Department and its advisers were. Consequently, when Japan demanded the exclusion of Manchuria and Inner Mongolia from the consortium's activities, Thomas Lamont, manager of the American Banking Group, warned Washington that his colleagues would certainly not want 'to put money there unless Japan desires to go along.'[15] A face-saving agreement was then worked out by the bankers, whereby Japanese interests, including the South Manchuria Railway—but not the region as such—were to remain outside the consortium's terms of reference. In other words, the bank consortium proved ineffective as a weapon against Japanese imperialism.

Japanese fears and suspicions on the subject of a possible East–West confrontation in the post-war world were given impetus not only by the State Department's apparent hostility, but also by British attitudes

[14] Quoted in Nish, *Alliance in Decline*, 287.
[15] Dayer, *Bankers*, 78.

towards renewal of the Anglo-Japanese alliance.[16] When London began to give consideration to renewal during 1920, objections to it came both from the Peking government (which held that the alliance had encouraged Japan in actions detrimental to Chinese sovereignty) and from British chambers of commerce in China (citing the damage to trade that arose from Chinese resentment). The Foreign Office found their pleas unconvincing, but this was not because it regarded Japan as a satisfactory ally. Curzon supported renewal on the grounds that the existence of the alliance made it easier 'to keep a watch upon [Japan's] movements in China . . . and to exercise a moderating influence on her policy generally'. Victor Wellesley, head of the Far East department, expressed himself as being in favour of a tripartite arrangement, bringing in the United States, to replace the alliance. It would, he said, put Britain and America 'in a far stronger position to exercise an effective restraint on Japanese ambitions and counter the insidious ramifications of their policy of peaceful penetration'.[17]

A Foreign Office committee, examining the options in the winter of 1920–1, came down on Wellesley's side. Its report[18] recognized that Japan 'stands little chance of industrial survival unless she can obtain control over the resources of China'. However, such an objective, if attained, might well make China a Japanese 'vassal state'. For Britain to give the appearance of helping to make it one would be disastrous for Britain's China trade. On the other hand, the use of force to prevent it was not a feasible alternative. Instead, the committee argued, 'the best safeguard against a danger which lies as much in the weakness of China as in the aggressive tendencies of Japan is to be found in a constructive policy for the rehabilitation of China'. Since Britain, exhausted by war, could not accomplish this alone, a triple entente, involving Japan and America, seemed the best way forward. This meant that the alliance would have to be sacrificed.

Curzon was not altogether persuaded. He still saw the alliance as a useful restraint on Japan. He also believed that it had a naval value, in addition to affording some insurance against German or Russian re-entry on the Far East scene. Nevertheless, criticism of it in Canada and Australia, reinforcing the opinions of his own officials, led him to give formal notice to Japan in May 1921 that renewal could not be taken to

---

[16] See Nish, *Alliance in Decline*, chaps. 17 and 18; Wm. Roger Louis, *British Strategy in the Far East 1919–1939* (1971), 37–49.

[17] Quotations in Nish, *Alliance in Decline*, 296–7, 307.

[18] The text, dated 21 Jan. 1921, is in FO 371, vol. 6672.

be automatic. The Japanese cabinet was both surprised and alarmed by this. It became even more so when it was proposed to absorb the question of the alliance's future into the wider range of issues to be considered at a Pacific conference. The move looked remarkably like an Anglo-American conspiracy to isolate Japan; or in the more emotive words of Lieutenant-General Tanaka Kunishige, one of the Japanese delegates, 'an attempt to oppress the non-Anglo-Saxon races, especially the coloured races, by the two English-speaking countries, Britain and the United States'.[19]

The Washington Conference, beginning in December 1921, which was the outcome of the exchanges in the spring and summer of that year, was therefore approached by Japan's representatives in a defensive frame of mind.[20] On naval disarmament, which was a major agenda item, they accepted in principle that Japan should have a smaller tonnage of capital ships than Britain or America (the 5:5:3 ratio), but devoted a good deal of energy to ensuring that it would not thereby be too much disadvantaged in any naval conflict with them. The result was a standstill decision concerning naval fortifications in the western Pacific, other than in Japanese territory, which precluded any strengthening of Guam, Manila, and Hong Kong. Against that, from Japan's point of view, had to be set the loss of naval and financial benefits deriving from the Anglo-Japanese alliance, which was replaced by a much looser four-power agreement, signed on 13 December 1921. Under its terms, Japan, Britain, France, and the United States were bound to nothing more than consultation, in the event of disputes in East Asia.

More important for our present purpose is the manner in which the conference dealt with the affairs of China. First, there was a nine-power treaty of 6 February 1922, to which China was itself a party, binding the powers to respect China's sovereignty, independence, and 'administrative integrity'. They were to abjure spheres of influence and to observe the principle of 'equal opportunity for the commerce and industry of all nations' in China. This was in reality no more than a formal declaration in favour of the Open Door, as the United States defined it. It ignored a Chinese plea that all existing 'special rights,

[19] Quoted by Hosoya Chihiro, in Ian Nish (ed). *Anglo-Japanese Alienation 1919–1952* (1982), 8.
[20] For a general account of the Washington Conference, see Nish, *Japanese Foreign Policy*, 133–45. Relevant documents are in Kajima, *Diplomacy*, III, Part 3. The nine-power treaty was signed by the USA, Belgium, Britain, China, France, Italy, Japan, the Netherlands, and Portugal.

privileges, immunities or commitments . . . be deemed null and void'. It also set aside China's demand for the termination of foreign leases.

The Japanese delegates later reported to Tokyo that during these discussions they had not sought any specific exemption for Japan's position in Manchuria, believing not only that this was already well recognized by the powers, but also that to raise the issue might give China 'a most powerful weapon for fanning anti-Japanese feeling and thus bring about a most difficult situation for us in dealing with the problem of the Twenty-one Demands.'[21] However, they did reach an agreement over Shantung in direct talks with the Chinese. Japan undertook to return the Kiaochow leased territory to China and to withdraw its troops from the Tsingtao–Tsinan railway. The railway itself was to be purchased by China, paying in government bonds. Former German mining rights were to be transferred to a Sino-Japanese company. This left Japan with substantial economic interests in the province, plus compensation for much of the investment it had made there.

The pressures which Japan experienced during the Washington meetings contributed to a significant shift of policy by the Hara government and its successors, one aspect of which was noted in the context of Siberia. Terauchi's ideas about a special Sino-Japanese relationship were hereafter to be relegated to the background. Instead, Japanese imperialism was again to be imperialism as conceived by the Foreign Ministry. That is to say, it was to concentrate on the exploitation of privileges within the treaty port system, save only for insistence on a sphere of influence in Manchuria (the nine-power treaty notwithstanding). Its chief executant in this new phase was to be Shidehara Kijurō, a career diplomat, who had been Vice-minister in 1915–19, then ambassador in Washington. He served as Foreign Minister in 1924–7, again in 1929–31. Like Katō Takaaki, who first gave him cabinet office, he had married into the Iwasaki family, owners of Mitsubishi, a circumstance that no doubt contributed to his interest in promoting Japanese trade.

Shidehara believed that Japan's progress and stability depended on the growth of industry; that this is turn relied on foreign trade; and that it was therefore the task of diplomats to avoid any action, notably territorial expansion, likely to deprive Japan of international sympathy in

21 Kajima, *Diplomacy*, III, 526.

pursuing its economic ends. This is what he described as 'economic diplomacy'. It applied especially to China. As he observed in 1924: 'Japan, being closest to China, has an advantage by way of transport costs and she also has the greatest competitive power because of her wages. It must therefore be a priority for Japan to maintain the great market of China.'[22] In the climate of the nineteen-twenties Shidehara could count on widespread support within Japan for such a pro-gramme, though not everyone—not even Shidehara, indeed—took it to mean that Japan must abandon its claims to superior rights. Matsui Iwane of the General Staff reflected a considerable body of opinion when he interpreted Japanese policy in 1923 as being to 'substitute economic conquest for military invasion, financial influence for mili-tary control, and achieve our goals under the slogans of co-prosperity and coexistence'.[23] It was language like this, offensive as it was to Chinese of every kind, which ensured that Shidehara's diplomacy, no less than that of his predecessors, would come into conflict with the force of Chinese nationalism.

Japan and Chinese nationalism

Chinese nationalists had always regarded the treaty port system as exploitative and semi-colonial, but their resentment of it received its greatest stimulus in 1919 from the news of what had been decided at Versailles. The May Fourth Movement, which began in that year, marshalled popular indignation against the willingness of the powers to recognize Japan's wartime gains. Therafter, hostility to foreigners and foreign firms in the treaty ports was regularly manifested in the form of strikes and boycotts, riots and demonstrations. Most were accompa-nied by violence. Violence in turn served to increase the pressures on Chinese leadership—of whatever political persuasion—to resist foreign privilege. Two political parties, the Nationalists (Kuomintang) and the Communists, made renunciation or radical revision of the unequal treaties a central element in their programmes.

For these reasons, the perpetuation of informal empire in China was in crucial respects related to the domestic struggle for power. Imple-menting the treaties depended, as it had done from the outset, on the existence of a stable Chinese government. Yet no Chinese government after 1919 could be stable unless it came to terms with nationalism,

---

[22] Quoted in Nish, *Japanese Foreign Policy*, 155.
[23] Quoted in Iriye, 'Failure of economic expansionism', 245.

which demanded that the treaties be revised. Coming to terms, of course, could be variously defined. For the nothern war-lords, including Tuan Ch'i-jui and Chang Tso-lin, who were engaged in a wearisome contest for the control of Peking, it did not preclude the possibility of a dependent relationship with Japan or one of the other powers. For their principal rivals in the south—leaders of a regime centring on Kwangtung, which brought together Sun Yat-sen's Kuomintang and the newly organized Communist Party, among others—it implied a much more radical opposition to foreign rights. But the southerners were less influential, at least before 1926. After that date the position was reversed, as Chiang Kai-shek, who had seized power in Canton two years earlier, began to bring about national unification by conquest. During the summer of 1926 his Northern Expedition drove into the middle-Yangtze valley and established the Kuomintang in headquarters at Wuhan. There followed a break with the Communist Party, whereupon Chiang set up his own independent Nationalist government at Nanking (April 1927). More military victories in 1927 and 1928 extended his authority as far north as Peking.

It was while these events were taking place that the United States, Britain and Japan were trying to put into effect the policies which they had formulated at Washington in 1921–2.[24] They did not find it easy. Chinese spokesmen, representing various Chinese governments, continued to press for an end to spheres of influence, for the abolition of consular courts and extraterritoriality, for an increase in customs dues and formal recognition of China's tariff autonomy. The powers were never able to frame a unanimous response.

The tariff question had been discussed at some length during the Washington meetings. It had for many years been apparent that the rate of customs duties laid down in earlier treaties had been rendered out of date by rising prices and the falling value of silver. There was no real demur about restoring it to a genuine 5 per cent *ad valorem*. More contentious was a Chinese request to raise the rate to 12.5 per cent. Britain was in favour, because improving the Chinese government's finances would increase its ability to repay foreign loans. Japan, however, objected to the burden such a change would impose on its own

---

[24] This discussion of the international politics of East Asia in the 1920s is based principally on Akira Iriye, *After Imperialism: the search for a new order in the Far East 1921–1931* (1965); Dorothy Borg, *American Policy and the Chinese Revolution 1925–1928* (1947); and Louis, *British Strategy*. On Japanese policy, see also Nobuya Bamba, *Japanese Diplomacy in a Dilemma . . . 1924–1929* (1972); and Morton, *Tanaka*.

exports. A compromise was finally reached, by which tariffs were to be set forthwith at a true 5 per cent (to be maintained by periodic revision), leaving any decision about a higher level to be taken at a separate tariff conference. This was to be convened in China and would be given authority to levy a surcharge of 2.5 per cent on Chinese imports, subject to certain conditions.

These proposals came forward for discussion at Peking in the winter of 1925–6, when Tuan Ch'i-jui was still Prime Minister. The United States, predictably, showed itself ready to approve tariff revision and tariff autonomy, provided there were promises about tax reform. Britain agreed, as it had done before, that the Chinese government urgently needed a larger revenue from customs dues, but would not accept full tariff autonomy without safeguards about how the revenue would be spent. These amounted to a continuing system of foreign supervision, linked in particular to the servicing of consortium loans. Japan took a quite different line. Shidehara was willing to accord tariff autonomy, in the belief that such a concession would be good for Sino-Japanese relations. About other customs arrangements he was altogether uncooperative. He wanted the increase in import dues to be phased, so as to reduce its effect on Japan's textile exports; the appointment of a Japanese as Inspector-General of the Chinese Maritime Customs (replacing a Briton); and an undertaking that part of the proposed customs surcharge would be used to repay non-consortium loans (such as those negotiated by Nishihara a few years earlier). All this reflected the fact that in arguing the case within Japan for working closely with the powers in China, Shidehara could not afford to let it appear that the treaty port system's benefits to Japan were being lessened. Only a week or two before he took office in 1924 the four Japanese Ministries concerned with mainland policy (Finance, Foreign Affairs, War, and Navy) had reaffirmed the need to cultivate a special relationship between Japan and China. Their statement envisaged further development of China's natural resources through firms under Japanese management; Japanese assistance with institutional reform, especially in finance and industry; military aid, if need be; and efforts to block any western moves towards international supervision of the Chinese government.[25] Given the strength of these ideas in Japanese ruling circles, Shidehara was constantly looking over his shoulder in his dealings with Britain and America.

[25] Text (May 1924) in *NGNB*, II, documents, 61–3.

Because of these divergent policies the tariff conference achieved very little. It was decided that China would be accorded tariff autonomy with effect from January 1929 and would in return abolish transit tax (*likin*) on foreign goods. Japan was encouraged to have bilateral talks with China on the nature and timing of changes in particular customs dues. But by April 1926, when the overthrow of the Tuan government brought the conference to an end, no headway had been made on working out how China would use its additional revenue, or to what extent it would be subject to foreign supervision in doing so.

There were similar difficulties over legal jurisdiction. An international commission had been set up to study extraterritoriality and related questions. This produced a report in September 1926 which made a number of recommendations, including the introduction of new civil and criminal codes, revisions in the working of the courts, and measures to protect the Chinese judiciary from political interference. Only when substantial progress had been made in all these things should the powers consider abolishing extraterritoriality, it was stated. And even then they should do so by stages, so as to give foreign residents time to adjust to change.

The British and American governments viewed these proposals favourably. The United States, while it had always shown sympathy towards Chinese nationalist aspirations, had little enthusiasm for abolishing extraterritoriality while China was still in turmoil. Britain was coming round to a similar position. In December 1926 it called publicly on the powers to 'abandon the idea that the economic and political development of China can only be secured under foreign tutelage'. They should recognize 'the essential justice of the Chinese claim for treaty revision', while bearing in mind 'the difficulty under the present conditions of negotiating new treaties in place of the old'.[26]

In practice this turned out to mean no more than a gradualist approach to the subject of legal jurisdiction, coupled with a determination to defend the foreign position at Shanghai at almost any cost. All the same, it did make possible a greater degree of Anglo-American accord. In 1928, when Chiang Kai-shek at last defeated his Peking rivals, Britain and the United States recognized the Kuomintang administration in Nanking as the legitimate government of China. In the same year they signed treaties conceding tariff autonomy, which

---

[26] Quoted in Borg, *American Policy*, 229. See also Louis, *British Strategy*, 151–4.

opened the way for China to declare revised rates of customs duties in February 1929. Legal questions took longer to decide, not least because of opposition from the residents of the treaty ports; but the talks were eventually brought to a conclusion when China announced that extraterritoriality would be abrogated unilaterally during 1932, if not ended by agreement earlier. Draft treaties followed in 1931, though in the diplomatic confusion caused by the Japanese occupation of Manchuria in September they were never signed.

Anglo-American actions threatened to leave Japan in isolation. Shidehara, starting his second term of office in July 1929, was conscious of the risks this carried. He had no desire to offend China. As he had told the British ambassador in Tokyo during April 1927, he considered China to be more important commercially to Japan than it was to Britain. It followed that Japan should do nothing likely 'to disturb this important China trade for any length of time'.[27] He was also fully aware that Japan was integrated into the world economy in a way that made necessary a substantial degree of co-operation with Britain and America, not only in East Asia: the United States was Japan's chief silk market; British India supplied both cotton and pig-iron for Japanese industry.

Nevertheless, Shidehara's commitment to preserving Japanese commercial interests in the treaty ports and Japanese dominance in Manchuria—he was no more willing than previous Foreign Ministers to see this undermined—hampered him in dealing with a Chinese regime that was determined to put an end to informal empire. This was especially so at a time when Chiang Kai-shek gave every sign of making Manchuria his next target. Matters moved slowly, therefore. In the spring of 1930 an agreement was reached about tariffs. Japan recognized China's tariff autonomy in return for a promise that customs dues on the most important items of Japanese exports to China would remain unchanged for another three years, thus giving Japanese business a breathing-space until 1933. Attention then turned to extraterritoriality. Shidehara tried to reserve Japan's position in Kwantung and south Manchuria, just as Britain had done about Shanghai. He also bargained for the full opening of China's interior as a price for the surrender of foreign leases and concessions. Before these questions could be settled, however, the Japanese army's seizure of Manchuria (September 1931) brought the negotiations to an end.

[27] Bamba, *Japanese Diplomacy*, 277.

Shidehara had gone on trying to preserve Japan's claims to privilege in China at a time when the treaty port system, on which they rested, was being abandoned by others as unworkable in the face of Chinese hostility. Recognizing that China was determined to abolish the unequal treaties, neither Britain nor America was in the last resort willing to uphold them by force. Instead, they negotiated as best they might to save what they could of their economic advantages. Shidehara followed their example, albeit grudgingly. By so doing he was helping to destroy the machinery through which one strand of Japanese imperialism had operated since 1895; and as neither he nor his political opponents within Japan had any intention of allowing this permanently to weaken their country's position on the continent, the result was to precipitate a search for alternatives. Working these out led to a new stage in the development of Japanese imperialism.

12

The Making of Manchukuo, 1931–1932

THE collapse of world trade, which was becoming evident at the end of 1929, had two important consequences for Japanese imperialism. One was to undermine the economic structures within which it had operated. By breaking up trading patterns, even if it only did so temporarily, and by giving a stimulus to the formation of regional economic blocs, the slump completed the process of Japanese disillusionment with the treaty port system. Some Japanese had always doubted whether the system's benefits were worth the self-restraint—with respect to Manchuria, for example—which the effort of preserving them imposed. Many more became so after 1930. For them, it ceased to be self-evident that the way in which the affairs of China were internationally regulated was more important than the prospect of securing immediate gains in north-east Asia. This did not mean that the resources of China were any less valued in themselves, of course. It was just that they should be tapped by other means. 'Co-prosperity', signifying an exclusive and unequal economic partnership between China and Japan, became the slogan of the decade.

The second consequence was political. The commitment of the Japanese people to a belief in the virtues of modernization had never been total. Conservatives among them resented the other face of 'national wealth and strength': the erosion of traditional values that it brought about, the subordination of the village to the town, the forms of corruption that seemed to be inherent in urban life and party politics. Recession gave feelings of this kind a fresh intensity and wider popularity. Deprived of American buyers for their silk, many Japanese farmers starved. Facing a sharp drop in overseas markets for their textiles, Japanese manufacturers laid off workers. The resulting discontents, whether they were feared as creating a potential for revolution, or seen as signs of a social injustice that had to be set right, introduced a note of stridency into Japanese politics. Foreign policy was affected by it, like everything else. Caution and conformity ceased to be the qualities thought appropriate in Japan's dealings with the outside world. Autonomy and self-reliance replaced them. Manchuria was the place where these could most readily be shown, as the army was to demonstrate in September 1931.

In all this it was the mood, the sense of purpose, the acceptance of risk that were new, not the ideas themselves. Co-prosperity in China and plans to create an independent Manchuria were aspirations which already had a history in Japan, as we have seen. Although both now acquired in some respects a fresh rationale—notably with respect to the relevance of self-sufficiency to total war—and were to be given wider geographical definition, it remains true that such changes were developments from what had gone before, not discontinuities with it. There took place, one might say, a reversal of priorities: coexistence with the West, which had been primary, became secondary; relationships with Asians, which had been secondary, became primary. The shift was manifest in nationalist attitudes some time before it was reflected in government policies.

Nationalism and militarism

Central to the consciousness of national identity in Japan was the Shintō myth: that the emperor was a descendant in the direct line of the sun-goddess, Amaterasu; that the people were also of divine descent, though from lesser gods; and that between emperor and people there was a mystical bond, superior to anything of the kind to be found elsewhere in the world. In one sense these ideas were as old as the historical record. In another they derived from modern politics. In order to give Meiji Japan unity and cloak its innovations in legitimate authority, there had been a constant reiteration after 1868—in imperial decrees, in schools, in the training of conscript soldiers—that a subject's duty and loyalty stemmed from this mystique, not from any concept of social contract or popular sovereignty. Around it, too, there clustered other virtues: the preservation of traditional values and behaviour; obligations to the family and community; respect for an inherited culture.

In so far as nationalism ensured a commitment to patriotic aims and a large measure of support for the decisions of the emperor's government, it contributed much to the emergence of orthodox imperialism in the early phase of Japanese expansion. After about 1918, however, it was becoming politically ambivalent. There was still agreement on all sides that Japan must be Great Japan. There was still the same amuletic vocabulary: 'the national polity', 'the national essence', 'the national family'. Nevertheless, as Japanese society became more bourgeois, so nationalism became in one of its guises a critique and a lament: that landlords had become absentees, exploiting villagers; that business men were *nouveaux riches*; that politicians were party men, seeking only power; that none of them put nation first. At schools and universities, it was said, the young were being taught to esteem individualism, which was a Western word for selfishness.

In these circumstances, nationalism became critical of contemporary leadership. It demanded a reaffirmation of what used to be and a call to Japanese to go back to it. This involved *inter alia* a return to the same kind of amibitions overseas and the same kind of imperialist policies in pursuit of them as had developed in the Meiji era. Nationalism was also revolutionary, however. It denied the validity of much that had been done in the name of modernization in the past; demanded once again a complete reordering of society, effected by force in the emperor's name; and condemned the whole world order as unjust. It therefore called upon Japanese to carry through to completion the tasks which the Meiji leaders had left half-done, both at home and overseas. The heroes it chose were the 'men of spirit' of the 1860s, who had helped to bring the Tokugawa down. Its methods, like theirs, were terrorism and the *coup d'état*. Patriotic assassination, never absent for long from modern Japanese politics, became frequent and respectable again.

The political movement, or perhaps one should call it the political activity, that took shape under these influences after 1930, has been variously described as 'ultra-nationalist' and 'fascist'. There was a strong element of agrarianism in it, reflecting a hostility to urban life and all it stood for. There were strands of socialism and Pan-Asianism. And as those statements imply, there was little coherence or unity. In this context, as in others, the Japanese were prone to form associations and societies, most of them small and clustering round one or two men of personality or charisma. Such groups rarely worked together. Certainly they never comprised a mass organization such as Hitler or Mussolini could command. What is more, their avowed function was not to seize power, but to destroy it. Out of chaos, they believed, would come in some mysterious way a better Japan.[1]

[1] There are some thoughtful essays in nationalism and kindred subjects in Maruyama Masao, *Thought and Behaviour in Modern Japanese Politics* (1963). The agrarian theme is considered in Thomas Havens, *Farm and Nation in Modern Japan* (1974). Richard Storry, *The Double Patriots* (1957), examines a wide spectrum of patriotic societies from the Meiji period to the end of the Second World War.

The most famous of these nationalist revoluntaries was Kita Ikki (1883–1937). Like many Meiji radicals, he came from a fairly well-to-do family. He had links with the Kokuryūkai (Amur Society); was much influenced when young by Social Darwinism; and spent several years in China after the 1911 Revolution. The outcome of these experiences was a book entitled *A Plan for the Reorganization of Japan* (*Nihon kaizō hōan taikō*), which was written in Shanghai in 1919, but not published in Japan until 1923, when it was banned by the police. Its theme was that Japan must be fundamentally reformed in order that it might be fit to give leadership to a resurgent Asia. The reform, Kita argued, would need to be initiated by a *coup d'état*, having as its objects a declaration of martial law and the suspension of parliament. This would remove the established cliques which interposed between the emperor and his people. Thereafter it would be possible for a reconstituted imperial government to destroy the landed and financial interests of the rich; to institute state controls over the economy in preparation for inevitable war; to carry out land reform, giving legal protection to tenant farmers; to introduce profit-sharing and the eight-hour day into industry; and to implement civil liberties.

Kita made a parallel analysis of the international system and the steps that were needed to correct it. The villains of the piece were Britain, 'a multimillionaire standing over the whole world', and Russia, 'the great landlord of the northern hemisphere'. Between them they had put all Asia in thrall, building empires that stretched from Turkey to Siberia. The countries of Asia could not overturn these empires on their own. Only through Japanese assistance could they do so: 'our seven hundred million brothers in China and India have no path to independence other than that offered by our guidance and protection'. Japan should accordingly 'lift the virtuous banner of an Asian league and take the leadership in a world federation'. Indeed, this would also enable it to solve problems of its own. Since its population had doubled in the previous fifty years, 'great areas adequate to support a population of at least two hundred and forty or fifty millions will be absolutely necessary a hundred years from now'.[2]

The programme of domestic policy which Kita put forward was attractive neither to men who had inherited from the Meiji period a place of prominence in Japanese society, nor to those who opposed

[2] Quotations from Tsunoda, *Sources*, 776. More generally, see G. M. Wilson, *Radical Nationalist in Japan: Kita Ikki* (1969); the *Plan* is discussed at 64–87.

them from the standpoint of the proletarian left. However, this was conspicuously not true of what he said about Japanese policy overseas. By way of example one might take, first, the ideas of Konoe Fumimaro. Konoe belonged to the Fujiwara line, which made him heir to centuries of office at the imperial court, and was subsequently the Prime Minister by whom Japan's New Order was proclaimed in 1938. He cannot be considered actually or potentially a social revolutionary. Nevertheless, from the time that he first published an article in a nationalist magazine in December 1918, he had been a bitter critic of what he saw as Western self-seeking and dishonesty. The policies pursued by Britain and the United States, ostensibly for the purposes of world stability, were, he argued, attempts by the 'haves' to keep out the 'have-nots'. They served to condemn late comers like Japan 'to remain forever subordinate to the advanced nations'; and unless something were done to change this situation—such as offering 'equal access to the markets and natural resources of the colonial areas'—Japan would be forced 'to destroy the status quo for the sake of self-preservation, just like Germany'.[3] Konoe returned to this theme in another article in 1933, in which he maintained that it was the failure to break Anglo-American control of the international economy that had compelled Japan to move into Manchuria in 1931.

A very different case is that of Sano Manabu and Nabeyama Sadachika. They were two communists, sentenced to life imprisonment in 1932, who in the following year publicly recanted their allegiance to the party. In an explanation of their action, which they issued at that time,[4] they said that they had done this, not because they had abandoned the struggle against 'the iron chains of violent capitalism', but because events on the mainland had led them to see Japan's world mission in a fresh light. The war that was taking place was designed to free China from British and American capital. This made it 'a progessive one for the peoples of Asia'. Japan, being strong, must inevitably take the lead in it. Other Asian countries, being backward, must accept a subordinate role. And since ideas of colonial independence and national self-determination were 'bourgeois' and 'outdated', the proper outcome would be for places like Manchuria to come to 'enjoy equal rights within a people's government of Japan, Manchuria,

---

[3] The article is summarized in Oka Yoshitake, *Konoe Fumimaro* (1983), 10–13.

[4] See George M. Beckmann, 'The radical left and the failure of communism' (1971), 164–73.

Formosa, and Korea, by merging with Japan, which is economically close to them'.

There is no way of telling whether this quasi-Marxist version of the New Order was honestly conceived, but it demonstrates the influence which radical nationalist imagery had on Japanese of all political groups. Young (and some not-so-young) officers in the army and navy also found it appealing. They, too, founded patriotic societies to debate its implications, treating Kita Ikki's fiery rhetoric as something akin to policy proposals. Since they took the view, long exemplified by their seniors with respect to Manchuria, that the responsibilities of the military were not confined to carrying out the orders of a civilian government, the *Plan* became for many of them the delineation of a future towards which it was their duty to work.[5]

Twice after 1930 there were abortive *coups d'état* in Tokyo. In the first, which took place on 15 May 1932, junior officers from a naval air station joined with civilian extremists in attacks on public targets and political figures, including members of the cabinet. The Prime Minister, Inukai Tsuyoshi, was assassinated. However, because no generals or admirals moved to exploit the situation, the coup failed. The second attempt came on 26 February 1936, when troops from the First Division, acting on the orders of their company commanders, occupied the centre of the capital and held it for three days. During that period they killed or wounded several leading politicians—though not on this occasion the Prime Minister, who escaped unrecognized—and distributed pamphlets calling for radical changes in Japanese society. The high command, prompted by the emperor, acted with unexpected firmness. Loyal troops were brought in to surround the rebels. When the latter surrendered, a number of their leaders were quickly tried and executed. So was Kita Ikki, who had been personally involved.

The officers who planned and led those operations had, it seems, been misled by vaguely worded expressions of sympathy from their superiors into believing that men of higher rank would come to their support once a coup had been carried out. That they did not so was partly due to the fact that the most powerful among them were more militarist than revolutionary. That is to say, they put the requirements of military strength before those of social change. Army leadership, in particular, was principally concerned with—and divided about—the

[5] On the Young Officers movement, see Ben-Ami Shillony, *Revolt in Japan* (1973), chaps. 1–4.

nature of modern warfare and the manner in which Japan should be made ready for it.[6] Under Ugaki Kazushige, who was War Minister in 1924–7 and again in 1929–30, there had emerged a nucleus of able officers on the General Staff who sought above all to give the Japanese army greater striking power through modernization. They later passed under the patronage of Minami Jirō, War Minister during 1931, in whose term of office the attack on Manchuria was carried out. Opposition to Minami developed for a number of reasons: because his military reforms had offended many old-fashioned generals; because he wanted to move cautiously on the mainland until Japan had reached full military preparedness; because he was more willing to restrain than to help the radicals. This opposition coalesced round a new grouping, the Kōdō-ha (Imperial Way Faction), led by Araki Sadao. Araki took over the post of War Minister at the end of 1931. Minami's followers, among whom the most prominent were Nagata Tetsuzan (assassinated in 1935) and Tōjō Hideki, then became part of what was to be called the Control Faction (Tōsei-ha). After 1936 this was the dominant group within the army.

Differences between the two factions were in many respects a matter of emphasis, since both acknowledged a common objective in creating a 'purer' and more powerful Japan. The Imperial Way faction gave greater weight to ideology and morale: an emperor-centred polity; anti-communism; co-operation (on Japan's terms) with China; the struggle against Soviet Russia. It was self-consciously Asian. The Control faction wanted a Japan better organized for global warfare: military reform; controls over capital and labour, as well as over the allocation of raw materials, such as would benefit strategic industries; a disciplined civilian population; territorial expansion. It was highly professional. And though there was a great deal of overlap in the slogans and patriotic terminology of the two, it was the Control Faction that played the more important part in reshaping Japanese imperialism.

The way in which it did so can best be illustrated by examining the views of Ishiwara Kanji.[7] Graduating from staff college in 1918, Ishiwara served in China in 1920–1 and returned sceptical of that country's

---

[6] Army factions and their policies are examined in James B. Crowley, *Japan's Quest for Autonomy* (1966), 82–91; also in Y. C. Maxon, *Control of Japanese Foreign Policy* (1957); Kitaoka Shinichi, 'Rikugun habatsu tairitsu (1931–35)'; and Sasaki Takashi, 'Kōdō-ha to Tōsei-ha' (1983).

[7] See Mark R. Peattie, *Ishiwara Kanji and Japan's Confrontation with the West* (1975), especially 49–74.

capacity to serve as a worthwhile partner to Japan, at least in the shorter term. Subsequent study in Germany from 1922 to 1925 gave him a better knowledge of modern warfare and an awareness of the Japanese army's technical deficiencies. He came home to become an instructor at the staff college in 1926. In the next few years, while teaching there, he won recognition as the army's leading theorist on strategy and military history. His next appointment was to the staff of the Kwantung Army, where he planned the operations undertaken in Manchuria in 1931–2. In 1935 he became head of the tactical section of the General Staff.

The main lines of Ishiwara's thought had already taken shape by 1931. Central to it was a belief that Japan, acting through the army, was destined to save the world from Marxism and other corrupting ideologies. This would require a series of wars, first against Russia, then against Britain, finally against the United States, in which Japan would stand as the champion of Asia and the embodiment of Confucian righteousness. The culminating struggle would be a holocaust in which warfare would take on a wholly new dimension—though one foreshadowed in western Europe in 1914–18—bringing into action entire populations and the totality of their resources. Preparing Japan to take part in it had both an internal and an external dimension. At home, it would be necessary not only to ensure stability and unity, but also to institute such controls over society and economy as would guarantee the most effective applications of available strength. Abroad, Asia would have to be brought under Japanese dominance, starting with Manchuria. As Ishiwara saw it, 'war can maintain war'. Each accrual to Japanese strength would make possible the next; and the process, when complete, would make available the economic resources on which final victory would depend.

By asserting the need to integrate political, military, and economic policy for purposes of 'defence', as defined in this way, Ishiwara was doing something more than bring together elements that had existed separately hitherto. He was also identifying the army as the principal actor on the national stage. Thus in so far as his ideas determined Japanese actions in the following decade—there was never unanimity concerning them—he was the prophet of what can appropriately be described as military imperialism. It began in Manchuria.

Japan and Manchuria before 1930

The decision taken by the Hara government in May 1921 to support Chang Tso-lin as war-lord of Manchuria was maintained in principle throughout Shidehara's first term as Foreign Minister. Japanese advisers were appointed to Chang's staff. One of them was told in 1924 that his duties, in addition to maintaining liaison with Japanese forces in Kwantung and Korea, were 'to facilitate the mutual co-operation of Japanese and Chinese armies in the event of emergency' by ensuring that military installations and organization in Fengtien province (the southern part of Manchuria) were modelled on those of Japan.[8] As a *quid pro quo*, the Kwantung Army took steps to bolster Chang's authority within Manchuria. When one of his subordinates, Kuo Sung-ling, rebelled in 1925, he found that Japanese troops were used to hamper his campaign. Matsuoka Yōsuke, then a director of the South Manchuria Railway Company, commented that 'where there is a move to overthrow someone advantageous to us and replace him with someone not to our advantage, we should prevent it'.[9] Even the cabinet, anxious as its Foreign Minister was to avoid action that might cause resentment in China, in view of the risks to Japanese trade, did not always refrain from meddling. A resolution of 8 December 1925, referring to the 'hundreds of thousands of Japanese subjects' and the 'immense amount of Japanese invested capital' in Manchuria, instructed the Kwantung commander-in-chief to make it clear to all parties that there were limits to Japanese non-intervention: 'should a situation develop as a result of hostilities or disturbances . . . calculated to jeopardize or seriously menace those important interests of Japan, the Japanese forces would be constrained to act as duty demands'.[10]

Unfortunately, affording protection to Chang Tso-lin did not *ipso facto* make it possible to control him. He had on several occasions taken steps to encourage Chinese commercial and industrial ventures which competed with Japanese ones, even in the railway business. He had deliberately set out to create a Chinese education system capable of reducing the appeal of Japanese-run schools. Nor did he seem very eager to suppress anti-Japanese activities by local Chinese nationalists. Yet none of these things was more than an irritant compared with his continuing determination to play a leading part in the politics of China Proper. During 1926 he again strengthened his position there, moving his own headquarters to Peking towards the end of the year. Since this coincided with the beginning of Chiang Kai-shek's expedition to the

[8] McCormack, *Chang Tso-lin*, 123–4.
[9] Ibid., 173.
[10] Ibid., 177.

north, it threatened to provoke a confrontation Japan might find embarrasssing. Chiang Kai-shek, after all, had the look of a possible Japanese ally, both as an anti-communist and a would-be unifier of China; but it would not be easy to make him one if he came to power as a result of fighting Chang Tso-lin. At least, to do so might make it necessary to jettison Chang.

From April 1927, choosing a path through these hazards became the responsibility of a new Premier, Tanaka Giichi, who was also Foreign Minister. As a soldier-turned-politican he was better equipped for it than most. From the army's standpoint, he was known to be 'sound' on the subject of Japan's position in Manchuria. He was prepared, as Shidehara had not been, to countenance firm action in China for the purpose of suppressing 'communists . . . [who] resort to terrorism with a view to building up an anti-foreign movement which will destroy order and break up the emperor system in Japan'.[11] Like Shidehara, however, he recognized the importance of trade and investment on the mainland to a greater extent than most army officers did, though he tended to give more weight to the interests of merchants in the treaty ports than to those of the *zaibatsu* and other large firms at home. One of his principal aides, Mori Kaku, had business interests in the Yangtze valley. Another, Yamamoto Jōtarō, whom he made President of the South Manchuria Railway Company, had earlier had experience in several Sino-Japanese concerns. Moreover, Tanaka was a militarist in something close to the sense in which one uses the word of Ishiwara Kanji. In July 1927, when inaugurating a study which was intended to prepare the way for a National Mobilization Plan, he expressed the view that 'control and development of resources' for purposes of national defence would be the means by which to 'establish the most orderly war structure to meet all the demands of this military nation'.[12]

Within a few weeks of taking office Tanaka sent troops to Shantung to protect Japanese there from danger during Chiang Kai-shek's march north. Despite the offence it gave to Chinese opinion, the move was not apparently intended to signal a reversal of Shidehara's policies as a whole. At about the same time (June 1927) Tanaka summoned officials from various posts in East Asia to discuss the affairs of China at a conference in Tokyo. One of them, Yada Shichitarō, consul-

---

[11] Tanaka (1927), quoted in Nish, *Japanese Foreign Policy*, 292.
[12] Quoted in Bamba, *Japanese Diplomacy*, 312.

general at Shanghai, produced the familiar Shidehara argument that the protection of Japanese trade and investment in that country was the first priority. It required, he said, the existence of a Chinese government which was not only capable of maintaining peace and order, but also possessed 'political, economic and social organizations similar to those in Japan', together with 'a certain durability'.[13] Neither Tanaka nor other members of the group made any demur about this. Nor did they about the proposition that the nature and extent of Japanese interests in Manchuria and Inner Mongolia made it necessary to insulate that region as far as possible from China's political instability. These were fundamentals of Japan's China policy, accepted on all sides. Disagreement only arose when it came to spelling out particular applications of them. Mori Kaku, supported by a memorandum from the Kwantung Army's staff, argued that China should be made to recognize 'self-government' for Manchuria, that is, its status as a separate political entity. This was farther than the Foreign Ministry was willing to go. Diplomats also had reservations about the role to be accorded Chang Tso-lin. The Japanese minister at Peking urged support for him as an independent war-lord in Manchuria, provided he withdrew north of the Great Wall. Tanaka himself went along with this. On the other hand, Yoshida Shigeru, consul-general in Mukden, who was about to become vice-minister in Tokyo, argued that Japan should not involve itself with Chinese puppets of any kind, since relations with them were always in some degree unsatisfactory. He preferred that it act directly through its own representatives. So did some others who were present.

It was often said during the 1930s that one product of this Eastern Conference was a memorial, submitted by Tanaka to the emperor, which set out plans for Japanese domination, first of Manchuria and Mongolia, then of the rest of China, finally of all Asia. There is nothing inherently improbable, either in the ideas or in this manner of stating them—Japanese policy-makers of the next decade were constantly drafting high-flown declarations of intent, capable of bearing this interpretation—but the nature of the document, as published variously in Chinese and English, does not carry conviction about its authenticity. Nor is there any satisfactory evidence that the conclusions reached by the conference, such as they were, had this degree of

---

[13] Quoted in Iriye, *After Imperialism*, 154. The Eastern Conference of June–July 1927 is considered in some detail in ibid., 151–72; Bamba, *Japanese Diplomacy* 293–9; and Eguchi Keiichi, *Nihon teikokushugi shiron: Manshū jihen zengo* (1975), 28–35.

generality. Tanaka summarized them innocuously enough in a tele-gram to the chargé d'affaires in Peking. Japan, he stated, looked to 'the maintenance of peace in the Far East and the realization of Sino-Japanese co-prosperity'.[14] Within this overall objective, China Proper and Manchuria-Mongolia must be regarded separately. In the first, Japan was willing to give countenance to any Chinese regime that was moderate, friendly, and likely to preserve stability. In the second, because of the importance of Japanese strategic and economic rights, it might become necessary to take direct action in the event of disorder. Short of that, however, Japan would support any effective Chinese leader who was willing to respect its special position.

One implication of this was that Chang Tso-lin was not indispens-able. All the same, Tanaka's actions during the next twelve months still suggest a desire to make use of him. In November there was a private meeting with Chiang Kai-shek in Tokyo, at which Tanaka tried, apparently without success, to get the Kuomintang leader to stop short of the Manchurian boundary, in return for formal recognition by Japan. When Chiang nevertheless moved north next spring, Tanaka once more sent troops into Shantung. The step this time led to clashes with Chiang's forces in Tsinan and to Japanese occupation of the Kiaochow–Tsinan railway.

Meanwhile, during the winter of 1927–8 Yamamoto Jōtarō of Man-tetsu, acting on Tanaka's behalf, had reached a wide-ranging agree-ment with Chang Tso-lin, giving Japan new railway rights in Manchuria and a promise of closer economic co-operation generally. Yamamoto believed that were the plan to materialize as he expected, it would be 'as if Japan buys up the whole of Manchuria'.[15] Even so, the agreement went unsigned for several months because of Foreign Min-istry objections to private diplomacy. It was eventually renegotiated in a more restricted form by the minister in Peking and signed in May 1928.

At this point Tanaka had to face the problem of what to do about extricating Chang Tso-lin from the consequences of his increasingly unsuccessful involvement in China's civil war. Chiang Kai-shek was still advancing on Peking. Tanaka therefore publicly warned both sides (18 May) that Japan was ready to intervene to prevent hostilities

[14] Telegram of 7 July 1927, in *NGNB*, II, documents, 101–2. On the Tanaka Memorial, see John J. Stephan, 'The Tanaka Memorial (1927): authentic or spurious?' (1973).
[15] Bamba, *Japanese Diplomacy*, 317–18.

spreading to Manchuria. Privately, he sent word that if Chang Tso-lin agreed to leave the capital before the fighting reached there, he would be allowed to withdraw into Manchuria with his army; but if he did not, Japan would close the frontier at Shanhaikuan, blocking his retreat. Having no realistic alternative, Chang accepted the bargain. At the same time Tanaka let it be known to the Nanking government that once back in Mukden the Manchurian war-lord would not be allowed to cross the frontier to the south again.

Clearly, what Tanaka was trying to accomplish by these complex manoeuvrings was a separation of Manchuria from China in everything but name. He set out his ideas in August 1928 in a note on the subject for Uchida Yasuya, who was to make appropriate explanations to Britain and the United States. Japan, this stated, had no intention 'of invading Manchuria territorially as a protectorate'. It was entirely willing to observe the Open Door there. However, there were two things it could not permit. One was the penetration of the area by communist groups, since they would not only cause disorder in the Manchurian provinces, but also impair 'our rule in Korea'. The other was the extension of Kuomintang authority north of the Great Wall, in view of the Nanking government's bad record on treaty rights and anti-Japanese activities.[16]

There was enough ambiguity about ideas like this, when taken in conjunction with Tanaka's readiness in previous months to use troops in China, or threaten to use them, to give encouragement to those who believed that a truly separate Manchuria under Japanese control would be the simplest and most satisfying solution. There was, as we have noted in previous chapters, a long tradition of such thinking among members of the Kwantung Army staff. On of them, Colonel Kōmoto Daisaku, who had attended the Eastern Conference, now came to the conclusion that the occupation of Manchuria by force was what Tanaka and his own superiors secretly wanted. He therefore took steps to give them a pretext for it. On the morning of 4 June, as Chang Tso-lin's train from Peking approached Mukden, a bomb, placed by troops working under Kōmoto's direction, was detonated under it. Chang died within a few hours.

Neither the Kwantung Army nor the authorities in Tokyo made any move to exploit the opportunity which Kōmoto had provided for them.

---

[16] Text partly translated in Nish, *Japanese Foreign Policy*, 293–4.

No attempt was made to 'restore order' in Manchuria. In fact, it was all that his friends on the General Staff could do to prevent the colonel from being court-martialled. What is more, the plan to provoke military intervention in Manchuria, because it failed, proved counter-productive even in terms of the aspirations of those who approved of it. Chang Tso-lin was at once succeeded by his son, Hsüeh-liang, who not unnaturally showed some reluctance about working with Japan. In December he declared allegiance to the Kuomintang. He repudiated the railway agreement signed by his father the previous May. And in south and central China, where there was already much indignation at Japanese actions in Tsinan, the murder prompted an extension of boy-cotts against Japanese trade. Loss of trade in turn brought Tanaka under pressure from commercial organizations at home. The result was a gradual shift in policy: a tariff agreement with Nanking (February 1929), withdrawal from Shantung (March), recognition of the Kuomintang as China's central government (June). By July 1929, when his cabinet resigned, Tanaka gave the impression of being more anxious to reach a settlement with Britain and America in China than to pursue separatist ambitions in Manchuria. The Japanese Foreign Ministry had good reason to be satisfied with the change. Its past warnings about the economic disadvantages of army actions on the mainland had been shown to have substance. Discipline with respect to foreign policy had been restored.

Or so it seemed. In reality, men who had been sympathetic to Kōmoto attributed his failure to bad planning, not mistaken thinking. His replacement as senior staff officer in the Kwantung Army, Itagaki Seishirō, together with the newly appointed chief of his operations section, Ishiwara Kanji, resolved that the planning would not be at fault again.

The Manchurian Incident

Japan's international position changed during 1930 and 1931 sufficiently to tip the scales against the Foreign Ministry's view of policy. One reason for this was the slump in world trade, which brought about a very sharp drop in Japanese exports: they fell 43 per cent by value between 1929 and 1931 (Table 8). This hurt manufacturers and merchants concerned with the sale of goods to China, who suffered more than proportionately. There were also catastrophic losses for farmers producing silk for the United States. One consequence was a shift in the political balance within Japan: business support for Shidehara was

Table 8. Japan's colonial and mainland trade, 1929 and 1931

	Total (yen millions)	Index (1910/14 = 100)	Totals in yen millions (% of total exports/imports)			
			Taiwan	Korea	Kwantung	China
Exports						
1929	2,513.4	423.8	140.4 (5.6)	315.3 (12.5)	124.5 (5.0)	334.6 (13.3)
1931	1,426.1	240.4	114.8 (8.0)	217.8 (15.3)	65.5 (4.6)	155.8 (10.9)
Imports						
1929	2,740.0	413.7	238.7 (8.7)	309.9 (11.3)	166.3 (6.1)	210.0 (7.7)
1931	1,662.0	250.9	201.4 (12.1)	249.0 (15.0)	90.2 (5.4)	145.7 (8.8)

Sources: Ohkawa, Shinohara and Meissner, *Patterns of Japanese Economic Development* (1979), Tables A 26 and A 27; Oriental Economist, *Foreign Trade of Japan* (1935); *Nihon Kindaishi Jiten* (1958), Table 42.

weakened, while the distress in rural communities was reflected in greater activity by nationalist groups, who claimed to represent them. There was mounting public pressure from all sides for a different approach to foreign affairs. Thus Shigemitsu Mamoru, consul-general in Shanghai, maintained that co-operation between the powers had broken down in China, leaving Japan no choice but to 'cope with East Asian matters on its own responsibility and at its own risk'. Matsuoka Yōsuke, addressing himself more specifically to the slump's significance for Japan, made a speech in the Diet in January 1931, arguing that 'economic warfare' was leading to the creation of 'large economic blocs', thereby making it necessary for Japan to create one, too, in order to survive. It must, he said, be ready to use force to assert 'its rights to a bare existence'.[17]

Changes in the patterns of trade helped to reinforce this argument. Although exports to China and Manchuria declined from 18.3 to 15.5 per cent of the Japanese total between 1929 and 1931, those to Taiwan and Korea rose from 18.1 to 23.3 per cent. Similarly, imports from the two colonies increased from 20 to 27.1 per cent of the whole in the same period, while the proportion from China and Manchuria

[17] Quotations in Iriye, 'Failure of economic expansionism', 261, 265.

remained almost unchanged. It was not difficult to draw the conclusion that foreign trade had resisted the depression best in those trades where Japan exercised political authority. It followed that to assert authority in other areas where trade was important might have equally beneficial results. There was therefore more frequent talk in these years of Manchuria being Japan's economic 'lifeline'. This was by implication to remove it from the context of 'special interests', which had connotations of the treaty port system, and put it into the quite different one of 'national survival'. Constant use of such expressions by journalists, politicians, and army officers helped to forge a link in the public mind between expansion and the avoidance of disaster.[18]

Another influence on the political mood was the chain of events leading to the London Naval Treaty of April 1930. Its purpose was to extend the Washington agreement concerning naval arms limitation to additional types of warships. The Navy General Staff objected to the proposals on the grounds that they would severely hamper Japan in any conflict with the United States. The Hamaguchi cabinet overruled it, however, for the sake of co-operation with the powers. This produced a constitutional furore. Military men (that is, not only the navy) claimed that the cabinet had no right to settle in this way an issue concerning the technical assessment of defence needs, for which the appropriate Chief of Staff was responsible directly to the emperor. Failing to block the treaty by this argument, they began to consider more seriously how they could bypass civilian policy-makers, when, as they saw it, national interests were at stake. Concern about this was to be found at this time in both services and among officers at all levels; but it was particularly important during the next few years among those whose duties took them to the Asian mainland, where the doctrine of 'command prerogative' was fashioned by field commanders and their staffs into what was in reality a form of sub-imperialism.

The 'colonialist' attitudes on which the actions of these men were based, in contrast to the 'internationalist' outlook of Japanese diplomats, was largely a product of training and institutional experience. A senior member of the foreign service, potentially a vice-minister or even minister in Tokyo, would have spent some years in at least one of the main Western capitals. His work there would have called for regular consideration of the policies of other powers, of their relevance to

[18] Eguchi, *Nihon teikokushugi*, 53–5; more generally on the reactions and influence of the press, see ibid., chaps. 6 and 7.

Japan, of the factors that fashioned them. Matters respecting China belonged within that framework. Against that, a senior army man, qualified to command a division or to fill one of the higher posts in the War Ministry or General Staff, would have spent a significant part of his career in Taiwan or Korea or Kwantung, where there was a permanent military establishment. As a member of it he would have acquired a sympathy towards the aims and expectations of those who had preceded him. He would also have made the acquaintance of civilian associates who shared many of his prejudices: directors of the South Manchuria Railway Company, or of colonial banks, or of large companies drawing their profits from the colonial economy. Such an environment reinforced both the continuities and the parochialism in military thinking about foreign affairs.

To men of this kind, the dangers faced by Japan in 1930 could best be met by political and military intervention on behalf of economic rights. The reasoning applied with special force to the situation in Manchuria. Since 1928 Chang Hsüeh-liang, while not actually admitting Chiang Kai-shek to a position of authority in the north-eastern provinces, had given free rein to local Kuomintang propaganda against Japan and had continued his father's policy of encouraging plans for Chinese railways and harbour installations which would compete with Mantetsu. The trade recession had brought a fierce competition over freight rates between Chinese and Japanese lines, in which the Chinese had the advantage of a currency tied to silver, not gold. Mantetsu also suffered exceptionally by the drop in world demand for soya beans, in the shipment of which it had a virtual monopoly. As a result, the company's profits dropped fom 45.5 million yen in 1929 to 12.6 million in 1931. Expressed as a return on capital, this was a fall from 11.8 to 3.3 per cent.[19]

These facts led many Japanese to conclude, not only that there was a concerted Chinese attack on Japan's privileges in Manchuria, but also that it might succeed. Shidehara's response was to seek a settlement with the Kuomintang. That of the Kwantung Army—or at least of some members of its operational staff, directed by Itagaki Seishirō and Ishiwara Kanji—was to complete contingency plans for what amounted to a pre-emptive strike.[20] Ishiwara's view was that the pre-

---

[19] Eguchi, *Nihon teikokushugi*, 55–9.
[20] The circumstances surrounding the outbreak of the Manchurian Incident in 1931 are examined in detail in Morley, *Japan Erupts*, especially the article by Seki Hiroharu; and in Sadako N. Ogata, *Defiance in Manchuria* (1964), chap. 4.

occupation of the powers with economic problems made a military seizure of Manchuria practicable. Strategic considerations made it necessary. Japan could not afford to risk losing its domination over the region, he believed. To do so would pose a threat to the Korean frontier and deprive Japan of Manchuria's resources of food and industrial raw materials in its struggle with the Western powers.

Because the Kwantung Army was heavily outnumbered and not particularly well equipped, an element of surprise was thought to be essential to success. This was interpreted as necessitating an overnight occupation of key points in the south, triggered by a manufactured incident on the railway, to be followed by a rapid extension of operations to other parts of Manchuria. During the summer of 1931 planning was carried out on these assumptions. Military movements were worked out; colleagues in the War Ministry and General Staff were consulted; co-ordination with Japanese commanders in Korea was discussed. It is not clear how far senior officers realized that this was something more than good staff-work, designed to anticipate possible future needs; but by early September rumours were undoubtedly circulating in Tokyo to the effect that the Kwantung Army was proposing action to prevent agreement over Manchuria with Nanking.

Responding to these rumours, the imperial court and the surviving elder statesman, Saionji Kimmochi, urged caution on the government. This led senior officials of the army high command, meeting on 14 September, to decide that it would be wise to lay a political groundwork, both in Japan and abroad, before anything more were done. Tatekawa Yoshitsugu of the General Staff was chosen to carry a warning to this effect to those in Mukden.

Itagaki and Ishiwara were given private notice of his coming and resolved to put their military arrangements into effect on the night of 18 September, when Tatekawa was due to arrive. There are conflicting accounts of what happened on that day: that Itagaki went to meet Tatekawa, delaying his journey and making sure that he was kept drinking at a restaurant until the troop movements had begun; that Tatekawa, being sympathetic to the conspiracy, knowingly allowed himself to be diverted from following his orders until next morning; even that he pretended to be drunk, then sneaked away from the restaurant to take part in the plan. Equally, there is uncertainty about how far the Kwantung commander-in-chief, Honjō Shigeru—who was not in Mukden—was play-acting when he authorised steps to deal with a sudden 'emergency' caused by a bomb on the railway. All one can be sure of is that there was indeed a conspiracy; that senior officers were not immediately in charge of it, or preferred to give that impression; and that by the morning of 19 September 1931 the Japanese military occupation of southern Manchuria was already well under way.

These events brought an immediate closing of ranks within the army behind the decisions taken in Mukden. On 20 September its three most senior representatives (the War Minister, the Chief of Staff, and the Director-General of Military Education) agreed that there could be no going back. A satisfactory solution would now have to be found to the problem of Japanese authority in Manchuria, though preferably one which did not involve the most northerly districts, because of the risk of provoking Russian intervention there. They therefore ordered reinforcement of the Kwantung Army—Honjō had only 10,000 men under his command—while instructing it not to move into the province of Heilungkiang. Even this degree of caution proved difficult to enforce, since it was almost impossible for the men in Tokyo to override claims of 'operational necessity' made by commanders on the spot. One division was in fact pushed forward as far as Tsitsihar.

If the War Ministry and General Staff had only a tenuous hold on the Kwantung Army, the cabinet had still less on the military as a whole. Protests from China and the powers were met by formal denials of territorial ambition. Japan, the Foreign Ministry claimed, was merely engaged in restoring law and order. It wished to respect China's integrity and the Open Door. This was generally regarded as disingenuous, especially after the Wakatsuki government resigned in December, bringing Shidehara's tenure of office to an end. The new Premier, Inukai Tsuyoshi, was believed to be personally in favour of compromise, but his War Minister, Araki Sadao, made no secret of his own enthusiasm for what his subordinates were doing on the mainland. Nor did the greater part of the Japanese press and pubic. So Inukai had little choice but to swim with the tide. In March 1932 he permitted Manchuria to become an independent state under the name of Manchukuo.

These developments made it unlikely that Japan would be able to come to terms with the Kuomintang in the immediate future. They also made co-operation with Britain and America with reference to China difficult, if not impossible, and set in motion a dispute with the League of Nations, which rather tentatively espoused China's cause. The affair culminated in Japan's withdrawal from the League in March 1933. All these things might be said to have been part of the

Kwantung Army's grand design, in so far as they contributed to under-mining 'internationalism' in Japanese foreign policy. And they estab-lished a number of precedents that were to be important for Japanese imperialism in its succeeding phase. Several times in the next decade the pattern was to be repeated: an initiative by army commanders in the field, endorsed by the high command and accepted—with varying degrees of reluctance—by the cabinet. What is more, once Man-chukuo was established, there existed a model of how the territories so gained might be run.

Manchukuo

The Itagaki–Ishiwara group within the Kwantung Army had always envisaged that once the occupation of Manchuria had been completed the area would come under Japanese military administration, which would be directed towards developing the Manchurian economy in a manner complementary to that of Japan.[21] This was a good deal more than the War Ministry and General Staff initially had in mind. Though they shared the desire to detach the region from the rest of China, they insisted that some kind of Chinese administration be retained. The army was not to get involved, they stated on 21 September 1931, in raising taxes, seizing customs revenues, or taking over local govern-ment. In other words, they saw the way forward as being through an extension of existing treaty rights and a reinforcement of the system of Japanese advisers. The cabinet concurred.

The Kwantung Army did not. However, recognizing the strength of the opposition they faced, Ishiwara and his colleagues decided to drop the idea of military rule and put forward instead a proposal for an 'independent' Chinese state in Manchuria, much on the lines sug-gested in 1912. It would have a Chinese figurehead: Pu Yi, last emperor of the Manchu house, who had abdicated at the time of the revolution. His representatives would be responsible for internal administration. Defence and foreign policy, together with transport and communications, were to be controlled by Japanese. It was a form of government which headquarters staff described as 'outwardly . . . under Chinese administration but actually under our control'; and they did not wait for Tokyo's permission before starting to set it up. An offi-

---

[21] On the steps leading to the establishment of Manchukuo, see especially the article by Shimada Toshihiko in Morley, *Japan Erupts*; also Ogata, *Defiance*, chap. 8.

cer was sent to Tientsin in October to bring back Pu Yi. Local Chinese 'provisional governments' were established, capable of being absorbed later into the new regime. Thus the Japanese cabinet was presented with a *fait accompli*, just as it had been over military occupation. A carefully fostered independence movement inside Manchuria gave the procedure a colouring of legitimacy.

Tokyo, fearing that the Kwantung Army was itself not far short of becoming a separate political entity, gave way. The Kwantung decisions were given broad approval in January 1932. In mid-February various Chinese and Mongol representatives met at Mukden, formed an administrative council, and declared their independence of China. They then invited Pu Yi to become chief executive of a republic with its capital at Changchun. These measures were confirmed at a national convention on 29 February, which was quickly followed by the installation of Pu Yi and a formal notification to the powers that he was the new Head of State. It was to be another two years before Pu Yi received the title of emperor.

The central body in the goverment of Manchukuo was an executive council, headed by the Prime Minister, who was Chinese.[22] Below this was a General Affairs Board, responsible for the budget, planning, and appointments. Its Director-General and the heads of its six bureaux were all Japanese. So were the vice-ministers of the departments concerned with public order, the economy, home affairs, and foreign affairs. Japanese also held key positions in the provinces and some of the more important prefectures. As soon as appropriate changes had been authorized—which was in some cases not until 1936 and 1937— these men were supported by a system of law codes and lawcourts modelled on those of Japan, plus a police force, of whose members one in ten were Japanese. The Manchukuo army, which was recruited from units formerly under Chang Hsüeh-liang, now given Japanese officers and equipment, had only peace-keeping duties.

Education was reorganized on much the same lines as had been followed in Taiwan and Korea. That is to say, there was separate (and superior) provision for Japanese residents, while schools for Chinese were designed chiefly to provide vocational training and inculcate loyalty. To ensure that it would serve the second of these ends, both teachers and textbooks were closely vetted; the curriculum was chosen

---

[22] On the government and administration of Manchukuo, see Jones, *Manchuria*, 23–54.

so as to emphasize Confucian values; and ideas that might be associated with the Kuomintang were replaced by invective against Marxism, republicanism and democracy. Higher education, in so far as it was available to Chinese, was mostly technical. Outside the education system, support for the link with Japan was fostered through the Concordia Association (Kyōwakai), founded in April 1932 to be an organ of political indocrination and a symbol of Sino-Japanese amity for local élites. After all, to Ishiwara Kanji and those who worked with him, Manchukuo was not merely thought of as a passive material resource. It was, if possible, to be an active partner, in the way that idealists had long hoped China would be. In Ishiwara's words, it was only 'by bringing about Japanese–Manchurian co-operation and Japanese–Chinese friendship that the Japanese people can become rulers of Asia and be prepared to wage the final and decisive war against the white races'.[23]

Japanese control did not of course rely exclusively on the presence of advisers and the use of devices like the Concordia Association. For one thing, the commander-in-chief of the Kwantung Army, who was also Japanese ambassador to Manchukuo, had at his disposal both the force and the authority to insist on having his own way in almost everything. In the protocol by which Japan recognized the independence of Manchukuo on 15 September 1932,[24] all previous Japanese rights there, deriving from treaties with China, were confirmed. In addition, an annexe provided that Manchukuo would bear the cost of Japanese units stationed in the country for its defence and the maintenance of order; would entrust to Japan the management of railways, ports, and airfields needed for these purposes; and would follow the advice of the Japanese commander-in-chief in the appointment of advisers.

From the viewpoint of the Japanese government, this left open the very important question of who was going to control the commander-in-chief.[25] Technically he was responsible to the Foreign Ministry in his civil capacity, to the War Ministry and General Staff in his military one. There were areas of uncertainty about his relationship with the South Manchuria Railway Company, with which the Finance Ministry and the Colonial Ministry were also concerned. The result was at times an awkward lack of co-ordination. General recognition of the disadvantages of this did not lead readily to a solution, however,

[23] Quoted in Peattie, *Ishiwara*, 166.
[24] Text in *NGNB*, II, documents, 215–23.
[25] On central organs of control for Manchurian policy, see Baba, *Nitchū kankei*, 231–302.

because there were constant bureaucratic disputes about who should have the deciding voice. The Foreign Ministry, for example, demanded that the commander-in-chief, when acting as ambassador, should operate from the embassy building, not from his headquarters, in order to demonstrate that Manchukuo was not legally a Japanese dependency. The army countered by calling for unification of Japanese agencies dealing with Manchukuo, by which it meant that executive responsibility should rest with the War Minister in Tokyo and with the Kwantung commander on the mainland. The dispute continued unresolved until the formation of the Okada cabinet in July 1934. Okada then put forward a compromise solution of his own, which was accepted at the end of the year. It provided for the creation of a special office under the Prime Minister, called the Manchurian Affairs Board (Tai-Man Jimukyoku). The commander-in-chief, who was to remain ambassador as well, would be subject to it in matters of general policy; the Board would be staffed by men seconded from the other ministries concerned; and the War Minister would be its president.

This represented a significant weakening of the Foreign Ministry's position, since everything but diplomacy in the narrowest sense, as applied to Manchukuo, now slipped out of its hands. It was a partial victory for the army, which gained some recognition of its involvement in non-military matters. So it was for the Kwantung Army, though not to the extent it would have wished. On the other hand, nothing was really solved, because the new agency was neither strong enough to fight its own corner, nor weak enough to fall under the domination of one of the existing ministries. The Prime Minister himself lacked the authority to treat it as his own preserve. The fact was that the acquisition of power in Manchukuo had posed a novel administrative problem for Japan, that of how to determine and supervise policy with respect to an area which was neither truly colonial nor truly independent. Since this was related to disagreements about the kind of international structure Japan was trying to build—the Foreign Ministry had a proprietorial interest in the treaty port system, or a derivative from it, while the army favoured something closer to direct Japanese rule—it was not a problem that could be easily shrugged aside. What is more, as the area of Japanese ambitions was extended, it inevitably recurred with regard to other parts of Asia.

13

Japan's New Order in North-east Asia

THE events leading to the creation of Manchukuo in 1931–2 changed the frame of reference for Japanese policy-making in several ways. Externally, they demonstrated that in certain circumstances the objections of the powers could be ignored. Because world trade had been reduced in volume and was becoming regionally fragmented, threats to exclude Japan from markets or to deny it access to finance were paradoxically less to be feared. Japan was already suffering such deprivations, regardless of its actions on the Asian mainland.

By the same token, it had become more difficult for the Foreign Ministry to cite such threats as an argument for checking the aspirations of the army. Army commanders had shown that they could disregard the cabinet with impunity. There were no elder statesmen who were highly enough regarded to be able to call them to order, as Itō had done in 1906. In fact, most decisions in the 1930s were made by groups of departmental ministers, many of whom were former bureaucrats. Each spoke for the 'national' interest in terms of his own segmental view of it; none had the authority to impose his own priorities on the rest. Nor had the Premier, who was commonly chosen because he was 'acceptable'. Thus Japanese government, although in theory authoritarian, came to rely increasingly on 'liaison' between one centre of power and another. And Japanese imperialism became the product of a multiplicity of policies, ill co-ordinated.

There were two ingredients in it which will be familiar to students of other cases of imperialism. The first, which had long been evident in Manchuria, was sub-imperialism: initiatives taken by men in positions of responsibility overseas, confident that a successful *fait accompli* would be ratified by their government at home. The second, related to it, was frontier imperialism: a habit of intervention in territories adjacent to those already held, on the grounds that they sheltered 'enemies', or were disorderly, therefore dangerous. Both phenomena had occurred in the building of Britain's empire in India and Russia's in

Central Asia. Both can be observed in the Japanese Army's moves from Manchuria into northern China after 1932.

If one were to accept that Japanese expansion in these years reflected nothing more than this—the removal of restraints upon long-standing ambitions, plus the kind of temptations that weakness usually offers to the strong—then there would be little that need be said about it. It was more than this, however. The very fact of exercising power in China raised difficult questions for many Japanese. One was practical: having committed itself to seeking a much larger measure of control over Chinese society than the West had done, what machinery could Japan devise for giving its wishes effect? Neither traditional devices, like founding a new dynasty, nor modern ones, deriving from informal empire, seemed particularly appropriate. A second question was the psychological one: how were the realities of Japanese power to be reconciled with emotive—and often sincere—slogans like 'coexistence and co-prosperity', or 'Sino-Japanese accord'? Could one reconcile the fact of empire with a sense of being Asian?

It was from such dilemmas that there emerged the concept of the New Order (*shin-chitsujo*). The expression was first applied to Japan, Taiwan, Korea, north China, and Manchukuo; and it will therefore be considered in that sense here, leaving its subsequent extension to the rest of East and south-east Asia for discussion when we examine the Greater East Asia Co-prosperity Sphere.

The advance into China

By the spring of 1932 it was clear to most senior political figures in Tokyo that there was no prospect of undoing what had been done in Manchuria. The powers, though obviously disgruntled, showed no signs of intervening. Hence the immediate question was how to win Chinese acceptance of the situation. In other words, the focus of policy debates shifted from the making of Manchukuo to the nature of Japan's relationship with China Proper: whether to seek, as in the past, to pursue Japanese interests by supporting a friendly Chinese government, or to extend the Manchurian pattern farther south, as many army leaders wished to do.

In August 1932 the Saitō cabinet approved a number of resolutions on this subject.[1] They set out two main objects: to develop the econ-

---

[1] The text of the cabinet resolution is in *NGNB*, II, documents, 206–10. The account of Sino-Japanese relations given in this chapter is based principally on Crowley, *Japan's Quest for Autonomy*; Morley, *The China Quagmire*; Boyle, *China and Japan at War*; and Lincoln Li, *The Japanese Army in North China 1937–1941* (1975).

omy of Manchukuo as a contribution to Japanese military strength; and to maintain trade with China in collaboration with the powers. They also—though in guarded language—authorized the cultivation of goodwill among Chinese officials in north China, independently of Nanking. The effect was to give a green light to the Kwantung Army's most recent ambitions. Early in 1933 it pushed some distance into Jehol and Hopei, on the pretext of guaranteeing defences for Manchukuo. It also established an office in Tientsin under Itagaki Seishirō, from which to try to win local war-lords away from their allegiance to Chiang Kai-shek. Finally, it negotiated a truce (May 1933) creating a demilitarized zone thirty miles wide to the south of the Great Wall.

Whereas the army on this evidence was aiming at piecemeal control over such parts of China as were thought necessary to its strategic and economic purposes, the cabinet, reflecting the views rather of the Foreign Ministry, moved towards something more like a protectorate over the country as a whole. In March 1933, when notifying its withdrawal from the League of Nations, Japan had asserted that in its present chaotic condition China could not be regarded as 'an organized state'. Therefore 'the general principles of international law which govern the ordinary relations between nations' had to be 'considered modified in their operation as far as China is concerned'.[2] Just over a year later a Foreign Ministry spokesman in Tokyo, Amau Eiji, drew out some of the implications of this. Japan, he said, claimed the right to prohibit 'any attempt on the part of China to avail herself of the influence of any other country in order to resist Japan'. It would even oppose technical and financial assistance to China by the powers, on the grounds that this might be made 'an opening wedge for direct international control'.[3]

In December 1934 a memorandum drafted for the cabinet by officials of the Army, Navy, and Foreign Ministries took the formulation of Japanese aims a step further. China was to be brought, it stated, together with Manchukuo, into an international structure of which Japan would be 'the nucleus'. To this end, it would be necessary to abandon the pretence of non-intervention in Chinese politics. Japan must 'exploit internal strife' as a means of overcoming China's anti-Japanese attitudes; induce Nanking 'to appoint persons friendly toward

---

[2] Nish, *Japanese Foreign Policy*, 299–300.
[3] Morley, *China Quagmire*, 79–80.

Japan to various offices within the government'; and seek to detach local leaders from their allegiance to the Kuomintang.[4]

Once again the Kwantung Army took this as the authority for doing what it wanted to do, namely, create a regional government in north China, subordinate to Japan and committed to promoting economic development on Japan's behalf. Despite Tokyo's continuing reluctance to push matters to extremes, it eventually had its way. On 6 December 1935 the Kuomintang agreed to permit the formation of a Hopei–Chahar Political Council, headed by Sung Che-yüan, and to give it a measure of financial autonomy. It also promised Sino-Japanese co-operation against communism, plus 'harmonization' of economic relations between north China and Manchukuo.[5]

This did not by any means ensure unanimity within Japan. Accordingly, efforts were made during the first half of 1936 to express policy in more generally acceptable terms. The discussions at once revealed disagreements between the Army and Navy General Staffs. Both believed that the resources of north China and Manchukuo were essential to Japan's defence and must be developed under Japanese supervision. Beyond that, however, they differed. The navy, looking to its oil requirements, urged economic penetration of south-east Asia. A corollary, it maintained, was caution in north China and Inner Mongolia, which should remain 'special regions under Chinese sovereignty'. The army, preoccupied with the question of control, insisted on the need for 'building a new China', which it saw as 'the key to administering East Asia'.[6]

In August 1936 the Hirota cabinet undertook the difficult task of reconciling these ideas with each other and with those of the Foreign Ministry concerning the necessity of a settlement of some kind with the Kuomintang. The outcome was a statement of principles, known as the Fundamentals of National Policy.[7] It was an important document, setting out the basic propositions from which both the New

---

[4] Ibid., 90–1.

[5] B. W. Kahn, 'Doihara Kenji and the North China Autonomy Movement' (1978),

[6] Documents in Joyce Lebra (ed.), *Japan's Greater East Asia Co-prosperity Sphere in World War II* (1975), 58–62. On Ishiwara's views at this time, see Peattie, *Ishiwara*, 267–86.

[7] There are variant translations of the document (dated 7 Aug. 1936) in Lebra, *Japan's . . . Co-prosperity Sphere*, 62–4, and Nish, *Japanese Foreign Policy*, 301–3. The full Japanese text, together with an associated statement on foreign policy of the same date, is in *NGNB*, II, documents, 344–7.

Order and the Co-prosperity Sphere were to develop. Central to them was the assertion that Japan must 'eliminate the tyrannical policies of the powers in East Asia' and substitute 'cordial relations' with the peoples of the area, 'founded on the principles of coexistence and co-prosperity'. It would also undertake economic expansion on its own account, both 'by creating a strong coalition between Japan, Manchukuo, and China' and by extending its interests into south-east Asia in 'gradual and peaceful' ways. There were some conditions. The army must be given forces in Korea and Kwantung sufficient to deal with any attack from Soviet Russia. The navy must have a fleet capable of maintaining 'ascendancy in the west Pacific' against that of the United States. At home, steps would have to be taken to unite public opinion behind the plans and promote 'sound thoughts'; to improve economic organization; to achieve 'self-sufficiency in important resources and materials needed for national defence and industry'.

Proposals for diplomatic action, approved on the same date, were in some respects more specific concerning China and south-east Asia. Sino-Japanese co-operation, designed to detach Nanking from its communist affiliations, though highly desirable, must not, it was said, be allowed to stand in the way of treating north China as a 'special region', to be brought into close relationship with Japan and Manchukuo. It was, for example, to provide strategic materials, in order to strengthen their defences against the Soviet Union. As to the south, the gradual and peaceful approach enunciated in the Fundamentals was intended to avert fears in the countries of the area concerning Japanese aims. There might be some advantage in giving cautious encouragement to moves towards Philippine independence. A non-aggression pact with Holland might be considered, as a means of reducing Dutch suspicions about Japanese designs on the Netherlands East Indies. Elsewhere, Japan should provide 'leadership and guidance' to 'backward peoples'.

From the point of view of ministers in Tokyo, none of this was meant to bring about territorial expansion. They still thought in terms of informal empire, that is, of securing an increase in Japan's privileges through pressure exerted on Asian governments, including that of China. Even authorizing negotiations with local Chinese leaders was primarily for the purpose of getting the Kuomintang to acknowledge the realities of Japanese power. However, this was not how things looked to people on the mainland, whatever their nationality. Japanese generals assumed that they had the authority to make their own arrangements with Chinese officials, virtually ignoring Nanking. Loyal members of the Kuomintang, witnessing this, took what was happening to be a planned dismemberment of their country. After December 1936, when Chiang Kai-shek reached agreement with the communists at Sian, their resistance to the practice stiffened.

It was as a result of such perceptions on both sides, not on this occasion as a consequence of conspiracy, that full-scale hostilities broke out between China and Japan in July 1937. Following a clash between troops at Marco Polo Bridge on the outskirts of Peking, the Japanese general commanding in north China seized the opportunity to demand greater control of the region's railways, apparently with a view to strengthening his position *vis-à-vis* the Hopei–Chahar Political Council. The Chinese resisted. What is more, they steadily committed more troops; and since the Japanese General Staff was able to persuade both itself and its government that a rapid and total victory was possible, in order to achieve a 'final' solution to the China 'problem', it was only a matter of weeks before the incident became a campaign. By September, Japan's newly created North China Army had 200,000 men in the field. Fighting spread to the Yangtze, culminating on 13 December in the capture of Nanking, where Japanese units were turned loose to murder, rape, and loot in one of the war's worst atrocities.

Our concern here is not with the military struggle, save to note that, contrary to Japanese expectations, it did not quickly end. During 1938 further Japanese victories secured most of the Yangtze valley, except Szechwan, and established command of the coastline as far south as Canton. Still Chiang Kai-shek's forces did not surrender. They withdrew into the south-west, keeping open lines of communication with India. Moreover, in the hinterland, especially in the north, the Chinese Communist Party organized guerrilla resistance on a considerable scale. Thus, although the Japanese army held the principal cities, ports, railways, and waterways of China, fighting continued in one part of the country or another until 1945. This fact was to be a major obstacle to Japan in trying to effect a political and economic settlement.

The New Order

Konoe Fumimaro became Prime Minister of Japan in June 1937 and so remained until January 1939. Advisers close to the imperial court had chosen him in the belief that while his views on Japan's proper place in the world would make him acceptable to army leaders, his lineage would ensure a commitment to the balance of political institutions established since 1868. They were disappointed. Konoe pursued a policy of 'government by acquiescence'. The army was left free to undertake expansion in China during the next two years, while a National Mobilization Law, passed in March 1938, gave the cabinet the powers which the Control Faction regarded as necessary in preparation for total war. To quote the *Tokyo Gazette*, it provided for 'control and operation of human and material resources in such a way as to enable the State to give full scope to the efficient use of its strength for . . . national defense in time of war'.[8] Specifically, it empowered the government to implement, when it thought fit, regulations covering the control of foreign trade; prices and profits; allocation of capital, labour, and raw materials; and the dissemination of news. Some were put into force almost at once.

It was during this period that a group of intellectuals, working under Konoe's patronage, was seeking to frame a set of ideas appropriate to the country's expansionist aims in Asia. Most were members of an association, the Shōwa Kenkyūkai, founded at the end of 1936.[9] They considered that in the task of creating its own economic and strategic bloc Japan had need of an ideology more positive than could be comprised in simple rejection of the West's liberalism, individualism, and communism, on which contemporary rhetoric blamed the world's ills. Nor was it desirable in their view that Asian peoples should be allowed to equate Japanese imperialism with Western imperialism, merely because both put their self-justification in terms of population growth and living-space. Hence they turned for an alternative to the traditionalist critique of modern society, which had become an element in Japanese nationalism. Western imperialism, they said, because it was self-seeking, was tyranny (*hadō*). By contrast, Japanese expansion, which sought to free Asia from the West, was just. Its object was a partnership. For practical reasons, this must be a partnership in which Japan led, resting on an ethic in Japanese form: on Japan's 'national polity' (*kokutai*), manifested in Japan's 'imperial way(' (*kōdō*). That is to say, the Confucian concept of what was just must be combined with a

[8] Hugh Borton, *Japan since 1931* (1940), 61.

[9] i.e. Shōwa Study Association (Shōwa being the reign-period of the emperor, Hirohito, starting in 1926). See James B. Crowley, 'Intellectuals as visionaries of the New Asian Order' (1971). Some relevant translations are in Lebra, *Japan's . . . Co-prosperity Sphere*, Part I, including the passage from a book by Miyazaki Masayoshi, which is quoted here.

Japanese idea of how to achieve it (implying that Japan was to take over China's historical role in Asia, as well as that of the West). Miyazaki Masayoshi, writing in 1936, had shown what this might mean in current conditions. Chiang Kai-shek, he argued, was unacceptable as a ruler of China because he represented the coming together of 'British and French imperialism and Soviet Red imperialism'. Only after he had been overthrown could China be absorbed with Japan and Manchukuo into an East Asian league, capable of being 'a free union of liberated East Asian nations', based on 'the rule of righteousness'. Within such a league, Japanese 'guidance' would replace Western dominance. And 'the Western concept of freedom' would give way to 'the Eastern concept of morality'.

Men like Miyazaki provided Japanese imperialism with a political vocabulary, but they did not shape its policies. These continued to emerge from the leadership's assessment of military imperatives and international pressure, though in the euphoria produced by Japanese victories during the second half of 1937 the latter did not impose any notable restraint. Following the capture of Nanking, the Konoe cabinet decided to offer the Kuomintang (not Chiang Kai-shek personally) peace terms which embodied Chinese recognition of Manchukuo and of Japan's position in the north. Acceptance of them, it was believed, would make possible the creation of a political authority in Peking, friendly to Japan and capable of being developed into an amenable central government for all China. Local autonomous councils as far south as Shantung and west to Shansi would be absorbed into it. Another similar authority would be needed in the lower-Yangtze basin, destined eventually to be brought into a close relationship with that in the north. Both were to be supervised through Japanese advisers, much like Manchukuo, and both were to have as one primary function the planning of 'co-prosperity', in order to co-ordinate transport, mining and energy supply in ways that would meet Japanese industry's needs.[10]

Much of this was a confirmation of policies which army commands on the mainland had already put in hand. During the campaign the Kwantung Army had established a separatist Mongolian government in Kalgan, mostly for the sake of giving Mantetsu access to the area's coal and iron. There was also a puppet regime in Peking, having its origins in a series of local Chinese committees, sponsored by the

---

[10] Cabinet resolutions of 24 Dec. 1937 in *NGNB*, II, documents, 381–4.

North China Army, acting under orders from the War Ministry and General Staff. These had been brought together under a Tientsin–Peking Liaison Committee in September 1937, then formed into the Peking Provisional Government in December, headed by a former Finance Minister, Wang K'o-min.

The situation in the Yangtze valley required more circumspection, since both the Kuomintang and the treaty powers were able to make things difficult there. Hence progress was slower, though the end-result was much the same: numerous local peace preservation committees, set up during the winter of 1937–8; a provisional and avowedly temporary Reformed Government in Shanghai from March 1938, which moved to Nanking in June. This had the same range of authority and was subjected to the same military supervision as the one in Peking, with which it was linked later in the year by yet another liaison committee.

The fact that the Kuomintang and the Chinese Communists continued to offer resistance, despite these moves, led to a further review of Japanese policy during the second half of 1938. As a result of it, on 30 November the Imperial Conference—senior members of the cabinet and service chiefs, meeting in the emperor's presence—approved a list of proposals designed to bring China into a close relationship with Japan and Manchukuo.[11] This was to be the New Order in East Asia. By way of preliminary, China would have to be persuaded to give diplomatic recognition to Manchukuo. This done, there would be established a federal structure for China itself: 'a composite of administrative parts' (*bunji-gassaku*). Separate Japanese-sponsored regimes in Mongolia, Shanghai, Tsingtao, and Amoy would all continue to coexist with those in Peking and Nanking. A Sino-Japanese military alliance would give Japan the right to station forces in China and Mongolia for the purposes of providing defence against Russia and suppressing communism within China's borders. It would be supplemented by Japanese provision of military advisers and munitions for a Chinese army limited to peace-keeping functions, like that of Manchukuo. In return, Japan would gradually relinquish its privileges under the unequal treaties. In economic matters—which will be considered more fully later in this chapter—Japan was to have special rights with respect to the exploitation of key raw materials in Mongolia

---

[11] The text is in *N G N B*, II, documents, 405–7. See also Boyle, *China and Japan at War*, 215–17, and Morley, *China Quagmire*, 327–9. For Konoe's public statement on the subject in December 1938, see Lebra, *Japan's . . . Co-prosperity Sphere*, 68–70.

and North China, as well as co-operating generally in the development of the Chinese economy.

These proposals constituted a surrender to the hard-line view that there was no immediate prospect of discovering in China a potential central government that was likely to be both effective and friendly to Japan. Japan's interests, it was argued, could best be served by a process of divide-and-rule After all, in terms both of the threat from Russia—its immediacy had been underlined during July and August 1938 by a clash near the Russo-Korean frontier at Changkufeng—and of the need for industrial materials, it was the north that mattered most. Hence the New Order would concentrate on the Japan–Manchukuo–North China triangle. Leaving the Yangtze valley and the south under looser control was tolerable, even advantageous. It might reduce the level of Anglo-American protests. It would enable Japan still to maintain a valuable export trade in consumer goods, by which to earn foreign currency.

There were nevertheless several attempts in the next two years to try the alternative, that is, to construct a 'suitable' government for China, which might, despite subservience to Japan, secure at least a partial loyalty from the country as a whole. They came to centre on winning over Wang Ching-wei, who had long been one of Chiang Kai-shek's senior colleagues.[12] When Konoe publicly announced the New Order in November 1938 he made it clear that this did not preclude peace talks with the Kuomintang, provided the latter dropped its claim to speak for all China and was willing to separate itself from Chiang Kai-shek (whom the Japanese Army believed to be irreconcilable). This was the beginning of a complex series of negotiations, in which different Japanese authorities—the army, the Foreign Ministry, the cabinet—pursued a variety of aims. It was obvious throughout that the army was unwilling to abandon the puppet regimes it had established in North China and Mongolia, chiefly because it did not want to share its power in those regions with any other Japanese organization. On the other hand, many men of influence in Tokyo wanted to keep the door open to a settlement with Chiang Kai-shek, which could hardly be done if firm arrangements were concluded with Wang Ching-wei. It required talks in Tokyo, Shanghai, and Chungking, lasting into 1940, before all this was sorted out.

[12] On Japan's dealings with Wang Ching-wei, see Boyle, *China and Japan at War*, 167–335; and more generally on Japan in north China, Li, *Japanese Army*, 95–117.

The agreement signed with Wang Ching-wei on 30 November 1940 embodied the principle of *bunji-gassaku* enunciated by the Imperial Conference two years earlier: separate councils in Peking and Kalgan, only nominally subject to Wang's own government in Nanking; and local committees in Shanghai, Amoy, and Hainan. All were in large measure under Japanese control, as was evidenced by the presence of Japanese garrisons. The North China Political Council in Peking was to have Japanese advisers; a specified share of China's central revenue; its own currency; even its own military force. Administratively it would be closely linked with Manchukuo and would implement similar domestic policies. They included the formation of a Sino-Japanese political support group, the New People's Society (Hsin-min Hui), much like the Concordia Association, plus an education system giving priority to technical training and Confucian values. Both the Hsin-min Hui and the schools were required to renounce the People's Principles which the Kuomintang had inherited from Sun Yat-sen, as well as Western liberalism and materialism. Confucian textbooks were revised and reintroduced, emphasizing common elements in the Sino-Japanese tradition; the political terminology of imperial China was widely used; so were its surviving bureaucrats and village headmen. Deliberately— though not very successfully—the people of north China were encouraged to think of themselves as members of a culture, Japan-centred and anti-Western, from which China's recent history had led them to deviate.

There was nothing comparable in central and southern China, where Wang Ching-wei's administration was treated as little more than a device for maintaining order in Japanese-occupied areas. The outbreak of the Pacific War in December 1941 gave it a better bargaining position, because China's internal conflict then became relevant to the wider struggle, so giving Japan a motive for generosity; but the only recognizable gain was a revision of the unequal treaties (January 1943), paralleling that which Chiang Kai-shek secured from Britain and America. The fact was that Wang Ching-wei never won the kind of independence from Japan that would have made it possible for him to compete with either nationalists or communists for Chinese popular support. This in turn made his role in the New Order an inconsiderable one.

Building the New Order also involved changes in Japan itself. Some of these were designed to rally the country behind the decisions which preparation for total war demanded: a one-party Diet; stricter censorship; enhanced political indoctrination in schools; a constant public reiteration of patriotic slogans. Others were meant to improve co-ordination in the framing and execution of policy. The Cabinet Planning Board (Kikakuin) was established in October 1937 to strengthen the bureaucracry in its central direction of affairs. The Imperial Headquarters (Daihonei) was activated in the following month to ensure better liaison between army, navy, and civil offices with respect to the campaigns in China.

In addition, there were attempts further to reduce the responsibilities of the Foreign Ministry,[13] just as there had been after the founding of Manchukuo. This was not unreasonable, in so far as Japanese relations with other territories within the New Order were not 'diplomatic' in the usual sense. Nor did they all emanate from the government in Tokyo: many of the decisions being taken on the mainland, especially in the north, were made by army special service units, operating almost independently. It was not difficult, therefore, for men in the capital to agree that something fresh should be done to regulate them. Problems arose, however, because of a familiar conflict of interests. The Foreign Ministry insisted that the affairs of China involved essentially Japan's relations with the powers, the army that they were first and foremost a matter of national defence (now extended to include the planning of a war economy). Hence proposals for a special government agency to deal with China, when they were put forward by the Cabinet Planning Board in January 1938, at once became a subject of controversy. The Foreign Ministry wanted economic development in China to be put under the supervision of one of its own bureaux, in that it touched upon international rights. The War Ministry argued for a separate institution—over which it expected to exercise a predominant influence—to deal with both occupied and supposedly independent zones there. It was not until September 1938 that Konoe was able to engineer a compromise between them. A new body, the China Affairs Board (Taishiin)—renamed the Asia Development Board (Kōain) in December—was to be created, having the Prime Minister as its president and the Foreign, Finance, War, and Navy Ministers as deputies. It would deal with all matters of policy concerning China, except 'pure' diplomacy; would liaise with other government departments as might be necessary; and would establish its own field

---

[13] Baba, *Nitchū kankei*, 303–9, 337–50.

representatives on the mainland, superceding the army special service units in due course.

The Asia Development Board proved one degree less effective than the Manchurian Affairs Board. There were more bodies for it to deal with: the Cabinet Planning Board, as well as various ministries; the Imperial Headquarters, as well as the General Staff; and at a distance, the North China Army, as well as the Kwantung Army. It had a wider range of problems to solve: the distinctions to be maintained between north China and the rest of that country; the contradictions between Japan's strategic and economic interests everywhere. As a consequence, its efforts to co-ordinate often failed. Even in economic policy, which was central to this phase of Japanese expansion, there were soon to be indications that Japan had taken on more than it could readily handle.

The industrial heartland

To some Japanese it was the unselfish objectives of national policy—establishing a special relationship with China, in particular, and thereby turning back the tide of Western imperialism—that were of first importance. To others it was the selfish ones: Japan's own security and economic survival, achieved at whatever cost to Asian values. Arguably, one could not exist without the other. Unless Japan were made strong, there was no way of saving Asia from the West; and making Japan strong involved economic exploitation of its neighbours.

There were nevertheless two different ways in which the economic relationship could be conceived. One was simply as trade, that is, an exchange of merchandise necessary to the functioning of the Japanese economy. Ever since Japan had entered the first stage of its modernization in the nineteenth century, it had depended crucially on other parts of the world for markets and raw materials. The slump of 1929–30 had put at risk its access to some of them. A sudden drop in sales of silk to the United States and of cotton goods to China, revealed in the export figures for 1930–4 (Table 9), was not only a disaster for Japanese farmers and textile manufacturers, but also a severe blow to the country's balance of payments, on which the import of raw materials depended. One response was devaluation of the yen at the end of 1931, stimulating a growth of markets through more competitive pricing. Equally significant, however, was a geographical redistribution of foreign trade. In colonial and semi-colonial areas exports could be supported by political pressure. Thus while the United

Table 9. *Japan's foreign trade 1925–1939: percentage shares by countries*

	Total* (annual averages in yen millions)	% shares						
		USA	Taiwan	Korea	Kwantung/ Manchuria	Rest of China	India	Rest of Asia
Exports								
1925–9	2,391.2	37.1	5.4	11.4	4.4	16.3	7.0	10.0
1930–4	1,987.5	22.8	7.0	15.4	7.9	9.9	8.8	13.7
1935–9	3,955.6	14.3	7.2	20.7	11.8	13.2	6.2	10.9
Imports								
1925–9	2,841.3	23.2	7.6	11.5	5.5	7.9	12.7	8.2
1930–4	2,182.7	24.6	10.6	13.7	3.1	9.0	8.5	7.4
1935–9	3,878.7	25.0	10.4	15.6	1.2	10.1	7.6	9.2

* Includes Japan's trade with Japanese colonies

Sources: *Nihon Kindaishi Jiten* (1958), Table 42; *Nihon Teikoku Tōkei Nenkan*, annual volumes; Ohkawa, Shinohara and Meissner, *Patterns of Japanese Economic Development* (1979), Tables A 26 and A 27; Oriental Economist, *Foreign Trade of Japan* (1935).

States' share of Japanese exports fell from 37 per cent in 1925–9 to just over 14 per cent in 1935–9, that of Taiwan and Korea, taken together, rose from 16.8 to 27.9 per cent over the same period. Similarly, the proportion going to China and Manchuria increased from 20.7 to 25 per cent.

A similar realignment of imports was not necessarily possible, as is shown by the continued high percentage drawn from the United States. After all, the distribution of cotton and iron and oil supplies was a fact of geography, not political circumstance. Even so, some adjustment took place. Taiwan and Korea provided 19.1 per cent of imports in 1925–9, but 26 per cent a decade later. To set against that, China and Manchuria showed a small decline, though, as we shall see, it reflected changed directions of development, rather than trading conditions. Altogether, the countries that were comprised within the New Order accounted for just over 37 per cent of Japanese imports in 1935–9, compared with 32.5 per cent before 1930.

There is another aspect to overseas trade, however. Since about 1914 it had become common for Japan's leaders to consider supplies of raw materials for heavy industry as being in a separate category from the rest, because of their strategic importance. From that viewpoint, it was highly desirable that Japan should have not only the means of paying for imports of them, but also some guarantee of a reliable supply.

This carried certain political implications. First, it was necessary as far as possible to ensure the security of the regions from which such materials were drawn, together with the routes running from them to Japan. Second, there had to be a measure of financial control, through which to influence production and development in a manner appropriate to Japanese needs. In essence, this meant investment in transport and mining, supported by military access.

Japan's requirements for petroleum could not be within north-east Asia, where Sakhalin had the only developed field. Of the total quantity imported in 1932, approximately 55 per cent by value came from the United States and 20 per cent from the Netherlands East Indies (Indonesia).[14] It is therefore more convenient to postpone consideration of oil supplies until the next chapter, where they can be considered in the context of Japan's advance into south-east Asia. Of other raw materials, coal and iron for the steel industry were of particular military concern. Japan was deficient in some grades of coal (though it had a surplus of other grades, available for export) and was almost wholly dependent on imports for iron. Apart from American scrap metal, the nearest major sources were Manchuria and north China. Further afield, pig-iron came from British India, iron ore from the Straits Settlements, some coal from French Indo-China. In 1929, total imports under this head totalled 90 million yen. Of this sum, approximately 55 million can be attributed to north China and Manchuria, another 28 million to the European colonial territories. Since the latter could hardly be considered a 'reliable' source in a period of potential conflict with Western imperialism, it is not at all surprising that Japan turned increasingly thereafter to its neighbours for these items. By 1940 the value of imports of coal and iron came to 382 million yen: 167 million from north China and Manchukuo, only 22 million from India and the Straits Settlements.

Such figures afford one explanation of why military planners gave priority to Japanese control of Manchuria, plus the adjacent regions of north China and Inner Mongolia. At the end of 1939 a memorandum by the Ministers of War, Navy, and Foreign Affairs described these areas as forming with Japan an 'economically self-sufficient national

---

[14] Statistical information in this section is drawn chiefly from the following: *Nihon Teikoku Tōkei Nenkan*, relevant years; J. B. Cohen, *Japan's Economy in War and Reconstruction* (1949); Kobayashi, *Dai Tōa Kyōei Ken*; *Ōkura zaibatsu no kenkyū*; and Schumpeter, *Industrialization of Japan and Manchukuo*.

defence sphere'.[15] This was certainly the army's intention. Ishiwara
Kanji, while serving on the General Staff in 1936 and 1937, successfully extended its functions to include the economic aspects of planning for war. Working in conjunction with Miyazaki Masayoshi,
formerly of Mantetsu, and bringing a number of senior bureaucrats
and representatives of the *zaibatsu* into the discussions, he drafted a
Five Year Plan covering the years 1937–41 (on the assumption that
Japan must avoid being drawn into major hostilities until that period
had ended).[16] It applied to all the major industries which were vital to
military strength: iron and steel, light metals, oil, coal, electric power,
chemicals, armaments (including aircraft), automobiles, railway
rolling-stock, shipbuilding, machinery, and machine tools. For each
there were production targets, separately for Japan and Manchukuo,
together with estimates of the capital investment that would be needed
to achieve them. Imports required from north China were also
specified.

The plan suffered a number of bureaucratic vicissitudes, with the
result that it was not formally approved by the cabinet until early 1939
(and then in modified form). Moreover, its original calculations were
seriously undermined by the outbreak of war with China in the summer of 1937. Nevertheless, it constituted the chief basis of government
policies for economic development during the next few years. Elabor-
ating it became one of the tasks of the new Cabinet Planning Board.
Implementing it was a primary purpose of the National Mobilization
Law. It can be regarded, therefore, as a statement of the economic
principles underlying Konoe's New Order.

In the context of a study of imperialism, these principles had one
very distinctive feature. An attempt to organize an industrial complex
spreading into several different territories is itself unusual. It becomes
still more so when it departs significantly from the 'imperialist' doctrine that the role of dependencies is to provide the homeland with
food for its work-force and raw materials for its manufacturing industries. Japan did not wholly abandon these doctrines, of course. Korea
and Taiwan were to remain suppliers of foodstuffs. North China and
Manchukuo continued to furnish coal and iron. In addition, however,
the Five Year Plan set targets for steel production in Manchukuo—at a

[15] Memorandum of 28 Dec. 1939 in *NGNB*, II, documents, 424.
[16] Peattie, *Ishiwara*, 197–219. For details of the Five Year Plan itself, see Takafusa
Nakamura, *Economic Growth in Prewar Japan* (1983), 268–85.

level about half that of Japan—and looked to the manufacture there of modest quantities of arms, aircraft, automobiles, and railway rolling-stock. This is not at all the standard pattern of a colonial economy.

In the colonies proper, the new planning had more impact on Korea than on Taiwan. In the latter there was a small increase in manufacturing industry during the 1930s, but more than two-thirds was still concerned with food processing in 1935–9, only about one-sixth with metals, machinery, and chemicals. Just under a half of Taiwan's production was accounted for by agriculture, chiefly rice and sugar.[17] In Korea, too, agriculture was much the most important industry, exporting 37 per cent of its rice crop to Japan in 1935–9. However, there was a significant growth in mining and manufacturing after 1930.[18] Apart from processed foods and cotton textiles, Korea was producing useful quantities of iron and steel by 1941, as well as chemicals, magnesium, and light metals. Japanese business investment there in 1942 is estimated at a little more than 2,000 million yen, of which about one-eighth was in companies associated with the three main *zaibatsu*, Mitsui, Mitsubishi, and Sumitomo, whereas three times as much was represented by one of the new *zaibatsu*, Nihon Chisso (Japan Nitrogen). This firm had moved to Korea in 1926 in search of cheap labour and electric power, then diversified into the production of explosives, zinc, aluminium, magnesium, and synthetic oil.

The development that took place in Manchukuo and north China differed from that of the two colonies both in scale and in the nature of its business structure. In 1930 over 60 per cent of Japanese investment in China was already located in Manchuria, approximately another 25 per cent being in and around Shanghai. After that year its value grew rapidly (Table 10). The figure for Manchuria (Manchukuo) increased fivefold between 1931 and 1941, that for the rest of China by only a little less. During the Pacific War this rate of increase was broadly maintained. Thus by the end of the war Japan had put over 10,000 million yen into Manchukuo alone, which at 1941 exchange rates would have been nearly 2,500 million US dollars. Total foreign investment in the whole of China, including Manchuria, had only been 3,200 million dollars in 1931. Comparing this with the colonies,

---

[17] Barclay, *Colonial development*, 28–42, Kobayashi, *Dia Tōa Kyōei Ken*, 338–41.
[18] Chang, 'Colonization', 171–8; article by Chul Won Kang in Nahm, *Korea*, 77–85; Kobayashi, *Dai Tōa Kyōei Ken*, 79–91, 201–12, 334–8.

Table 10. *Japanese investment in China and Manchuria,*
1931–1944

	Totals (yen millions at current prices)			
	at 1931	at 1936	at 1941	at 1944
Manchuria (Manchukuo)	1,400	3,000	7,300	10,400
Rest of China	800	1,600	3,500	6,400

Sources: Higuchi, *Nihon no tai-Shi tōshi* (1939); Kobayashi, *Dai Tōa Kyō'ei-ken* (1975); Okurashō, *Shōwa Zaiseishi* (1954–65), vol. 13. The sources do not in all respects agree, so figures are approximate.

Japanese public and private investment in Korea by 1944 came to about 7,000 million yen, that in Taiwan to 2,000 million.[19] When Japan occupied Manchuria in 1931, much the largest part of heavy industry there was under the control of the South Manchurian Railway Company (Mantetsu). In addition to the railway itself, this included a major coal-mine at Fushun, producing 7 million tonnes a year, and an ironworks at Anshan. The Ōkura company had a coal and iron plant at Penhsihu. There were also a number of industrial concerns founded on the initiative of the war-lord government in Mukden. This comprised the nucleus from which the Kwantung Army set out to create an industrial base to support its operations in the event of an attack by Russia.[20] Its chosen method—designed to avoid 'the baneful effects of unbridled capitalism'—was to establish a range of 'special' and 'semi-special' companies under the overall supervision of Mantetsu (in which the Japanese government held half the stock). Each company was to dominate a particular field of activity: coal-mining, electric power, petroleum, and so on. In this way, it was believed, the direction of development could be made to conform with the army's priorities.

Mantetsu's railway activities expanded greatly over the next few years. There was some building of new lines, mostly for strategic purposes in the north and to open up mining areas in the south; but much

[19] There is a useful summary of investment figures in *Ōkura zaibatsu*, 377–82, though there remain some unresolved discrepancies. The most detailed information is in Ōkurashō, *Shōwa Zaiseishi* (1954–65), vol. 13. Investment in China before 1930 is discussed in Chapter 9, above.

[20] On the economic development of Manchukuo after 1931, see Schumpeter, *Industrialization of Japan and Manchukuo*, 376–410; Kobayashi, *Dai Tōa Kyōei Ken*, 47–52, 66–78, 192–201; and *Ōkura zaibatsu*, 382–93.

the largest part of the increase came by virtue of taking over the management of Chinese railways in 1933 and of the Chinese Eastern Railway, purchased from Russia in 1935. An extension of Manchuria's road network was also undertaken. The Anshan ironworks, reorganized as Shōwa Steel in 1933, together with Penhsihu, doubled the region's output of iron ore and pig-iron, while making a start on producing steel. There was a more modest increase in the production of coal, of which some three or four million tonnes was exported annually to Japan. Of the other state-controlled companies operating between 1931 and 1937, the largest were in ancillary services, like communications, electric power, and banking.

The results achieved did not altogether satisfy the Kwantung Army. Nor did Mantetsu's management, which in the army's view gave too much attention to making profits. Steps were therefore taken to modify the arrangements after the first few years. One was to extract from Ishiwara's Five Year Plan the sections relating to Manchukuo, in order to implement them immediately, without waiting for more comprehensive decisions in Tokyo. It was agreed in January 1937 that additional investment should be made in coal, iron and steel, electric power, and synthetic oil production, designed eventually to make Manchukuo self-sufficient in the basic components of heavy industry. The bulk of the capital required was to be provided, as in the past, by Mantetsu and the government of Manchukuo.

The spread of hostilities in China a few months later forced some reconsideration of this plan. The long-term ambition of achieving self-sufficiency was set aside in favour of developing at once a capacity to supplement heavy industrial production in the homeland, especially in iron and steel. To this end, a sharp increase in mining investment was proposed, drawing more heavily on Japanese funds, including those of the *zaibatsu*. A new organization was created as a channel for it: the Manchuria Industrial Development Company (known as Mangyō), which was founded in December 1937, taking over from Mantetsu the supervision of the special and semi-special companies. These constituted the Manchukuo government's contribution to its initial capital. The rest was provided by the absorption of Japan's Nissan company, which now moved its headquarters to Hsinking (Changchun). Nissan's Ayukawa Yoshisuke assumed direction of the industrial development of Manchukuo as Mangyō's president.

Despite the considerable inflow of Japanese money after 1937 the targets set in the Five Year Plan for Manchukuo were never fully met.

This was partly because growing international tensions cut off access to western technology, partly because there were severe shortages of skilled labour. Japan, itself fully stretched, could not provide enough of either. Thus in coal-mining Manchukuo continued to rely to a large extent on older workings, like Fushun, instead of what were expected to be newer, low-cost ones. In order to maintain supplies to Manchukuo's own iron and steel industry, exports to Japan had to be reduced. Supplies even had to be brought from north China. Penhsihu and Shōwa Steel expanded to the point of producing just over 20 per cent of Japan's total output of pig-iron, but never exceeded 8 per cent in steel. Oil and light metal production failed to meet targets by wider margins. Outside these fields, which were mostly state-financed in one way or another—the Japanese government guaranteed a return of 6 per cent on Mangyō's capital for the first ten years—there were quite substantial business investments by major private companies like Mitsui and Mitsubishi, mostly in chemicals, machinery, cotton-spinning, pottery, and foodstuffs. Consequently, by the end of the war the southern part of Manchukuo was quite heavily industrialized.

In north and central China the conditions for a Japanese-sponsored development of this kind never really existed. The army—at first deliberately, but later because it lacked the resources to do anything else, in face of Chinese opposition—controlled principally the urban and mining areas, plus the transport routes connecting them. This pattern set limits to economic planning. Nor was there ever a single government in China which was able, like that of Manchukuo, to act as partner to Japan in a programme of industrialization, or to provide the legal and financial framework for it. Japanese economic penetration of China was carried out in regional segments, operating in each case through puppet regimes.

Some of what was done consisted simply of carpet-bagging and expropriation. Japanese entrepreneurs, enjoying army patronage, rapidly expanded their activities in the textile business and retailing in the 1930s. On a larger scale, the extension of Japanese political control after 1937 was accompanied by the seizure of Chinese companies in industries thought to be strategically significant. In most cases they were put under the management of well-established Japanese firms, such as Ōkura, supervised by military special service units.

In addition to all this, there were official attempts to ensure that China's resources of industrial raw materials were more fully exploited and made available to Japan.[21] The first steps in this direction were taken on the initiative of Mantetsu in 1934 and 1935, leading to the creation of a subsidiary in north China, the Hsing Chung Company, in August 1935. It made investments in electric power, coal and iron, and salt production. Mantetsu also moved into Inner Mongolia, taking over the important coalfield at Tatung and the Lungyen iron-mine near Kalgan. However, since Mantetsu proved no more acceptable to the North China Army than to the Kwantung Army as an economic agent, the Konoe government approved the formation of the North China Development Company on similar lines to Mangyō. It began operations in November 1938 under Ōtani Sonyū, a former Colonial Minister; drew half its capital from government contributions and the absorption of Hsing Chung; and concerned itself primarily with coal, iron, transport, and electric power. Another such concern, the Central China Development Company, was established at the same time to perform similar functions in the middle and lower Yangtze.

Substantial increases in production and supply were achieved under these arrangements. Coal produced in North China and Inner Mongolia totalled 10.7 million tonnes in 1937, rising to 22.8 million in 1941. About 30 per cent of it was exported to Japan and Manchukuo. The same two regions, together with central China, mined about one million tonnes of iron ore in 1939, and as much as 5 million tonnes in the peak year, 1942. Between 60 and 70 per cent of this came from the Yangtze valley, where the Hanyehping concern (see Chapter 10) had been put under the management of Nippon Steel. Again, the bulk of the output went to Japan and Manchukuo: between 75 and 90 per cent, according to year.

During the Pacific War it proved impossible to maintain these levels of production, still less to increase them further, as the Five Year Plan envisaged. Problems with the maintenance of transport and machinery, shortages of labour (partly reflecting inflation and difficulties with food supply), together with attacks by Chinese guerrillas, all contributed to a decline. It is true that China continued to provide crucial support for Japan's wartime industries, even though it did so under conditions which depended more and more on local labour and improvization, less and less on Japanese technology and skills; but because its contri-

---

[21] On Japanese acquisition of raw materials in China, see especially Takafusa Nakamura, 'Japan's economic thrust into North China 1933–1938' (1980); the article by Kimishima Kazuhiko in Asada, *Nihon teikokushugi-ka no Chūgoku*, 193–286; and Kobayashi, *Dai Tōa Kyōei Ken*, 92–9, 180–91, 213–30.

bution was smaller than Japanese planners had anticipated, the New Order did not become a springboard to victory. On the contrary, the resources of north-east Asia showed themselves inadequate in range, as well as quantity, thereby forcing Japan to turn elsewhere for some of its needs.

14

Advance to the South

EXPANSION into Korea, Manchuria, and north China was the inner ring of Japanese imperialism. It affected the powers in East Asia strategically, because it gave Japan a common frontier with Russia, and also politically, because it threatened the independence of China; but in the last resort it did not sufficiently endanger their economic interests—which were paramount in their dealings with the area—to make them willing to incur the risks involved in halting it. The extension of Japanese power to central and south China touched Western trade and investment much more nearly. Even so, it did not seem to threaten to exclude them altogether. Just as the West, when it had enjoyed unquestioned dominance in the nineteenth century, had made room within the treaty port system for Japan, so Japan after 1937 left opportunities for the West to continue a profitable, if more limited, relationship with China.

The prospect of Japanese penetration of south-east Asia, which was what creating an 'outer empire' involved, raised issues of much greater sensitivity. The southern region was for the most part divided into European colonial territories. And while Japan's motives for seeking access to it were much the same as those it had in China—namely, the acquisition of raw materials and the development of export markets through which to pay for them—the political obstacles it faced were of a quite different order. This was especially so in the atmosphere of protectionism and imperial preference that gripped the world after 1930. As a consequence, Japanese imperialism in this phase cannot be discussed without reference to the struggles between the powers.

Ishiwara Kanji, as we have seen (Chapter 11), had anticipated that Japan would have to fight wars successively against Russia, Britain, and the United States. Konoe Fumimaro had condemned the international structure as something that existed to preserve the privileges secured in the past by Britain and America. Both represented a broad spectrum of Japanese opinion. From such viewpoints it seemed logical that Japan should come to terms with other countries which resented the 'haves', that is, Germany and Italy. Thus in November 1936, following initiatives by the Army General Staff, Japan signed an anti-Comintern pact with Germany, providing for a measure of co-operation in the event that either was attacked by Soviet Russia. A year later Italy, too, acceded to it. The result was to align Japan with the Axis against Britain and France. In 1938, seeking insurance against possible Soviet intervention in China, the General Staff pressed for the arrangement to be made into an alliance. Opposition within Japan delayed any such move until September 1940—when military campaigns had made Germany dominant in Europe—but there was then concluded a treaty which bound Germany, Italy, and Japan to 'assist one another with all political, economic, and military means' if any one of the three were to be attacked by a country 'not involved in the current struggles'.

Japanese fears of Russia were a constant factor in these moves. During the 1930s there had been a steady build-up of Soviet military strength along the Amur, the effectiveness of which was demonstrated in the course of two major frontier clashes. The first was in July and August 1938 at Changkufeng, south-west of Vladivostock, the second at Nomonhan on the border between Manchuria and Outer Mongolia during the summer months of 1939. On both occasions there was fighting on a considerable scale. On both the Kwantung Army suffered a reverse. This reinforced the arguments of those in Tokyo—like Ishiwara Kanji—who wanted the strongest possible guarantees against a 'premature' Russo-Japanese conflict, on the grounds that Japan was not fully prepared for it. The Tripartite Pact went some way towards providing these. Then in April 1941 Japan concluded a non-aggression pact with Moscow, as Germany had already done; and although the German invasion of Russia a few weeks later threw Tokyo policies once more into disarray, the decision was eventually taken to press on with the task of rounding out the New Order, rather than take the opportunity of proceeding against the Amur frontier. Russian neutrality was an important condition of Japanese expansion into south-east Asia later in the year.

Japanese disputes with Britain in this period arose almost entirely with respect to China. Although many Japanese diplomats continued to believe that Britain would accept an assured but lesser role there, once convinced of Japan's resolution, British attempts to defend financial interests—by encouraging Chinese currency reform, or by insisting on dominating the Chinese Maritime Customs Service—persuaded most officials in Tokyo that the clash of interests was irreconcilable. It was also obvious that Britain stood to lose more than most from any extension of Japanese authority into south-east Asia. British hostility, therefore, had to be assumed. In September 1941, when the Japanese Vice-minister of Foreign Affairs was discussing the Atlantic Charter with the British ambassador, he observed that Britain had a long record of frustrating his country's legitimate claims, ranging from the issue of racial equality at Versailles to the closing of British colonial markets to Japanese trade. Both sides, he said, 'should be fully aware that Britain is an obstacle to Japan's natural development'.[1]

It is arguable that Anglo–Japanese rivalry, more than concern over China, accounts for the American government's growing hostility to Japan in these years. Certainly American economic interests in China do not seem to have been considerable enough to warrant full-scale confrontation. And it was only as Japanese moves towards south-east Asia were becoming a factor in Britain's ability to resist the Axis powers that the United States began reluctantly to intervene. In September 1940 the American ambassador in Tokyo commented in a telegram to Washington that 'American interests in the Pacific are definitely threatened by her [Japan's] policy of southward expansion, which is a thrust at the British Empire in the East.' Given that the existence of the British empire was an element in America's own security, 'we must strive by every means to preserve the status quo in the Pacific, at least until the war in Europe has been won or lost'.[2]

It is from the summer of 1940, when German victories suddenly improved the chances of a Japanese advance, that the United States put economic pressure on Japan. In July 1940 licensing was introduced for some scrap-metal and petroleum exports to that country. Later in the year iron and steel shipments were put under embargo. In January 1941 brass, copper, and zinc were added to the list. These actions related not only to the timing, but also to the motives of Japanese concern with south-east Asia.

South–east Asia and economic self-sufficiency

Whereas Japan's military penetration into China had behind it fifty years of continuous economic effort, its thrust into south-east Asia

---

[1] Quoted in Nish, *Anglo-Japanese Alienation*, 73. On the general issues of Japanese foreign relations raised here, see the relevant sections of Robert Butow, *Tojo and the Coming of the War* (1961); Akira Iriye, *Across the Pacific* (1967); Morley, *Deterrent Diplomacy*; and Nish, *Japanese Foreign Policy*.

[2] Quoted in Iriye, *Across the Pacific*, 207.

rested on an altogether flimsier foundation. True, there had been a modest amount of capital investment in the region since 1914, estimated by Higuchi at 130 million yen in 1924, rising to 300 or 400 million in 1936. This was approximately 6 per cent of Japan's total investment overseas. Figures for 1937 show its geographical distribution as follows: one-third in Malaya, two-fifths in Indonesia, and one-sixth in the Philippines. By industry, about two-fifths was in commerce (mostly retailing), a quarter in agriculture (mostly rubber and hemp), and a little over a fifth in mining (mostly Malayan iron ore). It amounted to only a tiny fraction of the investments made in the area by the Western colonial powers.[3]

With respect to foreign trade, a large part of that shown in the column headed 'Rest of Asia' in Table 9 (Chapter 13) was in fact with south-east Asia. It came to just over 10 per cent of Japan's exports in 1925–39, rather less than 9 per cent of imports.[4] Indonesia alone accounted for about a third of this. For a time after the devaluation of the yen in December 1931 Japanese textiles and other cheap manufactures had flooded into the region's markets, significantly reducing those of the Dutch and British. For example, Holland's share of Indonesian imports dropped from 18 per cent in 1929 to 12 per cent in 1933. Britain's experience in Malaya was similar. Both Holland and Britain then took steps to reverse the trend by tariff regulation. As a result, the rise in Japan's export totals was fairly short-lived, though it gave an important stimulus to Japanese expectations.

Japan's imports from the area were more significant for their nature than their value. In the years 1932–4 well over 30 per cent of the iron ore brought into Japan came from Malaya. Though there was a decline thereafter because of tariff changes, Malaya and the Philippines still provided 50 per cent of Japan's iron ore imports in 1937. Malaya was also a principal source of tin and rubber. There were substantial shipments of coal from French Indo-China. Even more important in the context of a possible naval conflict with America was the fact that the Netherlands East Indies contributed 20 per cent of Japan's oil imports in 1932, rising to 25 per cent by 1936. This made it a supplier second only to the United States (which provided more than twice as much).

[3] Japanese investment in south-east Asia is discussed in Higuchi, *Nihon no tai-Shi tōshi*, 564–9, 574–6, and Yano, *Nanshin no keifu*, 113–14.

[4] On trade, see J. M. Pluvier, *South-East Asia from Colonialism to Independence* (1974), 98–100; M. A. Aziz, *Japan's Colonialism and Indonesia* (1955), 100–4; Cohen, *Japan's Economy*, 114–17; *Nihon Teikoku Tōkei Nenkan*, vols. for 1931, 1936, and 1949.

Against this background, it is not surprising that the ideas of economic autarky that emerged in Japan during the 1930s included an element of *nanshin*, 'advance to the south'.[5] This, too, was seen as part of a policy for national defence, but the economic role allotted to south-east Asia within it was quite different from that of north China and Manchukuo. In north-east Asia Japan was to build an integrated industrial complex. In the southern regions (*nampō*) it was to have an empire, or at least an informal empire, which would provide markets and raw materials in much the same way as it had done over the years for Europeans.

The South was vital to the navy, in particular: because any operations there must necessarily be maritime; and because the navy depended on imported oil. Accordingly, during 1935 and 1936 a group of naval officers in Tokyo, working with representatives of the army and Foreign Ministry, began to study the implications of *nanshin*. They had no difficulty in confirming the overriding importance to Japan of securing materials like oil, rubber, and tin. They recognized, however, that doing so would almost certainly involve a clash with Britain and Holland, and probably with France and the United States as well. As a consequence, the defence plans formulated in June 1936 for the first time designated Britain as a potential enemy, ranking with China, but behind Russia and America (in joint first place).

This order was significant, for it carried the implication that the South was not yet worth a war. The point had been made clearly enough a few weeks earlier in a navy staff paper, which had argued that while south-east Asia mattered for purposes of 'strengthening our national defence and solving the population problem', Japan must nevertheless 'advance gradually' there, taking care 'not to stimulate the world powers unreasonably so as not to force them . . . to unite against us'. The same combination of caution and ambition was manifest in the statement of Fundamentals of National Policy, adopted by the inner cabinet in August 1936. Japanese expansion in the South was to be primarily economic, it said. It was to be achieved 'by gradual and peaceful means', avoiding provocation of other countries as far as possible.[6]

---

[5] Shiozaki Hiroaki, 'Gumbu to Nampō shinshutsu' (1983), 83–8; Yano, *Nanshin no keifu*, 146–52.

[6] The two documents are translated in Lebra, *Japan's . . . Co-prosperity Sphere*, 58–60, 62–4.

So matters remained for the next three years, while Japan's efforts and resources were devoted substantially to the affairs of China. The situation was then changed by the outbreak of war in Europe. For one thing, this created an opportunity, as it had done twenty-five years earlier. There was less reason after September 1939 to take account of the probably hostile reactions of the colonial powers. For another, war further disrupted the flow of world trade and capital, making it more than ever desirable for Japan to secure a position of advantage in south-east Asia. Some supplies (and some technology) were no longer available because of the fighting. And it was already becoming evident that self-sufficiency could not be attained within the territories that had been brought under Japanese control so far. Early in 1940 Koiso Kuniaki, then Colonial Minister, admitted publicly that it was not realistic 'to expect a perfect autarky . . . among Japan, Manchukuo and China'. It followed, he said, that Japan must 'rely on the South Seas for the supply of needed materials for the realization of the New Order in East Asia'.[7]

The basis for this statement is to be found in a Cabinet Planning Board study concerning the supply of raw materials, dated October 1939.[8] It argued that the war, because of the restrictions it had placed on exports from the European colonies and the United States, made it necessary for Japan 'to bring within our economic sphere areas on the East Asian mainland and in the southern region' which could contribute to Japanese self-sufficiency. In 1938 the southern region had taken 13 per cent of Japan's exports, other than those within the yen bloc. It had provided a similar proportion of imports, including 70 per cent or more of imported tin, rubber, bauxite, and chrome ore, plus anything up to 50 per cent of manganese, tungsten, nickel, copper, and petroleum. These quantities needed to be increased, the Planning Board believed. Among imports, special efforts should be made to secure the following: nickel, tin, rubber, and industrial salt from the Netherlands East Indies; tin and rubber from Thailand; tungsten from the Philippines. In order to make this possible, diplomacy should be directed towards persuading the governments of those countries to enter into closer economic relations with Japan. Foreign credits should be made available to Japanese companies for relevant kinds of trade and investment, while an investigation should be made of items that

---

[7] Quoted in James B. Crowley, 'A New Asian Order' (1974), 282.
[8] Text in *Gendai-shi Shiryō* (45 vols., 1962–80), vol 43: 172–6.

might be exported successfully to the East Indies and Thailand, in particular.

This brand of economic diplomacy began to take on a harsher note after Germany occupied Holland, Belgium, and much of France during the spring and early summer of 1940. In June the Foreign Minister, Arita Hachirō, issued a press announcement stating that the peoples of East and south-east Asia, who were related to each other 'geographically, historically, racially and economically', were 'destined . . . for their common well-being and prosperity' to unite in 'a single sphere'. Their destiny, he said, 'is a matter of grave concern to Japan in view of her mission and responsibility as the stabilizing force' in the region.[9] This was the language Japan had used in the past of China. If the parallel proved exact, it implied something more than an economic relationship.

So did the discussions that were taking place within the army and navy at this time.[10] Both services accepted the general desirability of 'defence in the north, advance to the south' in present conditions, though they continued to give priority to different parts of south-east Asia—the army to the mainland, the navy to the islands—and to envisage different ways of carrying policy out. The army, which was the more influential of the two, argued the need for an early occupation of French Indo-China, followed by war against Britain, which, it believed, could be pursued without involving the United States. A corollary was to be closer co-operation with the Axis. Once the second Konoe government was formed (22 July 1940), the new Foreign Minister, Matsuoka Yōsuke, supported these ideas. Within a few days of coming to office the cabinet approved a general policy statement embodying them, even to the extent of anticipating a resort to force in south-east Asia, 'if circumstances at home and abroad make that advantageous'.

The resolution on this subject[11] is of interest for its wording, which was more ideological than had been customary on previous occasions. It contained references to Japan's purpose of bringing 'eight corners of the world under one roof ' (*hakkō-ichiu*) and putting into effect 'the

---

[9] Quoted in Morley, *Fateful Choice*, 136–7.

[10] On Japanese policy-making concerning *nanshin* during 1940–1, see the article by Tsunoda Jun in Morley, *Fateful Choice*; Shiozaki, 'Gumbu', 95–107; Yano, *Nanshin no keifu*, 152–7.

[11] 26 July 1940, in *NGNB*, II, documents, 436–7.

principles of the national polity' (*kokutai no hongi*). To this ingredient of Shintō-based nationalism was added an Ishiwara-type strategic vocabulary. At home, Japan must seek to create a 'national-defence state' (*kokubō kokka*), giving priority to the development of heavy industry. Abroad, it must bring together Japan, Manchukuo, and north China to form the nucleus of a New Order in Greater East Asia (Dai Tōa Shin-chitsujo), self-sufficient in food supplies and raw materials.

Interestingly, there was no mention of the term 'co-prosperity sphere'. This appeared first in a press release by Matsuoka Yōsuke on 1 August,[12] when he declared that the aim of Japanese policy was to create a Greater East Asia Co-prosperity Sphere (Dai Tōa Kyōei-ken). He described it as being 'the same as the New Order in East Asia or the Security Sphere', except that its scope was to be extended to include 'areas such as the Netherlands Indies and French Indo-China'. During the next few months this became the standard government usage, though documents still occasionally contained variants. In August, for example, Koiso Kuniaki attached the label East Asia Economic Sphere (Tōa Keizai-ken) to his proposed 'economic federation' (*keizai remmei*), incorporating Indo-China, Thailand, Malaya, Burma, the East Indies, and the Philippines.[13] Though this was supposedly to assert the 'economic autonomy' of East Asia against Europe and the United States, Japan's own role within it was to be more than economic, since it would involve 'guidance' of the internal affairs of these countries and military protection of their territory.

It is clear from all this that during July and August 1940 Japanese officialdom was engaged in formulating more precisely than before its intentions with respect to south-east Asia. Part of the process arose from negotiations for the Tripartite Pact, which entailed discussion of the kind of world the signatories had it in mind to create, as well as how they would go about achieving it. The most thorough examination of this subject occurred in a draft by Matsuoka on 30 July.[14] It identified 'Japan's living sphere' as comprising French Indo-China, Thailand, Malaya, Borneo, the Netherlands East Indies, Burma, India, Australia, and New Zealand. Making it a reality would obviously involve removing British, French, and Dutch colonialism from the region (there was not at this stage any reference to the United States). There would be room for discussion of a possible Soviet stake in

---

[12] Translated in Lebra, op. cit., 71–2.
[13] Text in *Gendai-shi Shiryō*, vol. 10: 466–70.
[14] Morley, *Deterrent Diplomacy*, 283–8.

western India, however; and while there must be doubts about the practicality of pushing Japanese power as far as Australia and New Zealand,
there had at least to be an assurance that those territories would not
remain under 'the administration of any country outside East Asia'.

On 6 August the Cabinet Planning Board set out in greater detail
the economic elements in this policy.[15] It concentrated its attention on
a zone running from Burma through the Dutch islands to the Philippines and Indo-China, that is excluding India, Australia, and New
Zealand. Within this zone, the report stated, 'Japan's military and raw
material requirements' must take first place. To ensure that they
would be met, there must be guarantees for the unrestricted export to
Japan of specified commodities; special rights with respect to the
supervision of foreign trade, transport, and communications; improved
credit and exchange facilities; a number of mining concessions; and
undertakings about the employment of Japanese advisers. Management would need to be strengthened in those Japanese enterprises
concerned with oil, nickel, tin, bauxite, rubber, iron, and coal, but
capital for development was as far as possible to be raised within the
countries concerned.

What seems to emerge from this is a plan for a Japanese relationship
with south-east Asia which had more in common with the kind of
foreign privileges that had existed in China before 1930 than with the
western colonialism Japan was determined to destroy: systematic trade
advantages; management of transport and mining; a supervised financial structure; and political arrangements calculated to maintain these
things. There were differences, of course. The 'foreign' element was
to be exclusively Japanese, not co-operative. There was less emphasis
on investment being brought into the region, no doubt reflecting the
burden of capital commitments Japan had already made elsewhere.
There were more references to the strategic materials needed by Japan
than to trade simply as a source of profit. Yet despite these differences,
one is tempted to call this an 'old-fashioned' imperialist formula, compared with the kind of economic empire that was being attempted in
Manchukuo.

The point can be illustrated by examining what happened with
respect to Indonesia. Japan's immediate response to the German
invasion of Holland in May 1940 was to demand that the Dutch

---

[15] *Gendai-shi Shiryō*, vol. 43: 177–8.

government guarantee delivery to Japan from the East Indies of fixed annual quantities of petroleum, bauxite, nickel, manganese, and rubber. This set the stage for a series of talks, conducted in Batavia and lasting into 1941, in which the Dutch representatives, aware of the weakness of their position, consistently adopted delaying tactics in order to avoid a settlement. Oil supplies were the chief subject of contention. Japan wanted 3 million tonnes. Two million tonnes was the most the Dutch were ever persuaded to offer.

In August 1940 the Konoe government decided to send a special envoy to Batavia to conduct these talks, choosing Kobayashi Ichizō, Minister of Commerce and Industry. His instructions,[16] in addition to covering questions about the supply of raw materials and the regulation of trade, set out a proposed political framework for relations between Japan and the Netherlands Indies—Kobayashi was warned that force might have to be used to bring it into being—which would have revolutionized the colony's position *vis-à-vis* the Dutch. Batavia was to end its ties with Holland and give the Indonesians self-government. This done, the Indies were to become a member state within the Co-prosperity Sphere and conclude a treaty co-ordinating defence arrangements with Japan. Japanese subjects were to be put on an equal footing with the local peoples with respect to rights of residence, property, and the conduct of business.

Kobayashi made little progress and was recalled, to be replaced at the end of the year by Yoshizawa Kenkichi, a professional diplomat, experienced chiefly in the affairs of China. Meanwhile, the Japanese cabinet had carried its planning a stage further. On 25 October it resolved[17] that in addition to removing export restrictions on items needed by Japan, Batavia must be pressed to undertake agricultural development, in order to increase the population's purchasing power and so expand the market for Japanese goods. The islands were to have closer financial links with Tokyo, though not to become part of the Yen bloc. Other outside economic influences were to be excluded. Finally, Japanese advisers were to be attached to appropriate economic organs in Indonesia, including those which handled foreign trade, customs, taxation, finance, and transport.

The parallels that could be made between this and China's unequal treaties did not in any way make the demands acceptable to the Dutch.

[16] Approved by cabinet, 27 Aug. 1940; text in *NGNB*, II, documents, 440–6. See more generally the article by Nagaoka Shinjirō in Morley, *Fateful Choice*.

[17] Text in *NGNB*, II, documents, 462–3.

When Yoshizawa raised them in Batavia early in 1941 they only enhanced the resistance he was encountering over the export of raw materials. By June his mission had failed. The obvious conclusion was that nothing short of military action would enable Japan to get its way.

Experience in French Indo-China tended to confirm this view, in that force was used successfully there and produced significant economic gains.[18] Japan's original object in seeking a foothold in the colony was to close China's southern frontiers, as a means of blocking outside help to the Kuomintang. When France surrendered to Germany in June 1940 Japan demanded the use of airfields in northern Indo-China and the right to send troops through the area in furtherance of the China campaign. An agreement negotiated in Tokyo by the Vichy regime's ambassador on 30 August conceded this, in return for a Japanese promise to 'respect the rights and interests of France in the Far East, particularly the territorial integrity of Indo-China and the sovereignty of France over the entire area of the Indo-Chinese union'. Military details were left to be worked out in Hanoi.

It was by no means certain that the colonial authorities in Hanoi would accept the pact Vichy had signed, so while talks proceeded Japan made preparations for moving troops into Indo-China if they failed. They were to be provided by the South China Army, whose staff generally took the view that a military occupation of northern Indo-China would in any case be sensible and convenient. Accordingly, when Hanoi at last gave way (22 September 1940) the South China Army did not abandon its plans. On 23 September some of its units crossed the frontier near Lang Son and became involved in heavy fighting. Nor was any attempt made by army staff to call off an amphibious landing that had been planned to take place at Haiphong. When it looked like being frustrated because of separate instructions sent to the naval escort, the senior army commander, refusing to acknowledge any communication that did not come from his own superiors, hid in a storeroom to ensure that fresh orders would not reach him, even if received. The upshot was that the army landed and the navy promptly withdrew.

On the face of it, these incidents had something in common with what had happened in Mukden nine years earlier; but since the operations that followed were in accordance with the agreements Tokyo

---

[18] On Japan and Indo-China, see the article by Hata Ikuhiko in Morley, *Fateful Choice*; also Pluvier, *South-East Asia*, 110–13, 148–50.

had made with Vichy and Hanoi, they did not constitute 'military imperialism' in quite the same sense. One reason for this is that independent initiatives on the scale that had been witnessed in Manchuria were much more difficult to carry out in south-east Asia, because of problems of logistics, inter-service rivalry and quality of opposition. Another was that the existence of the Imperial Headquarters had marginally strengthened Tokyo's control over field commanders. Most important of all, however, was the fact that both the army and navy now had better ways of influencing decisions at the centre: through their links at intermediate levels with agencies like the Cabinet Planning Board; through their representatives on the Asia Development Board; and through the influence which the War and Navy Ministers—both of whom were serving officers—could exert by virtue of their membership of the inner cabinet. Sub-imperialism was no longer necessary, since the official policies of the state had shifted significantly towards those which the military thought proper.

Thus Japanese activities in Indo-China reflected the wishes of the central government, rather than those of its subordinates. They also led to an economic settlement, negotiated in May 1941, which gave Japan the kind of privileges it had failed to get in Indonesia: guaranteed supplies of rice and key raw materials (rubber, zinc, tungsten, manganese, tin, chromium, and coal); unrestricted access to the Indo-Chinese market for Japanese manufactures, especially textiles; and most-favoured-nation status for Japanese residents, who were to be allowed to establish businesses, undertake mining operations, and open schools.

Yet local economic dominance was not the only end in view: Indo-China was coveted as a base from which Japan could approach the rest of south-east Asia. Consequently, on 2 July 1941 the Imperial Conference resolved to extend its military operations further into French territory, in order to 'strengthen arrangements for advance to the south'.[19] The decision reflected a new willingness on the part of the Konoe government to pursue 'self preservation and self-defence', if necessary at the cost of large-scale hostilities. This made it a crucial step along the road to the Pacific War.

The action produced counteraction. An American freeze on Japanese assets in the United States (26 July) was quickly followed by an embargo on oil exports to Japan (1 August) and British abrogation of

---

[19] Morley, *Fateful Choice*, 236.

Japan's commercial treaties with India and Burma (27 July). The Netherlands East Indies introduced a system of permits for exports to Japan (28 July), then imposed a total ban on sending oil and bauxite there (28 August). These decisions prompted Tokyo and Washington into direct negotiations, though unavailingly. In the talks, which dragged on until December, Japan showed itself unwilling to dismantle the New Order without an acceptable solution to the economic difficulties which had made it attractive in the first place, while the United States refused to make economic concessions without a political quid pro quo, preferably in the form of a Japanese withdrawal in China.

Economic sanctions also put Japanese planners on notice that time was running out. Without oil and steel, Japan could not fight a war; and as the stockpiles ran down, war seemed to be the only way of renewing them. Hence failure to make progress in the Japanese–American talks became a countdown to hostilities. Early in September the army and navy agreed that the state of oil reserves and seasonal weather conditions would make it necessary to start any campaign in south-east Asia not later than December. This in turn required that a final decision to launch it be taken in October. When the moment for this came, the Konoe cabinet was deadlocked in a familiar way: the Foreign Ministry on one side, arguing the need for one more attempt at compromise; the services on the other, demanding firm resolve. Konoe resigned. On 17 October he was replaced as Premier by his War Minister, Tōjō Hideki. The appointment brought a renewal of debate, ending on 2 November in a decision to continue simultaneously the preparations for the use of force and the diplomatic efforts to avoid it; but this time it was made very clear that the failure of diplomacy meant war. On 1 December the Imperial Conference confirmed formally that diplomacy had failed.

Six days later planes from the Japanese fleet attacked the American base at Pearl Harbor in Hawaii with the object of ensuring that the United States Navy would be unable to interdict a Japanese seizure of south-east Asia. Operations in south-east Asia were also put in train. They were wholly successful. By the end of April 1942 the Japanese army had occupied Hong Kong, the Philippines, the Malay peninsula, Burma, the Netherlands Indies, and most of the islands of the central and south-west Pacific. Thailand and French Indo-China, though in theory neutral, were put unmistakably under Japanese domination. The result was to make possible practical steps towards organizing the Greater East Asia Co-prosperity Sphere.

15

The Greater East Asia Co-prosperity Sphere

IT is tempting to seek a meaning for the term 'co-prosperity sphere' in its historical associations. 'Sphere' (*ken*) echoes phrases like 'sphere of influence', that is, preponderance without direct rule. 'Co-prosperity' (*kyōei*) was used during the First World War to describe an unequal relationship between an industrial Japan and a backward China within the treaty port system. Presumably, therefore, the co-prosperity sphere was conceived as a type of informal empire, serving the needs of the Japanese economy, but rejecting—as Japanese propaganda constantly asserted—the models of European colonial government.

There is enough substance in this view of things to make a starting-point for analysis. Yet one needs to be wary of it. In the first place, there was never a blueprint towards which statesmen and their officials worked. The label emerged, as we have seen, from a clutch of similar ones, chosen, no doubt, partly because it had the right 'feel', but also partly because it was politically convenient, in the sense of inhibiting opposition from those who were to find themselves under Japanese dominance. Secondly, the sphere took shape in time of war, when policy-makers had more on their minds than constitutions and welfare. It had to serve the immediate purpose of gaining victory or averting defeat, which meant accepting military priorities. On both counts, any assessment of it must be tentative. Only if Japan had won the war could it have been judged realistically as a form of empire.

Political structures

In the two years before the attack on Pearl Harbour there had been a number of indications of how official ideas were evolving on the subject of a New Order in the south. An article in *Contemporary Japan* in 1939 emphasized economic complementarity: Japan's 'capitalistic system' and the 'agrarian economy' of its neighbours were described as 'mutually harmonious'. A political scientist, adviser to Konoe, wrote in 1940 of a bloc free from 'imperialistic exploitative control', in which each nation would play 'its proper role'; though he qualified it by observing that Japan would require 'the military bases necessary for land and sea operations over all Greater East Asia'. A navy research committee noted in 1939 that there would have to be 'complete recognition by the native peoples of Japan's real power'. On these terms Japan could conciliate Muslims, support Philippine independence, co-operate with Thais, even come to agreement with overseas Chinese.[1]

Such vague aspirations were not the building bricks of empire. Yet one is hard put to it to find anything more precise in the papers of the cabinet.[2] The decisions taken about the Netherlands East Indies on 25 October 1940 envisaged, in addition to the appointment of Japanese economic advisers there, hints of political control, like arrangements to ban anti-Japanese material from newspapers and magazines, or invitations to Indonesian dignitaries to come and study conditions in Japan. Proposals concerning Thailand in the following month included one that it should 'reform its internal structure gradually, so that an alliance with Japan can be effected smoothly'. A survey of foreign policy options by Matsuoka Yōsuke in January 1941 came closest to setting out a general scheme. It stipulated that Japan should have 'a preferential position in so far as resources for national defence are concerned', but would adopt 'the principle of the Open Door and equality of opportunity' in other matters; that it would assume responsibility for 'leadership and government'; and that other peoples would be granted 'as much autonomy as their ability allows'.

This in brief was Matsuoka's vision of a post-war world. Officials of the Foreign Ministry apparently made it the basis for a memorandum on long-term plans for occupied territories, dated 14 December 1941,[3] which proposed that Singapore, the Straits Settlements, British North Borneo, and Sarawak become Japanese, ruled by a Governor-General in Singapore, who would also supervise the rest of the Malay States and Brunei as Japanese protectorates. The Netherlands East Indies were to be grouped in a self-governing Indonesian federation, except that some outer regions (Dutch New Guinea, Borneo, and Timor), though nominally part of it, were to remain under Japanese control. The Philippines were to become independent, subject to the reservation of special military and economic privileges to Japan. Hong

---

[1] Documents translated in Lebra, *Japan's . . . Co-prosperity Sphere*, 25–30, 31–5, 64–7.

[2] For the documents cited in this paragraph, see *NGNB*, II, documents, 462–3, and Morley, *Fateful Choice* 218–19, 65–7.

[3] Jones, *Japan's New Order*, 332–3.

Kong was for the time being to be Japanese, though it might be restored to China once the war was over.

There is no evidence that this document was ever formally approved, but its contents correspond quite closely with decisions taken piecemeal in subsequent years. There are omissions, of course. For example, there is no reference to Thailand, Indo-China, or Burma. More immediately, there is not a great deal about the practical issues—military occupation of the region; keeping order there; ensuring that Japan had access to raw materials—which were engaging the attention of staff at the War Ministry. Late in 1941 the latter prepared a draft, approved at a Liaison Conference on 20 November, setting out a number of interim measures.[4] It recommended that the military authorities should make maximum use of existing governmental institutions in south-east Asia, leaving aside for the time being questions about the ultimate status of occupied territories and avoiding 'premature encouragement of native independence movements'. There was to be no change in policy towards Thailand and Indo-China, which would not be put under military government. The main lines to be followed in military administration elsewhere would be laid down in Tokyo and appropriate instructions passed to field commanders through their respective services. Occupation units were to make themselves as far as possible economically self-sufficient. In addition, they were to supervise trade, foreign exchange, transport, and communications, in order to divert to Japan 'important resources such as petroleum, rubber, tin, tungsten, and cinchona'. Acquisition and development of these resources would be under the overall direction of the Cabinet Planning Board. And—ominously—the hardship inevitably 'imposed upon native livelihood' as a consequence of this policy 'must be endured'.

Tōjō Hideki, as Prime Minister, pulled together the threads of short-term and long-term planning in a speech he made to the House of Peers in January 1942.[5] The object, he said, was to create 'an order of coexistence and co-prosperity based on ethical principles with Japan serving as its nucleus'. Areas which were 'absolutely essential for the defence of Greater East Asia' would be held under Japanese rule. Hong Kong and Malaya both came into this category. Indeed, priority must be given everywhere at first to the task of prosecuting the war.

---

[4] Translated in Lebra, op. cit., 114–16.
[5] Ibid., 78–81.

Alienated populations
not co-partners – not
allies

This involved securing strategic bases and dominating the regions which possessed key raw material resources, 'thereby augmenting our fighting strength'. Nevertheless, there would ultimately be independence for Burma and the Philippines, provided they were willing to co-operate with Japan. The Netherlands East Indies would be treated 'with full understanding for their welfare and progress' once they had submitted. In all these areas, military administration was only a beginning: 'as defence and maintenance of peace and order are firmly secured, the scope of civilian participation will be extended'.

In attempting to judge the reality that underlies these various statements, it is convenient to begin by considering the administrative arrangements made in Tokyo.[6] At several points in this book there has been occasion to note that disagreements over the machinery for implementing Japan's mainland policy had paralleled disagreements over policy itself. The same was to be true of south-east Asia. The principal contestants had been the Foreign Ministry and the army, especially the Kwantung Army and the General Staff. The latter had achieved a measure of success when the Colonial Ministry (Taku-mushō) was established in 1929, since this was entrusted with the supervision of Kwantung and the South Manchuria Railway, as well as colonies properly so-called. The next stage was the creation of the Manchurian Affairs Board in 1934, then the Asia Development Board in 1938. Both provided a means whereby the War Ministry could more effectively influence decisions at the centre, reducing the Foreign Ministry's autonomy.

The Asia Development Board, despite its broad title, had been devised to deal with the affairs of China and Manchukuo. In 1940 and 1941, as the geographical scope of Japan's ambitions grew, proposals were made for increasing both its responsibilities and its status. By October 1941 the Board itself was recommending that it be made into a ministry, which would work closely with Imperial Headquarters in co-ordinating all non-military aspects of the expected Greater East Asia war. This would have meant taking over many of the functions of the Foreign Ministry. Not surprisingly, the latter protested, counter-proposing a revision of its own structure which would in effect have incorporated into it most of the work of the Development Board.

Once hostilities began the latter's ideas about its own future

[6] The most detailed study is Baba, *Nitchū kankei*, 384–468. See also Jones, *Japan's New Order*, 334–7, and Lebra, *Japan's . . . Co-prosperity Sphere*, 82–7.

attracted support from the Cabinet Planning Board, as well as from the War and Navy Ministries, on the grounds—put forward before in 1938—that the activities which had to be directed from Tokyo were far more extensive than mere diplomacy. In March 1942 this resulted in a plan for a new Ministry of Foreign Administration (Gaiseishō). It was to absorb the Foreign Ministry, Colonial Ministry, Manchurian Affairs Board, and Asia Development Board; be staffed by secondment from them; and take over the formulation of diplomatic, economic, and cultural policies for the whole of the Co-prosperity Sphere, except military government in occupied areas, which was to remain the responsibility of Imperial Headquarters.

The objections to such an arrangement were stated by the Foreign Minister, Tōgō Shigenori, at a meeting with Tōjō Hideki on 12 July. They fell under three heads. First, foreign policy would be undesirably fragmented by separating out the affairs of the Co-prosperity Sphere in this way. Second, the duties proposed for the new Ministry were beyond the capabilities of a single organization, as the inadequacies of the Asia Development Board had already shown. Third, to bring together within a single department matters relating to avowedly dependent territories, on the one hand, and supposedly independent countries like Manchukuo, China, and French Indo-China, on the other, would cast doubt on the whole meaning of the term 'independence' within the Co-prosperity Sphere. Tōjō was unmoved. It was in fact true, he said, that 'independence' meant something different when applied to countries inside and outside the Sphere. So why should not their affairs be handled separately?

A few days later the cabinet decided in principle to establish a Greater East Asia Ministry (Dai Tōa-shō), much on the lines envisaged for the Gaiseishō in March. It was to take over all embassies and legations in Manchukuo, China, French Indo-China, and Thailand, plus the overseas agencies of the Asia Development Board. The Foreign Ministry would handle only 'pure diplomacy' in these places. This, Tōjō explained at a cabinet meeting on 1 September, when the final draft was presented for discussion, was in order to preserve 'the regular diplomatic forms', showing respect for 'their dignity as independent countries'. It was not to be allowed to weaken Japanese leadership. Nor was it to interfere with the overriding priority attached to winning the war: 'the whole of Greater East Asia, whether independent countries or newly occupied lands, must be made one with Japan, each being brought to contribute its own strength for the sake of Japan'.[7] *didn't happen*

Despite the resignation of Tōgō as Foreign Minister and a rearguard action by the Privy Council, Tōjō had his way. The Greater East Asia Ministry came into existence on 1 November. It had separate bureaux dealing with China, Manchukuo, and the southern region. It was given no jurisdiction over Korea or Taiwan, which were transferred to the Home Ministry, but Kwantung was included with Manchukuo. The Foreign Ministry lost nearly all its active functions, together with much of its staff, since the work of its European and American sections was now virtually in abeyance. There is some suggestion, however, that it regained some of the lost ground once the course of hostilities in the Pacific turned decisively against Japan. Until the summer of 1944, while Tōjō was in office, the Greater East Asia Ministry was under Aoki Kazuo, a former Finance Ministry official. Thereafter the post was held by professional diplomats, serving simultaneously as Foreign Minister: first, Shigemitsu Mamoru; then—a form of political revenge—Tōgō Shigenori.

The ministry's duties with respect to south-east Asia were more prospective than actual, in so far as military government continued in some form throughout the war.[8] The largest and most heavily populated regions, including the Philippines, Malaya, Java, Sumatra, and Burma, were under the supervision of the army, which in effect meant the army section of Imperial Headquarters, acting through the War Ministry. Remoter and smaller islands—Celebes, the Moluccas, New Guinea, the Bismarck archipelago—were under naval administration, the chain of command running similarly through the Navy Ministry. In the early months, while fighting was still in progress almost everywhere, responsibility in the field rested with military government sections attached to operational headquarters at appropriate levels. Later regulations (March and July 1942) provided for the addition of civilian staff, including political advisers, plus a more elaborate structure to deal with such matters as economic and financial policy, transport, and the disposal of enemy property. Thereafter there was a greater separation of military government from operational command.

[7] Baba, *Nitchū kankei*, 416–17.
[8] There are useful accounts of Japanese rule in south-east Asia in Jones, *Japan's New Order*, 337–91, and Pluvier, *South-East Asia*, Parts III and IV. Grant K. Goodman (ed.), *Imperial Japan and Asia* (1967), includes a stimulating essay on the subject by Harry J. Benda, at 65–79. Japanese military government is described in Ōta Kōki, 'Nampō gunsei no tenkai to tokushitsu' (1983).

Malaya and Sumatra were controlled by the 25th Army, which had its headquarters at first in Singapore (renamed Shōnan), then from May 1943 in Sumatra.[9] Since it had far fewer trained personnel at its disposal than the colonial regimes it replaced, it used them sparingly. Japanese were appointed as mayor of Singapore and as governors of provinces (ten in Malaya, ten in Sumatra), each with a small Japanese staff. At lower levels non-European officials were for the most part left in place. The local sultans were deprived of their hereditary political authority, but allowed to retain their religious functions, in order to avoid giving offence to the native population. A similar system was operated by the 16th Army in Java. A central administration, located in Batavia, appointed Japanese to be heads of units comparable to the former colonial residencies, leaving local government in the hands of Indonesians.

Neither in Malaya nor in Indonesia was any attempt made to establish indirect rule through a puppet government, no doubt because the political future of the territories was undecided. The usual pattern was to seek popular support without encouraging south-east Asian leaders to develop political ambitions. In Malaya, for example, Japanese distrust of the overseas Chinese led them to favour the choice of Malays as officials; but they preferred to reinforce this practice by giving their patronage to the Muslim religion, not to politicians. In Indonesia, such progress as the Dutch had permitted towards introducing a measure of representation on elected councils was ignored or specifically abandoned. Though there was already an active Indonesian nationalist movement, its leaders, like Sukarno, were given no opportunity to form a cabinet. Political parties were banned. The only mass organizations to enjoy any credit among Japanese officials were those based on the Muslim religion, as in Malaya, or those designed directly to promote the ideas of the Co-prosperity Sphere.

In Burma, which came under the 15th Army at Rangoon, the Japanese approach was entirely different. Partly because the country's natural resources were less critically important to Japan, partly because a campaign was continuously in progress against British India, it was from the beginning an object to win over 'prominent Burmese leaders' to form a regime that would 'have on the surface the appearance of

---

[9] There are two collections of translated documents on the subject of Japanese military government in south-east Asia: Harry J. Benda *et al.*, *Japanese Military Administration in Indonesia* (1965); and Frank N. Trager, *Burma: Japanese Military Administration* (1971). On Indonesia, see also Aziz, *Japan's Colonialism*, especially 152–62.

independence, but in reality . . . carry out Japanese policies'.[10] In July 1942 it was made clear that the Japanese army commander would retain extensive powers over defence, foreign relations, and some financial matters, plus a veto over legislation and major policy decisions, but that there was to be a Burmese central executive and deliberative assembly, supposedly governing the country. Key members of the executive—down to the level of assistant vice-ministers— were to be subject to appointment and dismissal by the Japanese. There were also to be Japanese advisers in the Prime Minister's office and central government departments. The instructions given to them, while warning against any 'sense of superiority toward Burmese officials', nevertheless made it clear that they were to play 'a nuclear role in guiding the affairs of the state'.[11]

A leader was found for this regime in the person of Ba Maw, a nationalist politician who had earlier been imprisoned by the British for advocating non-co-operation in the war against Germany. He was installed as chairman of an executive committee in June 1942, then as head of a provisional government two months later. The more extreme Burmese nationalist groups were disciplined or imprisoned. Others were brought into a new mass organization in support of Ba Maw, tempted by promises of eventual independence.

Much the same pattern was adopted by the 14th Army in the Philippines. However, because past American promises of independence had been more precise than those which Britain had made in Burma, it proved difficult to win popular acceptance of Japanese power. Jorge Vargas was installed as head of a Philippine government as early as January 1942, subject to the same kind of military controls as Ba Maw, rather better concealed; but when it emerged that the regime was ineffective as an instrument of Japanese policy, because of popular distrust, military officers began to intervene more obviously in affairs, thereby undermining it further. Filipino political activity was banned in July 1942; the national legislature was abolished; and neighbourhood associations were introduced on the Japanese model as a means of maintaining order through collective responsibility. By 1943 it appeared that installing a puppet government in Manila had been only a qualified success.

The navy was not tempted into experiments of this kind in the

---

[10] Southern Army instructions of 6 Feb. 1942, trans. in Trager, *Burma*, 31–3. For the more detailed instrucions issued on 22 July, see ibid., 113–17.
[11] Instructions of August 1942, ibid., 122–4.

islands it administered, because their occupation was directed towards 'permanent retention under Japanese control . . . [and] the organic integration of the entire region into the Japanese Empire'.[12] Its approach was similar to that used by the army in Malaya: direct rule, using existing administrative arrangements, where possible, and employing such 'native chiefs and officials' as manifested 'a sincere desire to cooperate with Japan'. Since the level of political consciousness in these territories was low, the policy provoked no great opposition.

That left principally Indo-China and Thailand. The former, as a French colony, was an anomaly within the Co-prosperity Sphere; but since Japan had secured the advantages it wanted there even before the outbreak of the Pacific War, there was no strong motive for making a change. The continued presence of Japanese troops—as many as 35,000 men—ensured that no extension of political authority was needed. Thailand, by contrast, was both Asian and non-colonial. When military operations were started against Malaya in December 1941, Japan had demanded passage for its land forces across Thai frontiers, then negotiated a military alliance under which it was able to secure economic rights and some control over lines of communication in Thailand. Care was always taken to emphasize—if not very convincingly—the voluntary nature of Thai co-operation under it. In due course Thailand had its reward. In the summer of 1943, while visiting Bangkok, Tōjō announced that four Malay and two Shan states, claimed by Thailand along its eastern and southern borders, were to be handed over.

Tōjō said during the war crimes trials after surrender that Japan had set itself to create in Greater East Asia 'governments which would be in accordance with the desires of the inhabitants, as was the government of Manchukuo'.[13] The great variety of what was done suggests that his statement was not an accurate recollection, except, perhaps, in so far as it related to the change of emphasis in Japanese policy after the summer of 1943. By that time the tide of war had clearly turned. The Japanese fleet had been defeated at Midway a year earlier. Japanese ground forces had been evicted from Guadalcanal in February. Shortages of munitions were becoming evident. In these circumstances, the Tōjō cabinet decided at the end of May that it was necessary

---

[12] Navy Ministry paper of 14 Mar. 1942: Benda, *Japanese Mil. Admin.*, at 29.
[13] Quoted in Aziz, *Japan's Colonialism*, 45.

to make political concessions in occupied areas in order to win greater co-operation from their inhabitants in an essentially defensive struggle. An Imperial Conference on 31 May 1943 resolved as follows: to conclude a revised treaty of alliance with China; to grant Thailand the border regions it claimed, in return for economic privileges; to implement the decision already taken to grant Burma independence; to move towards independence for the Philippines; and to permit greater participation in political affairs for the peoples of Malaya, Sumatra, Java, and Borneo. All this was to be done by October, so that a conference of leaders of the Co-prosperity Sphere could take place in Tokyo in November, reaffirming their unity and their will to victory.[14]

Japan and Burma signed a treaty of alliance on 1 August, formally ending Japanese rule, though there were still to be Japanese advisers, directed by the Japanese ambassador, and the Japanese army was to retain 'entire freedom of action in the execution of military operations in Burma'. Japanese were to have most-favoured-nation treatment (though not the right of extraterritoriality). Foreign policy and economic policy were to be co-ordinated with that of Japan.[15] The Philippines concluded a treaty of alliance on 14 October on very similar terms.

In Malaya, the creation of advisory councils in the provinces and some towns had been announced a few days earlier: bodies with Japanese chairmen, but Malay, Chinese, and Indian members, who were to be appointed by Japanese governors or mayors. In Indonesia there was to be a measure of elected representation, despite a firm decision—taken at the army's insistence and not made public—that the islands would remain Japanese territory. New regulations provided for the setting up of provincial councils, partly appointed by governors (all but two of whom were Japanese), partly elected by village heads. Above these would be a central advisory committee, having a majority of appointed members, but also representatives chosen by the provincial councils. It was to have a Japanese secretariat. Moreover, it would be empowered to discuss only those matters brought before it by the military administration.

These changes give one a better idea of how Japanese power was expected to be exercised: Burma and the Philippines to be controlled

[14] Text in *NGNB*, II, documents, 583–4.
[15] The relevant documents are in Trager, *Burma*, 145–55.

in the manner of Manchukuo; Thailand and Indo-China to be virtual protectorates; China, perhaps, the same, though more directly supervised in the north; Malaya, Java and Sumatra, together with the rest of the islands, to be colonies on the lines of Korea and Taiwan. Like the British empire, this was more an agglomeration than a system. Nor was anything more systematic proposed at the conference of leaders which met in Tokyo in November.[16] It was, in fact, a propaganda exercise. Tōjō welcomed the delegates in a speech contrasting the 'materialistic civilization' of the West with 'the spirit of justice' and 'the spiritual essence' of Greater East Asia. Much of what he said was devoted to an emotional attack on the 'aggression' and 'exploitation' that had characterized the actions of Britain and America in the region. The delegates responded by endorsing an appropriate public declaration. They would, they announced, build Greater East Asia on a basis of respect for each other's sovereignty, independence, and cultural traditions; on reciprocity in economic development; on racial equality and 'the opening of resources' in their relations with the rest of the world. There was not a word about government.

Ideology and economics

There was an obvious conflict between idealism and self-interest in Japan's approach to the problems of the Co-prosperity Sphere. Many Japanese genuinely believed *both* that saving Asia from the West was a crusade *and* that it could only be accomplished by asserting Japanese authority over other Asians. The result was a Japanese equivalent of the white man's burden. The same contradiction existed with reference to culture and the economy: on the one hand it was argued that Asian culture could only be defended through an insistence on Japanese values, which constituted its highest form;[17] on the other that economic development, whether for war or welfare, could only be achieved if the resources of an underdeveloped Asian periphery were made cheaply and reliably available to a Japanese industrial core.

Contradictions of this kind are inherent in the nature of empire. They inevitably had their place in the Co-prosperity Sphere, despite Japanese insistence that it was not an empire at all. Thus nearly all the instructions issued to military government officers contained some reference to the respect that must be shown towards local customs.

---

[16] For Tōjō's speech and the conference declaration, see Lebra, *Japan's . . . Co-prosperity Sphere*, 88–93.

[17] See, for example, a passage written by Ōkawa Shūmei in 1943, Lebra, op. cit., 40.

Typically, those issued by army headquarters in Singapore in August 1942 warned that care should be taken not to give offence in such matters as 'the hasty institution of public holidays, the casual changing of names, or the enforcement of Japanese morality and customs'.[18] Against that, there were practical and political reasons for ensuring that education systems should introduce the teaching of the Japanese language and inculcate loyalty towards the concept of the Co-prosperity Sphere. It was a principle firmly established in north China and Manchukuo, as well as in Korea and Taiwan. There was one important difference in south-east Asia, however. It was not possible there to appeal to a common Confucian heritage, as it had been in countries within the Chinese tradition. The Muslim and Buddhist religions, though Asian, therefore to be encouraged, would not serve the same social purpose, which made it necessary—and to many Japanese, desirable—to rely much more on ideas associated with Japan's own nationalism, suitably modified. For example, 'eight corners of the world under one roof ' (*hakkō-ichiu*), which Japanese could claim as a Shintō justification of empire, was sometimes translated 'universal brotherhood'.

The Japanese armed forces were quite explicit about what was needed educationally. A navy document recommended 'taking advantage of the prestige resulting from our military victories and the native hostility toward former colonial powers' to promote 'the dissemination of Japanese language and culture'.[19] One object would be to dismantle the European-style colonial education systems, except in so far as they were needed to give a modest technical training to 'native populations'. Another, as one army command saw it, was to provide a framework within which Japanese residents in the occupied areas could be given an education appropriate to improving 'the character of the people who are the guiding race'.[20]

Race, indeed, was a recurring problem for Japanese officials. A colonel from the War Ministry, addressing a group of senior bureaucrats and business men in April 1942,[21] expressed what might be called the Tokyo view of it. Because Japan was best equipped to guide the back-

---

[18] Benda, *Japanese Military Administration*, 191.

[19] Ibid., 33.

[20] Ibid., 192. See Aziz, *Japan's Colonialism*, 174–81, for an account of wartime education in Indonesia.

[21] Statement originally published in *Kokusaku Kenkyūkai Shūhō*, 18 Apr. 1942; reprinted in *Senji seiji keizai shiryō* (8 vols., 1982–3), vol. 4, 319–20.

ward societies of the southern region, he said, the relationship between Japanese and local peoples must be that of elder brother and younger brother. Acts of oppression must be avoided. Those Japanese who were sent to work overseas must be carefully chosen and impressed with the need for behaving well. If they failed to do so, they should be repatriated.

Actions in the occupied territories did not always match this paternalism. For one thing, not all Japanese shared the same enlightened attitudes. For another, the racial complexities of south-east Asia did not make it easy for administrators to remain even-handed between different racial groups. Malaya was especially difficult. Trying to redress the balance in favour of Malays with respect to appointment to minor government office further offended overseas Chinese, among whom there were already strong anti-Japanese sentiments because of the invasion of China. Brutal Japanese suppression of the resulting unrest turned part of it into an armed resistance movement. Frustration of nationalist hopes in Burma and Indonesia also prompted discontent, which made the Japanese little more acceptable in some circles than the British and Dutch had been. Ba Maw later wrote of the Japanese military that 'few people were mentally so race-bound . . . and in consequence so totally incapable of understanding others or of making themselves understood by others'.[22] A Japanese army officer, whose task it was to organize groups from mainland south-east Asia to fight against the British on the Burma front, also recognized failings on the part of the Japanese. What Japan ought to have been doing in Burma and Malaya, he wrote after the war, was 'seeking an understanding of the Asian peoples' aspirations for freedom and liberation'. What it actually did was to make them part of the Japanese war effort. This was both selfish and self-defeating: 'these operations were devoid of a principle that would inspire the co-operation of other nationals'.[23]

The same criticism can be levelled at Japanese economic policy. A cabinet paper of 12 December 1941[24] stated its purpose bluntly: 'to fulfil the demand for resources vital to the prosecution of the present war, to establish at the same time an autarkic Greater East Asia Co-prosperity Sphere, and to accelerate the strengthening of the economic power of the Empire'. It envisaged that Thailand and Indo-China would continue to be sources of foodstuffs, in particular. In the rest of

[22] Quoted in Lebra, *Japan's . . . Co-prosperity Sphere*, 157.
[23] Fujiwara Iwaichi, *F. Kikan* (1983), 10, 12.
[24] Trans. in Benda, *Japanese Mil. Admin.*, 17–25.

the area (the East Indies, Malaya, Borneo, and the Philippines) priority would be given to the acquisition by Japan of industrial raw materials and petroleum. Existing mines were to be restored to production (after war damage) and new ones developed for nickel, copper, bauxite, chrome, and manganese, but no attempt was to made to increase the output of iron or tin. For the sake of efficiency, control should be exercised by a small number of large-scale enterprises. On the other hand, in order to avoid the evils of monopoly there should in the southern region as a whole be at least two contractors concerned with each product. Other industry should be encouraged only where it had a part to play in extracting and transporting these ores. Shipbuilding was cited as an example.

There was, the document continued, to be strict control of foreign trade. The region was to be made as far as possible self-sufficient in foodstuffs, local deficiencies being made good by regional exchanges. There should only be application to other parts of the empire 'for those resources for which there are no alternatives'. Trade to and from Japan was to be on government account and subject to the control machinery already established in Tokyo (under the National Mobilization Law). Within the area, commerce was to be conducted on free trade principles, both Japanese and native merchants being allowed to take part in it. However, Japanese manufactures imported through this system were to go preferentially to 'mines, plantations, and other enterprises producing goods for export to Japan'.

Finally, there were a number of provisions concerning currency and finance. Japanese purchases were to be paid for in military scrip, issued at par in local currencies, but the amount of this in circulation was to be held down by assigning confiscated enemy property to Japanese credit. The central banking system in each country was to be regulated by Japan. The cost of defence and other military expenditure was to be borne in part by non-Japanese governments and public authorities, whose contributions were to be assessed on the basis of the payments, other than foreign trade, they had made under European rule. They were to be increased beyond that level wherever possible.

A representative of the War Ministry, who has been cited previously in connection with attitudes to race, made one significant addition to these points when he was summarizing occupation policy in April 1942.[25] The economic experts, sent to south-east Asia to oversee this

----

[25] Report cited in note 21, above.

programme, would be chosen in consultation with relevant government departments and private business firms, he said. It was not
intended to establish special government-sponsored development
companies, as had been done in China and Manchukuo. Instead,
development would be entrusted to Japanese enterprises already having experience of the area, though they would, of course, be expected
to act in conformity with directions issued by the various military commands. Moreover, capital would be raised within south-east Asia—by
a new organ, the Southern Region Development Bank (Nampō Kai-
hatsu Kinko), to be established by the Finance Ministry—not exported
from Japan.

It was the duty of military government to apply these principles to
the particular circumstances of occupied lands. Burma, which was not
specifically mentioned in the policy paper of 12 December 1941, was
the subject of two sets of Southern Army instructions in March and
April 1942.[26] These followed the Tokyo guide-lines with respect to
the kind of natural resources that were required, save that a section on
agriculture recommended an increase in the cotton crop at the expense
of rice (reflecting the loss of supplies from India and the United
States). The mining of iron ore was to cease, so making possible a
transfer of capital, labour, and technology to the production of copper
and lead. Oil was earmarked for Japan. Coal was to be the chief source
of energy locally. Heavy industry making use of iron or rubber was not
to be encouraged, but the production of textiles and soap for the Burmese market was to be maintained. In general it was envisaged that in
the long run the economy would be dominated by Burmese and Japanese, whose respective roles were indicated by the fact that Burmese
were said to be 'extremely inefficient in managing factories'. It followed that the influence of Indians and overseas Chinese would
gradually be reduced. Mines and factories were to be put under Japanese management wherever they were thought relevant to the provision
of strategic materials.

The Navy Ministry, issuing orders in March about the islands of the
south-west Pacific, had a somewhat different emphasis.[27] Oil, coal,
and phosphates were singled out for special regulation. As in Burma,
manufacturing industry was not to be encouraged. Moreover, where
Japanese management was installed the companies entrusted with it

[26] Trans. in Trager, *Burma*, 45–52, 65–72.
[27] Trans. in Benda, *Japanese Mil. Admin.*, 26–46.

were to be 'guided toward casting off their entrepreneurial, profit-seeking attitude' and becoming 'agencies of the State'. Japan was to assume 'the financial hegemony hitherto held by the enemy institutions'. It was also to impose price and wage controls, partly to facilitate the acquisition of materials, partly 'to prevent adverse effects upon price levels in Japan'.

In practice, implementing the core policies identified in these documents depended heavily on the participation of Japanese companies in mining and manufacturing.[28] Despite government reluctance, this in turn entailed transfers of capital from Japan: a little over 800 million yen in the three years 1942, 1943, and 1944. The Southern Region Development Bank, using military scrip, credits from confiscated enemy property, and its own debentures, contributed another 1,500 million yen or so. As a result, Japanese investment in the area eventually totalled about 3,500 million yen, some 60 per cent of it being in Malaya and Indonesia. To put the figure in perspective, this was rather less than half the amount attributed to Chinese residents in south-east Asia.

A list of the companies concerned includes the Manchukuo development company, Mangyō, with 400 million yen invested, mostly in mining, but for the rest the names are the familiar ones of Japanese domestic industry: Mitsui, Mitsubishi, Sumitomo, Nomura, and Furukawa, all with mining interests; Tōyō Spinning, Tokyo Shibaura Electric, and Hitachi in other fields. Much the largest were Mitsui and Mitsubishi. Mitsui, whose investments in the region amounted to more than 700 million yen in 1942, had nearly two-fifths of this in mining in Malaya and the Philippines, the rest largely in general trading. Mitsubishi had just under 600 million yen in all, about one-third in mining, but including also a large stake in Singapore's shipbuilding and other industries.

In exploiting the advantages which their country's political dominance gave them, these companies and their military government allies faced difficulties of two kinds. One concerned production. The widespread disruption and physical damage to plant which occurred during the first few months of fighting took a long time to make good. Even thereafter, mines and factories continued to suffer from the same shortages of technology and skilled manpower as were faced in

---

[28] See especially Kobayashi, *Dai Tōa Kyōei Ken*, 395–404, 505–9. On oil production and supply, see Cohen, *Japan's Economy*, 133–42.

Manchukuo and China. The second problem was transport. Attacks by enemy ships and aircraft, later also by guerrillas, ensured that damage grew greater, not less, as the war went on. This meant that materials produced in south-east Asia had increasingly to be used there, instead of being shipped to Japan. Rice exports to Japan from Indo-China, Thailand, and Burma fell from 1.4 million metric tonnes in 1942 to a mere 74,000 tonnes in 1944. Iron ore supplied from the Philippines dropped to 10 per cent of pre-war levels. Production of crude oil recovered remarkably well, reaching just under 50 million barrels in 1943, compared with 65 million in 1940; but less than 10 million barrels of crude and 5 million of refined reached Japan in 1943, while in the following year the quantities were 1.6 million and 3.3 million, respectively.

Thus south-east Asia contributed much less to Japan's wartime economy than it had been expected to do. Given the nature of the war that was being fought in the Pacific between December 1941 and August 1945—one in which industrial resources and technology were decisive—it is arguable that the failure of the Co-prosperity Sphere to fulfil the economic role assigned to it guaranteed Japanese defeat. What is more, the region's own economy was so distorted in the process as to make 'co-prosperity' in anything other than a military sense unrealizable. For the implications of substituting Japan for the colonial powers as an economic partner to south-east Asia were immense. The Japanese capital available for investment—especially in view of the more fundamental commitment to north China and Manchukuo—was pitifully inadequate. Japanese industry, overstretched by military demands upon it, had no prospect of supplying consumer goods on the scale previously accepted as normal in such countries as Burma, Malaya, Indonesia, or the Philippines. Nor could Japan absorb the specialized exports which had been developed in nearly a century of complementarity with the metropolitan economies of the West. The Japanese demand for strategic raw materials did not carry over into other staple products, like coffee, tea, and sugar.

Accordingly, Japan faced the task, not only of securing the minerals it wanted, but also of restructuring the south-east Asian economy while it did so.[29] One step was to cut back on the production of items for which there was no longer a sufficient overseas demand. Malayan tin production fell by nearly 90 per cent during the war. In Indonesia

[29] For a discussion of this point, see Pluvier, *South-East Asia*, 271–81.

the acreage under tea was cut by 50 per cent, that under coffee by nearly 30 per cent. Rubber production in 1943 was only one-fifth that of 1941. Java's sugar crop was reduced by even more and half the sugar factories were converted to making cement. In the Philippines sugar was no longer produced for export at all. An attempt to use the land for cotton-growing had little success.

The chosen alternative, which was to divert land and labour to food production for the sake of self-sufficiency, faced insuperable problems. One was lack of capital, compounded by a decline in tax revenues. Another was the fragmentation of the area, both politically—a heritage of western colonialism—and geographically. War damage, plus the priority given to Japanese military needs, destroyed or pre-empted the transport which would have been required to deal with it. The result was hardship far greater and more widespread than Japanese policy-makers had ever envisaged in December 1941, when they had stated uncompromisingly that it would have be 'endured'. The cut-back in plantation industries brought unemployment in the countryside, soon spilling over into the towns. The disruption of communications, coupled with the requisition of supplies for Japanese occupation forces, caused food shortages, especially in those districts which had concentrated on growing export crops and had therefore come to rely on foodstuffs brought from outside. Lack of consumer goods, hoarding, and black markets, together with the circulation of large quantities of military scrip, brought inflation everywhere. By the time hostilities ended the economy of the Co-prosperity Sphere was in total disorder.

So was that of Japan itself, of course. From July and August 1944, when American forces captured Saipan and Guam, the naval and air defences of the Japanese home islands had been in peril. With the loss of Iwojima in March 1945 and of Okinawa in June, they crumbled. Japan was thereafter in a state of siege. And battered by air attack, Japanese industry could no longer have made use of raw materials from the southern region, even if it had been able to obtain them. Indeed, some weeks before the atom bomb brought Japanese surrender, the scale of conventional bombing had demonstrated that the enemy's ability to destroy Japan's industrial heartland from the air made possession of an empire an irrelevance.

16

Conclusion:
The Nature of Japanese Imperialism

ANALYSES of imperialism too often treat it as static. True, those examples which were relatively short-lived can well enough be considered in this way, but others, including that of Japan, went through stages of development. Japan's began with what might be called a period of 'dependency', when a strength recognizably greater than that of the country's neighbours was combined with weakness *vis-à-vis* the other powers. In the decade after 1894 alignment with Britain and the United States was the necessary concomitant of putting together the rudiments of a Japanese empire. In the second stage, starting in 1905, Japanese imperialism became more self-assertive. Like Bismarck's Germany a generation earlier, Japan behaved after the Russo-Japanese War as an abrasive latecomer, seeking equality of esteem not only through an insistence on treaty rights, but also through the acquisition of spheres of influence. Finally, after 1930—though there had been indications of it as early as the First World War—Japanese leaders set out to substitute a Japan-centred system of imperialism in East Asia for that which they had inherited from the nineteenth-century West. To do so required both a restructuring of economic patterns and the promotion of a specifically 'Asian' ideology.

One general influence on these developments was the process of economic modernization within Japan. In 1894 Japanese capitalism was primarily commercial, despite the presence of important elements of industry. By 1930 it was industrial. Opinions differ as to when the shift took place—some scholars put it as early as 1905—but there is agreement that by 1918, if not before, Japanese expansion had come to be concerned as much with markets and raw materials for industry as with trading profit. There were corresponding changes in availability of capital for export. Yet capital was never plentiful—except, perhaps, in 1917 and 1918—so it is difficult to argue that Japan's aspirations overseas derived even then from a need to find outlets for a surplus of

it. Certainly in the first decade or so of the century Japanese investment in colonies and spheres of influence relied heavily on borrowing
in London and New York. Later it rested in part on contributions from
the areas under Japanese control, whether Manchukuo, or China, or
south-east Asia.

A second general influence was that Japanese governments always
had to have regard to the fact that East Asia was a region in which
western imperialism had become entrenched before Japan was in a
position to exercise power there. At the end of the nineteenth century
the treaty port system constituted an international framework which
could not be ignored. On the one hand, it had been, and possibly still
was, a potential threat to Japan. Thus Japanese imperialism emerged in
an atmosphere of wariness with respect to great power rivalries. On the
other, what had already existed defined the attainable. Japanese could
work within the system, or modify it, or, when they were strong
enough, seek to destroy it. They could not wish it away. Similarly,
European colonialism was a precondition of Japan's advance into
south-east Asia, in the sense that it was a phenomenon about which
Japanese policy-makers had to take a view. In some respects, therefore,
the New Order and the Co-prosperity Sphere were heirs to Western
empire: partly because they incorporated those ingredients in it that
survived, partly because the West's experience remained a factor in
Japanese thinking. There never was a time when Japanese empire-
builders could start with a *tabula rasa*.

Politics within Japan, in so far as they concerned foreign affairs,
focused on a choice of national objectives overseas within limits that
were determined by these internal and external circumstances. Economic modernization in the Meiji period was part of a wider programme
of reform, undertaken by men predominantly of feudal origin—that is,
ex-*samurai*—with the object of defending the country from foreign
threat. Brought up as members of a military ruling class, these ex-
samurai were inclined to give special attention to Japan's defence peri-
meter, hence to securing a foothold in Taiwan, Korea, Kwantung.
Simultaneously, however, a growing knowledge of the West had persuaded them of the need to overcome Japan's international weakness
by economic means, including the acquisition of commercial advantages in China.

These two elements were made difficult to reconcile with each other
by a divergency within the West's imperialism in East Asia. Its economically most advanced exponents, Britain and the United States,

GERMANY

The Nature of Japanese Imperialism 253

continued to insist on the overriding importance of equal opportunity in China, a policy which became characterized as the Open Door; but this was unattractive to those powers, like Russia and Germany, which gave greater weight to more nearly monopolistic rights, secured through spheres of interest. In the rivalry between them, beginning after 1895, Japan, as a late developer, might logically have been expected to belong to the second group. Against that, strategic considerations, identifying Russia as a potential enemy, constituted an argument for working with Britain and America. So did commercial ambition, reinforced as it was by the strong trade links established with those two countries during the previous thirty years. The result was ambivalence. First came the Anglo-Japanese alliance and a commitment to the Open Door. Then after 1905, without abandoning the Anglo-American connection, Japan began to turn towards creating a sphere of influence in Manchuria, partly to provide a defensive cushion for Korea, partly for the sake of those important business interests which could only match their Western competitors with government support. With this modification the objectives of Japanese imperialism came more obviously into line with the stage of national economic growth. In other words, whereas the first phase of Japanese imperialism was one of dependency, the second accorded much more closely with the patterns of European imperialism, as exemplified by Germany.

Meanwhile the two main facets of Japanese policy—the development of special rights in Manchuria and the exploitation of treaty privileges in the rest of China—had acquired separate power bases within the Japanese bureaucracy. The first, because it was closely related to defence against Russia, became very much a preoccupation of the army, backed by colonial officials and those companies which were most active in dependent territories. The second, which involved in particular Japan's relations with Britain and America, was a Foreign Ministry concern, though the ministry could usually count on the co-operation of banks and of firms in the export trade. The distinction between the two is sometimes presented in such a way as to suggest that the former was imperialist, the latter not; but it is more realistic to treat both as exponents of imperialism, albeit of different kinds. One consequence of doing so is to identify the change that took place between 1905 and 1930 as being a gradual strengthening of 'informal' and 'economic' imperialism at the expense of the 'formal' and 'strategic' variety. The growth of Japanese overseas trade and investment during that period parallels the greater weight attributed to commerce and industry in national life.

A corollary was military disaffection. As the Foreign Ministry and its allies set out to modify the treaty port system, so as to make it serve Japanese interests more effectively—thereby helping to arouse Anglo-American distrust and focus Chinese nationalist resentment increasingly on Japan—the army sought ways of implementing the policies it thought necessary to defence by asserting its own 'autonomy', that is, by resisting any interference from the civil authority. The potential for damage which this situation held was for a time contained by the ability of senior statesmen, the Genrō, to preserve discipline with respect to cabinet decisions; but the nineteen-twenties witnessed the removal of all but one of the remaining Genrō from the scene by death, and the diffusion of political power in Japan between rival institutional claimants (including the parliamentary parties, representing the emergent bourgeoisie). In these conditions the conflicting aims of the army and the Foreign Ministry became competitive, not complementary.

Army officers objected to the treaty port structure because it gave other countries a voice, even a deciding voice, in the disposal of territories which, they believed, Japan had to dominate for the sake of its own defence. Other Japanese saw a different objection: that it put Japan on the 'wrong side' in a exploitative relationship between the West and Asia. To them, a better alternative would have been Sino-Japanese partnership. There were many who advanced the idea as a denial of imperialism. To others it was a reformulation of imperialist intent, anticipating a state of affairs in which China's markets and resources would be put at the disposal of Japanese industry in the name of resistance to the West. This was much how it was seen by men like Terauchi and Nishihara, who first gave concrete form to the notion of 'co-prosperity'.

Thus by 1930 Japanese imperialism comprised three disparate elements: a network of colonies and spheres of influence, protecting the approaches to the home islands and guaranteeing certain food supplies; membership of an international system based on treaty rights, conferring trade and investment privileges throughout East Asia; and an incipient special relationship with China, geared in particular to the needs of Japan's industrial economy. The events of the next decade were to bring these ingredients together in such a way as to make Japan's case distinctive in the history of empire.

The precipitant was the Wall Street slump of 1929 and the policies of economic autarky which were widely adopted in response to it. Arguments in favour of 'co-operative imperialism' in China were seriously undermined by the collapse of international trade. Japanese social discontents were much enhanced by it, and easily blamed on a hostile world enviroment. At the same time, strategic planning acquired an economic dimension. To Matsuoka, Ishiwara, and the men who thought like them it seemed self-evident that 'saving' Japan required not only lines of military defence, such as Yamagata had identified, but also control over markets and resources, in order to sustain the industry on which modern warfare depended. Within a year or two the prospect of building an autonomous Japanese bloc to serve these ends had become a central theme in Japanese politics. It could, after all, satisfy those whose hopes and fears about the outside world were otherwise diverse: military demands on the subject of defence; business's need for markets and protection; and sentimental desires for Asian solidarity. There remained only the task of giving it geographical identity. Successive advances into Manchuria, China, and south-east Asia between 1931 and 1941, each representing an elaboration of the basic concept, performed this function.

So bare a summary tends to overstate the degree of co-ordination in the process, but it is nevertheless true that the Greater East Asia Coprosperity Sphere embodied a specific economic plan, which is highly unusual among empires. The countries of north-east Asia, comprising Japan, Korea, Manchukuo, north China, and Taiwan, were to constitute a region in which heavy industry was to be developed. It would be Japan-centred in the sense that the home islands would be the principal source of capital, technology, and managerial skills, but there would also be a measure of industrial decentralization. The rest of the area brought under Japanese rule—most of China and south-east Asia, plus the islands of the south-west Pacific—would serve the industrial heartland as a source of export earnings and raw materials. This was a natural extension of the idea of Sino-Japanese co-prosperity, in circumstances which gave Japan both the motive and the opportunity to apply it on a larger scale.

The division into 'inner' and 'outer' zones, which was part of this plan, gave economic substance to a long-standing distinction within Japanese policy between the areas immediately adjacent to Japan and those farther south. The same distinction was made—with slightly different boundaries—in the arrangements for dealing with non-Japanese peoples within the Sphere. There was enough commitment to Asian values on the part of Japanese to make them reluctant to describe what they were creating as an 'empire'. Yet they believed that not all Asians were equally qualified to be partners in it. Accordingly they behaved differently in north-east Asia and in south-east Asia. The inhabitants of the former were, like the Japanese themselves, bred to China's classical tradition. On this basis it was possible to appeal to them through education and propaganda to reform their societies as the Japanese had done, so that like could work wholeheartedly with like. Thus avoidance of direct Japanese rule in China and Manchukuo derived in part from an awareness of shared racial and cultural origins. The same approach was open to European governments only in white settlement colonies.

In south-east Asia, by contrast, the Japanese saw themselves as combining Britain's role as lawgiver with France's *mission civilisatrice*: the 'backward' peoples rescued from colonialism were to be led—cautiously—towards a measure of independence as they became more 'civilized'. There were difficulties, however. Japanese beliefs proved too particularistic to be readily exportable, while 'Asian' proved to be in this context a label almost without meaning, which made it ineffective as an ideological instrument. Hence defeat left behind remarkably few traces of the Japanese presence, in the sense of transplanted Japanese cultural or institutional traditions, notwithstanding the influence bequeathed to a few outstanding individuals of Japanese education.

If these were the differences, what were the similarities with other empires? One was the fact of preponderant power. It is impossible to read the record of Japanese actions without recognizing that in the last resort Japan commanded. When co-operation was not forthcoming, obedience was the only accepted substitute. To this might be added the fact of political diversity. Empires do not have blueprints, by and large. Japan's was no exception. Differences in the machinery of authority between one part of the Co-prosperity Sphere and another were to be expected: they reflected the varied historical experience of the region and were no greater, after all, than those to be found within the British Commonwealth. Constitutionally, the Sphere was ramshackle.

It does not follow, however, that Japanese imperialism left no significant mark on East and south-east Asia. Its most evident achievement was to undermine—decisively, as it proved—European colonialism there. Post-war attempts to restore Dutch, French, and British power faced not only American reluctance, but also better-organized independence movements in the territories themselves. These owed less to Japanese encouragement than to the Japanese example, it is true. All the same, wartime propaganda about the Co-prosperity Sphere, coupled with the replacement of European officials by Asians at many levels in local administration, had done a good deal to counter the effects of Japanese government coolness towards nationalist leaders. And government fears that the latter might too readily direct their criticisms against Japan were in any case pushed into the background once Japan was facing defeat. Thus the Japanese contribution to the subsequent disintegration of European empires, though it was undoubtedly self-serving, was real.

In China the political issue was not that of formal independence— the country had never been a colony, either before or after 1937—so much as the resolution of a struggle between Chinese rivals. In this, too, the Japanese presence played a part. Japanese control of the cities and communication routes reinforced the Chinese Communist Party's decision to seek a base in the countryside. By leading the peasants in guerrilla war against Japan it was able to add the argument of patriotism to that of social justice, with the result that the end of hostilities found it immeasurably stronger, whether measured in terms of discipline or popular appeal. By contrast, Chiang Kai-shek's Kuomintang, cut off from its former centres of support by retreat to the south-west, returned in 1945 with something of the look of an intruder, backed by foreign arms. Chinese communists made the most of their opportunity, seizing upon the hatreds aroused by Japan as alien conqueror and political reactionary, in order to redirect them against domestic enemies.

The fate of Japan's older colonies, together with Manchukuo, owed more to international circumstance than to the Japanese legacy or the actions of their own inhabitants. Taiwan and Manchukuo reverted to China, the one to become the last stronghold of the Kuomintang, the other to be a continuing source of disagreement with Soviet Russia. Korea was divided by the world's leaders into two zones, Russian and American. These quickly acquired governments of contrasting political complexion, their polarity reaffirmed after 1950 by a savage war. It is difficult to see in this anything for which Japanese imperialism can be particularly praised or blamed.

One cannot say the same of economic development, however. In north-east Asia, Japan—whatever its motives—had set out to establish industries, to provide an infrastructure of transport and power supply, to train a work-force (including to some extent managers and technicians).

What was achieved was inherited by successor states and made a foundation for efforts of their own. It is no coincidence that Taiwan and
South Korea are two of Asia's most successful recent examples of
industrialization, that the Manchurian provinces have remained a
centre of Chinese heavy industry, that Mao Tse-tung's Great Leap
Forward incorporated elements remniscent of Japanese industrial
policy for China, as modified during the later months of the war Even
in south-east Asia it is possible to trace influences of the same kind,
though the short life-span of Japanese rule there, plus the disruption
associated with attempts to sever the area's links with former metropolitan economies, make it more difficult to identify a specifically
Japanese contribution to the diffusion of modern techniques and
attitudes that European colonialism had begun,

These issues are not part of the subject-matter of this book, because
they belong to the study of the post-war world, but it is legitimate for
us to note by way of conclusion that the consequences of Japanese
imperialism did not end with surrender in 1945. Nor did the emotions
it aroused. Those who look back in bitterness on the Greater East Asia
Co-prosperity Sphere can easily persuade themselves, or be persuaded, that Japan's close association with the United States, following
military occupation, is a variant of 'dependent' imperialism; that commercial success in Asia signals an attempt by Japan to restore the
inequalities of 'co-prosperity'; and that militarism remains just below
the surface of Japanese life. Such suspicions are a price Japan con-
tinues to pay for fifty years of imperialist endeavour.

A book which began by discussing explanations of imperialism should
end, no doubt, by putting the Japanese case into a theoretical framework. It is not easy to do so convincingly. It is beyond question that the
stages of Japan's imperialism reflected those of its economic growth. If
a single 'cause' has to be found, this comes closest to it. Yet there was a
powerful strategic element in it, relating to the interests of what
Schumpeter would call an atavistic military aristocracy. And one could
make a case for saying that external circumstance, in the shape of the
example and the constraints deriving from the West's imperialism, was
a precondition. Those, like myself, who accept multiple causation, will
not find this diversity of argument discouraging. They can settle for
the conclusion that imperialism is like the blind men's elephant: its
nature depends on which part of it you study.

BIBLIOGRAPHY

Abbreviations. Where literal abbreviations are used for material cited in the notes (e.g. *NGNB*), the abbreviation is entered in the following list at the appropriate point alphabetically, cross-referenced to the full title.

Allen, G. C., *A Short Economic History of Modern Japan*, 3rd edn. (London, 1972).

—— and Audrey Donnithorne, *Western Enterprise in Far Eastern Economic Development: China and Japan* (London, 1954).

Andō Hikotarō, *Mantetsu—Nihon teikokushugi to Chūgoku* [The South Manchuria Railway—Japanese imperialism and China] (Tokyo, 1965).

Asada Kyōji, ed., *Nihon teikokushugi-ka no Chūgoku* [China under Japanese imperialism] (Tokyo, 1981).

Aziz, M. A., *Japan's Colonialism and Indonesia* (The Hague, 1955).

Baba Akira, *Nitchū kankei to gaisei kikō no kenkyū* [Sino-Japanese relations and the machinery of foreign policy] (Tokyo, 1983).

Bamba, Nobuya, *Japanese Diplomacy in a Dilemma. New light on Japan's China policy 1924–1929* (Vancouver, 1972).

Barclay, George W., *Colonial Development and Population in Taiwan* (Princeton, 1954).

Beasley, W. G., *Great Britain and the Opening of Japan 1834–1858* (London, 1951).

—— *The Meiji Restoration* (Stanford, 1972).

—— *The Modern History of Japan*, 3rd edn. (London, 1981).

—— *Select Documents on Japanese Foreign Policy 1853–1868* (London, 1955).

Beckmann, George M., 'The radical left and the failure of communism', in James Morley (ed.), *Dilemmas of Growth in Prewar Japan* (Princeton, 1971), 139–78.

Beers, Burton F., *Vain Endeavor. Robert Lansing's attempts to end American–Japanese rivalry* (Durham, NC, 1962).

Benda, Harry J. *et al.*, *Japanese Military Administration in Indonesia: Selected Documents* (Yale University, 1965).

Bix, Herbert P., 'Japanese imperialism and the Manchurian economy 1900–31', *China Quarterly*, 51 (1972), 425–43.

Blacker, Carmen, *The Japanese Enlightenment. A study of the writings of Fukuzawa Yukichi* (Cambridge, 1964).

Blaug, Mark, 'Economic imperialism revisited', in K. E. Boulding and T. Mukerjee (edd.), *Economic Imperialism* (Ann Arbor, 1972), 142–55.

Borg, Dorothy, *American Policy and the Chinese Revolution 1925–1928* (New York, 1947).

Borton, Hugh, *Japan since 1931. Its political and social developments* (New York, 1940).

Boulding, K. E., and T. Mukerjee (edd.), *Economic Imperialism. A book of readings* (Ann Arbor, 1972).

Boyle, John Hunter, *China and Japan at War 1937–1945. The politics of collaboration* (Stanford, 1972).

Brown, Michael Barrett, 'A critique of Marxist theories of imperialism', in Roger Owen and R. B. Sutcliffe (edd.), *Studies in the Theory of Imperialism* (London, 1972), 35–69.

Butow, Robert J. C., *Tojo and the Coming of the War* (Princeton, 1961).

Cain, P. J., and A. G. Hopkins, 'The political economy of British expansion overseas, 1750–1914', *Economic History Review*, 2nd ser., 33 (1980), 463–90.

Chang, Richard T., *From Prejudice to Tolerance. A study of the Japanese image of the West 1826–1864* (Tokyo, 1970).

Chang, Yunshik, 'Colonization as planned change: the Korean case', *Modern Asian Studies*, 5 (1971), 161–86.

Chen, Ching-chih, 'Police and community control systems in the empire', in Ramon Myers and Mark Peattie (edd.), *The Japanese Colonial Empire* (Princeton, 1984), 213–39.

Chen, Edward I-te, 'The attempt to integrate the empire: legal perspectives', in Ramon Myers and Mark Peattie (edd.), *The Japanese Colonial Empire* (Princeton, 1984), 240–74.

—— 'Japan's decision to annex Taiwan: a study of Itō-Mutsu diplomacy, 1894–95', *Journal of Asian Studies*, 37 (1977), 61–72.

Chi, Madeleine, *China Diplomacy 1914–1918* (Cambridge, Mass., 1970).

—— 'Tsao Ju-Lin (1876–1966): his Japanese connections', in Akira Iriye (ed.), *The Chinese and the Japanese* (Princeton, 1980), 140–60.

Chung, Young-Iob, 'Japanese investment in Korea 1904–1945', in Andrew Nahm (ed.), *Korea under Japanese Colonial Rule* (Western Michigan University, 1973), 89–98.

Cohen, Jerome B., *Japan's Economy in War and Reconstruction* (Minneapolis, 1949).

Cohen, Warren I., 'America's New Order for East Asia: the Four Power Financial Consortium and China, 1919–1946', in *East Asia Occasional Papers* (Michigan State University, 1982), 41–74.

Conroy, Hilary, *The Japanese Seizure of Korea: 1868–1910* (Philadelphia, 1960).

Coox, Alvin D. and Hilary Conroy (edd.), *China and Japan. A search for balance since World War I* (Santa Barbara and Oxford, 1978).

Costin, W. C., *Great Britain and China 1833–1860* (Oxford, 1937).

Cowan, C. D. (ed.), *The Economic Development of China and Japan. Studies in economic history and political economy* (London, 1964).

Crowley, James B., *Japan's Quest for Autonomy. National security and foreign policy 1930–1938* (Princeton, 1966).

—— 'Intellectuals as visionaries of the New Asian Order', in James Morley (ed.), *Dilemmas of Growth in Prewar Japan* (Princeton, 1971), 319–73.

—— 'Japan's military foreign policies', in James Morley (ed.), *Japan's Foreign Policy 1868–1941* (New York 1974), 3–117.

—— 'A New Asian Order: some notes on prewar Japanese nationalism', in Bernard Silberman and Harry Harootunian (edd.), *Japan in Crisis* (Princeton, 1974), 270–98.

Dayer, Roberta A., *Bankers and Diplomats in China 1917–1925. The Anglo-American relationship* (London, 1981).

Duus, Peter, 'Economic dimensions of Meiji imperialism: the case of Korea, 1895–1910', in Ramon Myers and Mark Peattie (edd.), *The Japanese Colonial Empire* (Princeton, 1984), 128–71.

Earl, David M., *Emperor and Nation in Japan. Political thinkers of the Tokugawa period* (Seattle, 1964).

Eguchi Keiichi, *Nihon teikokushugi shiron: Manshū jihen zengo* [Views on the history of Japanese imperialism: about the time of the Manchurian Incident] (Tokyo, 1975).

Feuerwerker, Albert, 'China's nineteenth-century industrialization: the case of the Hanyehping Coal and Iron Company Limited', in C. D. Cowan (ed.), *The Economic Development of China and Japan* (London, 1964), 79–110.

Fieldhouse, D. K., *Economics and Empire 1830–1914* (London, 1973).

—— 'Imperialism: an historiographical revision', in K. E. Boulding and T. Mukerjee (edd.), *Economic Imperialism* (Ann Arbor, 1972), 95–123.

FO 17, FO 46, FO 371: *see under* Great Britain, Foreign Office.

Fox, Grace, *Britain and Japan 1858–1883* (Oxford, 1969).

Fujiwara Iwaichi, *F. Kikan: Japanese army intelligence operations in Southeast Asia during World War II*, trans. Yoji Akashi (Hong Kong, 1983).

Gallagher, J., and R. Robinson, 'The Imperialism of Free Trade', *Economic History Review*, 2nd ser., 6 (Aug. 1953).

Gendai-shi shiryō [Materials on recent history], 45 vols. (Tokyo, 1962–80).

Goodman, Grant K. (ed.), *Imperial Japan and Asia: a reassessment* (New York, 1967).

Gordon, Leonard, 'Japan's interest in Taiwan, 1872–1895', *Orient-West*, 9 (1964), 49–59.

Great Britain, Foreign Office, *General Correspondence*. The following series have been used:

FO 17: China

FO 46: Japan

FO 371: Political.

Great Britain, *Parliamentary Papers*.
   References to diplomatic documents published in this series are given to the
   year of publication, volume, and command number. Where possible, refer-
   ences are also given to volume and page numbers in the Irish University Press
   [IUP] reprint, which includes the nineteenth-century material on China and
   Japan (arranged in separate series by country and numbered volumes by topic).

Hackett, Roger F., *Yamagata Aritomo in the Rise of Modern Japan 1838–1922*
   (Cambridge, Mass., 1971).

Halliday, Jon, *A Political History of Japanese Capitalism* (New York, 1975).

Havens, Thomas R. H., *Farm and Nation in Modern Japan. Agrarian nationalism
   1870–1940* (Princeton, 1974).

Higuchi Hiroshi, *Nihon no tai-Shi tōshi no kenkyū* [Study of Japanese investments in China] (Tokyo, 1939).

Hirschmeier, Johannes, *The Origins of Entrepreneurship in Meiji Japan* (Cambridge, Mass., 1964).

Ho, Samuel P. S., *Economic Development of Taiwan 1860–1970* (New Haven
   and London, 1978).

—— 'Colonialism and development: Korea, Taiwan and Kwantung', in
   Ramon Myers and Mark Peattie (edd.), *The Japanese Colonial Empire*
   (Princeton, 1984), 347–98.

Hō Takushu [Peng Tse-chou], *Meiji shoki Nichi-Kan-Shin kankei no kenkyū*
   [Study of early Meiji relations between Japan, Korea, and China] (Tokyo,
   1969).

Hoare, J. E., 'The Japanese treaty ports, 1868–1899: a study of the foreign
   settlements', Ph.D. thesis (London, 1971).

Hosokawa Karoku, *Gendai Nihon Bummei-shi 10: Shokumin-shi* [Cultural history of modern Japan, vol. 10: Colonial history] (Tokyo, 1941).

Hosoya Chihiro, 'Japanese documents on the Siberian Intervention,
   1917–1922: Part I, Nov. 1917–Jan. 1919', *Hitotsubashi Journal of Law and
   Politics*, 1 (1960), 30–53.

—— 'Origin of the Siberian intervention, 1917–1918', *Annals of Hitotsubashi
   Academy*, 9 (1958), 91–108.

Hou Chi-ming, *Foreign Investment and Economic Development in China
   1840–1937* (Cambridge, Mass., 1965).

Hsiao Liang-lin, *China's Foreign Trade Statistics, 1864–1949* (Cambridge,
   Mass., 1974).

Hunt, Michael H., *Frontier Defense and the Open Door. Manchuria in Chinese–
   American relations 1895–1911* (New Haven and London, 1973).

Hurd, Douglas, *The Arrow War. An Anglo-Chinese confusion 1856–1860*
   (London, 1967).

Ikei Masaru, 'Japan's response to the Chinese Revolution of 1911', *Journal of
   Asian Studies*, 25 (1966), 213–27.

Bibliography 263

Ikei Masaru, 'Ugaki Kazushige's view of China and his China policy, 1915–1930' in Akira Iriye (ed.), *The Chinese and the Japanese* (Princeton, 1980), 199–219.

Inoue Kiyoshi, *Nihon teikokushugi no keisei* [The formation of Japanese imperialism] (Tokyo 1972 [1968]).

Iriye, Akira, *Across the Pacific. An inner history of American–East Asian relations* (New York, 1967).

—— *After Imperialism. The search for a new order in the Far East 1921–1931* (Cambridge, Mass., 1965).

—— (ed.), *The Chinese and the Japanese. Essays in political and cultural interactions* (Princeton, 1980).

—— *Pacific Estrangement. Japanese and American expansion 1897–1911* (Cambridge, Mass., 1972).

—— 'The failure of economic expansionism: 1918–1931', in Bernard Silberman and Harry Harootunian (edd.), *Japan in Crisis* (Princeton, 1974), 237–69.

—— 'The failure of military expansionism', in James Morley (ed.), *Dilemmas of Growth in Prewar Japan* (Princeton, 1971), 107–38.

Itō Hirobumi Den [Biography of Itō Hirobumi], 3 vols. (Tokyo, 1940).

Jansen, Marius B., *Japan and China: from war to peace 1894–1972* (Chicago, 1975).

—— *The Japanese and Sun Yat-sen* (Cambridge, Mass., 1954).

—— 'Japanese imperialism: late Meiji perspectives', in Ramon Myers and Mark Peattie (edd.), *The Japanese Colonial Empire* (Princeton, 1984), 61–79.

—— 'Yawata, Hanyehping and the Twenty-one Demands', *Pacific Historical Review*, 23 (1954), 31–48,

Jones, F. C., *Extraterritoriality in Japan and the diplomatic relations resulting in its abolition 1853–1899* (New Haven and London, 1931).

—— *Japan's New Order in East Asia: its rise and fall 1937–45* (London, 1954).

—— *Manchuria since 1931* (London, 1949).

Kahn, B. Winston, 'Doihara Kenji and the North China autonomy movement 1935–1936', in Alvin Coox and Hilary Conroy (edd.), *China and Japan* (Santa Barbara, 1978), 177–207.

Kajima Morinosuke, *The Diplomacy of Japan 1894–1922*, 3 vols. (Tokyo, 1976–80).

Kang, Chul Won, 'An analysis of Japanese policy and economic change in Korea', in Andrew Nahm (ed.), *Korea under Japanese Colonial Rule* (Western Michigan, 1973), 77–88.

Kiernan, V. G., *The Lords of Human Kind. European attitudes to the outside world in the imperial age* (London, 1969).

Kim, Eugene, 'Education in Korea under Japanese colonial rule', in Andrew Nahm (ed.), *Korea under Japanese Colonial Rule* (Western Michigan, 1973), 137–45.

——, and Han-kyo Kim, *Korea and the Politics of Imperialism 1876–1910* (Berkeley, 1967).

Kim, Han-kyo, 'The Japanese colonial administration in Korea', in Andrew Nahm (ed.), *Korea under Japanese Colonial Rule* (Western Michigan, 1973), 41–53.

Kindai Nihon Kenkyū 1: Shōwa-ki no gumbu [Studies of modern Japan 1: The military in the Shōwa period] (Tokyo, 1979).

Kitaoka Shinichi, *Nihon rikugun to tairiku seisaku 1906–1918* [The Japanese army and mainland policy 1906–1918] (Tokyo, 1978).

—— 'Rikugun habatsu tairitsu (1931–35) no sai-kentō: taigai-kokubō seisaku wo chūshin to shite' [A re-examination of the confrontation between army factions 1931–35, with a focus on overseas and defence policy], in *Kindai Nihon Kenkyū* (Tokyo, 1979), 44–95.

Kobayashi Hideo, *Dai-Tōa-Kyōei-Ken no keisei to hōkai* [The formation and collapse of the Greater East Asia Co-prosperity Sphere] (Tokyo, 1975).

Komura gaikō-shi [A history of Komura diplomacy] (Tokyo: Foreign Ministry, 1968).

Kurihara Ken, *Tai-Manmō seisaku-shi no ichimen* [Aspects of policy towards Manchuria and Mongolia] (Tokyo, 1966).

Landes, David S., 'The nature of economic imperialism', in K. Boulding and T. Mukerjee, *Economic Imperialism* (Ann Arbor, 1972), 124–41.

Langer, W. L., *The Diplomacy of Imperialism 1890–1902*, 2nd edn. (New York, 1951).

Lebra, Joyce C. (ed.), *Japan's Greater East Asia Co-prosperity Sphere in World War II. Selected readings and documents* (Kuala Lumpur, 1975).

Lensen, George A., *The Russian Push toward Japan. Russo-Japanese relations 1697–1875* (Princeton, 1959).

Li, Lincoln, *The Japanese Army in North China 1937–1941. Problems of political and economic control* (Tokyo and London, 1975).

Lichtheim, George, *Imperialism* (Harmondsworth, 1971).

Lockwood, W. W., *The Economic Development of Japan. Growth and structural change 1868–1938* (Princeton and London, 1955, rev. edn. 1968).

Louis, Wm. Roger, *British Strategy in the Far East 1919–1939* (Oxford, 1971).

Lowe, Peter, *Great Britain and Japan 1911–1915* (London, 1969).

McCormack, Gavan, *Chang Tso-lin in Northeast China, 1911–1928. China, Japan and the Manchurian idea* (Stanford, 1977).

Maruyama Masao, *Thought and Behaviour in Modern Japanese Politics*, ed. Ivan Morris (London, 1963).

Matsushita Yoshio, *Meiji gunsei shiron* [On the history of the Meiji military system], 2 vols. (Tokyo, 1956).

Maxon, Yale Candee, *Control of Japanese Foreign Policy. A study of civil–military rivalry 1930–1945* (Berkeley, 1957).

Mayo, Marlene (ed.), *The Emergence of Imperial Japan* (Lexington, 1970).

Meiji ikō hompō shuyō keizai tōkei [Principal domestic economic statistics since Meiji] (Bank of Japan, Tokyo, 1966).

Michie, Alexander, *The Englishman in China during the Victorian Era as illustrated in the career of Sir Rutherford Alcock*, 2 vols. (Edinburgh and London, 1900).

Mizoguchi Toshiyuki, *Taiwan-Chōsen no keizai seichō—bukka tōkei wo chūshin to shite* [Economic growth in Taiwan and Korea—with a focus on the statistics of commodity prices] (Tokyo, 1975).

—— and Yamamoto Yūzō, 'Capital formation in Taiwan and Korea', in Ramon Myers and Mark Peattie (edd.), *The Japanese Colonial Empire* (Princeton, 1984), 399–419.

Morley, James W. (ed.), *The China Quagmire. Japan's expansion on the Asian continent 1933–1941* (New York, 1983).

—— (ed.), *Deterrent Diplomacy. Japan, Germany, and the USSR 1935–1940* (New York, 1976).

—— (ed.), *Dilemmas of Growth in Prewar Japan* (Princeton, 1971).

—— (ed.), *The Fateful Choice. Japan's advance into Southeast Asia 1939–1941* (New York, 1980).

—— (ed.), *Japan Erupts. The London Naval Conference and the Manchurian Incident 1928–1932* (New York, 1984).

—— *The Japanese Thrust into Siberia, 1918* (New York, 1957).

—— (ed.), *Japan's Foreign Policy 1868–1941. A research guide* (New York, 1974).

Morton, William F., *Tanaka Giichi and Japan's China Policy* (Folkestone, 1980).

Mutsu Munemitsu, *Kenkenroku. A diplomatic record of the Sino-Japanese War 1894–95*, ed. Gordon Mark Berger (Tokyo, 1982).

Myers, Ramon H., and Mark R. Peattie (edd.), *The Japanese Colonial Empire, 1895–1945* (Princeton, 1984).

—— and Yamada Saburō, 'Agricultural development in the empire', in Myers and Peattie, *The Japanese Colonial Empire*, 420–52.

Nahm, Andrew C. (ed.), *Korea under Japanese Colonial Rule. Studies of the policy and techniques of Japanese colonialism* (Western Michigan University, 1973).

Nakamura Takafusa, *Economic Growth in Prewar Japan* (New Haven and London, 1983).

—— 'Japan's economic thrust into North China, 1933–1938: formation of the North China Development Corporation', in Akira Iriye (ed.), *The Chinese and the Japanese* (Princeton, 1980), 220–53.

Nakatsuka Akira, *Nisshin sensō no kenkyū* [Study of the Sino-Japanese War] (Tokyo, 1968).

NGB See *Nihon Gaikō Bunsho*.

NGNB See *Nihon Gaikō Nempyō narabi Shuyō Bunsho*.

Nihon Gaikō Bunsho [Japanese diplomatic documents] (Tokyo: Foreign Ministry, 1936–, in progress). There is a volume for each year, sometimes subdivided into separately bound parts, e.g. vol. 27:1, 27:2. There is a special sub-series on the Russo-Japanese War (Nicho-Ro Sensō), having separate volume numbers. Cited as *NGB*.

Nihon Gaikō Nempyō oyobi Shuyō Bunsho [Japanese diplomatic chronology and principal documents], 2 vols. (Tokyo: Foreign Ministry, 1965). Each volume is divided into sections of chronology and documents, separately paginated. Cited as *NGNB*.

Nihon Kindaishi Jiten [Dictionary of modern Japanese history] (ed. Kyōto University, Tokyo, 1958). Includes extensive lists and tables.

Nihon teikoku tōkei nenkan [Japan statistical yearbook] (ed. Cabinet Statistical Office, 59 vols., Tokyo, 1882–1941 and 1949).

Nish, Ian, *Alliance in Decline. A study in Anglo-Japanese relations 1908–23* (London, 1972).

—— ed., *Anglo-Japanese Alienation 1919–1952. Papers of the Anglo-Japanese conference on the History of the Second World War* (Cambridge, 1982).

—— *The Anglo-Japanese Alliance. The diplomacy of two island empires 1894–1907* (London, 1966).

—— *Japanese Foreign Policy 1869–1942. Kasumigaseki to Miyakezaka* (London, 1977).

—— 'Japan's indecision during the Boxer disturbances', *Journal of Asian Studies*, 20 (1961), 449–61.

—— *The Origins of the Russo-Japanese War* (London, 1985).

Ogata, Sadako N., *Defiance in Manchuria. The making of Japanese foreign policy 1931–1932* (Berkeley, 1964).

Ohara Keishi, *Japanese Trade and Industry in the Meiji-Taisho Era*, trans. Ōkata Tamotsu (Tokyo, 1957).

Ohkawa Kazushi and Shinohara Miyohei, with Larry Meissner, *Patterns of Japanese Economic Development. A quantative appraisal* (New Haven and London, 1979).

Oka Yoshitake, *Konoe Fumimaro. A political biography*, trans. Shumpei Okamoto and Patricia Murray (Tokyo, 1983).

Okakura Kakuzō (Tenshin), *The Awakening of Japan* (London, 1905).

—— *The Ideals of the East* (New York, 1904).

Okamoto, Shumpei, *The Japanese Oligarchy and the Russo-Japanese War* (New York and London, 1970).

Ōkuma Shigenobu (ed.), *Fifty Years of New Japan*, 2 vols. (London, 1910).

Ōkura zaibatsu no kenkyū: Ōkura to tairiku [Study of the Ōkura concern: Ōkura and the mainland] (Tokyo, 1982).

Ōkurashō [Finance Ministry], *Shōwa zaiseishi* [Financial history of the Shōwa period], ed. Ōuchi Hyōe and Aoki Tokuzō, 18 vols. (Tokyo, 1954–65).

Oriental Economist, *The Foreign Trade of Japan: a statistical survey* (Tokyo, 1935).

Ōta Kōki, 'Nampō gunsei no tenkai to tokushitsu' [The development and special characteristics of military government in the southern regions], in *Shōwa-shi no gumbi to seiji* (Tokyo, 1983), 4, 41–76.

Owen, Roger, and R. B. Sutcliffe (edd.), *Studies in the Theory of Imperialism* (London, 1972).

Ōyama Azusa (ed.), *Yamagata Aritomo ikensho* [Memoranda of Yamagata Aritomo] (Tokyo, 1966).

Parliamentary Papers: see under Great Britain, *Parliamentary Papers*.

Peattie, Mark R., *Ishiwara Kanji and Japan's Confrontation with the West* (Princeton, 1975).

—— 'Japanese attitudes toward colonialism, 1895–1945', in Ramon Myers and Mark Peattie (edd.), *The Japanese Colonial Empire* (Princeton, 1984), 80–127.

—— 'The Nanyō: Japan in the South Pacific, 1885–1945', in Ramon Myers and Mark Peattie (edd.), *The Japanese Colonial Empire* (Princeton, 1984), 172–210.

Pelcovits, Nathan A., *Old China Hands and the Foreign Office* (New York, 1948).

Pierson, John D., *Tokutomi Sohō 1863–1957. A journalist for modern Japan* (Princeton, 1980).

Pluvier, J. M., *South-East Asia from Colonialism to Independence* (Kuala Lumpur, 1974).

Presseisen, Ernst L., *Before Aggression. Europeans prepare the Japanese Army* (Tucson, 1965).

Pyle, Kenneth B., *The New Generation in Meiji Japan. Problems of cultural identity, 1885–1895* (Stanford, 1969).

Remer, C. F., *Foreign Investments in China* (New York, 1968 reprint [1933]).

—— *The Foreign Trade of China* (Taipei, 1967 reprint [1926]).

Roberts, J. G., *Mitsui. Three centuries of Japanese business* (New York and Tokyo, 1973).

Sasaki Takashi, 'Kōdō-ha to Tōsei-ha' [The Imperial Way faction and the Control faction], in *Shōwa-shi no gumbu to seiji* (Tokyo, 1983), 1, 155–91.

Schumpeter, E. B. (ed.), *The Industrialization of Japan and Manchukuo 1930–1940. Population, raw materials and industry* (New York, 1940).

Schrecker, John E., *Imperialism and Chinese Nationalism: Germany in Shantung* (Cambridge, Mass., 1971).

Segai Inoue Kō Den [Biography of Inoue Kaoru], ed. Sakatani Yoshirō, 5 vols. (Tokyo, 1933–4).

Senji seiji keizai shiryō [Wartime political and economic materials], ed. Kokusaku Kenkyūkai, 8 vols. (Tokyo, 1982–3). A reprint of the Kokusaku Kenkyūkai's weekly reports [*Shūhō*] for the years 1940–45.

Shao Hsi-ping, 'From the Twenty-one Demands to the Sino-Japanese military agreements, 1915–1918: ambivalent relations', in Alvin Coox and Hilary Conroy (edd.), *China and Japan* (Santa Barbara, 1978), 35–57.

Shillony, Ben-Ami, *Revolt in Japan. The Young Officers and the February 26, 1936 incident* (Princeton, 1973).

Shinobu Seizaburō and Nakayama Jiichi, *Nichi-Ro sensō-shi no kenkyū* [Study of the history of the Russo-Japanese War] (Tokyo, rev. edn. 1972).

Shiozaki Hiroaki, 'Gumbu to Nampō shinshutsu' [The military and the advance into the southern regions], in *Shōwa-shi no gumbu to seiji* (Tokyo, 1983), 3, 83–117.

Shōda Tatsuo, *Chūgoku shakkan to Shōda Kazue* [The China loans and Shōda Kazue] (Tokyo, 1972).

Shōwa-shi no gumbu to seiji [The military and politics in Shōwa history], ed. Miyake Masaki *et al.*, 5 vols. (Tokyo, 1983).

Silberman, Bernard S., and Harry D. Harootunian (edd.), *Japan in Crisis. Essays on Taishō democracy* (Princeton, 1974).

Stephan, John J., *Sakhalin. A history* (Oxford, 1971).

—— 'The Tanaka Memorial (1927): authentic or spurious?', *Modern Asian Studies*, 7 (1973), 733–45.

Storry, Richard, *The Double Patriots: a study of Japanese nationalism* (London, 1957).

Sugiyama, Shinya, *Japan's Industrialization in the World Economy 1859–1899. Export trade and overseas competition* (London, 1987).

Suzuki Takeo, *Nishihara shakkan shiryō kenkyū* [Study of materials on the Nishihara loans] (Tokyo, 1972).

Tabohashi Kiyoshi, *Nisshin seneki gaikō-shi no kenkyū* [Study of the diplomatic history of the Sino-Japanese War] (Tokyo, 1951).

Trager, Frank N. (ed.), *Burma: Japanese Military Administration. Selected documents, 1941–1945* (Philadelphia, 1971).

Treat, Payson J., *The Early Diplomatic Relations between the United States and Japan 1853–1865* (Baltimore, 1917).

Tsunoda Jun, *Manshū mondai to kokubō hōshin* [The Manchuria problem and national defence policy] (Tokyo, 1967).

Tsunoda, Ryusaku *et al.*, *Sources of Japanese Tradition* (New York, 1958).

Tsurumi, E. Patricia, *Japanese Colonial Education in Taiwan 1895–1945* (Cambridge, Mass., 1977).

—— 'Colonial education in Korea and Taiwan', in Ramon Myers and Mark Peattie (edd.), *The Japanese Colonial Empire* (Princeton, 1984), 275–311.

—— 'Taiwan under Kodama Gentarō and Gotō Shimpei', in Harvard East Asia Research Center, *Papers on Japan*, 4 (1967), 95–146.

Tsurumi Yūsuke, *Gotō Shimpei*, 4 vols. (Tokyo, 1937–8).

Usui Katsumi, *Nihon to Chūgoku: Taishō jidai* [Japan and China: The Taishō period] (Tokyo, 1972).

Vevier, Charles, *The United States and China 1906–1913. A study of finance and diplomacy* (New York, reprint 1968 [1955]).

Wada, Teijuhn, *American Foreign Policy toward Japan during the Nineteenth Century* (Tokyo, 1928).

Wehler, Hans-Ulrich, 'Industrial growth and early German imperialism', in Roger Owen and R. B. Sutcliffe (edd.), *Studies in the Theory of Imperialism* (London, 1972), 72–90.

Willoughby, W. W., *Foreign Rights and Interests in China* (Baltimore, 1920).

Wilson, George M., *Radical Nationalist in Japan: Kita Ikki, 1883–1937* (Cambridge, Mass., 1969).

Wright, H. M., (ed.), *The 'New Imperialism'. Analysis of late nineteenth-century expansion* (Boston, Mass., 1961).

Wright, Mary C., *The Last Stand of Chinese Conservatism. The T'ung-chih Restoration, 1862–1874* (Stanford, 1957).

Yamabe Kentarō, *Nikkan heigō shōshi* [Short history of the Japanese annexation of Korea] (Tokyo, 1966).

Yano Tōru, *'Nanshin' no keifu* [The genealogy of 'the advance to the south'] (Tokyo, 1975).

Yim, Kwanha, 'Yuan Shih-k'ai and the Japanese', *Journal of Asian Studies*, 24 (1965), 63–73.

Yoo, Jong Hae, 'The system of Korean local government', in Andrew Nahm (ed.), *Korea under Japanese Colonial Rule* (Western Michigan, 1973), 54–66.

Young, John W., 'The Hara cabinet and Chang Tso-lin, 1920–1', *Monumenta Nipponica*, 27, 2 (1972), 125–42.

Yuan Tsing, 'The Japanese intervention in Shantung during World War I', in Alvin Coox and Hilary Conroy (edd.), *China and Japan* (Santa Barbara, 1978), 19–33.

INDEX

Abe Moritarō 108, 110
Aberdeen, Lord 21
Aizawa Seishisai 29, 32
Akashi Motojirō 111
Alcock, Sir Rutherford 20, 25
Amau (Amō) Eiji 200
America see United States
Amoy (Xiamen) 16, 76, 206, 208
Amur region 22, 41, 78, 84, 156, 158, 160, 161, 221
Anglo-Chinese wars 15, 23
Anglo-Japanese alliance 76–7, 78, 81, 89, 99, 109, 135, 165–7, 253
Annam 42
Anshan ironworks 139, 215, 216
Anti-Comintern Pact 221
Antung (Dandong) 93, 113
Aoki Kazuo 238
Araki Sadao 159, 181, 193
Arita Hachirō 226
army, Japanese: and Japanese expansion (before 1930) 11–12, 35–6, 56, 78, 94–100, 105–6, 108, 117, 120, 145, 159–60, 253–4; (after 1930) 180–2, 190–4, 196–7, 198–9, 200–2, 209–10, 217, 226, 230–1, 236, 238–40, 245; General Staff 36, 46, 104, 161, 181, 203, 210, 221, 236; see also Control Faction; Imperial Way Faction; Kwantung Army; North China Army; South China Army
Asia Development Board (Kōain) 209–10, 231, 236, 237
Australia 166, 227–8
Ayukawa Yoshisuke 216

Ba Maw 240, 245
Baikal, Lake 160
banks, Japanese, and foreign investment 51–2, 60, 73–4, 106–7, 118, 135–6, 151, 154; see also Dai Ichi Bank; Industrial Bank; Yokohama Specie Bank
Batavia 229, 230, 239
Beijing see Peking
Bismarck archipelago 238
Black Dragon Society see Kokuryūkai

Bonin (Ogasawara) Is. 142
Borneo 227, 234, 242, 246
Bowring, Sir John 18, 21, 23
Boxer crisis 76, 81, 135
Britain: and East Asia 41, 42, 52, 55, 56, 160; and the treaty port system 14–20, 24, 61, 63, 65–6, 69–71, 101, 170–3, 174, 252–3; imperialism of 1–5, 8, 51, 143, 198–9, 227, 243, 256; investment in China 103, 133, 134; relations with Japan (before 1911) 21–2, 23, 24, 26, 33, 58–9, 62, 76–7, 87, 89, 91–2, 94–5, 99–100, 251, 253–4, (1911–30) 105, 109–10, 114, 115, 126, 157, 165–7, 170–3, 188, (after 1930) 193, 220–2, 223, 224, 226, 227, 231–2, 243
Brunei 234
Burma 41, 42, 227, 228, 232; in the Greater East Asia Co-prosperity Sphere 235, 236, 238, 239–40, 242–3, 245, 247, 249

Cabinet Planning Board (Kikakuin) 209, 210, 213, 225, 228, 231, 237
Cain, P. J. 4
Cambodia (Kampuchea) 41, 42
Canada 166
Canton (Guangzhou) 15, 16, 18, 23, 25, 63, 64, 100, 170
Cao Rulin see Tsao Ju-lin
Celebes 238
Central China Development Company 218
Chang Hsüeh-liang (Zhang Xueliang) 188, 191, 195
Chang Tso-lin (Zhang Zuolin) 111, 162–3, 170, 182–8
Changchun (Hsinking) 92–3, 113, 158, 195, 216
Changkufeng 207, 221
Chefoo (Yantai) 115
Chekiang (Zhejiang) 76, 113
Chemulpo see Inchon
Chiang Kai-shek 170, 172, 173, 183–4, 186, 191, 200, 203, 205, 207–8, 257

China: and the Western powers (before 1911) 69–71, 79, 80–1, 82, 83, 92–3, 96, 98, 252–3, (after 1911) 103, 156–8, 163–4, 167–8, 208; foreign trade 14–16, 17, 45, 124, 127–30, 189–90, 210–12; Japanese investment in 92–3, 103, 106–7, 109, 112–13, 122–3, 132–4, 135–41, 214–15, 217–18, 258; Japanese puppet regimes in (after 1933) 201, 205–8, 217, 243; nationalism and the treaties 157, 169–70, 188; relations with Japan (before 1911) 42–8, 55–68, 75–6, 80–4, 92–3, 98, (1911–30) 103–8, 110–15, 116–20, 127–30, 158–74, 183–8, (after 1930) 191–3, 199–203, 212–19, 257; tariffs and extraterritoriality 16, 63, 64, 170–4, 188, 208; the treaty port system in 4, 6, 7, 14–20, 25, 26, 60–8, 69–71, 81, 100, 103, 122–3, 169–74, 252–3; tribute system 41–2, 42–3, 47; Western investment in 69–71, 103, 109, 122–3, 133–4, 138–9, 140, 214; *see also* Manchuria

China Affairs Board (Taishiin) 209

China Industrial Company 107

Chinese, in South-east Asia 234, 239, 242, 245, 247, 248

Chinese Communist Party 169–70, 203, 206, 257, 258

Chinese Eastern Railway (CER) 70, 82, 83–4, 99, 160, 162, 216

Chinese Revolution (1911) 101–8

Chinnampo 53

Chita 160

Chongqing *see* Chungking

Chōsen (Korea), Bank of 117–18, 151, 154

Chungking (Chongqing) 64

Clarendon, Lord 17–18, 19–20, 21–2

Cochin China 41, 42

Colonial Ministry (Takumushō) 144, 196, 236, 237

Concordia Association (Kyōwakai) 196, 208

Control Faction (Tōsei-ha) 181, 204

co-prosperity: concepts of 52–3, 118–20, 169, 175–6, 201–2, 233, 254; plans concerning 117–21, 162–3, 186, 205, 228

Co-prosperity Sphere *see* Greater East Asia Co-prosperity Sphere

Curzon, Lord 165, 166–7

Dai Ichi Bank 73–4, 106, 118, 151

Dai Tōa-shō *see* Greater East Asia Ministry

Daihonei *see* Imperial Headquarters

Dairen (Ta-lien; Dalian; Dalny) 142

Dandong *see* Antung

Darwinism, Social 9, 31, 178

Datong *see* Tatung

Duan Qirui *see* Tuan Ch'i-jui

Dutch *see* Holland

East India Company (English) 15, 21, 136

Edo (later Tokyo) 23, 24

education, in Japanese overseas territories 147, 148–9, 195–6, 208, 244

Elgin, Lord 18–19, 24

emperor system *see* Japan, emperor system

Fengtien (Liaoning) 183

Fieldhouse, D. K. 3

Finance Ministry (Ōkurashō) 95, 106, 118, 128, 135, 247

Five Year Plan, Japanese 213–14, 216–17, 218

Foochow (Fuzhou) 16

Foreign Ministry (Gaimushō) 96–7, 98, 108–9, 120, 127–8, 146, 185, 188, 190–1, 197, 209–10, 236–8, 253–4

Formosa *see* Taiwan

France: and China 16, 17, 18, 56, 69–70, 103, 133–4, 157, 167; and Japan 24, 26, 58–9, 75, 221, 224, 227, 230–1; empire and colonies 1, 41–2, 44–5, 143, 227, 230, 256; *see also* Indo-China

Fujian *see* Fukien

Fujii Shōichi 7–8

Fukien (Fujian) 55, 57, 75–6, 77, 80, 109, 111, 113, 115

fukoku-kyōhei see wealth and strength

Fukuzawa Yukichi 30–1, 32, 33

Fundamentals of National Policy (1936) 201–2, 224

Furukawa company 248

Fusan *see* Pusan

Fushun coal-mine 92, 98, 136, 139, 215, 217

Fuzhou *see* Foochow

Gaimushō *see* Foreign Ministry

Gaiseishō 237

Gallagher, J. 3–4

General Staff *see under* army, Japanese

Germany: imperialism 1, 5–6, 251, 253; in East Asia and the Pacific 17, 71, 103, 116, 133–4, 157; relations with Japan 59, 62, 65, 109–10, 114, 134, 220–1, 227; rights in Shantung 69–70, 110, 113, 115, 134, 142, 154, 164, 168

Gotō Shimpei 76, 97–8, 119, 136, 146, 147, 160–1

Greater East Asia Co-prosperity Sphere (Dai Tōa Kyōei Ken) 10–12, 121, 199, 252; economic policies in 243, 245–50, 255; idea of 201–2, 226, 227–8, 229, 233–4, 235–6; Japanese military government in 238–41; political structure of 233–43, 256

Greater East Asia Ministry (Dai Tōa-shō) 237–8

Grey, Sir Edward 99, 109–10

Guam 167

Guangdong *see* Kwangtung

Guangxi *see* Kwangsi

Guangzhou *see* Canton

gunboat diplomacy 18, 20, 21, 23–4, 43

Guomindang *see* Kuomintang

Hainan 208

Haiphong 230

hakkō-ichiu 226, 244

Hakodate 23, 24

Hamaguchi Osachi 190

Hangchow (Hangzhou) 63, 64

Hankow (Hankou) 134, 170

Hanoi 230–1

Hanyehping coal and iron company 106–7, 108, 113, 115, 137–8, 139, 218

Hara Kei 104, 145, 158, 160, 162,–3, 168, 182

Harbin 84, 90

Harriman E. H. 93–4

Harris, Townsend 23–4, 28

Hay, John 70–1

Hayashi Gonsuke 86

Hayes, Carlton 5

Heilungkiang (Heilongjiang) 193

Hepei *see* Hopei

Hioki Eki 112, 113, 114

Hitachi company 248

Hobson J. A. 1–2, 3

Holland: colonialism 1, 227, 239; relations with Japan 21, 24, 28, 202, 223, 224, 227, 228–30; *see also* Netherlands East Indies

Hong Kong 16, 70, 167, 232, 234–5

Honjō Shigeru 192, 193

Hopei (Hepei) 200, 201

Hopei-Chahar Political Council 201, 203

Horvat, Dmitrii 159

Hotta Masayoshi 28–9

Hsing Chung company 218

Hsinking *see* Changchun

Hsin-min Hui (New People's Society) 208

Hubei *see* Hupeh

Hunan 63

Hupeh (Hubei) 63

Hyōgo *see* Kobe

Ichang (Yichang) 64

Iguchi Shōgo 91

Ijūin Motohiko 104

Ilchinhoe 90

Ili valley 41

Imperial Headquarters (Daihonei) 209, 210, 231, 236, 237, 238

Imperial Way Faction (Kōdō-ha) 181

Imperialism, Japanese: and Asian values 32–3, 101, 110, 112, 178, 196, 199, 204–5, 208, 210, 243–5, 251, 254, 255–6; and central government institutions 96, 144, 196–7, 198–9, 209–10, 231, 236–8; and economic autarky 188–90, 192, 201, 206–7, 210–19, 222–32, 245–50, 254–5; and economic development 37–40, 66, 71, 82–3, 116, 119–20, 123–6, 134–5, 140, 175–6, 188–90, 251–2, 253; and Japanese responses to the West 27–34, 48, 99, 101, 118–19, 168–9, 176, 178–80, 198, 202, 239–41, 251, 256; domestic pressures on 56, 66, 78–9, 81, 95, 96–8, 171, 175–6, 188–90, 252, 254; economic factors in (before 1930) 45, 51–2, 60–8, 73–5, 79, 81–3, 85, 87, 91–9, 106–9, 117–21, 122–3, 163–5, 168–9, 173–4, 175–6, 251–4; general characteristics 6–12, 72, 85, 101–2, 122–3, 174, 175–6, 198–9, 224, 231, 251–8; influence of nationalism and militarism on 30–3, 118–19, 176–82, 184, 226–7; lasting effects of 256–8; strategic factors in (before 1930) 45–6, 56, 59, 79–84, 85–7, 95–7, 105–6, 120–1, 142–3, 146, 152, 182, 253; *see also* Greater East Asia Co-prosperity Sphere; New Order in East Asia

Imperialism, Western: and Japan 27–33, 43, 51, 90, 212, 220, 227–8, 233, 239–41, 249, 250, 252–3, 256–7; general nature of 1–6, 17, 51, 65–6, 67, 69–71, 198–9, 220, 252–3
Inchon (Chemulpo) 49, 53, 74, 75
India: and Britain 15, 18, 19, 22, 41, 65, 99, 136, 198; and Japan 29, 126, 129, 130, 212, 227–8, 231–2, 247
Indo-China, and Japan 212, 223, 226, 227, 228, 230–1, 232, 235, 237, 241, 243, 245, 249; see also France: empire and colonies
Indonesia see Netherlands East Indies
Industrial Bank of Japan 38, 91, 118, 136
Inoue Kaoru 50–4, 60, 71, 73, 93, 95, 106, 110
Inoue Kiyoshi 8–9
Inukai Tsuyoshi 180, 193
investment see China: Western investment in; Japan, foreign and colonial investment
Iriye Akira 10
Ishii Kikujirō 158, 163–4
Ishiwara Kanji 181–2, 184, 188, 191–3, 194, 196, 213, 216, 220, 221, 227, 255
Itagaki Seishirō 188, 191–3, 194, 200
Italy 17, 220–1
Itō Hirobumi: and China 55–9, 60–4, 94–6; and Korea 44, 49, 50, 72, 80, 87–9, 90
Iwanaga Kakujū 81–2, 83

Jansen M. B. 9–10
Japan, Bank of 52, 73, 106
Japan, colonies and dependencies: administration of 96, 143–9, 196–7, 209–10, 233–43; economies of 130–2, 149–55, 210–19, 243, 245–50, 255; see also individual territories
Japan, economic interest groups 38–40, 45, 66, 79, 81, 93
Japan, emperor system 7, 34–5, 144, 176, 177, 184
Japan, foreign and colonial investment: (before 1914) 51–2, 60, 61–2, 66, 73–5, 85, 87, 92–3, 103, 106–7, 122–3, 132–41, 251–2; (after 1914) 115, 149–55, 213–18, 223, 228, 248
Japan, foreign and colonial trade 25–6, 37, 39, 45, 87, 123–32, 149–54, 188–90, 210–12, 225–6, 246, 249;

negotiations concerning 23–5, 60–8, 82–4, 92–3, 229–30, 231
Japan, foreign relations see under individual countries concerned
Japan, industry, 37–8, 39–40, 123–6, 251; in the New Order and Co-prosperity Sphere 213–18, 245–50; raw materials for 119, 120, 123, 124, 126–7, 129–30, 132, 137, 143, 153–4, 155, 211–12, 223, 225–6, 228, 249
Japan, overseas borrowing 91–2, 135–6, 252
Japan, treaty port system in 14, 18, 19, 21–6, 27, 33–4; and the treaty port system in East Asia 60–8, 71, 81, 90–100, 101–2, 113, 120–1, 122–3, 168–9, 170–4, 187, 252
Java 238, 239, 242–3, 250
Jehol 200
Jiangxi see Kiangsi
Jiaoxian see Kiaochow
Jilin see Kirin
Jinan see Tsinan
Jones, F. C. 11, 12

Kagoshima 24
Kalgan 205, 208, 218
Kanagawa see Yokohama
Kanghwa, Treaty of 44
Karafuto 6, 142, 143–4, 145, 146, 154–5
Katō Kanji 159
Katō Takaaki (Kōmei) 95, 114, 168
Katsura Tarō 75–6, 77, 83, 90, 93, 96, 98, 105, 135, 137
Kawashima Naniwa 105–6, 116–17
Khabarovsk 160
Kiangsi (Jiangxi) 76, 113
Kiaochow (Jiaoxian) 110, 114, 115, 142, 154, 168, 186
Kirin (Jilin) 92–3, 113, 158
Kita Ikki 178, 180
Kōain see Asia Development Board
Kobayashi Ichizō 229
Kobe (Hyōgo) 24, 25
Kodama Gentarō 75–6, 96, 97–8, 136, 144, 146
kōdō 204
Kōdō-ha (Imperial Way Faction) 181
Koiso Kuniaki 225, 227
Kokuryūkai (Amur Society; Black Dragon Society) 78, 90, 111, 119, 178
kokutai 204, 227
Kōmoto Daisaku 187–8

Komura Jutarō 62–3, 72, 77, 79–84, 89, 91–4, 98–9, 128

Konoe Fumimaro 179, 203–4, 207, 218, 220, 226, 231, 232, 233

Korea: and the treaty port system 18, 44; anti-Japanese unrest in 88–9, 148–9; as Japanese colony 6, 89–90, 130, 142, 143–5, 148–9, 153, 238, 257; as Japanese protectorate 83–4, 86–90, 142; Japanese investment in 51–2, 60, 73–5, 87, 135, 151–4, 214–15, 257; Japanese relations with (before 1905) 29, 42–54, 56–7, 67–8, 71–5, 77, 78–81, 83–4; trade with China and Japan 45, 75, 87, 130–2, 149, 152–4, 211

Kuhara company 155–159

Kuo Sung-ling (Guo Songling) 183

Kuomintang (Guomindang) 102, 169–70, 172, 187, 188, 191, 193, 201, 202–3, 205, 206, 207, 257

Kurile Is. 142

Kwangsi (Guangxi) 63, 70

Kwangtung (Guangdong) 70, 170

Kwantung (formerly Liaotung) 94, 105, 130, 131, 154; Japanese administration 97, 98, 144–5, 146, 236, 238; Japanese lease 104, 108, 112, 115, 131, 142, 173

Kwantung Army: and central policy-making 94, 97–8, 196–7, 210, 236; and Manchuria 94, 112, 117, 183, 185, 187, 188, 191–6, 215–16, 221; in North China and Mongolia 200, 201, 205

Kyōwakai 196, 208

Lamont, Thomas 165

Landes, D. S. 3, 4

Langer, W. L. 3, 4

Lansing, Robert 163–4, 165

League of Nations 164, 193, 200

Lenin, V. I. 2, 5, 9

Li Hung-chang (Li Hongzhang) 44, 57–8, 59, 60, 63–4, 66, 67

Liaotung (later Kwantung) peninsula 48, 55–9, 60, 63, 67, 69, 70, 73, 82, 84, 92–3, 94, 98, 131, 142

Liaoyang 78

likin 61, 63, 64, 172

Lobanov, Prince A. 72

London Naval Conference 190

Loochoo *see* Ryukyu

Lungyen iron-mine 218

Lushun *see* Port Arthur

Makino Nobuaki 109

Malaya 116, 130, 212, 223, 227, 232; in the Greater East Asia Co-prosperity Sphere 234, 235, 238, 239, 241, 242–3, 245, 246, 248, 249

Manchukuo: economic relations with Japan 211–12, 212–17; establishment and administration of 191–6; in Japanese relations with China 193–4, 195, 199–201, 205, 206–7, 208; Japanese control of 196–7, 236–8, 241

Manchuria: Japanese interests in: (before 1911) 6, 29, 46, 55–9, 60, 78–84, 85, 89–90, 90–100, (1911–31) 104–6, 108–9, 111–13, 115, 116–17, 118–19, 120, 124, 129–32, 134, 135–6, 139, 141, 156–63, 165, 168, 173, 175–6, 182–8, 189, 211–12; Russian interests in 41, 63, 70, 71, 78–84, 89–90, 91, 92, 98–9, 156, 161–2, 193, 216; *see also* Manchukuo (for period after 1931)

Manchuria Industrial Development Company (Mangyō) 216, 217, 248

Manchurian Affairs Board (Tai-Man Jimukyoku) 196–7, 210, 236, 237

Manchurian crisis (1931–3) 191–4

Mangyō *see* Manchuria Industrial Development Company

Manila 167, 240

Man-Kan kōkan 79–80

Mantetsu *see* South Manchuria Railway Company

Mao Tse-tung (Mao Zedong) 258

Marco Polo Bridge 203

Maritime Provinces *see* Siberia and the Maritime Provinces

Matsui Iwane 169

Matsuoka Yōsuke 183, 189, 226, 227–8, 234, 255

May Fourth Movement 169

Meckel, Maj. Klemens 36, 45–6

militarism *see* army, Japanese: and expansion; imperialism, Japanese: influence of nationalism and militarism on

Minami Jirō 181

Ministry of Foreign Administration (Gaiseishō) 237

Mito 29, 32

Mitsubishi company 39–40, 74, 93, 95, 106, 107, 118, 120, 137, 155, 168, 214, 217, 248

Mitsui company 39–40, 52, 60, 74, 93, 106–8, 118, 120, 136, 137–8, 139, 151, 154, 155, 214, 217, 248
Miura Gorō 54, 71–2, 74
Miyazaki Masayoshi 205, 213
modernization, and Japanese imperialism 34–40
Mokpo 53
Molucca Is. 238
Mongolia, Japanese interests in: (before 1917) 78, 90, 104, 105–6, 108, 111, 112, 115, 119, 120; (after 1917) 160, 165, 185, 186, 205, 206, 212, 218
Mori Kaku 107, 184, 185
Morley, James 11
most-favoured-nation clause 16, 24, 59–60, 62, 64, 67
Motono Ichirō, 160, 161
Mukden (Shenyang) 75, 78, 93, 113, 162, 187, 192–3, 195, 230
Muraviev, Count M. 73
Mutsu Munemitsu 47–8, 49, 50, 52, 54, 55–9, 60–4, 65, 67

Nabeyama Sadachika 179–80
Nagasaki 21, 22, 24, 25, 28
Nagata Tetsuzan 181
Nagoya 38
Nanchang 113
Nanking (Nanjing): Chinese governments at 100, 106–7, 170, 172, 187, 188, 192, 200–1, 203, 206, 208; Japanese atrocities at 203; Treaty of 15–16, 17
nanshin (advance to the south) 29, 75–6, 116, 220–32
Nanyō (later Nampō) *see nanshin*; Pacific islands; South-east Asia
National Mobilization Law 204, 213, 246
nationalism *see under* China; imperialism, Japanese
Nationalist Party (China) *see* Kuomintang
navy, Japanese 36–7, 159–60, 190, 201–2, 224, 226, 231, 240–1
Netherlands East Indies: Japanese policy towards 202, 212, 223, 225–6, 227, 228–30, 232, 249–50; under Japanese control 234, 236, 238, 239, 242, 245, 246
New Guinea 234, 238
New Order in East Asia 179, 180, 198–9, 201–2, 227, 232, 252; economic aspects of 210–219, 225; establishment and organization of 203–8

New Zealand 227–8
Newchwang (Yingkow; Yingkou) 63
Nihon Chisso (Japan Nitrogen) company 214
Niigata 24
Ningpo (Ningbo) 16
Nippon Steel company 218
Nishi Tokujirō 58
Nishihara Kamezō 117–18, 120–1, 254
Nishihara loans 117–18, 158, 171
Nishi-Rosen agreement 73, 74
Nissan company 216
Nomonhan 221
Nomura company 248
North China Army 203, 205–6, 210, 218
North China Development Company 218

Ogawa Mataji 46
oil and petroleum 155, 212, 223, 224, 228–30, 247, 249
Oka Ichinosuke 111–12
Okakura Kakuzō (Tenshin) 32–3
Ōkoshi Narinori 61, 62
Ōkuma Shigenobu 110, 158
Ōkura company 74, 104, 106–7, 120, 136, 137–8, 139, 151, 215, 217
Ōkurashō *see* Finance Ministry
Open Door policy 70–1, 77, 79, 99, 140, 157, 164, 167, 253; Japan and 79, 85, 91–2, 97, 100, 109, 123, 156, 187, 193, 234, 253
Oriental Development Company 151, 153
Osaka 24, 38
Ōtani Sonyū 218
Ōtori Keisuke 49–50
Ōyama Iwao 48

Pacific islands 116, 142, 153, 154, 232, 238, 247–8
Pacific War 10–12, 231–2, 241, 250
Palmerston, Lord 16, 21
Peking (Beijing) 17, 19–20, 63, 64, 134, 206, 208
Penhsihu iron and steel works 139, 215, 216, 217
Perry, Cdre. M. C. 23, 29, 43
Pescadores Is. 57
Philippine Is. 56, 202, 223, 225, 227, 228, 232; in the Greater East Asia Co-prosperity Sphere 234, 236, 238, 240, 242–3, 246, 248, 249, 250
Port Arthur (Lushun; Ryojun) 48, 56, 57, 70, 78, 79, 84, 142

Portsmouth, Treaty of 84, 92
Pottinger, Sir Henry 16
Pu Yi 194–5
Pusan (Fusan) 43, 49, 53, 74, 75, 151
Pyongyang 48

Qingdao *see* Tsingtao
Qiqihar *see* Tsitsihar

Raffles, Thomas Stamford 21
railways: in China (excluding Manchuria)
    63, 69, 75–6, 107, 108, 109, 112–13,
    137, 154, 165; in Korea 49, 50, 53, 60,
    74–5, 79, 86–7, 135, 136, 151–2; in
    Manchuria 63, 70, 82–4, 92–4, 98–9,
    104, 108, 111–13, 135–6, 139, 146,
    158, 165, 186, 191, 215–16
Reorganization Loan 103, 107, 109, 164
Rezanov, Nikolai 22
Robinson, R. 3–4
Roosevelt, Theodore, 92, 100
Russia: and Korea 53, 59, 67–8, 71–3,
    89–90; and Manchuria 69–71, 76–7,
    78–80, 81, 89–90, 94–6, 98–9, 156,
    193, 216, 221; expansion in East Asia
    14, 17, 22, 41, 42, 44–5, 46, 73, 105,
    133–4, 198–9, 227–8, 253; relations
    with Japan (before 1917) 22, 23, 24, 53,
    54, 58–9, 62, 71, 76–7, 78–84, 89–90,
    97, 98–9, 105, 253, (after 1917) 156–7,
    158–62, 202, 207, 216, 220–1, 224,
    257
Russo-Japanese War 7, 8, 78–84, 85,
    90–100, 251
Ryojun *see* Port Arthur
Ryukyu (Loochoo) Is. 142

Saigon 41
Saionji Kimmochi 54, 67, 94–6, 104, 106,
    107, 192
Saitō Makoto 199
Sakhalin 6, 83, 84, 142, 155, 162, 212
sakoku 21
Sakuma Shōzan 28, 29, 32
Sano Manabu 179–80
Sarawak 234
Schumpeter, J. A. 5, 9, 258
Seoul 48–9, 53, 71–2, 74, 75, 88, 151
Shandong *see* Shantung
Shanghai: foreign investment in 134, 138,
    139–40, 214; in the treaty port system
    16, 17, 18, 19, 22, 25, 45, 61, 64, 172;
    Japanese control of 206, 208

Shanhaikuan (Shanhaiguan) 63, 141, 187
Shansi (Shanxi) 205
Shantung (Shandong): German rights in
    70, 110–11, 113, 115, 134, 142, 154,
    157, 164, 168; Japan and 134, 139,
    146, 154, 157, 158, 168, 184, 186, 188,
    205
Shanxi *see* Shansi
Shashih (Shashi) 64
Shenyang *see* Mukden
Shibusawa Ei'ichi 66, 73, 74
Shidehara Kijurō 168–9, 171–4, 183,
    184, 185, 188–9, 191, 193
Shigemitsu Mamoru 189, 238
Shimoda 23
Shimonoseki 24; Treaty of 58–9, 63–4,
    65, 66, 67, 71, 82
Shōda Kazue 117–18, 120–1
Shōwa Kenkyūkai 204–5
Shōwa Steel company 216, 217
Siam *see* Thailand
Sian (Xian) 203
Siberia and the Maritime Provinces 22,
    78, 82–4, 159
Sichuan *see* Szechwan
Singapore 234, 239, 244, 248
Sino-Japanese Industrial Company 107
Sino-Japanese War (1894–5) 31, 46–8;
    peace settlement 55–68
Soeda Juichi 91
Sone Arasuke 93
Soochow (Suzhou) 63, 64, 107
South China Army 230
South Manchuria Railway (SMR) 82–4,
    92–4, 97–8, 98–9, 108, 111–13, 136,
    139, 146, 158, 165, 215–16, 236
South Manchuria Railway Company
    (Mantetsu) 97–8, 135–6, 139, 154,
    183, 184, 191, 205, 215–16, 218
South Seas (Nanyō) *see nanshin*; Pacific
    islands; South-east Asia
South-east Asia 116, 201–2, 212, 220,
    222–32, 255–6, 256–7; *see also indi-
    vidual countries*
Southern Region Development Bank 247,
    248
Spencer, Herbert 5, 31
spheres of influence 70–1, 71–6, 79, 80,
    83, 85, 90–100; *see also* investment;
    Manchuria; railways; Shantung
Staley, Eugene 5
Straits Settlements *see* Malaya
Sukarno 239

Sumatra 238, 239, 242–3
Sumitomo company 39–40, 74, 119–20, 214, 248
Sun Yat-sen 102, 104, 106–7, 109, 118, 137, 170, 208
Sung Che-yüan (Song Zheyuan) 201
Suzhou *see* Soochow
Szechwan (Sichuan) 63, 203

Taft, W. H. 99, 100
Taiping (Taihei) company 106, 137
Taishiin *see* China Affairs Board
Taiwan (Formosa): annexation of 6, 55–9, 142; as Japanese colony 75, 143–5, 146–8, 149–51, 238, 257; economic relations with Japan 130–2, 149–51, 153, 211, 214–15, 258
Taiwan, Bank of 106, 118, 147
Ta-lien *see* Dairen
Tanaka Giichi 158–9, 161, 184–8
Tanaka Kunishige 167
Tanaka Memorial 185–6
Tanin, O. 7
Tatekawa Yoshitsugu 192
Tatung (Datong) 218
Terauchi Masatake 90, 96, 105, 116–20, 144–5, 158, 160, 168, 254
Thailand (Siam): and the treaty port system 18, 23; relations with Japan (1939–45) 225, 227, 232, 234, 235, 237, 241, 242–3, 245, 249
Tientsin (Tianjin) 44, 63, 134, 138; Treaty of 18, 24
Timor 234
Tōa Kōgyō company 137
Tōgō Heihachirō 78
Tōgō Shigenori 237, 238
Tōjō Hideki 181, 232, 235–6, 237–8, 241–2, 243
Tokugawa government and policies 21, 24–5, 28–9, 30, 34, 42–3
Tokugawa Nariaki 29
Tokutomi Sohō 31–2, 33
Tokyo Shibaura (Toshiba) Electric company 248
Tongking, 41, 42
Tōsei-ha (Control Faction) 181, 204
Tōyō Spinning company 248
trade *see under individual countries concerned*
Trans-Siberian railway 46, 70, 93, 159, 160
treaty port system: in China (before 1918) 4, 6, 14–20, 60–8, 69–71, 90–100, 101,

103, 108–9, 120–1, 122–3, 252, (after 1918) 156–8, 163–74, 208, 220; in Japan 7, 14, 22–6
treaty revision: in China 169–74; in Japan 33–4
Tripartite Pact (1940) 221, 227
Tsao Ju-lin (Cao Rulin) 118
Tsinan (Jinan) 114, 168, 186
Tsingtao (Qingdao), 142, 168, 206
Tsitsihar (Qiqihar) 193
Tsushima 43, 78
Tuan Ch'i-jui (Duan Qirui) 117–18, 120, 158, 162, 170, 171, 172
Twenty-one Demands 108–15, 158, 163, 168

Uchida Ryōhei 78, 90, 111, 119, 120
Uchida Sadatsuchi 48
Uchida Yasuya 162, 187
Ugaki Kazushige 119, 181
Uiju 75, 151
United States: and informal empire in East Asia 8, 14, 16, 17, 18, 61, 64, 70–1, 99–100, 101, 170–3, 174, 252–3; investment in East Asia 91–2, 99, 102–3, 133–4, 163, 164–5; relations with Japan (to 1911) 21–2, 22–4, 59, 62, 84, 87, 89, 91–2, 94–5, 99–100, 251, 253–4, (1911–30), 102, 114, 157, 160–1, 163–5, 166, 170–3, 188, (after 1930) 193, 202, 220–2, 224, 226, 231–2, 243; trade with Japan 26, 125, 126–7, 129, 210–12, 222, 223, 231–2, 247
Uraga 23
Ussuri River 41
Utsunomiya Tarō 105

Vargas, Jorge 240
Versailles Conference 142, 157, 164, 169, 222
Vladivostock 70, 78, 159, 160, 161, 221

Wakatsuki Reijirō 193
Wang Ching-wei (Wang Jingwei) 207–8
Washington Conference 142, 167–8, 170–1, 190
wealth and strength (*fukoku-kyōhei*), and Japanese modernization 30–2, 34–40
Wehler, Hans-Ulrich 5–6
Weihaiwei 70
Wellesley, Victor 166

Wilson, Woodrow 157, 160, 161, 163, 164, 165
Witte, Sergei 59
Wonsan 75, 151
World War (1914–18), and Japanese imperialism 8, 102, 109–12, 115–16, 119–20, 125, 134–5, 156–8, 233, 251
Wuchang 102, 170
Wuchow (Wuzhou) 63, 64
Wuhan 170

Xiamen *see* Amoy
Xian *see* Sian

Yada Shichitarō 184–5
Yalu River 48
Yamagata Aritomo: and Japan's relations with the powers 72–3, 110–11, 158, 160; and the Japanese army 36, 48, 96; views on mainland policy 46, 76–7, 79, 89, 104, 105, 118, 120, 158, 255
Yamamoto Jōtarō 60, 184, 186
Yangtze (Yangtse) valley 17, 18, 63–4, 70, 109, 114, 137; Japanese control of 203, 205, 207–8, 218
Yantai *see* Chefoo

Yasuda company 39–40, 107, 120
Yawata iron and steel plant 38, 106, 137, 139
'Yellow Peril' 81
Yellow Sea 18, 48
Yengtai coal-mine 92, 98
Yichang *see* Ichang
Yingkow (Yingkou) *see* Newchwang
Yohan E. 7
Yokohama (Kanagawa) 23, 24, 25
Yokohama Specie Bank 106–7, 118, 135–6, 137, 154
Yoshida Shigeru 185
Yoshida Shōin 29, 32
Yoshizawa Kenkichi 229–30
Yüan Shih-k'ai (Yuan Shikai) 45, 102–4, 106–8, 109, 110–12, 114, 116–17, 118
Yunnan 70

zaibatsu 7–9, 39–40, 74, 120, 137, 151, 184, 213, 214, 216; see also *individual companies*, especially Mitsubishi, Mitsui, Ōkura, Sumitomo, Yasuda
Zhang Xueliang *see* Chang Hsüeh-liang
Zhang Zuolin *see* Chang Tso-lin
Zhejiang *see* Chekiang